Sex, Money & Personal Character in
Eighteenth-Century British Politics

MARILYN MORRIS

Sex, Money & Personal Character in Eighteenth-Century British Politics

YALE UNIVERSITY PRESS
NEW HAVEN AND LONDON

Published with assistance from the Annie Burr Lewis Fund

For information about this and other Yale University Press publications, please contact:
U.S. Office: sales.press@yale.edu   www.yalebooks.com
Europe Office: sales@yaleup.co.uk   www.yalebooks.co.uk

Typeset in Adobe Caslon Pro by IDSUK (DataConnection) Ltd
Printed in Great Britain by Gomer Press Ltd, Llandysul, West Wales

Library of Congress Cataloging-in-Publication Data

Morris, Marilyn, 1957–
    Sex, money & personal character in eighteenth-century
British politics/Marilyn Morris.
        pages   cm
    Includes bibliographical references and index.
    ISBN 978-0-300-208450 (cl: alk. paper)
1.   Great Britain—Politics and government—18th century.   2 Press
and politics—Great Britain—History—18th century   3. Journalism—Political
aspects—England—History.   I. Title.
    DA480.M644 2014
    941.07—dc23
                                                    2014022290

A catalogue record for this book is available from the British Library.

10 9 8 7 6 5 4 3 2 1

Contents

Illustrations

1. *The C___t Shittle-Cock*, 1742, *Catalogue of Prints and Drawings in the British Museum: Division I: Political and Personal Satires*, ed. Frederic George Stephens, Edward Hawkins and M. Dorothy George, 11 vols. © The British Museum, 2451.
2. James Gillray, *The Fall of Wolsey of the Woolsack*, 24 May 1792. © The British Museum, 8096.
3. *The Festival of the Golden Rump*, 19 March 1737. © The British Museum, 2327.
4. James Gillray, *Bandelures*, 28 Feb. 1791. © The British Museum, 7829.
5. James Gillray, *God Save the King.—In a Bumper. Or—An Evening Scene, Three Times a Week at Wimbledon*, 27 May 1795. © The British Museum, 8651.
6. James Gillray, *Cincinnatus in Retirement: Falsely Supposed to Represent Jesuit-Pad' Driven Back to his Native Potatoes*, 23 Aug. 1782. © The British Museum, 6026.
7. Richard Newton, *The First Interview, or An Envoy from Yarmony to Improve the Breed*, 19 April 1797. © The British Museum, 9007.
8. *Solomon in his Glory*, 19 Dec. 1738. © The British Museum, 2348.
9. Isaac Cruikshank, *The Wedding Night*, 20 May 1797. © The British Museum, 9015.
10. James Gillray, *The Presentation—or—The Wise Men's Offering*, 9 Jan. 1796. © The British Museum, 8779.
11. *Frederick, Prince of Wales and Princess Augusta of Saxe Gotha*, 25 April 1736. © The British Museum, 2270.

Preface

During my first year in Denton, Texas, I received a summons for jury duty. Never having been west of Chicago prior to flying in for the job interview, I expected that participation in this necessary but vexing civic duty might prove a bit of a culture shock. I was unprepared, however, for the extent to which this would be the case. Ironically, this card-carrying member of the Fort Worth Lesbian and Gay Alliance had been assigned to a trial of an adult-video shop for selling a gay magazine. I sat through a three-day voir dire (pronounced 'vore dah-er', so as not to intimidate the average citizen, as a judge explained during one of my subsequent dips in the jury pool) to establish whether potential jurors understood the obscenity law and were free from prejudice, which would have provided grounds for appeal. For me, the Texan pronunciation of the French legal expression became metonymic for the interpretive assumptions operating in this courtroom. A placard citing Miller v. California, which set the standard for obscenity in 1973, stood exhibited before us. We would have to determine that 'the average person applying contemporary community standards would find the work taken as a whole to appeal to prurient interest', that the work depicted in 'a patently offensive way sexual conduct specifically defined by the applicable state law' and that the work lacked any artistic, political or scientific value. Over the course of the voir dire it became apparent that my perception of obscenity differed significantly from that of the jurors who had been selected, and who would duly bring a guilty verdict. Why was the shop prosecuted for this item rather than, say, videos that depicted sexual violence against women? The experience left me questioning how community standards become established and by whom, and shaped my enquiries into eighteenth-century Britain's manners and mores.

While conducting my earlier studies on the ideological and political evolution of the early modern British monarchy and watching the present-day royal family become more and more enmeshed in scandal, I deliberated whether the example set by royal courts did have an effect on general behavioural standards, as commentators then and now insisted. Because such an assertion would be impossible to prove empirically, its usefulness as a rhetorical position seemed potentially revelatory about the process that communities used to set down and police moral values. My research convinced me that the family life of the monarch first became a subject of national interest during the latter part of George III's reign because of increasingly personal press coverage, the upsurge in evangelical Christianity's movement for personal reformation, and the bloody demise of Louis XVI and Marie Antoinette. Paradoxically, even when members of the British royal family misbehaved, newspapers and pamphlets presented them as moral exemplars. The trope of the king as the father of his people, refurbished by George III's public displays of familial devotion, became central to anti-French propaganda. As I continued tracking the domestic idiom in eighteenth-century political argument, I began wondering to what degree public knowledge of the personal lives of politicians, not just monarchs, shaped perceptions of their ability to govern.

Then the Clinton-Lewinsky scandal hit. As I read the Starr Report and marvelled over the irony of the Republicans' unselfconscious circulation of sexually explicit material on the Internet, I reflected upon the many career-wrecking sex scandals that had erupted during my residence in Britain in the 1980s and in the US from the 1990s. How exactly had marital fidelity become a criterion for political leadership? Subsequent events in American politics led to further points of interrogation. The Bush presidential campaign of 2000 harped upon the theme of 'restoring the nation's core values'. Subsequently financial rapes and obscenities replaced sexual incontinence in the scandal mill, with greater consequences and less sensational representations—that is, until the recession commenced in 2009. I mulled over whether sexual and financial relationships operated according to different ethical standards. In the aftermath of the 2004 election, pundits seemed uncertain what participants in the exit polls meant when they selected 'moral values' as the most important factor in their decision. Louis Menand pondered the inconsistent application of the phrase in the *New Yorker* of 6 December. According to the National Election Pool questionnaire, 22 per cent (80 per cent of whom voted Republican) of those polled picked 'moral values' as the most important issue influencing their vote.

Forty per cent of the *Los Angeles Times* exit-poll voters chose this issue from a closed list. Yet the same percentage also did so in 1996 when Clinton was re-elected and only 25 per cent in 2000 when Bush won. The notion of core moral values appeared both nebulous and tenacious all at once. Notwithstanding, why did perceptions of political leaders' personal qualities continue to seem more important than the integrity, honesty and success of their public policies?

Eighteenth-century Britain provides the perfect locus for pursuing these questions with a salutary critical distance from current partisan squabbles. More importantly, philosophies underlying the representative systems now operating in the Anglo-American world derive from that century's conflicts and compromises. Those who make claims about fundamental rights and values often delve for precedents from this era, although many of the economic, political, social and cultural problems that it spawned remain unresolved. For example, current debates over US dependency on foreign oil sound a lot like the eighteenth-century arguments for the civilizing effects of unfettered commerce in opposition to warnings against the dangers of foreign luxuries. The nature and purpose of marriage continue to be as hotly contested at the beginning of the twenty-first century as they were in the latter half of the eighteenth. And considering the family pedigrees of most political candidates and the ridiculous allegations of the Birthers in relation to Barack Obama, I wonder how great the differences are between the American presidency and the British monarchy in light of the family connections and vast sums of money needed to run for the highest office.

Although I will refrain from drawing further analogies between eighteenth- and twenty-first-century issues until my concluding chapter, I hope that this study will help raise an awareness of the contradictions, self-deceptions and inconsistencies inherent in the ethical assumptions attached to the personalized politics that continue to flourish in the Anglo-American world.

Acknowledgements

Fellowships from the Huntington Library, Lewis Walpole Library, Yale Center for British Art and the Harry Ransom Center at the University of Texas at Austin, the latter two in conjunction with the American Society for Eighteenth-Century Studies, between 1998 and 2001, and a Faculty Development Leave from the University of North Texas (UNT) during the 1997–98 academic year made research for this book possible. I thank the librarians, archivists and administrative staff at these institutions as well as those who assisted me at the Beinecke Rare Book and Manuscript Library at Yale, British Library, British Museum Department of Prints and Drawings Study Room, London Metropolitan Archives, Guildhall Library, British National Archives and Lambeth Palace Library. Google Books, the Lewis Walpole Library's digital collection, Oxford Digital Library and temporary access to Eighteenth-Century Collections Online through the North American Conference on British Studies saved me much time and legwork during the writing process. UNT's libraries, particularly the book and microfilm collections and the Interlibrary Loan Office, have been indispensable to my work—those who want to cut their funding, please take heed. The UNT College of Arts and Sciences' computer lab provided essential assistance.

I appreciate the UNT History Department and Gloria Cox, Dean of the Honors College, for having given me opportunities to develop courses around my research interests, and my students for making me think more broadly. Commencement of this project overlapped with founding the Study of Sexualities, now the LGBT Studies programme at UNT, thanks to the generous initiative of Howard and Margaret Watt, which cata-pulted my research in a new direction. The conferences and journals that provided forums for my writings in this area generated feedback valuable to the larger project. Another Development Leave from UNT in 2007–08 permitted a stretch of uninterrupted time needed for me to determine not only that my original book plan was at war with my research findings but also that I should split the material I had collected into two books; the next, I hope, will not be so long in appearing.

Special thanks to those who read my manuscript in its various stages. William M. Kuhn and John Smail helped me work through the early false starts. Once the writing began to flow, James J. Sack reviewed chapters as I completed them, saved me from some embarrassing errors and cheered me on. Robert O. Bucholz then assessed the next draft; I benefited greatly from his expertise in royal courts and finances. My cherished colleagues D. Harland Hagler, Nancy Stockdale and Jennifer Jensen Wallach also read this draft, alerted me to details that would be obscure to non-specialist readers, and pushed me to submit the damn thing already. After I finally did so, Robert Baldock's enthusiasm and Yale University Press's anonymous reviewers' kind words and wise suggestions helped immensely. I also appreciate the help of Candida Brazil, Tami Halliday, Rachael Lonsdale, and Robert Shore.

Accolades go to all the conference organizers, especially Caroline Gonda and Chris Mounsey for Queer People at Christ's College, Cambridge, and Frank O'Gorman and Corinna Wagner for the annual meetings of the British Society for Eighteenth-Century Studies at St Hugh's College, Oxford. Aurora Wolfgang, Jackie Rhodes and the Queer Caucus always helped make the American Society for Eighteenth-Century Studies meetings fun as well as intellectually invigorating. The Making of the Modern Monarchy conference at Kensington Palace in June 2012 enhanced my appreciation of fashion history. I have benefited from conversations and shared sources in person and in cyberspace with Walter Arnstein, Katherine Barbieri, Penny and Hugh Carson, James Caudle, Elaine Chalus, Anna Clark, Joanna Innes, Declan Kavanagh, Jason Kelly, Thomas Laqueur, Judith Lewis, Chris Nagle, Deborah Needleman-Armintor, Clarissa Campbell Orr, Julie Peakman, Nicole Pohl, Steve Poole, Chris Roulston, Betty Schellenberg, Carole Taylor, Amanda Vickery, Rachel Weil, Kelly Wisecup and Judith Zinsser. I am grateful to Ann Knowlden for her hospitality in London and her friendship, to the many friends who shared comforting home-cooked meals with me during my travels, and to Aunt Louise for the birthday and Christmas cheques that encouraged splurges on adventurous dining and theatre tickets. Ellen Cohn, sounding board extraordinaire, made me feel at home during my trips back to New Haven. Karen Duval and Kate Ohno also helped turn those research trips into homecomings. Back in Denton, talking early modern political theory while whaling on tennis balls with Steven Forde exercised my arguments, cardiovascular system and sense of humour. Discussions of bluestocking virtue over lunches with Elizabeth Bennett always proved edifying as well as entertaining. Christopher Fuhrmann fielded innumerable questions about the ancients and has been a reassuring presence in the office next door.

Writing this book coincided with a series of health crises. My stalwart comrade Harland Hagler deserves a medal for shepherding someone best described as 'the impatient' through four surgeries, starting way too early in the morning. The accommodation by my chair, Rick McCaslin, has been critical to my well-being during treatment. Thoughtful gestures and helpful advice from Jen Wallach, Neilesh Bose, Melia Belli, Sandra Mendiola, Guy Chet, Donna Hauptmann, Mari Metzgar, Terri Sundberg, Jacqueline Foertch, Jennifer Way, Lisa Vining, Jacque Vanhoutte, Joey Phounsavath, Gail Sulik, Treacy Colbert, Susan Bianconi, Kathleen Wilson, Pam DeGregorio and Nancy Donelon, combined with the moral support of my EBHS and South River Stables peeps, have hastened my recovery.

My family's concern and care have surmounted the geographical distance between us. My mother, Stephanie Morris; sister, Stephanie Choma; niece Amy Mason; nephew Joe Choma and their families sustain me in ways I cannot begin to express. Although I do not get to visit them often enough, following the doings of my great-nieces and -nephews—Isabel, David, Sophie, Zachary and Elizabeth—has brought great joy. Finally, this period also saw the passing of my father, Charles M. Morris, Jr., who might be credited with planting the seeds for this study decades ago with his interest in my school paper on the Kennedy-Nixon debates and the media.

Note on Dates

Before the Calendar Act of 1751, Britain used the Julian calendar, which had the year beginning on 25 March and was eleven days behind the Gregorian calendar in use on the Continent. I have preserved the dates as they appeared in the sources, but for clarity indicate when dates between 1 January and 24 March actually fell on the following year according to the Gregorian calendar. Edited correspondence between individuals in Britain and on the Continent often note whether the date is Old Style (O.S.) or New Style (N.S.) corresponding, respectively, to the Julian and Gregorian calendars.

CHAPTER ONE

The Political and the Personal

The Appearance of Persons of Quality of both Sexes on Saturday at St. James's was so numerous, that several of the Prime Nobility could not get beyond the first or second Rooms. Their Habits, particularly those of the ladies, were extremely rich, and most beautifully fancy'd. Her Grace the duchess of Bedford was esteemed the finest, having a gold Stuff most curiously embroidered and valued at 200 Guineas. The Duchess of Portland appeared in Jewels of an immense Value. The Gentlemen wore for the most Part cut Velvets of flowered Silks; and 'tis assured, that there was hardly a Suit worn either by the ladies or Gentleman but was of our own Manufacture, which at this Time excels any in Europe.

In the Evening there was a Ball, which the Prince of Wales opened with the Princess Amelia. Their Majesties retired about 11 o'Clock.

London Journal, 8 March 1734/35

Never at any former period, did the British Court appear in greater splendour than on this auspicious day. The scene was magnificent beyond the most enlarged idea that could be formed.—All that was of elevated rank—of distinguished fashion—and of beauty were present.

There was a glow of satisfaction on every countenance that displayed the felicity of the mind, and at once exhibited what the Company felt—and what the Monarch and his family experienced [. . . .]

THE QUEEN. As is the etiquette of the Court on her Birthday, appeared as plainly habited as the dignity of her situation could allow. Her greatest ornament was the brilliance of her company—and her chief pride, the affections of her people. She had indeed, some natural jewels very near her heart—They glistened in the eyes of her beautiful offspring, who were the admiration of all present.

The Times, 19 January 1792

Customary celebrations of kings' and queen-consorts' birthdays changed little between the reigns of George II and George III—a drawing-room in the afternoon, supper and a ball in the evening, the firing of guns, ringing of bells, bonfires and illuminations—but newspaper coverage of these and other royal anniversaries and ceremonial occasions underwent a radical alteration in style in the same period. The accounts of queens' birthdays cited above encapsulate the different aspects of this journalistic trend. During George II's reign, both ministerial (supporters of the current administration) and opposition papers reported on the daily pursuits of the king and his family, but usually did so without editorial comment. The pro-government *London Journal*'s description of Queen Caroline's birthday in 1734/35 is exceptional, with its representation of the event as a reflection of Britain's economic robustness, but, markedly, it is focused on aristocratic splendour rather than on the appearance of the queen. In contrast, almost sixty years later, *The Times* projected sentiment on to Queen Charlotte, her family and the company, and dwelled on personal and familial attachments. The reference to 'natural jewels' implicitly chastised critics' allegations of her greed for diamonds and the related rumours that she sent gifts she received as queen as well as moneybags of hoarded specie to Hanover.[1] By the 1790s, royal rituals had become an opportunity not only for presenting assessments of the state of the realm but also for encouraging subjects to imagine what members of the royal family must have experienced and felt.

Scholars concur that George III cultivated the appearance of an accessible, responsible and family-oriented monarch, but disagree regarding the significance of this development given the complete reversal of quiet domestic virtue and sobriety in the palace thanks to the flamboyant excesses of his sons. Linda Colley attributes the new-found popularity George III enjoyed in the latter part of his reign to his ability to project the image of an ordinary gentleman of private virtue. John Barrell questions the efficacy of George III's efforts by presenting counter-evidence of people in the king's presence disturbed by his departures from regal demeanour and by his manic affability. He quotes at length the poems of John Wolcot, published under the nom de plume Peter Pindar, showing himself undeceived by the trickery of George III and his principal minister, William Pitt the Younger, affecting virtuous private characters to mask their despotic public policies. My own research demonstrates that loyalist representations of George III as a genial father-figure menaced by bloodthirsty Jacobins abroad and at home served as an effective weapon against proponents of parliamentary reform. As the wording of the treason and sedition statutes focused on the potential risk to the monarch's life, prosecutors emphasized George III's human vulnerability as well as the inhumanness of the radicals who threatened this good man. Reformers had to monitor their speech and writings carefully to avoid expressing any personal animus towards the king. As the number of reports of, and prosecutions for, seditious words attests, many subjects could not exercise such restraint and blamed the king personally for unpopular government policies and economic hardship. Mediated by loyalist propaganda, however, acknowledgement of George's personal foibles could render him a more sympathetic figure. Although not convincing to everybody, the ideals of domestic probity, private virtue and self-restraint emanating from the palace, as well as being energetically touted by Anglican Evangelicals, held sway in political debate.[2]

Clearly, considering the pretence involved, the practical effects of such representations and rhetoric on political culture require further investigation. In this study, I set out to understand why a virtuous private life continues to be a central criterion of fitness for holding public office in the Anglo-American world (nowadays manifested in the utility of a photogenic family) and came to suspect that this can in large part be attributed to the nature of the British monarchy, the foundation of both political systems. Although the Revolution of 1688–89 replaced the personal rule of the Stuarts with constitutional government—with commentators even embracing the idea of parliamentary sovereignty—and much subsequent political activity took place outside the palace, the structure and traditions of the court endured and continued to shape the mores of the ruling elite as well as public perceptions of them.[3] The culture of courtiers, a world of flattery, deception and intrigue, spread into the widening political arena. Because the growth of print culture brought increasing intrusion into the private lives of public figures, royal ceremonial occasions, especially weddings, became forums for discussing the principles of domestic oeconomy and probity, with such discussions becoming inextricably entwined with political argument.[4] Appearances often stood at variance with reality, which turned the court into a confusing ethical terrain with respect to conduct in matters of money and sex. Private writings of politicians and observers on the outskirts of political power further reveal the deleterious effects of the expanding personalization of politics in the press: the development of an institutionalized hypocrisy and the public's illusory idea of being able to know the true character of public figures through their outward mien.

To explain how and why personal lives became an issue in politics, and with what consequences, this book brings to light the interplay between these private and public realms at several key sites. The opening chapters chart the transformation that took place in political journalism from the accession of William and Mary to the end of George III's reign, in conjunction with the development of organized parties and extra-parliamentary political activities. Matters of character and trust, which featured so strongly when monarchs reigned supreme and ministers vied for access to the throne, remained important as politicians built alliances inside and outside parliament. The middle chapters of this book demonstrate the enduring legacy of court culture in constitutional government by comparing press coverage of royalty with what actually took place behind the scenes, first with respect to sex and second to money. In spite of the dominant discourse of connubial contentment and fidelity, extramarital liaisons, not only marriage alliances, still shaped relations between men. Correspondingly, the principles of oeconomy, so fulsomely preached, could not so easily be practised as the court retained its role in promoting the luxury industries, and commerce and trade became the backbone of the national economy. The concluding chapters consider the difficulties that these tensions between rhetoric and reality caused for individuals relegated to the sidelines of the political world, particularly female friends and relations of men in power. Although the press did help democratize politics, the use of human-interest reporting, based on its false premise of being able to read the character of public figures through appearances, also perpetuated this aspect of court culture. This is not to say that the press engaged in some grand conspiracy; on the contrary, it catered to a public desire for those in power to be human and knowable by peddling the illusion of access.

My analysis has required mapping continuity and change over the course of the Stuart and Georgian eras, with two periods in particular providing a fruitful basis for detailed comparison—the 'Robinocracy', Sir Robert Walpole's domination of government from 1721 to 1742, and Pitt's tenure as the 'pilot who weathered the storm' between 1783 and 1801—because of their remarkable parallels. Both ministers attracted accusations of usurping crown power. During their terms, debates raged over stockjobbing, national debt, public credit, ministerial corruption and the state of public morality, as well as the propriety and economic consequences of war. Both administrations also imposed censorship. The corresponding royal families faced analogous conflicts as well. In April 1736, the wedding of Frederick, Prince of Wales with Princess Augusta of Saxe-

Gotha brought a confrontation with George II over the inadequacy of his income, which led to the prince running up considerable debt. In April 1795, George, Prince of Wales married Princess Caroline of Brunswick in order to force George III to find a remedy for his perpetual state of indebtedness. Both unions generated family feuds, gossip, scandal and intense public interest in the larger issues of royal prerogative and the provisions of the civil list. The marriages of the two princesses royal—Anne in 1734 and Charlotte in 1797—offer further opportunities for comparing attitudes expressed in commentaries on royal splendour and the institution of matrimony. The points of difference between these two regimes reflect changing mores. George III's public displays of marital devotion and the unmarried Pitt's apparent sexual continence seem to represent a sea change after the openly adulterous George II and Walpole. Walpole's adeptness at amassing huge amounts of wealth and spending it lavishly bordered on the marvellous, whereas Pitt's personal finances featured a stunning combination of abstemiousness and perennial debt. The two Georges did not differ materially in their overall reputations for frugality, but each would attract criticism for either extravagance or meanness in different contexts owing to the ways that the print cultures of their eras used notions of personal character to further partisan interests.

The idea that a politician's private character should be the subject of broad public discussion initially met with some resistance during this period. In the early eighteenth century, the ethical positions expressed in political argument tended to be formal and abstract. Lofty disquisitions on Virtue and Corruption dominated the discursive field. On the occasions when a newspaper, pamphlet or play made reference to specific irregularities in a political figure's personal life, some form of censure or censorship came crashing down upon the author, editor or printer. At this time, politicians considered ad hominem attacks ungentlemanly, but in their private writings they included details of sexual behaviour and personal financial habits in their assessments of one another's character and political acumen. Inevitably, observations of this nature slipped into the public domain under the auspices of evaluating party leaders' ability to maintain confidence. The anti-party rhetoric of 'not men, but measures' did little to curb the growing concern with reputation or to prevent personal peccadilloes, real and imagined, from making their way into newspaper and pamphlet debates. Some dismissed 'not men, but measures' as cant as they defended party organization and loyalties. The utilitarian philosopher Jeremy Bentham's ridicule of the principle in his *Handbook of Political Fallacies*, written between 1808 and 1821, made merry with the absurdity of separating the two: 'Now it must be confessed that few things are more provoking to a man who wishes well to his country than to see a set of bad men in power gain credit and continuance in office by virtue of their sponsorship of a single comparatively unimportant but, as far as it goes, beneficial measure.' He went on to reason that 'the badness of their measures is the only real warrant one has for calling them bad men. And if they are really the bad men they are supposed to be, one need only have a little patience, and they will come out with some bad measure which can be openly attacked as such. Furthermore, if no such bad measures ever do come from them, the imputation that they are bad men is rather premature.'[5] While Bentham sought to expose the adage's masking of the true source of political corruption, the system of crown patronage, rather than to investigate the correlation between private character and political ability, by the early nineteenth century when he was writing, the connection appeared entrenched. As Paul Langford observes, with journalists having made their private lives public property, politicians resorted to a 'cult of personality' involving carefully managed appearances and reputations.[6] Politicians' aloofness and attendance to propriety, however, only stimulated the imaginations of journalists and readers, and they never seemed to want for material for speculation.

Notwithstanding their example of domestic virtue and thrift, George III and Queen Charlotte's efforts to promote morality at court and in the kingdom at large only went so far. The recurrent conflicts between the Hanoverian kings and their heirs apparent undermined the appearance of familial harmony. Well-publicized incidents of flouting sexual and financial morality by George, Prince of Wales and Frederick, Duke of York, under the influences of Charles James Fox, Richard Brinsley Sheridan and other opponents of Pitt, became sites of resistance against the sociopolitical status quo as others joined in. Considering the degree to which the analogy between the household and the state provoked philosophical contestation, it is not surprising that virtues associated with an idealized domesticity did not provide practical standards for behaviour in politics.[7] Elements of the social mores common in Walpole's milieu persisted behind the scenes. Despite women's increased participation in politics during the latter half of the eighteenth century, gentlemanly sociability had become such an important aspect of elite masculinity that Dr Samuel Johnson had been inspired to coin the word 'clubbable'.[8] By the end of the century, a familial devotion sufficiently excessive to undermine a man's clubbability could damage his political prospects to the same degree as could indulgence in indiscreet libertinism.[9] The Foxites helped destroy their political viability with their gambling, dissipation and consorting with demireps, but a closer examination of the personal writings of ministerial and opposition politicians alike reveals that in spite of the trend towards companionate marriage, in the highest political circles advancement depended on participation in convivial masculine association. A clubbable man offered greater availability and attention to his allies than an uxorious one. Moreover, men often built lasting bonds as they assisted one another with the consequences of their transgressions. Morally censorious home-bodies did not win personal loyalty. At the same time, political aspirants felt compelled to follow the unsmooth path to true love, which could cause rifts with disapproving fathers more concerned with connections and fortune. Assisting friends along this bumpy road drew political allies into greater intimacy, but after the marriage, the supporting bachelors often felt shut out. Other politicians managed both to achieve a stable happy house-hold and to roister about with their allies, which sometimes involved cavorting discreetly with exciting, politically savvy women when away from their wives. The press contributed to the moral ambiguity with its selective reporting on who kept mistresses.

The accelerating expansion of commerce, with its accompanying worries about a greater proportion of the populace having access to luxury goods, created further ethical conundrums for the Georgian monarchy. Although luxury had been de-moralized by the end of the seventeenth century, much ink continued to be spilled over its effects on the balance of trade and the maintenance of the social order; specifically, regarding the problem of supporting domestic innovation and industry while guarding against the perilous consequences of emulation, overspending, excess and debt.[10] By the latter part of George III's reign, press assessments of whether or not the royal family had achieved the proper degree of splendour during public appearances fed into broader moral debates over indebtedness, patronage, spending and the dress appropriate to each station. Writers often drew analogies between personal and public habits of expenditure as they argued over the dangers of, and remedies for, the national debt. Although monarchs traditionally had the closest relations with, and affinity to, the aristocracy, as George III embraced bourgeois values and tastes as well as the agricultural pursuits of rural folk, he and some members of his family took on a malleable class identity that propagandists could exploit. Hence, even when royal personages took care to consider the needs of domestic manufactures and other economic conditions in planning their galas, decorations, clothing and adornment, they seldom got it completely right. Journalists had little consistency in the ethical principles they touted, preferring to practise a base species of casuistry by assessing and deploying whatever moral precept best suited their argument as circumstances dictated.

Political observers who had been relegated to the edges of power documented many of these phenomena. Former intimates of the royal family described the moral predicaments of court life and its personal tolls. Their complaints boiled down to the posturing and pretence therein that did not allow knowledge of anybody's true character. In contrast, those who attended court celebrations, toured palaces and socialized in the proximity of royalty and political leaders wrote as if they knew them intimately, even as they judged them by outward appearance, manners and style. Public images in some cases generated in their observers expressions of affection usually reserved for loved ones. The interrelated trends of sensibility, domesticity and consumerism had brought shifts in thinking about ethics during the eighteenth century that encouraged such reactions. By grounding a person's moral sense in his or her capacity for feeling, the ideology of sensibility justified the examination of everyone's personal passions. Taste became defined as a sensitivity to, and consequent appreciation of, beauty, and as such a reflection of inner character and virtue.[11] The political ramifications appear most dramatically in accounts of Warren Hastings's trial, held intermittently between 1788 and 1795, for alleged acts of extortion and cruelty committed while governor-general of India. Participants and observers each expected the trial to be a moral performance, with politicians as the actors, in a spectacle both entertaining and edifying. Speculation on the inner lives of all involved abounded. Those convinced of Hastings's guilt saw him as the embodiment of the monstrous tyrannies practised on the Indians and as a man who had purchased a showy wife. Hastings's supporters saw a loving husband and man of taste, good conversation and gentle manners persecuted by personal enemies. Spectators also assessed the sincerity of speeches based on the speaker's demeanour. The casuistic arguments that the press often employed in matters of money and sex, noted above, reflected the same mix of reasoning and personal sentiment that individuals used when making ethical judgements in private life.

A host of scholars have identified broader literary trends that parallel and help explain the evolution in political discourse investigated in this book. Changing practices in self-writing led to an increasing preoccupation with human character and passions. Between the seventeenth and eighteenth centuries, diaries evolved from being solely exercises in spiritual devotion and self-examination to individualistic chronicles and self-analyses. Material matters crowded upon spirituality, and private events mixed with public ones. Correspondingly, from the seventeenth century, biography and portraiture, in seeking to capture inner character, interrogated the relation between a man's public persona and his family life.[12] As a growing number and variety of personal narratives emerged, literary conventions moulded the burgeoning self-consciousness of writers. The genre of autobiography, which had come into its own by the end of the eighteenth century, reflected a belief in the existence of the self and the capacity to represent it in words. Although the unstable relation between representation and reality continues to preoccupy philosophers and literary critics, for the average reader, autobiography promises an authentic, coherent self embodied in a text.[13] Political propaganda, with its increasing attention to private behaviour and personal character, came to share qualities with the various genres of self-writing, and drew upon their techniques to render ethereal public figures flesh-and-blood people. The personalized representation of political leaders had a practical appeal as an increasing percentage of the populace involved itself in politics, whether as petitioner, demonstrator, spectator or voter. These images gave emotional clout and, with it, a moral force to political principles that enhanced their accessibility to a wider audience.

Concurrently, the development of the novel as a genre encouraged readers to trust representations of the inner lives of protagonists struggling with ethical dilemmas that could be solved by correctly divining the characters of others. In a long digressive footnote tossed into the miscellany of her *Memoirs* (1824), Laetitia-Matilda Hawkins recounted her launch into authorship sometime before 1780. She explained: 'being in want of a sum of money for a whim of girlish patronage, and having no *honest* means of raising it, I wrote a downright novel. It could do nobody any harm—indeed *I* thought it a marvellous moral performance, as it punished the culprits and rewarded the virtuous of my *dramatis personae*—but it was a temerarious undertaking, as descriptive of matters and situations of which I knew little but by hearsay.'[14] Her breezy declaration encapsulates a number of the phenomena examined in this book. Hawkins's characterization of her novel as a 'moral performance' reflects a perception of the reading public's demand for its stories to have an edifying sheen. Her use of the word 'temerarious', with its connotations of both recklessness and chance, and her profession of having no first-hand knowledge of the experiences of which she wrote indicate that she realized in retrospect that she had possessed sufficient instinctual confidence in the fundamental difference between real life and its depiction in narrative to gamble on it. She could construct her moral performance from things she had picked up from both, presumably, oral and written discourse. The admission that acquisitiveness had been her motivation, coupled with the acknowledgement of the irony inherent in this moral performance's underlying dishonesty, suggest Hawkins's appreciation of the perennial discrepancies between public pronouncements of ethical principles and the actual observance of them, something not lost upon courtiers, as is evinced by their writings.

Novels primed the imagination of the reading public. Readers accustomed to depictions of fictional characters' interiority by an omnipotent observer would be receptive to similar representations of political leaders. Patricia Meyer Spacks likens the bond that forms between a novel's narrator and the reader to the affinity between gossips as they share 'a set of responses to the private doings of richly imagined individuals'. David A. Brewer shows this imaginative practice to extend even further as he reconstructs how eighteenth-century readers envisioned the inner lives of characters in literature beyond what lay on the page. Popular fictional characters inhabited a make-believe common space that might be compared to traditional village common land open for grazing and gleaning. These figures provided a focal point around which to build a 'virtual community' in which 'readers who imagine characters as common, and hence available to the public, also conceive of themselves as part of a public'. Brewer, however, carefully distinguishes this public from the idea of a monolithic, conformity-seeking public sphere, which he characterizes as 'a powerful political fiction'.[15] As I will show, politicians and royalty too became fictionalized and richly imagined like characters in novels as multiple publics observed and discussed their images. At the time that more Britons moved from small agricultural communities to large urban centres, human-interest stories in newspapers and journals replicated village gossip for this new 'national society'.[16] Discussions of public figures' marriages and financial affairs intermingled with debates over the nation's moral and economic welfare. Prescriptive literature now had a new set of moral—and immoral—exemplars.

Eighteenth-century readers expressed the desire to know about the personal characters of noteworthy persons. In the course of their burgeoning friendship, Henrietta Louisa, Countess of Pomfret wrote to Frances, Countess of Hertford, her equally bookish, fellow former lady-in-waiting to George II's consort, Queen Caroline: 'It is too much the fault of historians to neglect those little incidents, that serve to enliven and raise reflexions in reading their books, which can never be produced by a dry relation of facts only. For my own part, I must confess, that I always want to know as much how a great person thought and spoke, as what he did.' She considered French scholarship superior 'from their admitting private characters into their historical works'.[17] British historians would try to follow suit. One of the six attempts at autobiography that Edward Gibbon left behind in manuscript began with the proclamation that he embarked on a narrative of his life for his own amusement, although he knew that he would be charged with vanity: 'Yet I may judge, from the experience both of past and of the present times, that the public is always curious to *know* the men who have left behind them any image of their minds: the most scanty accounts are compiled with diligence and perused with eagerness; and the student of every class may derive a lesson or an example from the lives most similar to his own.' Indeed, he continued, the self-portraits of numerous ancients and moderns far surpass their philosophical writings in their interest to readers. The earliest draft of his memoir, dated 1788–89, ruminated: 'In the study of past events our curiosity is stimulated by the immediate or indirect reference to ourselves; within its own precincts a local history is always popular, and the connection of a family is more clear and intimate than that of a kingdom, a province, or a city.' In spite of Gibbon's intentions, one of his readers, a self-proclaimed 'Lover of Literature', wished that his memoirs contained more anecdotes of 'such acquaintances as were distinguished characters', which he thought could be of no harm if done with propriety.[18] The pleasures of reading simulated the pleasures of good company. Elizabeth Montagu, queen of the bluestocking circle, thought it fortunate that her sister Sarah Scott would be among numerous 'titled persons' at Bath as 'pictures with mottoes entertain with presenting one with something more than mere faces. The only objection I have to the people *nobody knows* is, that as I do not know them they can not give me any sort of pleasure unless they are handsome, genteel, or dressed with peculiar elegance. The Persons whose characters one is acquainted with raise a certain set of thoughts and recollections.'[19] The persons portrayed in histories, newspapers, journals and novels filled the gap for those without access to such fascinating coteries.

Journalists, belletrists and satirists all held up a mirror to the paradoxical mores of fashionable society, what eighteenth-century Britons referred to as 'the World'. Increasingly popular from the 1730s onwards was the conversation piece: a group portrait of family and/or friends that showed off its commissioner's orderly, harmonious domestic or social life as well as the wealth and taste of his material possessions.[20] Simultaneously, the century saw a rise in trials for criminal conversation, the common-law action for trespass by which a cuckolded husband sued his wife's lover for damages. The lurid court testimony against adulterous couples supported the growing number of pamphlets and journals that traded in titillating, graphic narratives and visual depictions of illicit sexual liaisons.[21] In the theatres, domestic comedy rose in popularity and became a locus for debate over women's role and power in courtship and marriage. Plays dramatized innumerable sources of antagonism between the sexes before reaching the requisite happy resolutions. Representation of character types by actors who had their own public reputations, coupled with the deceptive surfaces on stage that facilitated the twists and turns of plot, fed into cultural anxieties regarding the ability to judge moral worth and truly know another's character based on reputation, actions and words. Questions of personal character intruded upon ideological considerations, most visibly in theatre censorship, which shifted from suppressing oppositional political ideas to cutting out any potentially slanderous depictions of members of the ruling elite.[22] Ironically, as domestic duty and sexual continence became de rigueur for political leaders, many genres of writing portrayed both the genteel and the commercial ranks of society becoming increasingly licentious.[23]

The degree to which graphic satire reflected the trend towards personifying politics has attracted some controversy. Vincent Carretta's analysis of oppositional poetry and prints places the transition from not-men-but-measures rhetoric to personal attacks at the end of 1742 after the fall of Walpole, inspired by suspicion that the Great Man still wielded power out of office. He points to the emergence of caricature, with its emphasis on what lay behind the masks individuals wore in public, which would eclipse allegory and symbolism by the 1760s. Carretta presents an array of prints, as well as verse satires, that rendered the fallen minister as a grotesque indulging in excesses of food and drink and an improper relationship with Lady Mary Churchill (the daughter he had with his mistress, later wife, Maria Skerrett), and financial corruption. While, during the Robinocracy, Walpole often appeared as a colossus, caricature now served to diminish him. Eirwen E.C. Nicholson has taken Carretta and other scholars to task for, among many other things, failing to differentiate consistently among the different print genres, privileging caricature and representing earlier political prints as somehow less evocative. In particular, she disputes Carretta's notion that in the 1740s and 1750s political rivals differed so little in terms of their principles that attention shifted to their personalities, and challenges the assumption that caricature conveyed personality more effectively than iconography.[24]

Notwithstanding Nicholson's contention regarding the power of metonymical representation of individuals by inanimate objects, it seems significant that the rise of caricature paralleled the increasingly personalized treatment of political figures in the press. Reading symbols and getting visual puns depended on a sophisticated visual literacy and a familiarity with the figures depicted. The exaggerated features of caricatured subjects made them comprehensible to a broader audience and gave the illusion of the viewer's ability to know their true characters. Take, for example, two prints that portray Walpole and Pitt, respectively, using the king's influence to take revenge on an enemy.[25] *The C___t Shittle-Cock* (1742) (fig. 1), published shortly after Walpole's fall, shows him having lobbed the duke of Argyll in the shape of a shuttlecock to George II, who has then sent him flying out of the court. Frederick, Prince of Wales in the background declares: 'My Reconciliatory Friend is Mounted.' The king seems insensible to his mistress, Madame Wallmoden, making an assault upon his breeches and a lewd suggestion while Walpole's illegitimate daughter proposes to her father that she take Yarmouth's place. All wear court dress and assume stilted poses. In contrast, James Gillray's *The Fall of Wolsey of the Woolsack* (24 May 1792) (fig. 2), published after Pitt told George III that either he or the lord chancellor, Edward Thurlow, would have to go, conveys a vivid kinetic energy with its discarded formality. George, engaging in a tug-of-war with 'Neddy' for the seat of office, chastises him for his resistance while Pitt tries to pull out from under Thurlow the common woolsack on which he sits. Pitt's cousin William Wyndham Grenville claws at the judicial wig, declaring that he would like to wear it. The shift towards immediate, stereotypical representations repeated over and over in an increasing volume of prints helped render the political more personal.

Studies of sensibility, domesticity and commercialization tend to present these movements in opposition to court culture, or to treat the Georgian monarchy as a social and cultural irrelevance. As David Kuchta sums it up: 'In attacking the court's conspicuous consumption, political, social, religious, and economic critics undermined the cultural foundations of monarchy in seventeenth-century England, subverting the crown's ability to pose as the arbiter of culture, the guarantor of a visible social order, the center of trade, and the moral regulator of ceremonial conformity.' He sees this as a fait accompli by the eighteenth century.[26] Likewise, while Michael McKeon traces the origins of the eighteenth-century domestic novel to the 'secret histories' of the Stuart era—scandalous stories about public figures presented as romantic fiction—he does not mention the House of Hanover's contributions to real-life domestic drama. McKeon contends that the family crisis of the Stuart dynasty undermined the analogy of state as family and prepared the way for the family to be a site of resistance against state encroachments into private lives: lives that collectively formed a disembodied public.[27] This interpretation epitomizes the influence that Jürgen Habermas's model of the rise and fall of the bourgeois public sphere in the West has had on eighteenth-century studies. From feudal times, Habermas argues, princes, nobles and churchmen displayed their authority through what he calls 'representative publicness': 'representation pretended to make something invisible visible through the public presence of the person'.[28] By the turn of the eighteenth century, state authority had become depersonalized and private individuals met in public to conduct trade, engage in rational debate, create public opinion and thereby blaze the trail to democracy. The expansion of commercialization, organized private interests and mass media in the following centuries, however, eventually undermined the freedom and accessibility of the public sphere. The state invaded the social order by imposing regulations and structuring the distribution and administration of communication. Citizens turned into consumers and publicity became associated less with rational public discussion than with representations, Habermas concludes.

The fall of the Stuart regime might have depersonalized sovereignty by re-establishing it in the balanced constitution of king or queen, Lords and Commons. In addition to this, the court no longer dominated artistic and literary life through patronage and as the central venue for exhibiting the latest poetry, music, drama and fine arts in elaborate entertainments and display. Nonetheless, the monarchy retained significant influence over fashion, artistic, literary and scientific endeavour, and the maintenance of the social hierarchy through its traditional means of conferring distinction. In addition to this, representations of George III and his family in print restored to monarchical rule a strong persona. Habermas does acknowledge the legacy of the earlier era: 'The aura of personally represented authority returns as an aspect of publicity; to this extent modern publicity indeed has affinity with feudal publicity. Public relations do not genuinely concern public opinion but opinion in the sense of reputation. The public sphere becomes the court *before* whose public prestige can be displayed—rather than *in* which public critical debate is carried on.'[29] In an intervention against oversimplifications of Habermas, Dena Goodman reminds us that he did not set up a dichotomy between the public and private spheres; rather, he presented them as part of the same open discursive realm opposed to the secrecy of a state that hypocritically claimed to represent the public.[30] Yet this seems more descriptive of *ancien régime* France. In England, parliamentary elections, active opposition parties and, during the second half of the century, publication in newspapers of parliamentary debates made the separation of the state and the public sphere less distinct than it was in France.

Accounts of the expanding political arena after 1688 usually shove the court far into the background. In reaction to interpretations of the eighteenth century that present patronage and family connections as dominating politics, epitomized by the work of Sir Lewis Namier, historians have recovered evidence of a greater involvement of the populace in politics in the shape of the increase of contested elections, development of party organization, access to news and opinion with the expansion of print, new non-royal political anniversaries for public celebration, a burgeoning urban political culture in the provinces, and the proliferation of coffeehouses as well as new clubs and associations for charity, self-help and debate. In this model, the commercial ranks of society eroded the patrician elite's hold on political power as aristocratic patron-client relations gave way to the bourgeois entrepreneurial spirit of the free market.[31] Barrell sees private conduct increasingly overturning public action as the central standard for judging men 'as part of the process whereby the moral values of the middle classes became increasingly hegemonic even in the sphere of high politics'. His focus, however, is on the impact of this trend on the public after the Pitt administration and its supporters exploited it in the 1790s: 'private opinions, and even private life itself, were represented as the proper object of the intrusive authority of the loyalist public and the state.'[32] Was this not simply an extension of the conditions in which courtiers had long lived?

By taking a longer view of high politics, I will show that the idea of personal character as a central criterion for political leaders' fitness to rule had its roots in the royal court itself, where personal relations customarily determined access to the monarch and to political power. I do not mean to imply that the structure of politics allowed the elite to hold sway over a deferential populace. Rather, when applied to politics, the idea of a virtuous private life reflected in dutiful and affectionate domesticity (discursively associated with the bourgeoisie) allowed the court's legacy of connections, intrigue and gossip to endure. This is also not to say that political principles were just a smokescreen for personal ambition. On this front, H.T. Dickinson makes a helpful qualification after reviewing how historians have asserted the importance of ideology in judicious challenges against the cynical Namierite view of politics as a selfish struggle for office: 'Those who accept that ideas and principles do motivate men do not claim that this applies to all men or even to a majority of them. Neither do they seek to divorce ideology from personal ambition or vested interest.'[33] In this book, I bridge the chasm between models of high and popular politics as I investigate how the domestic idiom had an impact both on the careers of MPs and on the images and ideas broadcast to society at large through words and images.

A resurgence of interest in court studies has brought a salutary reassessment of the monarchy's place in popular culture and politics after 1688. In spite of the image of the early Hanoverians' legendary dullness cultivated by contemporary detractors and gleefully believed by generations of historians, loyalist activities never ceased. Nor did the press ever lose interest in the royal court.[34] Still, their impressive coronation ceremonies aside, the first two Georges appeared to lack the ability or the desire to employ royal ritual, the arts or propaganda to project positive images of themselves as personalities as George III would later do.[35] No longer God's vicegerents, monarchs and their heirs apparent had become political players, and thus had to share the public stage and the representational realm with members of both Houses.[36] Anna Clark's work on political sex scandals shows domesticity and monarchy coming together to form new loci for popular politics. She commences her analysis with the Wilkes and Liberty movement of the 1760s that began with John Wilkes's attacks on John Stuart, Earl of Bute's alleged liaison with the princess dowager and consequent undue influence over the young George III, and evolved into a campaign defending parliamentary privilege and liberty of the press. Clark argues that the agitation for constitutional reform challenged royal and aristocratic authority and for the first time made the exposure of a ruler's scandalous domestic life a threat to the political hierarchy. In spite of all the rhetoric proclaiming that only service to the state, not private life, had any relevance to public leadership, political antagonists publicized their opponents' scandalous sexual activities whenever it suited their purposes. Clark demonstrates that the depersonalization of sovereignty remained contentious, however John Locke might have distinguished governmental from familial authority and the Revolution of 1688–89 validated the ideology of constitutional balance. As she observes: 'personal and familial relationships still structured politics, both literally and metaphorically'.[37] Clark concludes that publicizing private transgressions could be beneficial to public life. Scandals brought larger principles to the fore, made political issues more accessible to the public, and stimulated wider interest in participation in debate on principles of national import. Rejecting the Habermasian model of civil society's independence from the royal court, her analysis shows how causes célèbres drew these two spheres together.[38]

Scholars employing the methodologies of sociology, anthropology and communication studies to assess the effects of scandal on politics and society stress the peculiar conditions produced by the modern mass media, but many of their findings already obtain in the comparatively limited print culture of the eighteenth century. Like Clark, they stress that criticism of the private lives of individuals could serve as the basis for questioning the principles underpinning the socio-political order. Studies of audience reception indicate that serious public discussions about power relations and social and political practices can emerge out of incidents that some might dismiss as trivial tabloid-fodder. John B. Thompson argues for scandal's significance as 'struggles over symbolic power in which reputation and trust are at stake'.[39] Mediated scandal sometimes resembles a trial by ordeal, with the wrongdoer's political survival depending on tenacity, toughness and a more compelling story. He further observes how scandal-mongering sometimes blows up in the faces of self-appointed moralists who fail to notice or accept shifts in societal attitudes, or over-intrusive journalists who push 'gotcha' tactics further than the public can stomach. Resolution of moral conundrums in debate generated by one scandal can produce attitudinal changes that result in unexpected public reaction to the next. S. Elizabeth Bird classifies scandal as a subset of the larger genre of human-interest stories, so-called 'soft' news: 'it is *one* type of narrative that helps people structure their view of what the world is and how it should be.' When individuals perceive elements of a news story directly relating to their personal lives they are more prone to become engaged in the dialectic and may modify their original opinion as the story unfolds new details.[40] Thus, analyses of political scandal stemming from sexual or financial misconduct or abuses of power suggest, ironically, that political leaders have an impact on moral standards less by adhering to them than by transgressing them. Indiscretions promote outcry, statements of outrage and regret, respectively, from accuser and accused, and then public debate and resolution.

Before scholars of the eighteenth century took up Habermas, Richard Sennett issued his classic diatribe against the 'tyrannies of intimacy' that helped bring about the erosion of a civil, impersonal public sphere. While he and Clark describe the same process of personalization in politics, they could not be more different in their interpretations of its consequences. Sennett presents it as a symptom of the going-to-hell-in-a-handbasket diagnosis he gives to modern life:

> We may understand that a politician's job is to draft or execute legisla-
> tion, but that work does not interest us until we perceive the play of
> personality in political struggle. A political leader running for office is
> spoken of as 'credible' or 'legitimate' in terms of what kind of man he is,
> rather than in terms of the actions or programs he espouses. The obses-
> sion with persons at the expense of more impersonal social relations is
> like a filter which discolors our rational understanding of society; it
> obscures the continuing importance of class in advanced industrial
> society; it leads us to believe community is an act of mutual self-
> disclosure and to undervalue the community relations of strangers,
> particularly those which occur in cities. Ironically, the psychological
> vision also inhibits the development of basic personality strengths, like
> respect for the privacy of others, or the comprehension that, because
> every self is in some measure a cabinet of horrors, civilized relations
> between selves can only proceed to the extent that nasty little secrets of
> desire, greed, or envy are kept locked up.[41]

Sennett sees this sorry state of affairs as having commenced with the mid-nineteenth-century charismatic leaders who harangued street crowds. The developments that made this possible, he avers, came a hundred years beforehand, when Locke's idea of natural liberty collided with the notion of 'individual character as a social principle'. The Wilkes and Liberty movement presaged things to come in the way that Wilkes's sexual libertinism became a symbol of his stand against the established order. Secularism, self-absorption and the valorization of individual feeling conspired to turn the Enlightenment idea of natural character into the Romantic notion of personality, paving the way for its ensuing cult. Sennett argues that politics became, and continues to be, a form of seduc-tion, with audiences distracted by the compulsion to determine who their leaders are as people. Audiences fixate on the motivations that politicians project through careful manipulation of appearances, rather than evaluating their actual policies.[42]

Habermas rejects Sennett's depiction of public life based on an impersonal civility maintained by stylized role-playing and the masking of true emotions. Sennett, he insists, 'does not grasp the specifically bourgeois dialectic of inwardness and publicness that in the eighteenth century, through the ascendancy of the audience-oriented privateness of the bourgeois intimate sphere, begins to capture the literary world as well'.[43] Sennett's observations on emotional performances appear solid, however, in light of subsequent studies that chart the rise and fall of sensibility. Early modern natural philosophers at first referred to sensibility as an individual's ability to process sensory knowledge through the nerves as feelings. Moral philosophers then pronounced the capacity for feeling sympathy in particular as the wellspring of virtue, whereupon sensibility descended into sentimentality. Its critics warned against interpreting the artificial emotions encouraged by art, literature and fashionable manners, and the temptation to indulge in emotional excess as a sign of moral worth.[44] Habermas, more interested in establishing the communications apparatus necessary to facilitate the free exchange of ideas essential to a democracy than in the state or its propaganda methods, does not concern himself with the interchanges—often wildly irrational—among governmental propagandists and the various critical publics of the eighteenth century.[45] My research suggests that the workings of partisan political opinion in these dialectics and the emergence of political parties known by the names and personalities of their leaders might be the great spoilers of Habermas's dream of rational, productive communication. Furthermore, the scholarship on scandal reinforces my perception of how practical application of moral precepts often changes their meaning. A private act made public turns into a story. The actor's morality becomes a performance constructed in language and appearance as it moves further from the offending or commendable act into the discursive realm. Public discussion places the story in different contexts and its implications multiply. J.L. Austin, the father of speech-act theory, explains that statements appearing to be straightforward presentations of fact often are not, noting that, 'for example, "ethical propositions" are perhaps intended, solely or partly, to evince emotion or to prescribe conduct or to influence it in special ways'.[46] The quality of performance, appearances and media representation, as well as the individual experiences of their audience, all shape public discussion, and ultimately the moral judgement of an act, and help determine its consequences. In my survey of a broader field of political representations, Sennett's warnings against the distortive practice of judging persons, instead of principles and policies, seem more judicious than the optimistic conclusions of scholars who have focused on scandals alone.

The political and the personal afford the most productive categories of analysis for this study. I employ these designations first in the sense originally invoked by the sociologist C. Wright Mills in his explanation of how individuals begin to see their personal concerns in the broader context of society and politics:

> The sociological imagination enables its possessor to understand the larger historical scene in terms of its meaning for the inner life and the external career of a variety of individuals. It enables him to take into account how individuals, in the welter of their daily experience, often become falsely conscious of their social positions. Within that welter, the framework of modern society is sought, and within that framework the psychologies of a variety of men and women are formulated. By such means the personal uneasiness of individuals is focused upon explicit troubles and the indifference of publics is transformed into involvement with public issues.[47]

The prescience of Wright's thesis is borne out by Bird's empirical research, cited above, on audience reaction to human-interest news stories. Bird demonstrates that the dialectic between personal experience and outside events does promote formation of a worldview. My study will further document how individuals interrogated their own experiences and observations as they formed judgements of others based on appearances and reputation.

Secondly, I draw upon the notion of the personal-as-political in the feminist sense by adopting a broad definition of the political to include all negotiations concerning power, status and the allocation of resources. As noted earlier, in the eighteenth century, political activity extended well beyond the court, Houses of Parliament and municipal corporations. Elaine Chalus affirms: 'Women took part in a range of politicised activities, extending from writing, publishing and debating, through membership of charities and joint-stock companies, to the more "traditionally" political areas of social politics, patronage and electoral politics.'[48] Her research on women's involvement in electoral campaigns shows that even marriage could serve as a political tool beyond its traditional role in reinforcing connections between political families and, in the case of royalty, nations. She observes: 'In close election contests, marriages might even be encouraged and expedited by patrons, candidates or agents in order to increase the number of their voters.'[49] Areas traditionally placed in the private sphere, such as family, friendship and formal and informal socializing, could be hotbeds of political consciousness and activity. Likewise, women had some presence in public spaces traditionally considered male enclaves. Steve Pincus claims that the public sphere described by Habermas developed earlier, in Restoration England, out of political contestation, not capitalistic development, which stimulated the hunger for intelligence that supported the newspaper industry. He finds no evidence of the exclusion of women from the coffeehouse culture that catered to this new taste by disseminating written political information and opinion and by serving as a venue for discussion, debate and gossip.[50] My investigation shows that interactions between men and women in public and in private affected politics in unexpected ways as liaisons created bonds, sparked jealousies, had financial repercussions, affected character assessments and formed reputations.

Viewing the tensions within moral discourse as resting on the axis of the personal and the political provides a useful framework for analysing autobiographies, diaries, memoirs and letters. Political writings—confidential, propagandistic or literary—aim for specific, immediate gain (which includes support for a policy or an idea) through negotiation or persuasion. Personal writings, on the other hand, may engage with political controversy but with the purpose of keeping account or working out the writer's opinions. Personal writings perform self-examination or self-justification, but not as part of a negotiation with others for power, status, support or material gain. Of course, these categories are not mutually exclusive; indeed, when they overlap in a text, the complex interrelation between the personal and political emerges. Eighteenth-century writings of all genres tend to flit back and forth between matters of individual and general interest, and can reveal multiple intentions and objectives through careful critical reading and attention to their wider context. Likewise, drawing distinctions between the two categories by subject matter depends upon context. Discussion of a marriage, for example, would be personal or political depending on whether it concerned the union's individual emotional dimensions or its wider ramifications regarding power, status or wealth.

As with the public and the private and the personal and the political, money and sex often intertwine, most noticeably in the institutions of monarchy, matrimony and prostitution. The ethical principles regulating sexual and financial responsibility share a foundation in doing what is best for the family or the nation, but sex and money receive very different treatment in political discourse. Analyses of scandal posit that, with sexual mores constantly under contestation and shifting, and the ease with which sex scandals fall into familiar melodramatic narratives, they attract wider interest than financial scandals. The latter usually involve breaking the law, which renders them less compelling; their byzantine detail, moreover, restricts their accessibility to the general public.[51] This book raises the question of whether in some ways the discussion of money is more taboo, being more baldly revelatory of personal character and of power relations in society than is sexuality. In order to compare standards of financial and sexual probity effectively, as well as to get a sense of the day-to-day negotiations in matters of character and morals away from the overcooked atmosphere of royal scandal, I have broadened the focus of this analysis to include general discussions of marriage, adultery, divorce, charity, spending and debt relating to political leaders and those near to them. Building upon the considerable current scholarship on the impact of commerce, consumerism and capitalist ideology, I venture beyond the eighteenth-century luxury debate and the political rhetoric of public-versus-private interest to look more closely at the ways in which political and personal writings incorporated attitudes towards money into notions of character. I hope to present an alternative view of morality's place in politics, liberated from the Pocockian model of civic virtue derived from classical republicanism and civic humanism.[52] To understand the nature of the democracy that took root in the Anglo-American world, we must consider the residual structures, customs and expectations that the institution of monarchy defended and upheld alongside the development of republican thought.

The criteria determining good character evolved over the course of the century as writers continued to peer through the keyhole of the self's 'cabinet of horrors' and record in increasing detail what they saw. Whereas the moral principles mooted in political writings became more wrapped up in individual circumstances and complexity as the century progressed, the personal writings examined in this study suggest that individuals changed little over this time in their modes of ethical calculation. To some degree, political discourse grew to replicate interior thought processes, although published ethical discussion by its nature continued to be less angst-ridden and more dogmatic than personal reflections. Despite Blaise Pascal and others condemning casuistry as Jesuitical duplicity, its practice continued to thrive in Protestant Britain.[53] When confronted with an ethical issue, individuals often displayed a consciousness of what the World would say on the point. After weighing the particular circumstances and using or abusing logic, however, they might well make a different independent judgement, sometimes cloaked in fashionable moral tropes. Yet these writings show that engagement with political events did shape personal values. Moral performances could be disingenuous or sincere, public or private, but always they are at once personal and political.

CHAPTER TWO

The Politics of Personal Character

As party organization became essential to the practice of politics and a partisan press steadily grew, political writers faced a dilemma over how much personal information about opponents they should reveal in public forums. Consequently, from the coronation of William and Mary in April 1689 to the launch of the *North Briton* in June 1762, which commenced the Wilkes and Liberty movement, the act of making a correlation between an individual's domestic life and capacity for public service became contentious. The libel laws and the gentleman's code of honour to keep the secrets of one's peers only went so far in deterring publication of scandalous private behaviour. Journalists who published eloquent newspaper essays decrying personal libels on one day might well produce anonymous ad hominem attacks on another. At the same time, moral posturing against private peccadilloes could well turn scrutiny back upon the personal life of the censurer. Beneath the surface of political debate, politicians and their hired pens noticed one another's personal fortunes, financial, marital and sexual. As party feeling intensified in Anne's reign, so did the temptation to allow such observations to slip into print.

Subsequent trends increased the relevance of personal lives to politics. Under the first two Georges, the consolidation of the Whig oligarchy and the patronage system kept government under the control of a network of elite families intertwined in kinship and familiarity by generations of courtships, intermarriages, rivalries, and favours bequeathed and received or not. The domination of Sir Robert Walpole, the 'Great Man', seemed a new personal rule that justified intimate scrutiny, but innuendo rather than explicit detail usually appeared in the press. The attempt to transcend personal politics through the principle of 'not men, but measures' would be

made in vain, however, because it not only seemed to undermine the foundation of party allegiance but also to run counter to how men actually thought
and acted. Political memoirs show that, however they might claim otherwise,
politicians often judged one another by their personal characters as well as on
their principles. Politicians often used words such as 'intimacy', 'friendship'
and 'love' to describe party alliances among men. Temperament, appearance,
manner and capacity for friendship all influenced a politician's success.
Sexual or financial habits out of keeping with current codes of masculine
behaviour might undermine a man's reputation, and with it his power and
influence over others. Probably the most visible effect of the increasing
publicity attending politicians' lives was the rise and fall of sodomy as a metaphor for improper power relations. With the expansion of the reading public
and politicized crowds, the possibility of having the metaphor taken literally
carried more danger.

   Those who took to the moral high ground often found themselves
balancing on a slippery slope. After the ambiguous and unprecedented
proceedings of the Revolution of 1688–89 barred James II and his Catholic
heirs from the throne, William III's partisans asserted the legitimacy of his
rule with a propaganda campaign that had a strong moral component.
Invoking Hadrian's reign of virtue, which had helped to restore order to
Rome after the depravity and tyranny of Caligula and Nero, Bishop Gilbert
Burnet's coronation sermon heralded the commencement of a national
godly reformation, which, the prelate proclaimed, William would lead by
example. Mary II aided this struggle for moral authority as her genuine
piety and modesty contributed to a godly household. She increased the
performance of prayers and divine service, which she expected all servants
at court to attend. William did not heed Burnet's advice to issue a proclamation against vice immediately, however, which allowed reforming
members of local corporations and MPs to steal a march on him with societies for the reformation of manners that seemed an implicit reproach to the
court's laxity. Jacobites responded to the innuendos Whigs made about the
corruption of the Stuart courts—rumours about James I's male favourites
that had limited circulation during his reign now appeared in public
prints—by representing William's close relationships with his Dutch
favourites as sodomitical: a personal manifestation of his political taste for
conquest and usurpation. Tony Claydon argues that, nonetheless, Burnet
and his team commandeered the moral purchase of the reformation societies with royal proclamations in their support, in spite of the court's misgivings about using voluntary organizations for the vigorous enforcement of

laws against vice. By presenting William as the champion of legal reformation, his supporters could head off allegations that he was indifferent to moral issues as well as curb the excesses of the societies. Claydon speculates that those who protested against hypocritical magistrates, the use of the law to regulate private life, the seeming revival of puritanical persecution and the unjust targeting of the poor probably spoke for the majority of subjects. Nevertheless, Queen Anne too issued a proclamation against vice and supported the societies.[1]

With Anne's accession in 1702, accusations of personal hypocrisy began flying in many directions as politicians bought up the most talented writers of the age as propagandists, which often produced antagonisms between old friends. A few months after the king's death, Daniel Defoe, who had enjoyed generous compensation for his writings in support of William and Whig principles, published a lengthy poem called *Reformation of Manners*. It accused the societies' rich and powerful members of an array of moral transgressions: taking pleasure in the whipping of bare-breasted prostitutes, accepting bribes, practising in private what they prosecuted in public and lording it over the helpless poor. Defoe's exposure of magistrates' disorderly domestic lives resembled the sort of material in this era's *romans-à-clef* or secret histories. For example, he served Sir Robert Clayton, parvenu sheriff, lord mayor of London and Whig MP, thus:

> *Clayton* superbly wise and grave of Life,
> Cou'd every one reform, except his Wife:
> Passive in Vice, he Pimps to his own Fate,
> To shew himself a Loyal Magistrate.
> 'Tis doubtful who debauch'd the City more,
> The Maker of the Masque, or of the Whore.
> Nor's his Religion less a Masquerade;
> He always drove a strange mysterious Trade:
> With decent Zeal, to Church he'll gravely come,
> To praise that God which he denies at home.[2]

Defoe's moral outrage would cost him. He found himself standing before judges whose personal vices he had pilloried in the poem after his satires against the government's treatment of Protestant Dissenters made him liable to charges of seditious libel. When facing prosecution, Defoe felt abandoned by the religious nonconformists he had championed as well as by the Whigs. After a triumphant session in an actual pillory placed in his old neighbourhood, where the crowd purchased his writings instead of humiliating him, and a less happy stint in prison, he accepted the aid and patronage of Robert Harley, who was working to build what would become a new, moderate Tory party. The need to please his masters without betraying his principles, while fending off accusations of double-dealing from his cohorts, would be one of Defoe's lifelong battles.[3]

The personal relationships among writers of this era contributed to its schizoid print culture: scurrilous pamphlets, poems and *romans-à-clef* circulating alongside high-toned newspaper essays that condemned personal libels. Politicians and literati mixed in convivial drinking and dining clubs that had steadily grown in number since the Restoration.[4] That some men combined careers in journalism and parliament put additional pressure on boundaries between public and private life. When he launched the *Tatler* in 1709, Richard Steele, who became MP for Stockbridge in 1713, attempted to separate his moralizing from his political commentary by demarcating the journal's different departments geographically. For entertainment and tales of gallantry, one looked to White's Chocolate-house; for poetry, Will's Coffeehouse; for learning, the Græcian; and for foreign and domestic news, St James's Coffeehouse. Other subjects would appear under the head of '*my own Apartment*', that is, the virtual domicile of Isaac Bickerstaff, the contributors' collective persona. The reports that issued from White's contained anecdotes of the ill-natured and the foolish, whose identities readers could sometimes discern beneath the clever sobriquets, as well as generic character sketches of obnoxious social types. Bickerstaff's political commentary at first consisted only of the odd word of praise of Whig statesmen and their policies offered in passing—but not for long.

When it appeared that Harley would be replacing Sidney Godolphin as the head of the government, White's and St James's collided. On 29 June 1710, from Bickerstaff's apartment emerged the character of Polypragmon in an essay that marvelled at a man who would wish to appear cunning and awful:

It is certain *Polypragmon* does all the Ill he possibly can, but pretends to much more than he performs. He is contented in his own Thoughts, and hugs himself in his Closet, that though he is locked up there and doing nothing, the World does not know but that he is doing Mischief. To favour this Suspicion, he gives Half-Looks and Shrugs in his general Behaviour, to give you to understand that you don't know what he means. He is also wonderfully Adverbial in his Expressions, and breaks off with a Perhaps and a Nod of the Head upon Matters of the most indifferent Nature. It is a mighty Practice with Men of this Genius to avoid frequent Appearance in Publick, and be as mysterious as possible when they do come into Company. There is nothing to be done, according to them, the common Way; and let the Matter in Hand be what it will, it must be carried with an Air of Importance, and transacted, if we may so speak, with an ostentatious Secrecy. These are your Persons of long Heads, who would fain make the World believe their Thoughts and Idea's are very much superior to their Neighbours, and do not value what these their Neighbours think of them, provided they do not reckon them Fools.

Readers would recognize this as a portrait of Harley. In Steele's next newspaper, the *Guardian*, on 12 May 1713, while countering the Tory *Examiner's* demand that he be turned out of the Stamp Office for his libels, Steele took responsibility for the portrait of Polypragmon but denied that he had anyone specific in mind in making it and claimed it to be 'the most odious Image I could paint of Ambition'. He added: 'I have not [. . .] fixed Odious Images on Persons, but on Vices.' The *Examiner* had dug up examples of the *Tatler's* assaults on personal character to counteract the *Guardian's* moral outrage over the *Examiner's* witticisms about signs of the earl of Nottingham's lukewarm commitment to the Church, including the spectacle of his daughter, Lady Charlotte Finch, knotting in St James's Chapel during divine service in the presence of the queen. The *Guardian* of 28 April had presented this as an assault on all virtuous women and, by extension, all civilization:

If Life be (as it ought to be with People of their Character, whom the *Examiner* attacks) less valuable and dear than Honour and Reputation, in that proportion is the *Examiner* worse than an Assassin. We have stood by and tamely heard him aggravate the Disgraces of the Brave and Unfortunate. We have seen him double the Anguish of the unhappy Man, we have seen him trample on the Ashes of the Dead; but all this has concern'd greater Life and could touch only Publick Characters, they did but remotely affect our Private and Domestick Interests; but when due Regard is not had to the Honour of Women, all human Society is assaulted.

The 'him' here was Jonathan Swift, who was the editor of the *Examiner*, and had occasionally contributed to the *Tatler*. Or, as Steele went on to call him, 'the fawning Miscreant'. It became clear as the essay of 12 May continued that Steele's rancour marked the climax of the quarrel smouldering between the two friends over Swift's support of Harley. Steele asserted: 'I have carried my Point, and rescued Innocence from Calumny; and it is nothing to me, whether the *Examiner* writes against me in the Character of an estranged Friend, or *an exasperated Mistress.*' Here he lumped together Swift with his fellow writer at the *Examiner*, the notorious Tory scandalous memoirist Delarivier Manley, who in the *New Atalantis* (1709) had presented a lurid account of the financial and sexual incontinence of the younger days of Steele (styled 'Monsieur l'Ingrate') in revenge for refusing her appeal for a loan.[5]

It is difficult to assess the relative degrees of personal feeling and party spirit operating in the political propaganda of Anne's reign. Swift and Defoe separately admired the writings of Joseph Addison and Steele and each expressed frustration when they were attacked by the Whig journals. Both of them believed that Harley had not betrayed fundamental Whig principles, unlike Addison and Steele's beloved Junto Whigs, a group formed during William's reign in support of the war against France and heavily involved in its financing. The *Tatler* of 22 August 1710 attacked Defoe's *Review* for presenting Harley's ouster of Godolphin as, in principle, the formation of a Whig administration. The *Tatler* made pointed observations about the sorry sort of person who would abandon personal loyalties and beliefs to support whoever rose to power. Defoe fired back with a pamphlet titled *A Condoling Letter to the Tatler: On Account of the Misfortunes of Isaac Bickerstaff, Esq.* Parodying the Bickerstaff style, Defoe turned the 'Censor's' gaze upon Steele's habits of luxury, profusion and debt to twit him for hypocrisy while simultaneously commiserating as someone who had also suffered from the same vices that he condemned in others. Having been in a similar situation, he knew Steele's vulnerability. Defoe had attracted scathing personal attacks while acting as Harley's agent in Edinburgh to help bring about the Union of England and Scotland. Opponents to the Union had represented Defoe as vain, foppish and susceptible to flattery as they reminded their readers of his origins as a bankrupt hosier and of his stint in the pillory. Pamphlets cited the grammatical lapses in his writings and repeated the rumours that he had cuckolded his best friend to illustrate his disregard for rules and his lack of restraint, marks of a treacherous character.[6] In an early expression of the cult of domesticity that would flourish during the second half of the century, Defoe's *Condoling Letter* argued for the importance of family as the locus of a man's moral grounding in contrast to the morally bankrupt code of politeness that Addison and Steele promulgated.[7]

Bertrand A. Goldgar's dissection of Swift's falling-out with Addison and Steele posits that 'what Swift called "that damned business of party"' actually masked a number of fundamental differences in their worldviews. Most significant to the present study, Goldgar relates their contrasting propaganda styles to contemporaneous debates about human nature. The Tory satirists maintained the traditional Christian belief in man's fallen nature and susceptibility to vice, best battled with ridicule and shaming. The Whig moralists tended more towards the latitudinarian view of man as naturally benevolent, with virtue best promoted through cultivation of sentimental feelings. One of Steele's defenders against Swift depicted wit as inimical to Christian virtue and satire as the opposite of charity.[8] In an essay against libels published during George I's reign, Addison argued that writers attacked their adversaries' persons when they were unable to dispute their principles.[9] Nonetheless, as we have seen, he and Steele shared a preoccupation with matters of character in their moral essays; hence, they easily became drawn into matching Swift's personal invective while discussing political matters. They did not directly address the question of how far one could go into a politician's personal life to assess his character, but the *Tatler*'s reaction to the *Examiner*'s treatment of Nottingham implied that families should be off limits. Yet with the competition for power through favourites, with its accompanying intrigues and gossip in Anne's court, a clear boundary between public and private life did not always exist. The *Examiner*'s observations on Lady Charlotte's indulgence in the eighteenth-century equivalent of texting in the chapel royal, although presented as an invasion of her father's domestic realm, actually took place in an area not entirely private. Significantly, the *Tatler*'s Polypragmon focused on Harley's manner of conducting state business.

Elsewhere, however, Swift indulged a taste for embarrassing domestic detail, as, for example, in his anonymous character sketch of the Junto Whig Thomas, Earl of Wharton: 'He bears the gallantries of his lady with the indifference of a Stoic, and thinks them well recompensed by a return of children to support his family, without the fatigues of being a father.' Swift then dissected Wharton's character: 'He has three predominant passions, which you will seldom observe united in the same man, as arising from different dispositions of mind, and naturally thwarting each other; those are love of power, love of money, and love of pleasure: They ride him sometimes by turns, and sometimes all together.'[10] Given the colourful libertine reputation that had put Wharton out of favour with the queen, Swift's decision to focus on his wife's infidelity indicates its importance to a politician's authority. Wharton only became lord lieutenant of Ireland after the death of Anne's consort weakened her resistance to the Junto.[11]

In the *Examiner* and his writings elsewhere, Swift used allegory and innuendo to evade the libel laws.[12] In reply to critics who called personal invective the recourse of a scoundrel, Swift pointed to the absurdity of separating acts from their perpetrators. The *Examiner* of 30 November 1710 began: 'WHEN I first undertook this paper, I was resolved to concern myself only with things, and not with persons.' Claiming that he quickly found this impossible due to the malfeasance of individual ministers, he offered a parable aimed at John Churchill, Duke of Marlborough, hero of the Junto Whigs, whom the Tories had to discredit in order to secure Harley's position. 'Suppose I should complain, that last week my coach was within an inch of overturning, in a smooth, even way, and drawn by very gentle horses; to be sure, all my friends would immediately lay the fault upon John, because they knew, he then presided in my coach-box.' Given Marlborough's heralded military victories, poking around in the dark corners of his domestic life, where rumour suggested scandal lurked, might have seemed petty and mean. Sarah, Duchess of Marlborough's tarnished reputation as the queen's fallen favourite, combined with the huge financial rewards they both reaped for service, the monumental estate they were building at Blenheim and the duke's request for the office of captain-general of the armed forces for life, gave propagandists more than enough public actions to illustrate the couple's overweening ambition and greed. Swift then went on in this piece to criticize the rest of the administration by analogizing its members variously as a receiver of rents, a cashier, a messenger and clerks of different descriptions, whose collective incompetence imperilled an estate. Unable to resist a personal jibe, he styled Earl Cowper 'Will Bigamy' in an allusion to rumours of a clandestine marriage he had made early in life.[13]

Whereas Swift's pessimistic view of human nature manifested itself in vented spleen, Bernard Mandeville, in *The Fable of the Bees* (1714), offered a serious philosophical challenge to the connection that Addison and Steele drew between private virtue and public spirit.[14] As M.M. Goldsmith sums up his position: 'Mandeville contends that vice produces not only prosperity but civilization as well. "Vice" is essential to a flourishing society in two senses of the word: firstly, vice in the sense of physical deficiency, privation and need makes society necessary for human survival; secondly, vice in the sense of moral defect (greed, vanity, pride, selfishness, lust, luxury and envy) stimulates production and improvement.'[15] By implication, traditional notions of personal virtue would be irrelevant when assessing political leaders, something that Mandeville returned to in the second part of his fable, published in 1729 in response to his detractors. In this dialogue, his alter ego, Cleomenes, compared the English system of government to a knitting frame. Thanks to the efforts of generations of ingenious men, 'the greatest Artist at it can furnish us with no better Work, than may be made by almost any Scoundrel after half a Year's Practice'.[16] This remark made his foil, Horatio, press for clarification:

> *Hor.* But supposing the Government of a large City, when it is once establish'd, to be very easy, it is not so with whole States and Kingdoms: Is it not a great Blessing to a Nation, to have all Places of Honour and great Trust fill'd with Men of Parts and Application, of Probity and Virtue?
>
> *Cleo.* Yes; and of Learning, Moderation, Frugality, Candour and Affability: Look out for such as fast as you can: But in the mean time the Places can't stand open, the Offices must be served by such as you can get.
>
> *Hor.* You seem to insinuate, that there is a great Scarcity of good Men in the Nation.
>
> *Cleo.* I don't speak of our Nation in particular, but of all States and Kingdoms in general. What I would say, is, that it is the Interest of every Nation to have their Home Government and every Branch of the Civil Administration so wisely contriv'd that every Man of midling Capacity and Reputation may be fit for any of the highest Posts.[17]

A person of any class could participate in a well-constituted government, so all the party rhetoric about one group's superior honour and virtue was just so much hypocritical posturing. With an apparently cynical disregard for the foundation of Christian teachings, Mandeville treated vice as something people should exploit rather than suppress. Hence, he excited the same revulsion as Thomas Hobbes had with his notion of human nature dominated by lust for power. Nevertheless, Adam Smith and other moral philosophers would massage Mandeville's theory into a less offensive formula. They combined the seemingly antipathetic beliefs in man's innate propensity to vice and man's natural benevolence to form the theory that the human capacity for empathy helped to regulate selfish passions. Mandeville's astute observations on the hypocrisy of moralizers such as Steele would go disregarded, however. As the next chapter will show, a growing interest in analysing the passions in order to determine the best means of encouraging virtue would eventually make the examination of the personal lives of public figures appear less the province of libellers and more a matter of promoting the public good.

Sex, Money, the 'Great Man', his Enemies and his Minions

The scandal of the South Sea Bubble of 1720, born of political rivalry and a greed-fuelled frenzy of stock speculation, generated the rhetoric of public spirit as an antidote to party spirit, forming the basis of the nebulous entity called public opinion that increasingly took hold in political argument.[18] Political writing began making stronger connections between public and private morality. The insistence of Swift and Defoe that after the Glorious Revolution everyone was a Whig did not seem so ingenuous now. George I did not trust Tories and would dismiss many of that party from office. At the same time, between 1717 and 1720, the Whig party split over foreign-policy issues, with Robert Walpole leading the opposition and James, Earl of Stanhope and Charles Spencer, third Earl of Sunderland promoting a scheme for the South Sea Company to take over the national debt at a reduced rate of interest. The plan was fundamentally unsound in allowing speculation rather than trade to determine the value of company stock. The company directors then made matters worse by bribing members of the court and the ministry to stimulate sales. George I, his mistress, Ehrengard Melusina von der Schulenberg, Duchess of Kendal, their two daughters (officially her nieces), and his illegitimate half-sister, Sophia Charlotte Kielmansegg, Countess von Platen, made Countess of Leinster in 1721 and Darlington in 1722, and other members of his family all received discounted stock on 'credit' with no pressure to pay for it and reaped the profits. Bequeathed the title of governor in 1718, the king's involvement could not have been more public.[19]

In order to satisfy public outrage and preserve the integrity of the government and the system of finance, the corruption would need to appear isolated in particular individuals who could be punished and removed. Walpole had regained a place in the government shortly before the Bubble burst. His demonstrated skill in fiscal management, his initial opposition to the South Sea scheme and his failure to make any money during the boom placed him in the perfect position to assume a leadership role in restoring public credit. In the process, however, he did long-term damage to his personal reputation because cleaning up the mess involved covering up the court's involvement. Although Walpole loathed Sunderland, he managed to have him acquitted of corruption charges and to suppress publication of the parliamentary investigation report. The image of Walpole – dubbed the 'Skreen-Master General' – as a corrupt political fixer never faded. The reputations of Stanhope and Sunderland fared much worse. Stanhope dropped dead of apoplexy as he tried to defend himself in the Lords, which some undoubtedly interpreted as a smiting from on high.[20] Newspapers, pamphlets and poetical squibs represented the company directors and the ministers they had corrupted as a gang of sodomites. Significantly, accusations of so-called unnatural relations, formerly used to attack royal favourites' influence, as in the cases of King William and Queen Anne, were now repurposed to take aim at the conspiracies among politicians and financiers.[21] Suspicions of profligacy at court now ranged further afield in the widening political arena. The Bubble gave credence to the moral panic of the societies for the reformation of manners and their claims that the South Sea Company conspirators bankrolled licentious clubs in London that drew young men into debauchery and blasphemy.[22]

During the Bubble crisis, journalists continued to denounce personal libels in some contexts while drawing associations between political and personal behaviour in others. In *Cato's Letters*, which originally appeared in the *London Journal* from November 1720 to September 1722 and then in the *British Journal* to December 1723, John Trenchard and Thomas Gordon appealed to a range of Whiggish principles.[23] Although staunch supporters of freedom of the press, they acknowledged the danger of personal libels: 'they fly at men rather than things; which proceeding is as injudicious as it is unmanly. It is mean to be quarrelling with faces, names, and private pleasures; things perfectly indifferent to the world, or things out of a man's own power; and 'tis silly, as it shews those whom we attack, that we attack them not for what they do, but for what they are.'[24] This letter averred that the private vices and weaknesses of governors should only be an issue insofar as they became a factor in public administration, by which Trenchard and Gordon presumably meant private frailties made public by overt acts in the course of governing. They observed that most tyrants had not been cruel men in private; rather, their excessive dominion over other men made them ruthless.[25] Furthermore, personal misbehaviour simply was not on a par with political malfeasance when one considered their respective consequences. They derided George I's proclamation of 28 April 1721 against 'scandalous clubs or societies of young persons, who meet together, and, in the most impious and blasphemous manner, insult the most sacred principles of our holy religion, affront Almighty God himself, and corrupt the minds and morals of one another'. The harm inflicted on society by the private debauchery of 'a few giddy, unthinking, young wretches' paled in comparison to the public robbery perpetrated by the South Sea Company's directors. They enquired 'whether it had not been better for England, that the late directors, and their masters, had spent their nights and their days in the Hell Fire Club, than in contriving and executing execrable schemes to ruin England?'[26]

The tenor of Gordon's other writings makes this letter seem either ironic or duplicitous—or solely the work of Trenchard since scholars have identified Gordon as the author of scurrilous publications linking indulgence in the sexual dissipation of such clubs with the financial treachery underlying the Bubble. *The Conspirators; or, The Case of Catiline* (1721) begins with a dedication to the earl of Sunderland, but, as one reads on, it becomes clear that the author is setting up an analogy between the earl and Catiline, the bankrupt aristocrat of antiquity who plotted to murder and then usurp the power of the Roman consuls. The description of Catiline's several marriages, contracted for the sake of building alliances with powerful men rather than any love for the ladies in question, and of his expensive pampering of a series of Ganymedes, echoes the rumours then in circulation about Sunderland.[27] *Love-Letters between a Certain Late Nobleman and the Famous Mr Wilson*, which appeared the year following Sunderland's suspicious death in April 1722, not only presented a vivid picture of one of these Ganymedes and the villainy that sodomitical tastes engendered; it also drew a personal link between the earl and the notorious Scottish gambler-adventurer John Law, architect of the Mississippi Bubble in France, which also burst in 1720 after its miraculous earlier profits had inspired the South Sea scheme.[28] Law had absconded across the Channel in April 1694 after murdering in a sham duel one Edward 'Beau' Wilson, a young man of limited means who gained notoriety when virtually overnight he began carrying himself about London in clothes and equipage fit for a nobleman. Obviously, someone of great wealth kept him and London buzzed with speculation over who that might be; his murder intensified interest in the mystery. Law returned to England unexpectedly in November 1721 and Sunderland helped secure him a royal pardon for the murder. In a traditional depiction of court corruption, Delarivier Manley in 1707 had produced a *roman-à-clef* entitled *The Lady's Pacquet of Letters*, which insinuated that Wilson's keeper had been William III's mistress, Elizabeth

Villiers. That she should engage in a secret love affair at great expense and risk and then hire Law to murder Wilson when he discovered her identity, Manley implied, indicated the high level of her sexual dissatisfaction with the king, feeding speculation regarding his relationships with his favourites. *Love-Letters*, in turn, relocated sodomitical villainy to the aristocratic townhouse. As Cameron McFarlane observes of *Love-Letters* and contemporaneous pamphlets: 'sodomitical practices constituted a complex signifying economy in which the sodomite appears as a refigured representation of a variety of social concerns and anxieties.'[29]

Perhaps Gordon and the others could convince themselves that they were not libelling the persons responsible for the Bubble but simply using allegory and metaphor to convey more powerfully the immorality that made the financial fraud possible by constructing a tale of illicit and mercenary sex, secrets and intrigue. Earlier moralists, when they broached the topic of sodomy, often associated it with sins of excess such as gluttony and drunkenness, the evirating effects of luxury, a loss of manly independence, a lack of steady principles, and treachery.[30] *Cato's Letters* cited a number of examples from antiquity to illustrate how general corruption of the people paved the way for tyrannical power. One featured an honest, talented man, tired of hard work and poverty, who, 'turning pimp and pathetick, instantly prospered, and got great riches, power, and places'.[31] On the other hand, any sign of a political enemy's weakness for his own sex could not but be exploited, even by Steele, whose aspirations to genteel politeness went by the wayside when he began writing for Walpole. Steele published the *Plebeian* in spring 1719 as part of an effort to defeat Sunderland and Stanhope's Peerage Bill, which would have limited the number of peers a monarch could create and thus increase the House of Lords' power. In the first number, Steele presented a lesson from antiquity: the Lacedæmonian State coming to ruin because the Ephori (magistrates) usurped the king's power and implemented constitutional changes. A sharp correction from his old friend Addison, who supported the bill in his paper the *Old Whig*, gave Steele an opportunity to make a more pointed attack. In a tone of injured innocence, he protested: 'I always thought that bringing Examples from History was look'd upon as the most impartial and unexceptional Method of arguing, as it is abstracted from the Passions and Interests of the present Times.' He went on to contend ingenuously that the *Plebeian* had gone out of its way to avoid affront, then proceeded to supply the offensive material excluded from the first number: how the Ephori instituted regular inspections of naked fifteen-year-old boys and lived with those they favoured: '*Iis* (Ephebis) *assiduo fere adhaerebant* [the magistrates were almost constantly clinging to the teenage boys] . . . However, it is very plain all this was omitted to avoid the least Appearance of personal Reflection.' G.S. Rousseau explains that this clearly alluded to a rumour accompanying Stanhope back from his valorous service in the War of the Spanish Succession, that young soldiers had received promotion after spending the night in his tent, a behaviour said to continue with the appointment of court pages. Rousseau points out that Steele 'elsewhere described the trope of sodomy as encoding forms of excessive political dependence on an older and more established political statesman'.[32] Nonetheless, claiming to avoid 'personal Reflection' was the effrontery that Steele had once derided in Swift.

The literature of political contestation from Anne's accession to Walpole's ascendancy contained a tangle of political principles, philosophical and ethical theories, cultural prejudices and personal piques. Simon Targett challenges the traditional view of Walpole as the inveterate pragmatist with a closer look at his hired journalists. Their work contained elaborate deline-ation of Whig principles and varied ideas regarding human nature and the origins of government. Walpole's hirelings found it most useful to argue that men were greedy and self-interested in order to represent the English constitution, preserved by the Revolution of 1688–89 and, by extension, Walpole's government, as a discretionary power exercised by necessity.[33] Walpole's ability to hold on to power after George I's death in 1727 by securing the favour of George II, however, made the 'Great Man' vulnerable to the rhetoric of corrupt dependency that Steele had used against Stanhope.

The next time the spectre of the sodomite appeared in a political dispute, its conjurer, William Pulteney, used the metaphor in a way that could be read figuratively and constitute a personal attack, which did more damage to his own character. Yet, in the controversy that ensued, both sides eventu-ally conceded that politicians' private lives had some bearing on the quality of their leadership. Pulteney had allied with Walpole in the Whig Split of 1717, but, by 1720, relations between the two were so fractious that Walpole left Pulteney out of his new ministry and would continue to pass him by for office. Pulteney began by sniping from the backbenches of the Commons and then joined the press war against Walpole. In 1726, he teamed up with the notorious Tory and erstwhile Jacobite Henry St John, Viscount Bolingbroke and others to form the *Craftsman*, which became the leading opposition newspaper.[34] In January 1731, Pulteney published a pamphlet under the name of Caleb D'Anvers, the suppositious editor of the

Craftsman, which used the trope of sodomy in more personal terms than had been directed at Sunderland and Stanhope or even William III, as their accusers had not been intimates. His attack against John, Lord Hervey, one of Walpole's chief propagandists and once a close friend (Pulteney was godfather to his eldest daughter) and political ally, warrants detailed analysis for what it reveals about the legacy of Stuart court culture and the inescapable influence of ostensibly private personal relations on party politics.[35]

The set-to between Hervey and Pulteney took place after the ministry, having failed to suppress the *Craftsman* with libel writs or by answering its criticisms in the ministerial press, tried to defeat the paper at its own game by personally discrediting its writers as it prepared a new case against its printer. The *Craftsman* had become increasingly bold in allowing its mud-slinging campaign against Walpole to besmirch George II, thereby leaving the paper open to charges of seditious libel. Additionally, the *Craftsman* provided potential evidence of treasonable intent when it published the 'Hague letter', which contained information that Pulteney had obtained from the French ambassador exposing details of the secret negotiations Britain had undertaken to resolve the conflict with Austria.[36] Hervey publicly interpreted Pulteney's lack of discretion as a serious character flaw. In *Sedition and Defamation Display'd: In a Letter to the Author of the Craftsman*, Hervey penned a dedication addressed to the paper's patrons that set out in simple, personal terms the allegations that in the main text would be detailed with ample supporting evidence by William Yonge, another ministerial writer. Mocking the *Craftsman*'s tactics by observing that it was 'so much the modern Fashion to consider *Persons* rather than *Things*', Hervey represented its writers as being moved to sedition and rebellion out of personal malice.[37] Of Pulteney he observed:

> Let me then suppose a young Gentleman coming some time since into the World, with all the Advantages that recommend Men to the Esteem, Favour, and Approbation of Mankind, caress'd and espoused by the *Ministers*, loaded with the Favours of the *Crown*, promoted to some of the most considerable Employments of Honour, Profit, and Trust, and particularly supported by *One*, who heaped upon him all the Obligations that a cordial Friendship could ask or give: But being in his own Nature ambitious and aspiring, a Slave to his Passions, impatient and irresolute, unable to bear a Superiority; conceiving unjust Jealousies and Discontents, full of himself, and his own extraordinary Merit, and

determined to hold the highest Offices in the State, or to censure and confound *all* the Measures of the Government, under any other *Administration*; he at length renounced at once all former Friendships and Principles, vowing the Destruction of those who had distinguished him by a peculiar Regard, betraying private Correspondencies, and endeavouring to distress and disturb *that Prince and that Family* to whom he owed the highest Obligations.[38]

Hervey used metaphors of courtship, marriage, infidelity and marital breakdown to describe Pulteney's relations with the government, and hauled in the figures of the king and his family to make personal Pulteney's betrayal (he had been a favourite of George I). In doing so, he implicitly reminded his former political ally of the emotional bonds and confidences the two of them had once shared.

The personal umbrage that Pulteney took in reaction to what he called 'a Late Scurrilous Libel', which he assumed Hervey had authored on his own, seems to have gathered in intensity as he wrote. Metaphor exploded into explicitness. He began by explaining his prior disinclination to notice the author's 'pretty Declamations'. He compared them to the scribblings of schoolboys in order to introduce a gratuitous allusion to Walpole's youngest son, Horace, at Eton, rumoured to have sprung from the loins of Hervey's late, elder half-brother, Carr Hervey.[39] Pulteney's tone then shifted from condescending to shrill: 'I was afterwards inform'd that They were the Samplar-works of a forward, little, *Boarding-School Miss*; who was ambitious of becoming, one Time or other, a *Maid of Honour*; and indeed some dainty *virgin Expressions* in those Performances, (as the *same Writer* observes) render'd it far from being improbable. But at last I was told by a Person, in great Confidence, that They were the Productions of pretty Mr. *Fainlove.*' Pulteney described him as a delicate creature, not up to '*rough Encounters*', and one favoured by the ladies. Indeed: 'He is a *Lady* Himself; or at least such a nice Composition of the two Sexes, that it is difficult to distinguish which is more prædominant.'[40] Just in case his readers failed to catch his drift, Pulteney quoted classical verses that depicted monstrous confusions of gender, and then, on the next page, spelled it out: 'But though it would be barbarous to handle such a *delicate Hermaphrodite*, such a pretty, little, *Master-Miss*, in too rough a Manner; yet you must give me Leave, my Dear, to give you a little, gentle Correction, for your own Good.' An urbane reader of the time would have associated this patter (which today we might label as a mix of camp and sadomasochism) with the subculture of the molly houses: meeting places for common men to solicit sex with one another, a far cry from the rarefied circles in which Hervey travelled.[41] In this way, Pulteney suggested that Hervey had sunk to the level of his patron, whom the *Craftsman* regularly portrayed in the guise not only of great historical villains, but also of the wide range of lowlifes and undignified characters who hustled the London streets.[42]

Pulteney's innuendo became more explicit in further discussion of the patron-client relations between Walpole and Hervey. After parodying Hervey's characterization of him by turning the same language against Walpole, Pulteney mocked the specific arguments set out in the body of *Sedition and Defamation Display'd*, written by Yonge as if authored by Hervey: 'you seem, *pretty Sir*, to take the Word *Corruption* in a limited Sense, and confine it to the *Corrupter.*—Give me Leave to illustrate This by a parallel Case.—There is a certain, unnatural reigning Vice (indecent and almost shocking to mention) which hath, of late, been severely punish'd in a neighbouring Nation. It is well known that there must be *two Parties* in this Crime; the *Pathetick* and the *Agent*; both equally guilty.'[43] In 1730–31, the Dutch Republic had undertaken mass capital prosecutions of men nabbed at molly houses (*lolhuysen*) and cruising grounds, so Pulteney's allusion would seem unmistakable.[44] Pulteney's use of sodomy as a metaphor for corruption took on the force of a criminal accusation.

For his part, Pulteney appeared surprised at the adverse reaction to his pamphlet. Public opinion temporarily favoured Hervey for defending his honour. A fortnight after Hervey had issued the challenge and the two crossed swords in St James's Park, the author of *A Proper Reply* wrote a letter to Swift implying (inaccurately) that it had been *Sedition and Defamation Display'd* that had started the name-calling. Pulteney insisted: '*Villain, Traytor, Seditious Rascal*, and such ingenious appellations, have frequently been bestow'd on a couple of Friends of yours. Such usage has made it necessary to return the same polite language.'[45]

Pulteney's explanation might seem ingenuous—even childish—but it is plausible that his personal relationship with Hervey had precipitated his critical lapse of judgement. In 1729, while Hervey was in Italy with his lover, Stephen Fox, Pulteney had schemed with Hervey's wife and Hervey's father, Lord Bristol, both of whom loathed Walpole, to bring Hervey into the opposition.[46] For Hervey then to turn around and be party to a publication that impugned Pulteney's personal character caused Pulteney to snap. Styling Hervey as 'Mr. Fainlove' expressed his sense of personal betrayal. In the course of hurling further insulting personal allusions—to Hervey's family's career at court and his recent loss of a tooth—Pulteney seized upon his allegations of 'betraying private Correspondencies'. He raged: 'for though the Persons who once *distinguish'd you by a peculiar Regard*, had, I believe, more Discretion than to trust you with any *Secrets*, in the greatest Height of their Partiality towards you; yet you have given us very plain Indications how ready you would have been to *betray private Correspondencies*, if it had tended to serve any laudable Purposes of the *Court*, or the Interests of *Those*, in whose Cause you are now so zealously embark'd.'[47] Pulteney evidently feared Hervey repeating any indiscreet remarks he might have made at the time of their political rupture in 1729. Indeed, in his memoirs, which remained private during his lifetime, Hervey alleged that Pulteney anticipated a successful Jacobite insurrection. He quoted Pulteney characterizing the prince of Wales as 'the timid, poor, mean, weak wretch' and declaring that 'as stout as our shitten monarch pretends to be, you will find we shall force him to truckle and make his fat-arsed wife stink with fear before we have done with her'.[48]

It also must have crossed Pulteney's mind how allegations of sodomy implicated the accuser. As a precaution, he answered a remark Yonge made in the body of the pamphlet: 'How far the Principles of Honour may engage some Men not to blast the Reputation of others with whom they have lived in Friendship, I will not determine; in that Case some Regard ought to be shewn to their own Character, lest the World should imagine they had formerly been Sharers in the Guilt of those with whom they lived in Amity.'[49] Clearly, guilt in this case referred to the political principles once shared by the now-antagonists. Addressing Hervey, Pulteney stretched this into another complicit guilt in order to distance himself from it:

Will it not be natural to ask if you never had any particular and very great Obligations to a *certain Person* [Pulteney]? Was you not taken into his House like one of his own Family? Did He not in every Thing show a Disposition, perhaps more, to serve you? Did He not almost singly support your Character, when the little Finicalness of your Person had made you the Joke and Contempt of Mankind? Might not This be carried still farther?—But here I will stop;—Only thus much may be said—This *former Patron* of yours was, at least, the remote Cause of your obtaining the very *Employment* you now enjoy; and your *present Patron*, as destitute as he is of *Friends*, would have thought you too insignificant an Acquisition to have been purchas'd at so high a Price, if it had not been for the Additional Satisfaction of having purloin'd you from his *next Door Neighbour*.[50]

Too greedy to concede any of the obligations he thought Hervey owed him, and too intent on ridiculing his former protégé's effeminacy, Pulteney dug himself in deeper. If Walpole had coveted his neighbour Pulteney's property in Hervey, and if Hervey were now Walpole's whore, what then did this make Pulteney? His self-damning line of attack harks back to the rumours of 'some dark Deeds at Night' that the duchess of Marlborough threw in the face of Queen Anne after Abigail Masham replaced her as favourite.[51] Jill Campbell observes that Pulteney's attack 'uncannily anticipates Eve Kosofsky Sedgwick's thesis about the uncomfortable juncture between "homosocial" relations in the all-male preserves of government or commerce and the homosexual bonds which those establishments so fiercely reject; and the most insistent complaint of opposition writers during Walpole's ministry suggest that this juncture was under particular pressure in the period'.[52] Visual satires of the 1730s had sodomitical resonances, whether intended or not. The most infamous print of the era, *The Festival of the Golden Rump* (fig. 3), published in *Common Sense* on 19 March 1737 with an interpretive essay that extended into the issue of the 26th, has George II on a pedestal as Pagod, a satyr with an ample posterior. As the lengthy commentary explained, the high priestess (Caroline), adorned in jewels, has taken the opportunity to administer the golden clyster to his fundament as he kicks at his servants. The magician (Walpole), with belly as prominent as Pagod's rump, *Common Sense* points out, brandishes the rod with which he had stroked said rump to make it grow large enough for a statue in Grosvenor Square and make Pagod grunt with pleasure. The anal fixation in political satires would evolve over time into a less homoerotically suggestive scatology.[53]

The duel fought between Hervey and Pulteney on that frosty morning at the end of January only temporarily repaired masculine honour. Pulteney's indiscretion raised questions about his character and placed the opposition on the defensive. The *Craftsman* of 22 May 1731 addressed what it called malicious 'billingsgate' made 'by private closet whispers'. Pulteney, the vindication countered, did not desert his friends out of disappointed ambition; actually, they had abandoned their principles and forced him to go into opposition. Echoing the claim that Pulteney's nurturing had made Hervey's career, it posed the rhetorical question: 'May not *this Gentleman* think Himself the more obliged to contribute to *this* M____r's Fall, for having contributed so much to his Elevation?' The *Craftsman* then turned to the accusations of Jacobitism against Bolingbroke with the assertion that his slanderers had the advantage that 'arises from the various Scenes of Life, through which he has passed; some distant in place; some secret in their Nature. Here Calumny hath more Room to assert, and Innocence less opportunity to defend.' A pamphlet long mistakenly attributed to Hervey spat these words back with the exclamation 'What poor and contemptible Sophistry have we before us', and enquired: 'shall they then complain of this, whilst they torture another Gentleman's Actions in the most cruel and merciless manner? What Distance of Time or Place, what Privacy or Intricacy of Transactions, have ever moved their Candour, have ever restrained their Calumnies?' The author professed a desire to demonstrate how the two had abandoned the characters of true Englishmen and Whigs. It claimed: 'I have shewed this *altogether* from their *publick Behaviour*. I scorn to enter into *private Life*; I abhor to copy from their ever memorable PROPER REPLY, or from any of their other *Filthy Libels*, which have spared no *Family Affairs*, no *Personal Secrets*, or *Private Correspondencies*.'[54] Because the pamphlet referred to his private conversations with Walpole, Pulteney erred in supposing that the minister had written it or closely collaborated on its contents. With his characteristic hot-headedness, he blasted back with an intemperate pamphlet refuting the allegations against him point by point, including, ironically, that he had an unsteady temper. As for refraining from family affairs, Pulteney claimed that his accuser simply feared retaliation in kind because he had more secrets to hide.[55]

Family affairs and 'private Correspondencies' shifted in meaning as the controversy progressed over the first six months of 1731, illustrating how personal and political relations so easily became indistinguishable. Although one of the central questions under debate was whose family had enriched itself more at the nation's expense, the family under discussion became the one on the throne. Pulteney alleged conversations with Walpole during the time of the reconciliation between George I and the prince of Wales in which the minister had spoken contemptuously about the future George II. Repeating these alleged conversations actually hoisted Pulteney with his own petard. The pamphlet's printer, who also published the *Craftsman*, suffered arrest and George II struck off Pulteney's name from the list of privy councillors.[56] The *Craftsman* of 3 July made yet another attempt to salvage Pulteney's reputation by drawing distinctions among the range of negotiations that fell into the category of 'private Correspondencies'. These conversations had nothing to do with intimate friendship, the paper insisted, so a man could, and indeed should, divulge them to defend his reputation, something as dear as his life, liberty and property. Unrepentant, the

Craftsman went on to assert that the slanders of a ministerial hireling would have no more effect on 'this gentleman' than 'the impotent Rage of a *scolding old* woman'. The language of political contestation displayed in these public exchanges demonstrates how dangerous the emotional connections among men in power had become with the expansion of print culture and the opening up of the political arena beyond the court to public scrutiny.

Journalists eventually ceased trying to argue that politicians' private lives had no bearing on their capacity for public service. In the *Craftsman* of 14 August 1731, a letter addressed to Caleb D'Anvers opened:

> Tho' I agree with you in what I perceive to be the Opinion of most of your Readers, that your Discourses ought chiefly to turn on the Merit of *Facts*, not of *Names*, and therefore that all personal Enquiries should be avoided; yet, I cannot help thinking that there are some Cases, where it may not only be very justifiable to examine the *private Characters* of Men, but even necessarily apprize the Publick of them. The People have undoubtedly as just a Right to enquire into and be inform'd of the private Virtues and Vices of a Person, who is instructed with the Care of their *Liberty* and *Property*, as any Gentleman can have to demand the Character of the *Steward*, who is to manage his Estate. We know by *History*, we feel by daily Experience, how much *private Passions* influence *publick Actions*. If a Man is covetous, cruel, timorous, dissolute, immoral, insincere and unjust in *private Life*; it may, without Breach of Charity, be presumed that some of these Vices will stick to his *publick Character*.

The writer went on to reason that power and wealth often furnished the means to indulge the passions as well as enhanced the inclination to do so. A man of bad heart given arbitrary power would risk all to maintain it and would meet any opposition to his will with malice and rage. As discussed above, *Cato's Letters* a decade earlier had argued that absolute power rather than a man's personal inclinations promoted tyranny. This letter now declared the exact opposite: the coward in private inevitably turned bully in public; likewise, only a spendthrift could imagine bribery as an expedient of government. In response, the pro-Walpole *Free Briton* agreed that 'a wicked and unjust Man, one who is very bad in private Life, will hardly be good in a public Capacity. The Vices of his Nature will certainly be seen in his Office, and Change of Condition will not probably change his Manners.' The *Free Briton* assured its readers that 'whatever private Vices stick to publick Characters', opening up the minister's life would not show him at a disadvantage 'as a Husband, a Father, a Neighbour, or a Friend'. No sign had emerged of the minister being harsh, ill-natured, severe, unjust, haughty or deceiving, or guilty of betraying intimacies or gossipmongering. It referred to Steele's earlier description of him as an honest English gentleman and lauded his preservation of the nation's credit after the mad speculation on South Sea Company stock and the resulting financial crash.[57] The paper thundered: 'And when they have opened every Scene of his Life, when all his most concealed Affairs are brought forth to publick Censure, let that Man, *if any such shall be among them*, who hath acted a *fairer*, a *worthier*, and more *unblemished* Part as him to the World, the *honourable Person* will never be unjust to so much Worth; but will readily allow the Right of Power belongs to him, who, by that kind of Claim, can advance a better Title.' Hence, examination of the private character of men in power must extend to those who opposed them, particularly 'since nothing keeps the Passions more awake than opposition'.[58]

Personal Assessments of Political Characters

An examination of writings unintended for immediate publication indicates that men simply could not help making judgements of one another's political prowess based on their personal qualities, including their levels of sexual and financial continence and conquest. Hervey's memoirs of George II's reign, which opened with the accession in 1727 but which he began writing in 1733, show how politicians assessed character and how this way of thinking had classical roots. Hervey introduced himself as more qualified to write an account of the reign than those 'only acquainted with the chief people of this Court in the theatrical pageantry of their public characters, and never saw them when that mask of constraint and hypocrisy, essential to their stations, was enough thrown off for some natural features to appear'.[59] Much later on in the memoirs, while recounting in detail the royal family's internal squabbles in 1736, he bade persons who would dismiss such details as 'mere trifles' to stick to the gazettes:

> Let them enjoy their great reflections on great events unenvied, and seek them elsewhere; and let those only hope for any satisfaction or amusement in my writings who look with more indifferent eyes on the surface of those splendid trifles and pry less metaphysically into the bottom of

them, for it is to those only I write who prefer nature to gilding, truth to refinement, and have more pleasure in looking upon these great actors dressing and undressing than when they are representing their parts on the public stage.

Let Machiavels give rules for the conduct of princes, and let Tacituses refine upon them; let the one embellish their writings with teaching, and the other with commenting on these great personages; let these make people imagine that letter theory can be reduced to common practice, and let those pretend to account for accidental steps by premeditated policy, whilst I content myself with only relating facts just as I see them, without pretending to impute the effects of chance to design, or to account for the great actions of great people always by great causes.[60]

In his avowed intention to present personal details without didacticism, Hervey showed himself to be a student of Suetonius, not just Tacitus.[61] Roman historiography had an overarching moral purpose and, because individuals played such a dominant role in both Republic and Empire, a strong biographical component. For Tacitus, the best moral teachings came from learning about the noble deeds of antiquity rather than from philosophy or religion. As Hervey intimated, Tacitus did not shrink from passing moral judgement on his subjects' behaviour. Suetonius, on the other hand, dispassionately amassed detail to establish patterns that revealed a man's ethos. In Hervey's memoirs, as in Suetonius's histories, biography, anecdote and the construction of character engulfed the narrative.[62]

Like the ancients, Hervey suggested that the underlying reasons for the course that the 'great events' covered by the gazettes took lay in the personal characters of their actors. He dubbed the introduction to his memoirs 'a sort of *dramatis personæ*'. He listed the key politicians of his era, complete with character sketches evaluating their 'parts' (scholarly accomplishments), capacity for public business, trustworthiness, temperament and principles based on personal, not just public, successes and failures. Pulteney came first. Hervey wrote that he was 'naturally not generous, and made less so by the influence of a wife whose person he loved but whose understanding and conduct neither had nor deserved his good opinion and whose temper both he and every other body abhorred—a weak woman with all the faults of a bad man, of low birth, a lower mind, and the lowest manners, and without any one good, agreeable, or amiable quality but beauty'. He went on to describe how Pulteney 'never liked the people with whom he acted chiefly in his public character, nor loved those with whom he passed his idler hours'. In the former category, Walpole and Bolingbroke merely suffered Pulteney's want of esteem for them. In the latter,

> Lord Chesterfield and Mr. George Berkeley, with whom he lived in the most seeming intimacy, he mortally hated; but continued that seeming intimacy long after he did so, merely from a refinement of pride and an affection of being blind to what nobody else could help seeing. They had both made love to his wife, and though, I firmly believe, both unsuccessfully, yet many were of a contrary opinion; for her folly, her vanity, her coquetry, had given her husband the same jealousy, and the world the same suspicion, as if she had gone all those lengths in private which her public conduct, without one's being very credulous, would naturally have led one to believe.[63]

A domestic life that featured sexual and financial insecurity could not but make a man jealous, suspicious and incapable of forming firm alliances with other men.

Hervey's approach reflected both ancient precedent and modern practicalities. In the chronicles of ancient Rome, few aspects of a politician's life escaped scrutiny. 'Habits of eating, drinking and sexual behaviour, cultural interests and religious practices were very much conventional topics.'[64] Roman moralists made little distinction between sexual and sumptuary surfeit, and ideas associated with *incontinentia* (self-indulgence in either area) reflected cultural ambivalence. Excesses could signal a lack of manly self-control in some circumstances; but, in others, they were an assertion of masculine power and domination. In either case, a man's status could be compromised by an unruly wife, or be enhanced by his sway over the wives of his political opponents.[65] In Hervey's time, politicians not only had to curry favour with princes, they also had to win the confidence and respect of one another as they built alliances and negotiated party objectives. Their performances took place outside as well as inside the court in the social milieus of London townhouses and country estates. As they ate, drank, hunted game, attended sporting and cultural events, married, produced children, flirted and intrigued, they judged one another as men, not just political functionaries. If Pulteney could have chosen a wife of such a character, Hervey suggested, how could he possibly be a judge of others? Moreover, his consciousness of the mistake he had made in marrying her now impaired his dealings with other men, both personally and politically.

Struggling with his own place in the narrative, Hervey declared that he would assume the role of chorus in ancient tragedy, rather than actor, and sought to enforce a sense of his critical distance by referring to himself in the third person. At a later point in the manuscript, he reverted to the first person as he recorded his embarrassment at 'the frequent use I find myself obliged to make of my own name, notwithstanding all the resolutions I made against it when I undertook this work'.[66] As a memoir of a reign, the work aspired to history, but quickly slipped into autobiography (his enemies and, I dare say, some historians and biographers would have said fiction). Hervey could not resist the fashion for self-conscious, confessional writing. The memoirs illustrate how the untoward passions wrought from the complex bonds among family and friends influenced political relations and tested a man's mettle.

Hervey's explanation of the rift between himself and Pulteney commenced in a tone of objectivity: 'His [Hervey's] wife loved Mr. Pulteney and hated Sir Robert Walpole. Sir Robert had formerly made love to her, but unsuccessfully, which had produced the mutual enmity generally consequential on such circumstances, love in these cases being like a ball, which the greater strength it comes with, if it meets with resistance the farther it rebounds back from the point at which it was aimed.'[67] As the dowager duchess of Marlborough had facilitated the peerage of Hervey's father, Lord Bristol, in 1703, Pulteney also enlisted her help in convincing Bristol to bequeath a £600 pension for life upon Hervey to bring him over to the opposition. In this passage of the memoirs, Hervey starred in his own moral performance. To enhance his credibility, he admitted to a fault 'which little geniuses and young politicians are very apt to fall into from thinking it as possible for those who act an under part to avoid being explicit as it is for those who act the highest, and that people who are to bestow favours are as easily put off with indirect answers as those who are to receive them'.[68] He admitted error in not having informed Pulteney straightaway that he had started receiving £1,000 per annum from the court and, with ill health having prevented him from yet being of service, he felt obliged to fulfil the promises he had made to Walpole. Instead, he had made vague references to 'the ungiving temper of his father' as an excuse. Pulteney then persisted in believing that he simply had to prove the compliance of Lord Bristol and to convince Hervey that the administration would not last six months. This led to the colourful, indiscreet 'private Correspondencies' that generated so much discussion in the papers, discussed above.[69] By graciously taking the blame, Hervey portrayed himself as the man who was not a slave to his passions or susceptible to the importuning of family interests; he had a higher loyalty to public service.

As he unfavourably compared Pulteney's behaviour and character traits to those of Walpole, Hervey set out the personality he thought most conducive to good leadership. He thought that Walpole 'pursued his ambition without curbing his pleasures, and his pleasures without neglecting business; he did the latter with ease, and indulged himself in the other without giving scandal or offence. In private life, and to all who had any dependence upon him, he was kind and indulgent; he was generous without ostentation, and an economist without penuriousness; not insolent in success, nor irresolute in distress; faithful to his friends, and not inveterate to his foes.'[70] Regarding Lady Hervey's rejection of Walpole's advances, Hervey explained (referring to himself in the third person): 'Sir Robert Walpole's behaviour to his [Hervey's] wife he resolved not to know, in great points being always determined to let nothing interfere with what he thought just, and in little matters to suffer few checks to his pleasures. These two keys will serve to account for all his actions, prudent and imprudent.'[71] While making the point that Walpole's interest in women did not interfere with his judgement or personal loyalties, Hervey showed himself superior to Pulteney in having a wife both attractive and faithful. Hervey presented Sir Robert as a kindred spirit, another who was somehow above it all. In the upheaval of the royal courts separating in 1737, after Frederick took extraordinary measures to prevent his consort giving birth under his parents' roof, Hervey discussed the character flaws they each exhibited—Walpole's vanity in thinking the schism enhanced his indispensability and Hervey's own obsessive resentment of the prince of Wales—in a way that suggested comradeship. Hervey's sensitivity to the Great Man's vanity, he insisted, in spite of La Rochefoucauld's maxim that this would indicate a wound to his own, 'was a weakness that made him feel the difference between them less'.[72]

In support of his disinterested stance, the high regard that Hervey professed for Walpole's qualities did not extend to Walpole's kin. Again, the quality of a man's marriage reflected his character. On the topic of the diplomatic acumen of Walpole's brother, he recounted how Cardinal Fleury admired Horace for his sincerity and morality as exhibited, respectively, by his blunt speech and by his devotion to his wife. Hervey observed with venomous incredulity: 'So that Horace had the good fortune to succeed abroad by the very two qualities which drew the most contempt and ridicule upon him at home, which were the coarseness of his manners and the depravity of his taste. For the wife to whom he showed all this goodness was a tailor's daughter, whom he had married for interest, with a form scarce human, as offensive to the nose and the ears as to the eye, and one to whom he was kind, not from any principle of gratitude, but from the bestiality of his inclination.'[73] Hervey did not comment upon the infidelity of Sir Robert's first wife or pass judgement on the mercantile origins of his second, who had borne him a daughter while still his mistress. He noted casually: 'I must premise that Sir Robert Walpole at this time kept a very pretty young woman, daughter to a merchant, whose name was Skerret, and for whom he was said to have given (besides an annual allowance) £5000 by way of entrance money.'[74] For Hervey, neither wife impaired Walpole's character: 'Sir Robert was really humane, did friendly things, and one might say of him, as Pliny said of Trajan, and as nobody could say of his brother or his master [George II], "amicos habuit, quia amicus fuit": "He had friends, because he was a friend."'[75]

Although *sui generis* in myriad ways, Hervey did not seem so in the manner in which he judged other men. The odd collection of private, personal sketches by his inveterate enemy Philip Stanhope, fourth Earl of Chesterfield, published posthumously as *Characters*, shows the two men often targeting similar behaviours and traits, albeit with completely different interpretations. Walpole, Chesterfield observed,

> was the easy and profuse dupe of women, and in some instances in-decently so. He was excessively open to flattery, even of the grossest kind, and from the coarsest bunglers of that vile profession; which engaged him to pass most of his leisure and jovial hours with people whose blasted characters reflected upon his own. He was loved by many, but respected by none; his familiar and illiberal mirth and raillery leaving him no dignity. He was not vindictive, but on the contrary very placable to those who had injured him the most. His good-humour, good-nature, and beneficence, in the several relations of father, husband, master, and friend, gained him the warmest affections of all within that circle.[76]

Less Suetonian than Hervey, Chesterfield did not elaborate. Moreover, whereas he did describe the tastes in women of George I and George II as indicators of their character flaws, when it came to his fellow politicians, he expressed more concern over their sumptuary habits, in keeping with the opposition's fixation on fiscal probity.[77]

Like Hervey, Chesterfield derided Pulteney's lack of generosity, but made it all his own rather than blaming Pulteney's wife. He opined: 'His breast was the seat of all those passions which degrade our nature, and disturb our reason. There they raged in a perpetual conflict; but *avarice*, the meanest of them all, generally triumphed, ruled absolutely, and in many instances, which I forbear to mention, most scandalously.'[78] He cited avarice as the ruling passion as well for George II, Walpole, Lord Hardwicke and Henry Fox, the younger brother of Hervey's beloved Stephen.[79] In contrast, Chesterfield's friend and political ally Charles, Viscount Townshend had 'cleaner hands' than any other minister: 'Mere domestic oeconomy was his only care as to money, for he did not add one acre to his estate, and left his younger children very moderately provided for, though he had been in considerable and lucrative employments near thirty years.'[80] Hervey too judged men by their ability to handle money, not just their wives and mistresses. To Hervey, Bolingbroke 'was one to whom prosperity was no advantage, and adversity no instruction. He had brought his affairs to that pass that he was almost as much distressed in his private fortune as desperate in his political views.'[81] Similarly, Chesterfield remarked that Bolingbroke's ambition 'destroyed both his fortune and reputation' in the same way that the licentious dissipation of his youth had 'impaired both his constitution and his character'.[82] The two antagonists had very different concerns, so the frequency with which they coincided in the qualities that they noticed in others suggests that the political world had relatively uniform standards for judging character.

Notwithstanding this consistency, personal agendas, including impulses to compensate for shortcomings and errors, in addition to political interests, often lurked behind the decision to drag a man's marital and extramarital situations into evaluations of his public worth. Hervey and Chesterfield did agree upon Townshend's haughty, coarse manner and quickness to anger but judged his fundamental character in very different ways. Hervey related an anecdote of Walpole's raillery in the presence of the queen insinuating Townshend's design on the ugly, pious and aged Lady Trevor, which, given its absurdity, would have been 'impossible to shock my Lord's prudery, let him pique himself ever so much on the chastity of his character'. Chesterfield, in contrast, insisted that in spite of Townshend's 'seemingly brutal' manners, 'his nature was by no means so; for he was a kind husband to both his wives, a most indulgent father to all his children, and a benevolent master to his servants, sure tests of real good-nature, for no man can long together simulate or dissimulate at home'.[83]

Chesterfield could well have been thinking of himself: his unsung efforts to inspire greatness in his equally mediocre illegitimate son and godson, and to enjoy some appreciation for the gracious civility and support he imagined he had lavished upon his wife and mistresses. He began these pen portraits, perhaps the start of a memoir, after he resigned as secretary of state in 1748 and, in a retired solitude intensified by his increasing deafness, contemplated his legacy.[84] His biographer, Samuel Shellabarger, adjudges Hervey astute in his assessment of Chesterfield's affectations. He quotes a letter that Chesterfield wrote to his son in 1747 cautioning him not to fall into the error of cultivating false appearances of fashionable rakishness, suggesting the earl's regret of his own youthful follies.[85] The reputation stuck, however. As Sir Robert's son Horace Walpole observed in retrospect, Chesterfield 'had early in his life announced his claim to wit, and the women believed in it. He had besides given himself out for a man of great intrigue, with as slender pretensions; yet the women believed in that too—one should have thought they had been more competent judges of merit in that particular!'[86]

Hervey too seemed engaged in damage control of his legacy as he penned his memoirs. Alexander Pope had perpetuated Pulteney's characterization of him with references in his verse to 'Lord Fanny' (a double piece of wordplay on a slang term for vagina and on Fannius, Horace's unworthy rival), Sporus (Nero's castrated concubine), 'Amphibious Thing' and 'one vile Antithesis'.[87] In his memoirs, Hervey appeared to be channelling Suetonius's image of a masterful Augustus conquering women in political calculation, not lust, as he described the resumption of his affair with Anne Vane, who, he implied, had jilted him to become mistress to the prince of Wales in 1732.[88] Hervey claimed that, in 1735, Frederick used his impending nuptials as an excuse to discard Vane; he had already taken up with the jealous and cunning Lady Archibald Hamilton, who wanted her gone. Frederick had failed to discern that Vane already had grown bored with him, 'telling Lord Hervey that she wished nothing so much as to be disembarrassed of the Prince, except the being at liberty to see his Lordship with more ease, so this proposal of separation from H.R.H. would have given her much more pleasure than ever she found in his acquaintance had it not been for this conditional article of going out of England'. As he flaunted the superior virility to which Vane's preference attested, Hervey indulged in a confessional digression written in the third person that countered the Lord Fanny image:

> Lord Hervey and Miss Vane met constantly all this summer once or twice a week. The Prince had taken her a house at Wimbledon where all her servants were, except one old fellow and a maid, who were left in

her house in town. This made it easy for her to let Lord Hervey into her house in town unperceived and thither once or twice a week she constantly came to meet him, who used to be admitted as soon as it was dark and go away before it was light.

But the difficulty of getting tea, fruit, and supper, at her house made them soon change the scene of their meeting to his lodgings at St. James's, and his wife being gone into France with the Duke and Duchess of Richmond for three months, this coast was quite clear. Miss Vane used to walk thither, Lord Hervey himself letting her in and out; and in this manner they used to pass whole nights together, as little apprehensive of danger as if no eyes had been upon them and that at this juncture it would not have been as convenient to the Prince as destructive to her to have traced this commerce and proved it upon her.

Whether or not Hervey intended the 'in and out' as a double entendre, he did make clear that Vane was not visiting him for tea and cards and that she was ardent. He went on to describe a night together in bed at St James's when she had a fit of colic so severe that she fell into convulsions and a swoon, making him fear that she would die in his lodgings. He managed to revive her sufficiently to bundle her off home where, presumably, she could die unobtrusively if it came to it. Hervey boasted: 'But even this accident did not prevent these indiscreet people from exposing themselves in the same manner to the same dangers, or from meeting as frequently as they had formerly done.'[89] These were hardly the feats of a Sporus or a Pathetick. Hervey also chalked up a triumph over Pulteney in this torrid tale. Pulteney took blame for the letter that Hervey composed on Vane's behalf in his grand design of 'exposing and fretting the Prince'. Soon after the prince granted her a generous settlement, Vane and her infant son sickened and died within a week of one another. Hervey cold-bloodedly recorded these events, noting the surprise that the prince's affliction over the loss of the boy occasioned, without a single reference to any feeling of his own.[90] Political, not sentimental or carnal, passions prevailed.

Hervey reflected upon 'how much character and reputation depends sometimes on unaccountable accident and the caprice of mankind' as he considered his co-author in Sedition and Defamation Display'd, whom the king had dubbed 'Stinking Yonge'. '[W]ithout having done anything that I know of remarkably profligate—anything out of the common track of a ductile courtier and a parliamentary tool, this name was proverbially used to express everything pitiful, corrupt, and contemptible. It is true he was a great liar, but rather a mean than a vicious one. He had been always constant to the same party, was good-natured and good-humoured, never offensive in company, nobody's friend, nobody's enemy. He had no wit in private conversation, but was remarkably quick in taking hints to harangue upon in Parliament.' Hervey observed that Sir Robert 'caressed him without loving him, and employed him without trusting him', so having Walpole's favour did nothing to elevate Yonge's character. Hervey saw Yonge as one of the few exceptions to 'a pretty general rule—that is, that however preju-diced some particulars may be for, and others against, such men in public stations and characters, yet the true merit of such men commonly finds and settles in its own weight, as much as any commodity in a market; and is generally rated according to its real value in public opinion, as much as the other in public sale'.[91]

The use of the market metaphor indicates Hervey's awareness that poli-tics had become a business, with public opinion having become akin to a tradesman's credit, its maintenance dependent on good relations with others in one's trade as well as the consumers of one's product. Perhaps he wished to distance himself from the patronage-clientage relations at the foundation of Pulteney's attack. Having retained his place at court in spite of the assaults upon his personal character, Hervey could take comfort in the belief that the extremes of reputation ultimately balanced out and that usefulness coupled with fidelity guaranteed a man's worth. Time after time in Hervey's *dramatis personæ* a man's capacity for friendship determined his political success: Walpole possessed it; Yonge did not. Indeed, he attributed Chesterfield's failures at politics to a vain, undiscerning 'propen-sity to ridicule' that made him 'sought and feared, liked and not loved'. Queen Caroline 'always disliked Lord Chesterfield, owned it, and used to say that it was because he had always disliked her'. Marvelling at the lack of political sense he displayed in courting the king instead of the queen, and Townshend instead of Walpole, Hervey professed to find only one expla-nation possible: Chesterfield 'thought the people that were easiest deceived were the likeliest for him to please, and that nobody was capable of being made his friend but in the same degree that they were capable of being made his dupes'.[92] It would seem that Chesterfield became his own dupe.

Men or Measures?

That the man who allowed his personal distastes for Walpole and the queen to influence his political positions so greatly should be credited with coining the maxim 'not men, but measures' gives Chesterfield's biographer, Shellabarger, pause.[93] Considering the slipperiness of this principle in its various applications, however, the ambiguous and contradictory politics of its inception makes perfect sense. In a letter of 6 March 1742 to his chaplain, Dr Richard Chenevix, after Walpole's fall and the formation of a new ministry that did not include him, Chesterfield expressed a sentiment that he would develop in print the following year:

> The public has already assigned me different employments, and among others that which you mention; but I have been offered none, I have asked for none, and I will accept of none till I see a little clearer into matters than I do at present; I have opposed measures not men, and the change of two or three men only is not a sufficient pledge to me that measures will be changed; nay, rather an indication that they will not; and I am sure no employment whatsoever shall prevail me to support measures I have so justly opposed. A good conscience is in my mind a better thing than the best employment, and I will not have the latter till I can keep it with the former; when that can be, I shall not decline a public life, though in truth, more inclined to a private one.[94]

In questioning the veracity of this assertion, as well as whether Chesterfield deserved the accolades of the opposition as a defender of 'patriot' virtues when he joined its ranks, Shellabarger points out that, whatever he might declare, Chesterfield did accept honours and office from Walpole. Additionally, his inconsistent voting record could only be explained as motivated by factiousness.

Chesterfield must have known that marshalling support against a measure, Walpole's Excise Bill, in 1733, the Great Man's first significant defeat, would cost him the lord stewardship, but even if he did so out of honest conviction, he also did so in full expectation of the minister's ouster. The maxim, then, seems more the product of Chesterfield's growing disillusionment with party politics, which Shellabarger ably chronicles, than a statement of lifelong principle. In a letter written to a friend as he toured the Continent seeking spa waters, culture and diverting company to buoy up his flagging health and spirits in 1741, Chesterfield expressed pain over the politics of personal character: 'One thing that helps me a great deal here is my extreme indifference as to what any people I meet with may either think or say of me: whereas I confess that, in England, my consciousness that, of late I have not only been dispirited, but almost stupefied and incapable of either attention or imagination, made me uneasy and unwilling to appear among those whose good opinion, if I ever had, I was unwilling to lose. I had that diffidence and distrust of myself which never fail to make one appear still worse than one really is.' Chesterfield went on to say that, if his health did not improve, 'the honest comforts of a private life shall be my determination, as they have long been my wish'. Yet, if his health allowed, he would be ready to serve his friends if called.[95] The true politician never issues a declaration without an escape clause. The constant attention to one's image that made this flexibility requisite, however, came at some personal cost.

An early inspiration for Chesterfield's maxim might have been *Men and Measures Characterised from Horace. Being an Imitation of the XVI*[th] *Ode of his Second Book*, an eight-page, sixpenny opposition pamphlet that appeared in 1739 during the debate over the concessionary treaty Walpole made with the Spanish at the Convention of Pardo. Chesterfield wrote to the poet Robert Nugent: 'As I know of certainty that *Men and Measures* was not Pope's, I really thought it might be, and took it for yours, but I am glad it is not, because I am glad we have anybody who can write well enough to be mistaken for you.'[96] In Horace's ode, mariners out on a dark sea long for repose; neither the riches nor the grandeur of a regal court can assuage the tumults that swirl around them faster than a stag or a storm wind. What, the poet asks, causes the avaricious ambition of men? Only the joy of a simple, frugal life allows one the calm to meet whatever fate brings. He contemplates fallen heroes and undeserved fortune and, from his small country estate, disdains the mean spirit of the vulgar. In the imitation, the author superimposed these images and sentiments upon the British sailors in pirate-infested waters, the 'shameful' peace with Spain bought with bribed votes, Walpole's greedy henchmen and the ill-starred opposition:

> In vain thy Spirit, Strength, and Ease,
> O *P_ult_y*, warm, persuade and please
> While the resistless Nod of *B_b*
> Directs the Vote; and rules the Job.

The original and imitation both capture the longing for withdrawal from a corrupt world into a virtuous rural idyll that Chesterfield increasingly felt and Pope's verse at the time epitomized.[97] Although the poem does not articulate the political adage, it does set apart the independent man of principle from the ambitious acolytes of the powerful:

Whence then thy Schemes, deluded Man,
This noisy Chace in Life's short Span;
From Clime to Clime, from Pole to Pole;
Where Tempests Sweep or Billows roll;
Pursue you Bliss? Know, bustling Elf,
To gain it thou must lose thy self.

Whether by bad luck, an unfortunate manner, an inability to inspire trust and fidelity or by hitching his wagon to the wrong star, Chesterfield found himself left out in the cold by the personality-driven party politics of this era. 'Not men, but measures' was for him a face-saving philosophy by which he could reject the system that failed him while creating for himself a platform kept warm with self-righteous indignation.

William Pitt the Elder spun this maxim into another moral performance that proved effective as an oppositional tool, although his usage was as self-contradictory as Chesterfield's. In a wonderful irony, Walpole had actually been the first to deploy this principle as he fended off the motion for his removal on 13 February 1741. Sir Samuel Sandys, who introduced it, asserted that Walpole's dictatorship rendered inconsistent the constitutional principles that the king had the right to choose his ministers and that the king should govern. Walpole had the confidence of the king but usurped his powers; hence, parliament should have the power to remove him. Opposition politicians alleged that Walpole's unpopularity, evidenced by the tumults over his Excise Bill and his concessions to Spain, confirmed that he was 'weak and wicked'. Walpole and his supporters retorted that his only 'crime' was longevity of office; the opposition really only wanted a change of ministers, not measures. Furthermore, to judge the public utility of measures based on the minister's popularity rather than the king's favour would be to impugn his majesty's wisdom, undermine royal prerogative and countenance mob rule. When parliamentary losses finally drove Walpole out a year later, Pitt made 'not men, but measures' his battle cry, but turned Walpole's application of the principle on its head by claiming popularity as well as independence. He united these seemingly mutually exclusive qualities by contrasting himself with placemen who did the bidding of corrupt patrons out of a personal loyalty begotten of dependency. Paradoxically, it took a larger-than-life character to sustain the claim that personality or personal ties should not influence politics. For over twenty years, this principle justified Pitt's maverick behaviour. Yet, when Pitt invoked 'the people' with whom he was popular, he appealed to country gentlemen, not the commonality, and when he accepted a peerage from George III to become earl of Chatham in 1766, his image as the 'Great Commoner' lost its lustre.[98]

With the advent of 'not men, but measures', the debate over the relation between personal character and political probity became enfolded in discussions of party. In an essay first published in 1741, David Hume used the words 'party' and 'faction' interchangeably, but made a distinction between personal and real associations. He made the blanket statement, 'Men have such a propensity to divide into personal factions, that the smallest appearance of real difference will produce them.' At the same time, Hume declared factions to be characteristic of small republics rather than monarchies. 'Every domestic quarrel, there, becomes an affair of state. Love, vanity, emulation, any passion, as well as ambition and resentment, begets public division.' Yet he added the qualification that 'in those factions, which are founded on the most real and most material difference, there is always observed a great deal of personal animosity or affection'. Nonetheless, one quality—either emotional or material—would be dominant and thereby determine whether a faction was personal or real.[99] He went on to state that interest, principle or affection stood as the basis of a real faction. The last category, Hume explained, referred to 'those which are founded on the different attachments of men towards particular families and persons, whom they desire to rule over them. These factions are often very violent; though, I must own, it may seem unaccountable, that men should attach themselves so strongly to persons, with whom they are no wise acquainted, whom perhaps they never saw, and from whom they never received, nor can ever hope for any favour.' Here Hume was referring to the 'close and intimate' bond individuals *imagined* to exist between themselves and their sovereign.[100] Increasingly, as we will see, leaders of parties or factions would inspire this same imaginary emotional bond as more people became involved in partisanship through contested elections, crowd actions and press coverage of politics.

CHAPTER THREE

The Measure of Men

Changes at court after George III's accession in 1760 furthered the personalization of politics. Young, British-born and chaste, the king raised expectations for national moral regeneration. His elevation to the ministry of his 'dearest friend', John Stuart, Earl of Bute, as secretary of state for the northern department in March 1761, however, would be interpreted as a return to Stuart corruption. This act provoked politicians into a furore of irrational, xenophobic, misogynistic and highly sexualized personal abuse against this new favourite that would fan out and strike other ministers. The first king since Charles I not to keep mistresses, George III, with the full support of Queen Charlotte, did not receive women of questionable reputation at court. The new directive from the palace against extramarital liaisons allowed for fresh lines of attack against political adversaries. Yet the king quickly learned that marital fidelity alone did not make the perfect paterfamilias. Contemporary perceptions of the War for American Independence as a civil conflict produced partisan images of George III as a tyrannical father on the one side of the debate and the rebelling colonists as ungrateful children on the other. Faction, often presented in terms of personal friendship, destabilized the cabinet as the king warred against the great Whig families and their formidable patronage network to the detriment of colonial policy. Although some may argue that masculinity is *always* in crisis, with its self-definition, performance and defence, particular events cause anxiety to spike. After the loss of America, the ruling elite, criticized for effeminate aristocratic manners and mores, responded by closing ranks and reinventing itself in a manly, heroic mould. In response to the French Revolution's assault on traditional hierarchies, George rehabilitated his image by endorsing a model of manliness based on familial responsibility. He regularly appeared in public with queen and children in tow, allowing the loyalist press to represent him as the devoted father of his people.[1] By the 1790s, political propaganda routinely measured a man's character according to his ability to uphold this new, domesticated masculinity.[2]

The increasing number of venues for sociability and for journalistic reporting placed politicians under greater public scrutiny. Gillian Russell finds the crisis of masculinity brewing well before the humiliations of the American war as women grew into an unruly force in the world of fashionable public entertainments—theatres, pleasure gardens and exhibitions— that proliferated during the 1760s and 1770s, and joined the coffeehouses, taverns and clubs as loci for the new commercialized politics of the Wilkes and Liberty movement. The outlandish dimensions of modish feminine headdress epitomized the aggressive commandeering of public spaces by the so-called gentler sex and the once-shadowy figure of the mistress transformed into a disruptive public icon: the demirep.[3] The wives and mistresses of elite men became objects of public interest. Paul Langford notes the press's increased prying into the private lives of politicians as the post–1688–89 system of party management gradually moved political culture from the public space of the court to the privacy of the club, an all-male enclave. The admission of journalists into parliamentary debates, thanks to the Wilkite agitation of the 1770s, encouraged readers' familiarity with individual MPs as personalities. This, in conjunction with the growing presence of women in the political sphere as hostesses, canvassers, writers and patrons, spawned gossip columns that stimulated popular fascination with West End society. As the interest in private lives intensified, politicians by the turn of the century had become standoffish in public. In Langford's interpretation: 'Propriety, decency, modesty, were the approved terms for the coldness, correctness, and unpretentiousness which made modern statesmanship superior. At bottom this claim is to a higher virtue; it is about morals as much as manners.'[4] Beneath this orderly veneer, however, lay much turmoil.

The court's campaign for domestic virtue, on top of the sociability outside the palace that the business of party necessitated, placed politicians in an awkward position. Few could combine true marital fidelity and a devoted home life with the sustained accessibility and conviviality—encompassed in Dr Johnson's notion of clubbability—that traditionally supported bonding among men. The temptations, moral dilemmas and deceptions in many politicians' lives sometimes resembled the plots of popular novels. Conduct manuals and fiction of this era illustrate how the very natures of domesticity,

marriage and familial duties had become matters of debate among the aristocratic, genteel, professional and commercial ranks of society. Scholars of
the domestic novel have drawn correlations between the range of familial
relations and their dysfunctions the genre depicted and the different stages
of the Stuarts' succession crisis and its resolution. Ultimately, while some
exalted the importance of a warm, loving family, others exposed the oppression lying beneath its deceptive comforts. The tensions that played out in the
wider political world resemble the struggles between individual identity and
familial obligations dramatized in domestic fiction.[5]

Although by the end of the century men had to be discreet about their
extramarital affairs in public, they continued to assess one another's sexual
prowess in private. As shown in Chapter 2, the self-imposed restraints
against personal invective had been hard to maintain because of the long
tradition of viewing political relations in personal, often sexualized terms.
The danger of this language became manifest with John Wilkes's unfettered use of the sodomy trope against the king's ministers in a political
arena that now included the London mob. After witnessing the consequences of the frenzied hatred against Bute, politicians drew back in self-
protection. Insinuations about the sexuality of William Pitt the Younger
and Edmund Burke flared in the mid–1780s but never ignited—a marked
change from the escalations of personal abuse in political screeds of the
Walpole and the Wilkes and Liberty eras. Metaphors of sodomitical
corruption receded in political discourse at the same time that blackmailing
and judicial persecution of non-elite men suspected or convicted of 'the
crime not fit to be named' heightened in ferocity. Thomas A. King explains
this trend as the relocation of effeminacy from the aristocratic courtier to
the public, foppish, woman-hating figure of the sodomite who rejected
the now-privatized domain of domesticity.[6] As the political invective of the
1760s and 1770s shows, the exigencies of the moment and individual
circumstance shaped political discourse more than any hard-and-fast moral
principles did. Moreover, a closer look at the shifting political alliances of
the following decades reveals how financial and sexual behaviour condemned
in public could promote and sustain political attachments in private.
Principles might have been the bricks that built party, but personality
became the mortar.[7]

Intent upon representing George III's favour of Bute as a throwback to
pre-1688 court tyranny, Wilkes revived the scurrility of the Restoration
period and broadcast it to a now further-reaching political nation via an
expanding print culture. In prose and verse he portrayed Bute in possession

of a phallus of monstrous Scottish proportions used to seduce the princess dowager and thereby usurp the power of the royal sceptre, images then depicted graphically in visual satire.[8] In Wilkite propaganda, the sexual metaphors of political power mixed with gossip, innuendo and scandal, both real and imaginary. The inconsistency and selectivity with which political argument applied moral standards became more blatant than ever. The Wilkes phenomenon also demonstrates even more spectacularly than the set-to between Lord Hervey and William Pulteney the dangers of soured friendship between politicians. When Sir Francis Dashwood, John Montagu, fourth Earl of Sandwich and others among his partners in dissipation obtained places in the government and distanced themselves from him, Wilkes published lurid details of their exploits.[9] At the same time, he could not deny his own libertinism, so he carefully managed his image to distinguish his manly tastes from the alleged unnatural vices of his old associates. His personal life, an odd fusion of sexual conquest and domestic devotion to his daughter, Mary, spanned aristocratic and mercantile mores. Wilkes's libertinism became symbolic of political liberty and manly independence, held up in contrast to the sodomitical dependency and submission that he claimed characterized the ethos of the royal court and its debauched aristocrats. When prosecuted on charges of blasphemy for *An Essay on Woman* (1763), however, he based his defence on the right to private opinion. Hypocritically, Wilkes and his supporters contended that his private views and pursuits had no bearing upon his public role and thus were irrelevant, while simultaneously publicizing their enemies' financial and sexual concupiscence. They justified doing so with the argument that the system of favouritism, granting high office based on hereditary privilege and personal connections, turned ministers into the king's private servants, so personal vices, potentially corrupting of the whole realm, had to be matters of public interest.[10] Much of this is reminiscent of the earl of Chesterfield nursing his personal resentments as he insisted that measures, not men, really mattered. The Wilkites shouted aloud the judgements that earlier politicians had only whispered in private unless severely and personally provoked.

The anti-Bute agitation amplified the tendency to see politics in terms of competition, seduction, domination, propagation and inheritance. Over a decade after Chesterfield composed his other 'characters', he examined Bute's in the context of his administration. Perhaps his own personal dynastic failure made Chesterfield represent Bute's heritage and its perpetuation as a mark of crass, common appetite:

THE EARL OF BUTE was of an ancient family in Scotland. His name was Stuart, he called himself a descendant of that Royal House, and was humble enough to be proud of it. He was by his mother's side, nephew to John and Archibald, Dukes of Argyll. He married the daughter of Wortley Montagu, by Lady Mary Pierrepont, eminent for her parts and her vices. It was a runaway love match, notwithstanding which, they lived very happily together: she proved a very good wife, and did in no way *matrizare*. He proved *a great husband*, and had thirteen or fourteen children successively by her, in as little time as was absolutely necessary for their being got and born, though he married her without a shilling, and without a reasonable probability of ever having two, for she had a brother, who is still alive. She proved an immense fortune by the death of her father and mother, who, disinheriting their son, left her five or six hundred thousand pounds.[11]

Chesterfield then went on to describe how the couple had lived in frugality for eight or nine years beforehand as Bute studied 'agriculture, botany and architecture, the employments rather of an industrious than of an elevated mind'. Once they moved to town, Bute insinuated himself into Prince Frederick's 'little idle, frivolous and dissipated Court' and became a favourite:

The Scandalous Chronicle says, that he was still a greater favourite of the princess of Wales: I will not, nor cannot decide upon that fact. It is certain on one hand, that there were many very strong indications of the tenderest connection between them; but on the other hand, when one considers how deceitful appearances often are in those affairs, the capriciousness and inconsistency of women, which make them often be unjustly suspected; and the improbability of knowing exactly what passes in *tête-à-têtes*, one is reduced to mere conjectures. Those who have been conversant in that sort of business, will be sensible of the truth of this reflection.

This professed scepticism shows the sexual liaison to be beside the point, given Chesterfield's tendency to place sexual and political relationships on similar hierarchical grounds in which appearances were all. Later on in this account, while discussing negotiations between George III and William Pitt the Elder, Chesterfield opined that 'these political *tête-à-têtes*, like amorous ones, *à huis clos*, leave room only for conjectures, but none for certainty; and the performers only are able to tell, what, by the way, they never do tell, the truth, the whole truth, and nothing but the truth'.[12] Appearances of secrecy in political and personal alliances attracted speculation, conjecture, rumour and interpretations shaped by self-interest.

Chesterfield also dissected Bute's manner as an indicator of behaviour and character. He observed that Bute 'never looked at those he spoke to, or who spoke to him, a great fault in a Minister, as in the general opinion of mankind it implies conscious guilt; besides that, if it hinders him from being penetrated, it equally hinders him from penetrating others. The subaltern Ministers whom he employed under him, particularly in the management of the House of Commons, were most of them incapable of serving him, and others unwilling to do it.'[13] Although in this sense penetration refers to intellectual acuity, or the gaining of insight, Chesterfield's usage in the context of the male gaze and the domination of subalterns coupled with the word's other denotations cannot but bring to mind the part of Bute's anatomy that had become such an object of obsession. As other 'characters' of his discussed in Chapter 2 demonstrated, Chesterfield might have had a greater than average tendency towards the language of gallantry, but he certainly was not alone in viewing political contestation in this way.

Others followed suit. James, 2nd Earl Waldegrave, whom Bute had displaced as Prince George's tutor, employed the old genre of the secret history as an outlet for his resentment. His allegory of Leicester House featured Bute as Vigorosus and emphasized his physical attributes, 'which sometimes may have attracted vulgar widows'.[14] Horace Walpole, noting the irony and injustice of Waldegrave dying on 8 April 1763, the day that Bute stepped down from office, described the 'severe satires' against Princess Augusta and Bute that Waldegrave had shared with him. Walpole described Waldegrave as 'so thoroughly fatigued with the insipidity of his pupil the King, and so harassed and unworthily treated by the Princess and Lord Bute, that no one of the most inflammable vengeance, or of the coolest resentment, could harbour more bitter hatred and contempt than he did'.[15] Whatever the distorting lens of antipathy wrought, Walpole anticipated that Waldegrave's memoirs would corroborate many of the incidents related in his own. One of Walpole's manuscripts covering events of 1756 observed Augusta's marks of favour and signs of attraction, which, he further noted, Bute took no pains to conceal. 'His bows grew more theatric, his graces contracted some meaning, and the veins in the calf of his leg were constantly displayed in the eyes of the poor captivated Princess, and of a

Court, who maliciously affected to wonder that they preserved so much roundness.'[16]

In investigating the origins of the rumour of a sexual liaison, which he traces to Waldegrave, John L. Bullion helps explain the persistent link between sex and politics. He draws upon Patricia Meyer Spacks's observation that in the eighteenth century gossip thrived because of a prevailing inclination towards judging inner character via analysis of outward behaviour. Hence, politicians and courtiers habitually recorded the minutiae of what they observed in order to assess the motives and intents of persons with whom they collaborated and competed. Waldegrave, Bullion argues, was accurate in his observations of the princess's and Bute's behaviour, including the opportunities they seemed to create for tête-à-têtes, but wrong in his interpretation of a sexual liaison. Princess Augusta and Bute actually risked their reputations in order to conceal his secret tutoring of her son. George II would have taken custody of his grandson had he known the truth.[17] Bullion's analysis reminds us that gossip and intrigue remained an integral part of political power brokering. Even after 1688–89, sexual appeal and appetite as well as untoward emotional attachments, whether in appearance or reality, could help make or break political fortunes. Courtier mores persisted.

Although, compared to earlier reigns, the courts of the first three Georges had lost their political, cultural and social dominance, royal palaces remained important sites in each of these three spheres for the ruling elite. Invoking an expression employed by the countess of Leicester circa 1746, Hannah Smith observes: 'While the court continued to be used as a space to broker patronage and politics, it was also a venue for politics in another way—as a "Publick Place" where actions were performed in the glare of the public gaze and an arena where political transactions and events could be made known.' Smith notes how behaviour at court continued to provide an index of who was in and who was out of favour. The regular court rituals of levees, drawing rooms and commemorative entertainments on anniversaries and other celebratory occasions brought out the elite in droves where they reinforced their political and social status as they showed off their sartorial splendour and rarefied taste. As she concludes, models of the court as an institution in decline need readdressing in light of its role as a venue for extra-parliamentary politics.[18] Additionally, newspapers, pamphlets and graphic satire broadcasted the minutiae of the courtiers' observations into the public sphere.

The fallout from the Bute controversy illustrates how a court alliance could have wide-ranging effects. While politicians blamed him for the subversion of constitutional balance between king and parliament, Bute came to represent a whole range of injustices resented up and down the social hierarchy.[19] Rumours of illicit sex provided evocative metaphors for elite privilege and the abuse of power. Reflecting the prevailing moral standards of the time, anti-Bute propaganda did not castigate his adultery; instead, perceptions of Princess Augusta's ambition made petticoat government, with its suggestion of the Frenchified, tyrannical Stuart court, the dominant trope. The controversy also represented a clash between old and new codes of morality on another level. Male bonds of private friendship and confederacy usually mediated politicized sexual gossip and rumour. Now, as Jason M. Kelly observes, Sandwich's counterattack on Wilkes through making the *Essay on Woman* public 'represented the betrayal of a libertine code of conduct, which, while reveling in public rumor, did not make private activities a matter of political debate, as long as private activities did not corrupt public conduct. At the same time, a gentlemanly code of honor proscribed the betrayal of confidence and friendship, an act as offensive to Wilkite supporters as arbitrary arrest and seizure of goods.'[20] Paradoxically, the Wilkes and Liberty movement drew upon building animosity against aristocratic privilege as it lamented the demise of its ethos.

Having this moral combat conducted in the full glare of publicity helped endow Sandwich with an incommensurate and enduring reputation for licentiousness. Letters preserved in his archives show that, even up to a couple of years before his death in 1792 at age seventy-four, women looking for a sexual adventure continued to proposition him. Another great professor of the dictum that private morality had no effect on a man's capacity for public service, Sandwich had brought the *Essay on Woman* to the Lords' attention with a sensational oral rendition of the obscene poem in the House. He justified this act as incumbent upon him as a public official, given that in this work Wilkes had appropriated the name of William Warburton, Bishop of Gloucester in contravention of parliamentary privilege. Wilkes had not published the manuscript for general distribution, however, and Sandwich brandished a copy purloined from a private residence. The tales that the Wilkites spread relentlessly in retaliation sealed Sandwich's public persona as debauched, perfidious and a downright buffoon, although he was by no means the most abandoned, depraved or ridiculous of the libertines. As an aristocrat, he could not present his sexuality as anti-authoritarian in furtherance of the cause of liberty as Wilkes had done. In the end, paradoxically, a man who kept a mistress in the manner of a wife became more execrable than one who whored around. His lawful wife institutionalized for insanity, Sandwich lived openly in adultery with Martha Ray, a singer of humble origins, for sixteen years, producing numerous illegitimate children. In spite of Ray's efforts to preserve appearances, their relationship provided fodder for Sandwich's enemies. Portrayals of him dominated by a scheming, money-hungry vixen trafficking in naval promotions had a deleterious impact on assessments of his work at the Admiralty. In fact, Ray felt insulted by Sandwich's parsimony, particularly his reticence regarding making a financial settlement for her and their children. Her murder by a deranged young clergyman in front of Covent Garden Theatre in 1779 excited publicity and speculation. This fed into the already-fervid public interest in the lives of eminent men and their lower-class mistresses, so vividly apparent in the success of *Town and Country Magazine* (1769–91). Sandwich's displays of grief brought him much unaccustomed public sympathy. At the same time, the pages of *Town and Country* and other publications conveyed fears of aristocratic corruption and fashionable vice trickling down into other classes of society. What the magazine had once peddled as entertainment became a sign of dangerous moral decay, which brought about the temporary demise of fashionable scandal sheets in the mid-1790s.[21]

Spectacular Domesticity and Public Opinion

Embellished stories circulating about members of the ruling elite gave them the qualities of fictional characters, whose lives readers could imagine, discuss and judge. The tribulations of the duke of Grafton, made first lord of the Treasury in 1766 and assuming leadership of the ministry in 1768 after William Pitt the Elder, now the earl of Chatham, had withdrawn into one of his nervous states, epitomize the growing pains in the transition to a more democratized polity and the accompanying cultural shift from libertinism to domesticity. Lawrence Stone's introduction to his case study of the Grafton divorce evokes the heritage of the prior era: 'Augustus Henry Fitzroy, 3rd Duke of Grafton, was the third in direct line of descent from the second bastard son of Charles II by the latter's mistress Barbara Villiers, Lady Castlemaine, later Duchess of Cleveland in her own right. Of all Charles's many mistresses, she was the most sexually and financially voracious, and she took good care to see that her younger son was handsomely rewarded for his paternity.'[22] Albeit Grafton gained £40,000 and the promise of more by his marriage in 1756 to Anne Liddell, heir to Lord Ravensworth, the couple had professedly married for love.

Nevertheless, while the duke indulged his passion for the turf, the hunt and gallantry, the duchess developed a passion—but not, alas, a skill—for cards. Stone observes that, while Grafton had no inclination to surrender the sexual prerogatives of his class, he expected his wife to uphold the ideals of a companionate marriage. Aside from her ruinous debts, what unsettled him most was regularly coming home exhausted from political business around midnight to find her in the midst of a rout that would continue for hours. After much quarrelling, they began negotiating the terms of a separation at the end of 1764, whereupon the duchess, who had already been turned out of the house, found out that her husband had installed in her rooms Nancy Parsons, a notorious demirep. By 1767, the duchess had taken up with the earl of Upper Ossory, who got her pregnant, which precipitated the divorce proceedings that finally ended the marriage in March 1769. The duke, apparently exasperated with his mistress's infidelities, immediately evicted Parsons. Three months later, he married the daughter of Sir Richard Wrottesley, Bart., Dean of Worcester, and, early in 1770, he resigned from office.

Notice in the press of Grafton's disorderly domestic life reflected the ethos of two different eras. While in office, one of Grafton's fiercest antagonists, who maintained anonymity famously under the pen name 'Junius' in the *Public Advertiser*, most likely Sir Philip Francis, censured him both for treating his mistress shabbily and for showing her off in public. On the first count, it allowed Junius to harp further upon the theme of the duke's betrayal of his political allies. Alluding to the story that Parsons had rejected with contempt his suggestion that they remain friends, Junius implored him to resign and go back to his life of ease: 'Take back your mistress;—the name of friend may be fatal to her, for it leads to treachery and persecution.'[23] On the second count, Junius's sardonic depiction of the duke's obliviousness to changing manners and mores illustrates how George III and Queen Charlotte's marital fidelity and promotion of strict moral propriety at court invited public scrutiny of cabinet ministers' private lives:

> The example of the English nobility may, for aught I know, sufficiently justify the duke of Grafton, when he indulges his genius in all the fash-ionable excesses of the age; yet, considering his rank and station, I think it would do him more honour to be able to deny the fact, than to defend it by such authority. But if vice itself could be excused, there is yet a certain display of it, a certain outrage to decency, and violation of public decorum, which, for the benefit of society, should never be forgiven. It

is not that he kept a mistress at home, but that he constantly attended her abroad.—It is not the private indulgence, but the public insult of which I complain. The name of Miss Parsons would hardly have been known, if the First Lord of the Treasury had not led her in triumph through the Opera House, even in the presence of the Queen. When we see a man act in his manner, we may admit the shameless depravity of his heart, but what are we to think of his Understanding?[24]

More interested in mockery than public morals, the comments of Junius and other writers on politicians' personal relations were opportunistic and lacking in any consistent principle. Claiming such licence in print challenged the physical licence that the political elite had traditionally enjoyed. Lack of political acuity rather than scandal ended Grafton's turn at the helm, but his example shows that, at this point, politicians in office had to keep up appearances of probity lest they wound up pilloried in the virtual market square of the popular press.

With political power gained by family connections now at issue, a politician could also have his character impugned by association. Junius gloated over the former duchess of Grafton's marriage into the family of John Russell, fourth Duke of Bedford, an unpopular figure repeatedly menaced by mobs after serving as a principal negotiator of the reviled Peace of Paris of 1763 and blocking legislation in 1765 that would have protected Spitalfields weavers from the menace of cheaper imported French silk. In a collection of his epistles published in 1771, Junius added a footnote: 'His Grace had lately married Miss Wrottesley, niece of the *Good Gertrude, Duchess of Bedford*', although, at the time of the original letter of May 1769, the marriage had not yet taken place. The earl of Upper Ossory, lover and subsequently second husband of the former duchess of Grafton, was the new duchess of Grafton's cousin. In subsequent writings Junius expressed mirth as he contemplated the duke's marriage with 'a first cousin of the man, who had fixed that mark and title of infamy upon him, which, at the same moment, makes a husband unhappy and ridiculous'. Junius speculated upon the etiquette that they might observe should the cousins meet at their uncle's table, observing: 'It would be a scene in Œdipus, without the distress.'[25] The irregularities that had long featured in aristocratic intermarriages and remarriages used to stay within the family; now they attracted public scrutiny and invited the ugly labels of adultery and incest.

Public opinion aggravated tensions within elite families, multiheaded, tentacled monsters that they could sometimes be. According to Horace

Walpole, an intimate of the new countess of Upper Ossory, Bedford's personal conduct had earned him the opprobrium of Sir Thomas Pelham-Hollis, Duke of Newcastle back in 1751 because of his 'intimate connections' with Sandwich through 'intrigues, cricket-matches, and acting plays'. Sandwich once drew men of fashion into his orbit through invitations to Woburn and the Huntingdon races when George II was in Hanover. Walpole asserted: 'These dangerous practices opened Mr. Pelham's eyes; and a love-affair between one of his daughters and a younger brother of the Duchess of Bedford [Richard Leveson Gower], fixed his aversion to that family.'[26] Walpole's chronicles highlight how family connections constituted a virtual arsenal of political weapons, and thus elucidate why they attracted gossip and innuendo. He explained that the greatest impediments to the match between Grafton and Elizabeth Wrottesley were also its greatest attractions for a man bent on revenge. Grafton knew that the duchess of Bedford would expect to influence him through his new wife, a niece she had raised herself, but in order to do so she would have to distance herself from Grafton's ex-wife, now married to her nephew. Walpole gleefully reported that Grafton 'judged so well, that having made a visit to the new Lady Ossory, now her niece, the Duchess of Bedford had the meanness to excuse that visit to the Queen, pleading her affection to her nephew, Lord Ossory'. Grafton's personal feeling, however, had compromised his political purchase. He could indulge in the petty satisfaction of blocking Ossory's ambassadorship to Spain, but his association with the Bedfords ruined George III's perception of him as a man independent of faction wrought by family connections. Walpole intimated that the king's confidence in Grafton's independence had been misplaced anyway; before his marriage, droves of his 'creatures' had paid court to Parsons in the hope of future preferment.[27]

Although ridiculing men for the inability to check wayward mistresses, wives or daughters was a long-hallowed custom, something more transpired four months later when Junius turned his sights directly upon the duke of Bedford. Members of the Bedford faction had joined forces with Grafton in 1767, but, by 1769, the duke himself, at age sixty, was going blind and fading from public life. In the course of a critique of his entire political career, Junius alluded to the callousness Bedford had displayed after the accidental death of his son, Lord Tavistock, in March 1767 by appearing at India House two weeks later to vote. Junius then found himself under attack for his own callousness and needing to defend his character. In a pamphlet collection of his letters, he reprinted the criticism made against him and appended a long footnote that opened with the pronouncement: '*Measures and not men* is the common cant of affected moderation;—a base, counterfeit language, fabricated by knaves, and made current among fools. Such gentle censure is not fitted to the present, degenerate state of society. What does it avail to expose the absurd contrivance, or pernicious tendency of measures, if the man, who advises or executes, shall be suffered not only to escape with impunity, but even to preserve his power, and insult us with the favour of his Sovereign!' He supported his case by quoting a 1734 letter by Alexander Pope insisting that reform came only by example: hence the necessity for chastisement. The poet proclaimed: 'To attack vices in the abstract, without touching persons, may be safe fighting indeed, but it is fighting with shadows. My greatest comfort and encouragement to proceed has been to see that those, who have no shame, and not fear of any thing else, have appeared touched by my satires.' Junius used the word 'shame' frequently in his letters, Exposing a man's domestic life, where his character was naked or, as Chesterfield had put it, he was least able to 'simulate or dissimulate', seemed best calculated to evoke that sentiment.[28]

Personal attacks replicated, virus-like. A month after his initial assault upon Bedford, Junius questioned a hostile respondent's own personal affiliations:

> Had *he* been a father, he would have been but little offended with the severity of the reproach, for his mind would have been filled with the justice of it. He would have seen that I did not insult the feelings of a father, but the father who felt nothing. He would have trusted to the evidence of his own paternal heart, and boldly denied the possibility of the fact, instead of defending it. Against whom then will his honest indignation be directed when I assure him, that this whole town beheld the Duke of Bedford's conduct, upon the death of his son, with horror and astonishment.

Junius proclaimed public opinion the foundation of morality: 'The people are seldom wrong in their opinions,—in their sentiments they are never mistaken. There may be a vanity perhaps in a singular way of thinking;— but when a man professes a want of those feelings, which do honour to the multitude, he hazards something infinitely more important than the character of his understanding.'[29] The Wilkes and Liberty movement had transformed political discourse into a virtual charivari, with an actual mob at the ready to enforce the point physically. Junius's professed confidence in the moral sense of the multitude would become increasingly untenable, however. Expressing surprise when Wilkes won the Middlesex election in March 1768, Burke made a sagacious observation about the larger consequences of the personalization of politics. He interpreted the victory as the expression of hatred for Bute by 'the people'. 'Besides,' he added, 'the crowd always want to draw themselves, from abstract principles to personal attachments; and since the fall of Ld Chatham, there has been no hero of the Mob but Wilkes.'[30] After the mob violence of the Gordon Riots and the French Revolution, Burke would present elaborate arguments on the dangers of such appeals to 'the people'. Yet his writings in defence of party suggest that the elite and the commonality shared a need for personal attachments. The elite too desired a hero.

Party Men and their Measuring

On behalf of his patron, Charles Watson-Wentworth, Marquis of Rockingham, leader of the eponymous Whig party, Burke in 1770 attacked 'not men, but measures' as cant, 'a sort of charm by which many people get loose from every honourable engagement' and 'a doctrine which has a tendency to destroy all test of character as deduced from conduct'.[31] The political landscape had undergone a seismic shift. Sir Robert Walpole's antagonists had condemned party on the grounds that he had used it to maintain the Whig oligarchy by convincing the first two Georges that Tories were open or closeted Jacobites who continued to pose a threat to the Hanoverian succession. When George III ascended the throne, however, he dismissed Walpole's successors, the Pelhamite Whigs (an event christened 'the slaughter of the Pelhamite Innocents'), to put Bute in power with the intention of pursuing a reign of virtue, with kingship liberated from the tyranny of party machinations. With party now under siege by the court, the opposition moved from assaulting to embracing it.[32]

In *Thoughts on the Cause of the Present Discontents* (1770), Burke famously posited the existence of a double cabinet, with the interior one harbouring a 'new Court corporation', with members of this faction presumptuously calling themselves the '*King's men*, or the *King's friends*'. He took the position that attacking Bute personally did not address the larger problem of a '*system of Favouritism*' that allowed 'insulated individuals, without faith plighted, tie, or common principles [. . .] to destroy the connexions of men and their trust in one another'. Party and connection, Burke argued, had artfully been associated with faction by 'unconstitutional Statesmen' in order to undermine the communication and coordination needed to resist any 'evil design' in government. He declared that effective and good political action depended on the personal associations of party: 'Where men are not acquainted with each other's principles, nor experienced in each other's talents, nor at all practiced in their mutual habitudes and dispositions by joint efforts in business, no personal confidence, no friendship, no common interest, subsisting among them; it is evidently impossible that they can act in a public part with uniformity, perseverance, or efficacy. In a connexion, the most inconsiderable man, by adding to the weight of the whole, has his value, and his use; out of it, the greatest talents are wholly unserviceable to the publick.' True, a party could degenerate into faction, he acknowledged, but duty compelled its members to correct this evil, not flee from it. 'Every profession, not excepting the glorious one of a soldier, or the sacred one of a priest, is liable to its own particular vices; which, however, form no argument against those ways of life; nor are the vices themselves inevitable to every individual in those professions.' Burke invoked the ancient Romans, who 'believed private honour to be the great foundation of public trust; that friendship was no mean step towards patriotism; that he who, in the common intercourse of life, shewed he regarded somebody besides himself, when he came to act in a public situation, might probably consult some other interest than his own'. Party connections encouraged public and private virtues by making them mutually supporting.[33] Burke declined to enumerate specific personal qualities that rendered men fit or unfit for public service beyond a capacity for communication, friendship and trust. As he learned after Rockingham's demise, more went into friendship than professions of loyalty. Moreover, exigencies of party could trump personal connections.

The vicissitudes of the Whig party further confirm how profoundly personal feelings could influence politics. Grafton's resignation from office at the end of January 1770 came after Chatham returned to the political scene and allied himself with the Rockingham Whigs, the spiritual heirs of the Pelhamites, which lost Grafton the support of the Chathamites in the cabinet. George III, loath to surrender control to this Whig faction, gave one of 'the King's Friends', Frederick, Lord North, then chancellor of the Exchequer, the lordship of the Treasury. George felt comfortable with North personally and wished to assert the royal prerogative to choose his own ministers in defiance of the Whigs' ostensible determination to deprive him of that right. Thus, he clung to North through the darkness of the American conflict until March 1782 in spite of the opposition's efforts to unseat him and the minister's own desperation to resign. Military defeat in America

finally allowed North relief from office and the Rockinghamites the opportunity to storm the cabinet. Angered by the Whigs' agenda, particularly
Burke's Economical Reform Bill, seemingly designed to prune back his influence, the king did all he could to thwart them until Rockingham's death on
1 July 1782 abruptly ended their regime. George then dipped into the pool
of 'the King's Friends' for William Petty, 2nd Earl of Shelburne (later
Marquis of Lansdowne), in spite of this politician's attraction to French
Enlightenment principles and the personal repulsion he provoked in others.
The latter quality proved lethal. Charles James Fox and other Rockinghamites
resigned their offices and Shelburne could not pass the peace preliminaries in
the Commons, so he stepped down in February 1783. The unholy alliance
of the Fox-North coalition that followed did not survive the year because
the king simply could not abide Fox. George engineered the defeat of Fox's
East India Bill, dismissed the coalition when it would not resign, elevated
Pitt the Younger to the first lordship of the Treasury and stubbornly retained
his ministry in defiance of its initial defeats in the Commons. The resulting
sense of betrayal and outrage left deep emotional scars all round as well as
some moral ambiguity.[34]

Politics devolved into a personal rivalry between Pitt and Fox. George
III consolidated Pitt's position by dissolving parliament in March 1784
and pouring money into what Leslie Mitchell characterizes as 'the most
acrimonious and bitterly contested election of the century'. Mitchell's
analysis of the contest exposes the bricks and mortar of party. 'The King,'
he observes, 'less public in his manoeuvres, with an assured power base
within the constitution, could appeal to a whole range of traditional values,
which made sentiment stronger than argument. Fox, by contrast, had to
find theories to fit new situations as they unfolded.' Did the king's exercise
of his prerogatives to choose ministers and dismiss parliament compromise
the harmony between the executive and legislative branches of government
in contravention of the spirit of the constitution, as Fox alleged, or simply
stir personal pique? Electors seemed to believe that Fox had overstepped
his bounds: his associates received a trouncing in the polls. Mitchell sees
the events of 1782–84 as the defining factor in Fox's politics, 'the reference
point for decisions' resulting in a tendency towards obsessive self-
vindication and a loathing for George and Pitt 'so profound as to be sometimes destructive of good judgement'.[35] His examination of Fox's role in
the disintegration of the Whig party and his subsequent biographical
treatment of the statesman underline the primacy of ideology but also
show personal loyalties and antagonisms as central to party cohesion.

Fox's obdurate support of French revolutionary principles in the face of escalating violence abroad and alarm at home sundered old alliances. The vote on the war against France split what had been the Rockingham party, which in essence had become the Foxite Whigs by 1792, although William Henry Cavendish, Duke of Portland stood as its nominal head. By the summer of 1794, most of its core members, including Portland, had reluctantly defected to the Pitt administration. Fox would not emerge from the political wilderness until 1801, when Pitt stepped down over his disagreement with the king over Catholic emancipation, and would gain office again only briefly in 1806, the year when both he and Pitt died. In a review of the biography, James J. Sack marvels over Mitchell's discovery of how frequently Fox dunned his friends and could not be troubled with repayment when they in turn faced ruin. How Fox could '(both living and dead) engender such extreme political and personal loyalty' given that he was so financially malfeasant as well as 'indecisive, indolent, often unconcerned with politics or political issues' constitutes the 'mystery at the core of Mitchell's biography, never quite explained even by its subject's personal charm'.[36] All of this, however, becomes comprehensible by placing the Fox phenomenon in the larger context of how men of this milieu interacted with and measured one another as men.

Mitchell's studies show how Fox's high-stakes gambling and his dereliction of duty when ensconced abroad or at St Anne's Hill, Surrey with his mistress (from 1795 to 1802, his secret wife), Elizabeth Armistead, did cause inconvenience, annoyance and bad press. On the other hand, because Fox possessed the energy and daring to live large—able to deliver a rousing improvised speech in the Commons fresh from nonchalantly dropping a bundle in a marathon gaming session at Brooks's—he inspired awe. He appeared to live a life about which other men could only fantasize. As Mitchell inquires rhetorically: how many English politicians in their mid-thirties saw themselves starring in a racy pamphlet loosely based on their teenage sexual exploits on the Grand Tour? *Les Amours et les aventures du Lord Fox* (Geneva, 1785) kept his swashbuckling image alive when he was settling into domesticity with Mrs Armistead. This publication seemed fitting for a life lived in many respects as an open book. Observers might tut-tut over Fox's indulgent upbringing and resulting profligacy but they also could joke that his astronomical gambling losses brought back into circulation funds that his doting papa, Henry, had allegedly peculated while he was paymaster general from 1757 to 1765. Fox rejected his family's anti-Pelhamite interests. He defied North, antagonized the king, and embraced the causes of American independence and Whiggism. In retrospect, it seems almost inconceivable that Fox entered politics throwing punches at Wilkes in 1768 and sponsored Pitt's candidacy to Brooks's in the early 1780s. On the other hand, and more significantly, his friends from Eton, many of whom grew to be distinguished political figures, remained constant.

The personal feelings Fox inspired would be his greatest strength as well as his undoing. George III's disgust with him for his self-serving political antics in the early 1770s blossomed into intense personal hatred for the corrupt influence he saw Fox exerting over George, Prince of Wales. During the Regency Crisis of 1788–89, moreover, had the king not recovered, strong personalities and jealousies might well have been just as disastrous for the Whigs. Burke, who had recruited Fox into the Rockingham fold, felt abandoned, suspecting Fox's preference for Richard Brinsley Sheridan and both colleagues' loss of interest in his moral crusade against Warren Hastings and colonial policy in India. Sheridan became morally compromised by appearing to gain undue influence with the prince by catering to him and to Maria Fitzherbert after Fox had alienated her by denying their secret marriage in the heat of parliamentary inquiry. James Gillray's satire on this relationship depicts Sheridan as a political and sexual predator making crude advances on a complicit Fitzherbert, who has one arm around the insensible prince as he lounges against her on a couch and distracts himself with a child's toy. The verses below warn against falsehood in love and friendship (fig. 4).[37] Ultimately, it became clear that Fox disagreed with Sheridan's strategy for bringing the Whigs into office, which made Sheridan resentful, but only temporarily. Burke, on the other hand, with good cause, continued to feel left out of the discussions. On paper, at least, the anticipated Whig regime had no office set aside for him. Mitchell attributes Burke's early provocative departure from the party line over the French Revolution and Protestant Dissent to his sense of exclusion. The extreme difficulty with which the duke of Portland and other prominent Whigs followed Burke in June 1794, when events in France became insupportable, attests to the degree of attachment men felt towards Fox and his personal style in private, however they might criticize them in public. Fox's secession from parliament in 1797 did provoke anger, but a small group of party faithful in the Lords and Commons continued to keep his principles alive after the Whig split.

The Evolution of Sexual Metaphor

The long-term outcome of the Pitt-Fox rivalry might suggest the triumph of the new moral standards when one considers the strong public images held by the combatants. Pitt, the forbidding, hard-labouring ascetic, faced Fox, the unkempt, high-living roué. Two other figures cast a shadow over this contest: King George III, the morally self-righteous paterfamilias, and George, Prince of Wales, the self-indulgent, vice-ridden wastrel. As the next chapter details, the king's indomitable performance of devoted fatherhood in public, notwithstanding the personal toll that his behaviour would take on his offspring in private, made up for and provided a distraction from Pitt's shunning of matrimony and mistresses. Concurrently, the Whigs' association with the prince of Wales compromised them morally and kept them unbalanced as princely caprices had them lurching from one crisis to the next. On the other hand, whatever public appearances might demand, men quietly continued to bond in their various pursuits of women. In the press, the preoccupation shifted from sodomitical corruption to female chastity.

Judith S. Lewis's analysis of the gender politics of this era posits two models of masculinity as being in contention, one performed in hard drinking, womanizing and sport, and the other in austerity and independence from sexual appetite—hence, from women. Elite women, battered by the sexual double standard when they engaged in political activities publicly in the 1780s, behaved more discreetly by the opening decades of the nineteenth century, operating within salons and dinner parties. Lewis unpacks the contradictory meanings of the duchess of Devonshire, her sister Lady Duncannon (later countess of Bessborough) and Mrs Frances Crewe, a popular Whig hostess, canvassing for Fox in the infamous 1784 election. Welcomed with enthusiasm by the electorate but pilloried in print, Fox's deployment of female canvassers drew attention to the anomaly of a woman's being able to wear a crown but not to cast a ballot. This strategy also had the more dubious intention of exposing Pitt's unmanliness by demonstrating his lack of interest in alluring women. Opponents to his tax on maidservants that year similarly depicted him as indifferent or hostile to the female sex. Lewis argues that these tactics backfired. Showcased for their beauty, exposed to a lower-class male gaze and *giving away* kisses to constituents (in contrast to the male candidate *taking* them, as the proprietary status of upper-class males dictated), these female politicians could be represented by their opponents as something akin to prostitutes. Ultimately, Foxite libertinism would be associated with the political licentiousness of revolutionary France.[38]

Political propaganda turned away from representations of corruption as one man's weakness for, or subservience to, another man. Jokes about 'backstairs influence' and other sexual innuendo aimed at Pitt, popular in Foxite circles and reminiscent of anti-Walpole and Wilkite invective, made their way into print in muted tones.[39] For example, in arguing that Pitt's popularity rested on untried virtue, the *Gazetteer and New Daily Advertiser* of 24 March 1784 noted archly: 'Every new day, says a correspondent, produces a fresh instance of the duplicity of that immaculate Minister, who is unhacknied in the ways of men, aye, and of women too.' Satirical verse depicted Pitt foppishly taking tea at Brighthelmstone Castle with Tom Steele, his old friend from Cambridge, whom he had appointed joint secretary of the Treasury. Whereas his close friendships with men gave ample material for speculation, gossips assumed him a virgin rather than a sodomite.[40] John Barrell cites writing from the mid-1790s that 'remarked on his "maiden coyness"; described him as "Prettygirlibus indifferentissimus"; compared the childless minister with the philoprogenitive king; and linked all this to a presumed preference for masturbation'. In visual satire of the early 1800s, Barrell observes, Pitt appears to lack male gender distinction.[41] One radical handbill I found implied that Henry Dundas might have been more than Pitt's drinking partner. *A Political Creed*, distributed on 19 December 1794, began: 'I believe in *Billy Pitt*, Chancellor of the Exchequer, Master of Lords and Commons, and of all Court Intrigues, visible and invisible; and in *Secretary Dundas*, the only beloved of *Billy Pitt*, beloved before all Women, Men of Men, Heads of Heads, Ministers of Ministers, beloved not hated, being of one opinion of his Patron, by whom all Ministers are made; who, for us Men and Our Taxation, came out of Scotland.'[42] Along the same lines, Gillray's *God Save the King.—In a Bumper. Or—An Evening Scene, Three Times a Week at Wimbledon*, published on 27 May 1795, has Pitt sprawled suggestively on Dundas's dining table, with both so inebriated as to be oblivious to Pitt pouring from the wrong end of the bottle (fig. 5).[43] Nonetheless, the innuendo in these prints regarding the nature of the relationship between Pitt and his closest political ally pales in comparison to the insinuations traded in the writings of Pulteney and Wilkes.

Treatment of Burke's sexuality followed a similar trajectory. In some ways, Burke's situation resembled that of Lord Hervey. He had emotional, loving relationships with other men, but married nonetheless, and attracted aspersions that appeared more political than personal on the surface, as they did not refer to his specific romantic connections. When Burke rose in the House of Commons in 1780 to decry the treatment of two men convicted of sodomy, locked in the pillory and savaged by a mob, one fatally, the

Morning Post questioned why he would be so sympathetic to a vice that men and women should both hold in the highest detestation. Burke successfully sued for defamation of character. Visual satirists commonly depicted Burke as an effeminately attenuated figure in Jesuitical trappings, which outwardly alluded to his Irish Catholic roots but also carried associations of Roman vice (fig. 6).[44] Again, the sexual innuendo is comparatively oblique. Ironically, a decade later, Burke appeared as an idealized patriarch, held up in contrast to Thomas Paine, in loyalist propaganda. Whatever his proclivities, Burke sired a son while Paine remained childless. In order to discredit *Rights of Man* (1791–92), the Pitt administration had commissioned a scandalous biography of the author that pilloried him for alleged depraved behaviour and disgusting personal habits. Reflecting the modification of political metaphor and the shift in the dominant concerns of the time, the work did not try to link Paine to any sodomitical network; rather, it told tales of his monstrous, sadistic treatment of women.[45]

Clubbability, Domesticity and Political Eros

The loss of the American colonies precipitated a change in moral climate. The sense that a sinful nation had suffered God's wrath stimulated the revival of societies for the reformation of manners. The evangelical William Wilberforce's lobbying brought a royal proclamation against vice and immorality on 1 June 1787 and the launch of the Proclamation Society's crusade to promote morality in society and government, national and local.[46] After the scurrility of the Wilkes and Liberty era, even politicians not on board with this new movement understood that it was in their best interests to keep the intimacies between public men free from any insinuations of perversion. The perennial cabinet reshuffling of George III's reign involved delicate negotiations of personal loyalty facilitated by bipartisan sociability. Unfortunately, we will never have a complete picture of what went on behind the scenes in this political milieu. Under the influence of George Otto Trevelyan, the keeper of Fox's papers destroyed much of their personal content in order to preserve his political reputation.[47] Nonetheless, extant diaries and letters of Foxite Whigs and their friends from the 1780s onwards provide glimpses into these intimacies. Politicians still depended on the approbation and support of their peers.

Personal affections surfaced when reputations stood exposed, most visibly in the House when green or nervy speakers were on their legs. That the first of these efforts should be called a member's *maiden* speech makes the event seem something akin to that first trip to a brothel in the company of male relations or friends for performance of that act that will make him a man. At the same time, the expression evokes feminine vulnerability. As Chesterfield wrote to his son: 'I heartily congratulate you upon the loss of your political maidenhead, of which I have received from others a very good account.'[48] Sir Gilbert Elliot, who when in town or abroad wrote rambling gossipy letters to his wife who preferred the country, used a metaphor that was ambiguous in the same way. In December 1787, he announced himself 'safely delivered' of 'a fine boy' after opening the charge against Sir Elijah Impey, the chief justice of the Supreme Court at Calcutta implicated with Hastings. He then described his performance anxiety:

> I knew the sort of expectation which the greatness of the subject, and length of the preparation, and the partiality of my particular friends had raised; and I felt pretty sure that the moment was come when I was to kick it all down, and disgrace myself and them. My voice was very much weakened and muddled, as it were, either by my stomach or my fears, so that I did not expect to be well heard, and my mouth was as dry as parchment, in spite of an orange which I kept sucking. All this was before I began.

As soon as he rose, his mind went blank 'for a time, which *seemed to me* about the length of a moderate sermon'; he swore under his breath to Fox, seated at his side, and recommended worrying his orange. Elliot assured his wife: 'You need not be very unhappy about this little halt, as it is a thing that happens to everybody, and never does the smallest prejudice.'[49]

He went on at length about the essential support he received from his friends cheering him on as he spoke and congratulating him later. After conveying Burke's effusive praise, Elliot directed his wife: 'For God's sake do not show this to anybody else, for it is a little too bad to repeat even to you, though I do not think it fair to rob you of anything that will give you pleasure.' The pleasure, however, was not all Lady Elliot's. Her husband gushed:

> But Burke's praises in other points, which I think more material, are really both pleasing and affecting to me—in a word, as to the *substantial* points which go to *character*. I went home with him afterwards to dinner, and he could not at all contain himself. He was darting every now and then across the room to embrace me. At dinner, without any

provocation, he had his hand every now and then across the dishes to take my hand. From the rest of his family you will believe I had a warm reception, when I tell you that the passage of my speech which was by far the most admired was a panegyric on Burke, which *you know* did indeed come from the heart, and which I have long had it in my mind to acquit myself of once in my life, as a debt due to unsuccessful virtue.[50]

The following June, when Sheridan's oratory was the toast, Elliot reported: 'Burke caught him in his arms as he sat down, which was not the least affecting part of the day to my feelings, and could not be the least grateful testimony of his merit received by Sheridan. I have myself enjoyed that embrace on such an occasion, and know its value.'[51] Eager to promote uxorial approbation, Burke had written to Lady Elliot himself in order to deliver his commendation directly, and in the process acknowledge her husband's generosity towards him in his speech. He had done the same after Philip Francis 'was two hours and an half or rather more, on his Legs, and he never lost attention for a moment' in the crusade against Hastings. Burke began his letter to Mrs Francis by invoking cosy domesticity: 'I cannot, with an honest appetite or clear conscience, sit down to my Breakfast, unless I first give you an account, which will make your family breakfast as pleasant to you as I wish all your family meetings to be.' After describing Francis's triumph, he concluded with an encomium to lineage: 'Permit me most sincerely to congratulate you and the ladies, and Mr Philip of Cambridge, if he is yet among you; He has a great example before him, in a father exerting some of the first Talents, that ever were given to a man, in the cause of Mankind.'[52] All this familial warmth, however, only went so far.

Beyond patronage, relations between politicians involved competition, courtship and navigation around delicate egos. For Elliot, the direct expression of approbation from Fox, 'who is not apt to praise to anybody's face', seemed to mean more than Burke's embrace. After Fox 'broke out with the most violent expressions of admiration I have undergone yet from anybody', Elliot relished the favour of 'those formidable wits and critics of whom I have always stood in awe'. He declared to his wife: 'I have the pleasure of seeing that all these testimonies in my favour are not mixed nor poisoned by the least degree of jealousy or envy in anybody.' William Windham and Thomas Pelham, he thought, 'seemed as highly delighted at Fox's breaking out in the way I have mentioned as you could have been, and as much pleased that I should have no means left after this of doubting about the figure I had made'. Windham too would send a congratulatory letter to Lady Elliot, which Sir Gilbert seemed to take more seriously than Burke's, noting that it was not Windham's usual practice.[53]

Windham's gesture had further significance: his and Pelham's performances in parliament served as Elliot's benchmarks. Back in March 1787, while lamenting his troublesome nerves as he anticipated his own oration, Elliot noted how Windham and Pelham had both fallen short of the high expectations that their friends had entertained for them. A man's reputation, indeed, his very sense of self, was on the line when he spoke in the House. Elliot privately dissected Windham's performance, diagnosing the 'defects which flowed from defects in his character or constitution'.[54] In contrast, Fox's speechmaking, he later declared, 'excels all other men's in its kind [. . .] nature and simplicity being indeed the true characteristic quality of his eloquence'. Elliot made this observation as he reported on Sheridan's publicity-grabbing speeches of June 1788 in the case against Hastings, where he 'displayed powers yesterday hardly to be conceived, and perhaps never equalled in their kind'. Having said that, Elliot proceeded to pick apart Sheridan's speech at length, pronouncing it overprepared and '*theatrical*' in composition. He included details of Sheridan's vomiting the night before and consequent strained chest, almost gleefully positing: 'I believe that he has suffered as much from anxiety, labour, and nervousness even as me.' Loyal to his friend and mentor, he proclaimed Burke's speeches, in comparison, full of 'fine passages' and even more fired by imagination, but without 'the least trace of preparation'.[55] Windham's diary suggests that he would have agreed with Elliot's criticisms. Torment and self-recrimination dominated his experience of the Commons, whether he sat paralysed when he had intended to speak or managed to rise.[56]

Windham's account of his part in the motion on the Rohilla War of 1 June 1786 indicates that, from early on in his career, he did not relish House gamesmanship in the way that Elliot did. He breakfasted with Francis in order to gain clarity, but was suffering from a disordered mind and agitated spirits by the time he arrived at parliament. When his turn came, he still felt 'in no good state to speak', but, as he recorded:

> I contrived somehow to steady and recover myself in the course of speaking, and so far executed what I had prepared, that I conceive it to be a fashion to talk of what I did as rather a capital performance. 'Tis a strong proof on what cheap terms reputation for speaking is acquired, or how capricious the world is of its allotment of it to different people. There is not a speech of mine which, in comparison of one of Francis's,

would, either for language or matter, bear examination for one moment; yet about my performances in that way a great fuss is made, while of his nobody speaks a word.

Windham made a similarly cynical remark at the end of February 1792 after, in his judgement, lacking inspiration and memory in a speech: 'Such as it was, however, it was thought by some, the best of what I have ever done and even gained great credit. So easy is credit gained with us at least by public speaking.'[57] A man's clubbability could remedy defects elsewhere. Other politicians liked Windham in spite of his melancholic disposition, incessant dithering and odd obsessions. His diary catalogues a varied, active social life and a surprising capacity for spontaneity. He would allow himself to be led astray from his duties when friends proposed amusements, most famously when James Boswell inveigled him 'to explore, as he called it, Wapping' in 1792 in pursuance of the directive Samuel Johnson made back in 1783 that they should go thither to behold the variety of life that London held.[58]

In spite of his warmth, Burke was incapable of the conviviality and verve that inspired the strong loyalty that Fox enjoyed. Even Elliot, his dear friend, who enjoyed his assistance and nurture, dreaded his dinners. Shortly before his triumphant speech, Sir Gilbert reported that he had called in at Burke's for a 'chance dinner' for the first time in two winters, although he 'had always professed to intend it'. He explained to Lady Elliot: 'But, in the first place, their hours are very irregular, and next, though I admire him so much and like all the rest of his family, yet it is not lively society, and dinner does not go off so lightly as in Park Street or Russell Street'—the residences, respectively, of Lord Palmerston and Henry Gally Knight, where he often dined. Underlining the contrast, he wrote next: 'I was yesterday in the luck to see Charles Fox.' Elliot described a high-spirited party where an unnamed Scottish lord acted the coxcomb, and 'entertained me with the affected familiarity but real servility and adulation with which he bored Fox, whose natural rejection but good-natured toleration of it was entertaining also in its way'.[59] One could imagine Burke sitting there tight-lipped had he been present. After joining the some five hundred diners at the Shakespeare Tavern, Covent Garden to celebrate the fourth anniversary of Fox's victory in the Westminster election of 10 October 1780, Burke had commented to Windham on the numerous attendees' steadiness of cause and good humour, but complained that their leaders seemed oblivious to the need for a plan of action. His social discomfiture caused anxiety to Boswell years later when, sensing that Burke had been avoiding him, he pressed him to dine the following Saturday or any other. Burke begged off with the explanation that the Hastings business would not allow him to commit to a particular date and suggested Boswell include him when he had others to dine. Burke then turned up in a hackney coach the next Saturday, learned from a servant that no dinner party was in progress and fled, much to Boswell's consternation.[60]

Burke's rise from the professional ranks and habitual deference to what he called a natural aristocracy contrasted sharply with Fox's descent from Charles II and self-confidence wrought by an indulged, luxurious upbringing. Nathaniel Wraxall summed it up best as he ranked Fox and Burke first and second in the 1781 opposition. 'Infinitely more respectable than Fox, [the latter] was nevertheless far less amiable. Exempt from his defects and irregularities, Burke wanted the suavity of Fox's manner, his amenity, his placability. The one procured more admirers. The other possessed more friends.' Wraxall reported that Burke would leave the House 'exhausted, chagrined and often irritated', and retire 'to his family, or to the duties and avocations of domestic life'. Fox, invigorated by long debate, would make haste to Brooks's. The two worked well together, however, which he thought attested to Fox's accepting nature. As for the flaws that undermined his career, Wraxall cited only Fox's financial, not his sexual, irregularities, but thought his inability to cultivate George III his fatal fault.[61] As we shall see, he would amend his assessment when he compared Fox to Pitt.

In this milieu, spotless domesticity could make a man appear potentially censorious, less accessible personally, and lacking in a sense of fun and daring. As mentioned above, Fox kept his marriage to his mistress secret for seven years, perhaps to preserve his mystique as well as his approachability. Back in 1771, Horace Walpole speculated that 'his vices were affected': 'He drank hard, because it was a vice, gamed to attain a name from the excesses of his losses, and followed women but little because nature had not distinguished him from other young men by superior potency in love.' Nevertheless, appearances reigned. It was to Fox that young Windham turned for sympathy as he received mercury treatment for what appeared to be the clap in 1783. The Whig habit of passing around mistresses perhaps gave the impression of greater sexual prowess than was merited. When George, Prince of Wales joined this circle, press coverage and rakish reputations intensified.[62] Significantly, Elliot expressed his greatest frustration with Fox for his absence at the beginning of the Regency Crisis because of Mrs Armistead's indisposition and Fox's indulgence, Elliot remarked bitterly, of his own pleasure. Conversely, he criticized Fox's habitual indecisiveness but did not take personal umbrage when Fox did not turn up to support him as speaker of the House, a vote that went against Elliot.[63]

Francis, on the other hand, bore some personal resentment, so Fox's secession from parliament in 1797 unleashed his wrath. Like Elliot, he laid blame for Fox's propensity to shirk his responsibilities on his relationship with Armistead, whom he dismissed as 'a simple person'. Francis gave Fox a private, posthumous Junius treatment. In an assessment of Fox's character and career found in manuscript and copy among his papers, Francis claimed that in 1806 Fox 'was under the influence of a *clique* of women and others, who lived with him out of sight, who having all the easy access and gentle opportunities, beset him perpetually for their own purposes'. Francis distinguished between Fox's honourable old friends and the dubious new allies who 'paid court to his wife' and took advantage of his inability to 'resist assiduous whining importunity face to face', especially from her. Francis drew a larger principle:

> As to the influence of women, when it is allowed to interpose, and predominate over questions not within their province, I am sure it is a case that would rarely, if ever, happen with a man of sound understanding, who had no compensation to make for other deficiencies. They who cannot excite either love or respect must pay for it by submission to their wives. It is not for *me* of all men to be inexorable on this subject; for who is it has loved, admired, and esteemed as I have done? I know that women are the best of the human species, I know that a well-principled, well-educated English woman has more virtues, and is capable of a more disinterested attachment even to the sacrifice of herself, and more good sense too, in questions within her reach, than many of the most eminent men whom I have been acquainted with.
>
> But these are not the women by whom men are governed, nor do such women ever think of it. In England I am sure there never was an example of a young and beautiful woman attempting to govern a man of common understanding proportioned to her in age, and otherwise accomplished, if she were really in love with him.[64]

Marrying a courtesan, a woman whose very survival depended on her ability to bargain with and manipulate men, carried implications of an unnatural submission akin to sodomitical relations. For his own part, Francis combined familial solicitousness (particularly after his first wife became a semi-invalid) with long periods away when necessary, a liberty to roister about with male friends and some spicy sexual intrigue. He made a second marriage in 1814 to a woman forty years his junior.[65]

Elliot stands as the best example of how a man might have it both ways with the careful cultivation of his image. Publicly uxorious—christened 'Sir Bashful Constant' by Lady Palmerston—he played the gallant in society with a certain irony, as he related with wry humour to his wife, who in her missives expressed herself secure in his affections. He sent heart-tugging love letters when he could not stay by her side as she recovered after barely surviving a dangerous delivery of twins who did not themselves survive, kept her apprized of the latest gossip and bucked up her spirits with teasing accusations about a mutual attraction she shared with Pelham.[66] Yet, on 5 April 1792, not quite a year after the dramatic break between Burke and Fox, Elliot sent her a letter that might have raised suspicions in a less trusting mind. He wrote that he had seen more of 'Fox and his set' than usual at a new Friday dining club for ministers at the Star and Garter and occasionally at Brooks's. He explained: 'I should wish to get over the little reserve, both on his side and mine, which has kept us at a distance so long; but I imagine, that without living something of the same life, which I am not equal to, this is not very easy to accomplish.' While one could interpret this as Elliot's avowed eschewing of Fox's mores, it shows that nonetheless he could tag along with the fast set. The letter then turned to dinner-party gossip, mocking George James, 4th Earl (later Marquis) of Cholmondeley, who would become the prince of Wales's chamberlain, for being 'more absurdly uxorious than ever', behaviour consisting of ostentatious hand-holding (including squeezing and shaking) under the table 'and if he quitted hold an instant to make some gesture or action, he snatched it again as if they had met after a long separation'. Sir Bashful Constant's censorious regarding what, given Cholmondeley's history of rakishness, seemed hypocritical displays might have indicated his own sensitivity to such charges. Two years later, after having been stationed in France since August 1793, Elliot's account of the retreat from Toulon, where he had just arrived to serve as civil commissioner, neglected to mention how he had importuned Lady Elizabeth Webster (from July 1797, Lady Holland) with such violence that she had to flee their shared carriage. According to her diary entry of 14 February: 'his last words were, "Be *kind and discreet*." He is in great alarm at his wife's knowing this *écart*, as he affects great conjugal felicity.' Elliot told Lady

Webster that his long absence from home on a secluded posting had conspired with the sudden, resplendent sight of a countrywoman to stimulate memories and feelings that caused this uncharacteristic 'alienation from sense and propriety'. The incident seems plausible, notwithstanding the future Lady Holland's reputation for exaggeration, in light of the adulterous second family that Sir Gilbert managed to keep secreted away.[67] When a politician had extended assignments abroad, which Elliot professed to dislike but continued to take, for financial reasons as he claimed, brooding over distant home fires would do him little practical good. To succeed, a politician in both his personal and his political life had to adapt to circumstances, make the most of whatever resources were at hand, and be comfortable with multiple versions of truth.

Perhaps not coincidentally, Tom Pelham and Windham, the most acute sufferers of nerves in the House, were the greatest masochists in matters of the heart. Both recorded their torment in private diaries. At the same time that Lady Webster was fulminating against Elliot's hypocrisy, she was having an affair with Pelham. She continued to string him along from the Continent while she took up with Lord Holland, which led to Pelham's depression, illness and inability to cope with the Whig party split. In his diary, his references to her by cryptic initials usually feature some expression of anguish, whether from her taking umbrage at something he had written or his inability to convey the fullness of his heart. Pelham would not marry until 1801. He reluctantly broke with Fox in early 1794 and had a career marked by clashes and awkward relations with ministers in power.[68]

Whereas Elliot tended to confide his personal piques to his wife, Windham had no such outlet and so dissembling took its toll. Elliot's dig at Cholmondeley's uxorious display came out of an appreciation of his premarital depravities, behaviour that distressed Windham, A line in the betting book at Brooks's encapsulates Cholmondeley's bachelor manners: 'Ld. Cholmondeley has given two guineas to Ld. Derby, to receive 500 Gs. whenever his lordship fucks a woman in a Balloon one thousand yards from the Earth.'[69] While Cholmondeley was contemplating sexual aeronautics, Windham, in anticipation of his own balloon ascent in May 1785, had his mind on the damage that Cholmondeley's libertinism had wrought on terra firma. In a letter intended for his friend should he not survive the flight, Windham went on at length in tortured prose about his need to make sure he left with an affectionate farewell, why he had kept his flight secret—thus practising deception, which he hoped would not be misinterpreted but for which he apologized—and what the adventure meant to him. Eventually he got to the point of his letter: his outrage over Cholmondeley trifling with the affections of 'a great and noble mind, whose only weakness has been too fond an attachment to you'. Windham quickly worked himself into a lather: 'That you should prefer a life of vanity and voluptuousness to a connection with such a woman as Miss Forrest, is no very honourable mark of your choice of happiness: That you should think yourself at liberty to pursue that choice, to the utter ruin and extinction of her peace of mind, is, in the circumstances, in which you stood, no very favourable evidence of your regard to duty.' After cataloguing minutely the shock dealt to Miss Forrest, which Cholmondeley with all his shortcomings could never remedy, Windham announced that he had rewritten his will and reduced Cholmondeley's bequest 'till it ceases almost to be considerable: but I have not done more, than a regard to the merit, the wants, or the virtues of the parties, rendered, I thought, incumbent on me'.[70] After the adrenalin rush of the flight (the balloon almost drifted out to sea), Windham does not appear to have confronted Cholmondeley. He did spring to Cecilia Forrest's assistance, however, with his typical alacrity; they married in 1798. Prior to this, his obsession with a young woman whom he had met on a walk in the woods while touring Scotland with Burke had Sir John Sinclair and Henry Dundas shaking their heads in disbelief.[71]

Windham's odd, impractical approach to women distracted him and undermined his efficiency at work, as indicated by his diary entry for August 1790:

Just previously to my setting off for the Assizes and almost, I may say, on the very evening (Saturday, 24th July), I felt that strong sense of the unhappiness of my own celibacy—that lively conception of pleasure I had lost—that gloomy apprehension of the conviction which I should feel of this hereafter, clouding all my prospects, relaxing all my motives and in an especial manner destroying all enjoyment, that I might ever have in residence here, that unless I could resolve manfully to fight against such images, and force my mind from the contemplation of evils, admitting no remedy, the most fatal mischief must ensue, both to my happiness and to my powers. Of this resolution the necessity was not at first foreseen, nor the resolution of consequence fully taken. These images, accordingly, continued to pursue me during the time of my absence at the Assizes. It is, indeed, sufficiently plain, that wisdom must condemn the thinking on uneasiness, which thinking cannot mend.[72]

As the regular gloomy musings of his diary show, he seemed unable to follow this plan. A flair for political expediency seemed to go hand in hand with a pragmatic approach to desire.

Pitt's chastity became the ultimate form of sexual pragmatism. Wraxall's hatchet job on the minster in his account of 1783 is amusing after his unfavourable comparison of the domestically dutiful Burke to the footloose-and-fancy-free Fox of 1781, quoted above. Wraxall asserted: 'During the whole course of the eighteenth Century, and I believe I may say, since the Accession of Elizabeth, he is the only English First Minister who lived and died in a state of Celibacy. He was not therefore attached to the Commonwealth by those endearing ties, which blend the Statesman, with the Husband and the Father; thus giving a species of compound security for good conduct, to the Country.' Wraxall praised the fecundity of the duke of Newcastle and Henry Pelham, and then claimed Fox at heart a family man:

> though he remained long unmarried yet finally entered into that state; and he aspired to have done it much earlier in life, if his efforts for the purpose had not proved unsuccessful. During the early part of Hastings's Trial, in 1787, he raised his eyes and hopes to the Duke of Newcastle's Box in Westminster Hall, where usually sat Miss Pulteney, afterwards created by Pitt, Countess of Bath in her own right; then justly esteemed one of the greatest Heiresses in the Kingdom. After exhibiting his powers of Oratory, as a public Man, in the Manager's Box below, he sometimes ascended in his private capacity, to try the effect of his Eloquence under the character of a Lover. All his Friends aided a cause, which, by rendering their Chief independent in his fortune, would have healed the wounds inflicted by his early indiscretion.

Wraxall noted that General Fitzpatrick always contrived to seat Fox and Miss Pulteney together, so 'the Courtship assumed so auspicious an appearance' that James Hare speculated on the complexion of their future children, Miss Pulteney being as fair as Fox was swarthy. In contrast: 'Pitt, though, at different periods of his life, he distinguished certain Ladies, some of whom I could name, by marks of predilection; and in one instance seemed even to meditate Marriage, yet, never persisted in the attempt.' Thus, Wraxall contradicted the innuendo regarding Pitt's indifference towards women on which the opposition feasted and which Wraxall had mocked but not disputed twenty-odd pages earlier. He concluded that

Fox's 'Name, Descent, Abilities, and private Character, surmounted every impediment to his elevation'. But Fox's lack of high moral character, a deficiency to which the statesman admitted, Wraxall concluded, disqualified him from high office.[73] These tergiversations epitomize the tensions that characterized political life as appearances held sway over reality and old-style masculinity lurked beneath the valorization of domestic probity.

Wraxall described Pitt coming into office 'surrounded by a chosen phalanx of young men who participated in his triumph, pressed near him on a day of expected Debate, and constituted the resource of his leisure hours'. He repeated quips on this constituting a bodyguard that shot arrows against all who opposed their master, and Pitt emulating Louis XIV at Versailles as he rewarded them with peerages and sinecures.[74] The letter-journal begun at the end of 1793 by the most famous of them, the twenty-three-year-old George Canning, for his uncle and aunt, Reverend William and Elizabeth Leigh, rivals Elliot's letters to his wife in its depictions of political sociability and its naked desire for reassurance. These letters and others show a surprising degree of bipartisan sociability, belied by Wraxall and other memoirists. More importantly, they attest to the value of clubbability. Canning started out with more strikes against him than did Burke. Whereas Burke had the stigma of an Irish Catholic mother to overcome, Canning had an impoverished widowed mother who became an actress and produced five illegitimate offspring with an actor with whom she cohabited, and then five legitimate children with a silk-mercer husband from whom she then separated. Unlike Burke, Canning aggressively and confidently ascended from the excellent education that the Leighs and his other guardians, Stratford and Mehitabel (Hetty) Canning, provided. Like Fox, Canning made lifelong friends at Eton (as well as at Christ Church, Oxford), who became politicians and mainstays of support. Canning continued to mix with Foxite Whigs—his Aunt Hetty remained their ardent partisan and he dined regularly at the home of the leading Whig hostess Mrs Crewe—although he made the decision to decline the patronage of the duke of Portland and made overtures to Pitt, who took him under his wing. After a dinner chez Crewe in February 1794 when Lady Caroline Fox had been the only other guest, Canning noted how comfortable they were with one another as she voiced the sentiments of her brother Henry, third Lord Holland. He speculated that politics would never set them 'at variance'. As Susanna, Countess of Stafford, a steadfast Pittite, remarked to her son, Granville Leveson Gower, one of Canning's Christ Church friends, shortly after Canning's maiden speech: 'All the great Whigs, middle aged and young Politicians are paying him Court, inviting him to Dinner, &c., &c. We may expect to see him soon very fat, if constant Dinners can have that Effect. The Duke of Bridgewater is so pleased with his Speech in the H. of C. that he came here the next Morning to talk of it, and concluded with saying: "How the Devil did Pitt get him? He is an acquisition." '[75]

A week after commencing his letter-journal, Canning bubbled over with excitement about his first dinner at Holwood with Pitt, which led to an invitation to sup with Dundas at Wimbledon. Indeed, where and with whom he should take his meals became a steady preoccupation: his first journal entry of 15 November assured his aunt and uncle that the dining club at the Crown and Anchor did not have the 'bad character' they had heard tell while in London. The following July, he chided himself for not leaving a debate in the House early, 'whereby I lost my dinner at the Lord Chancellor's, on a turtle'. Trying to coordinate eating with the right people with attending the House posed a perennial challenge for this hungry young man of limited resources and great ambition. He suffered an illness from February to March 1794 that his doctor attributed to fasting before attending the House.[76] Disappointment over the lost opportunity to feast upon turtle, however, would pale in comparison to his anxiety over the possible damage that this missed engagement did to his relationship with Lord Loughborough. Almost a year later, Sir Ralph Payne, a Foxite who had gone over to Pitt in 1793, informed him that the lord chancellor had the impression that he had offended Canning or that Canning had some predisposition against him. Canning wailed to the Leighs that he had made sure to do everything right by Loughborough, but feared his apology for missing the supper because of a prior engagement constituted an error. He paid a courtesy call immediately. When the summons to dine again arrived a few weeks later, Canning took great trouble to rearrange travel plans in order to avoid confirming Loughborough's idea that he meant to slight him.[77] One wonders whether the coddling that Canning received from Pitt and his friends made others inclined to rough him up. Parliamentary life was difficult enough without having to work so hard to preserve, while getting full use out of, his formal attire and to be properly habited for appearances in the House and any social events that might follow.[78]

Canning habitually evaluated other men's performances at dinner parties. At Mrs Crewe's he was pleased to find that Thomas Erskine, the famous Whig lawyer, was not the bore that others had led him to expect. He averred that Erskine had talked about himself at great length, but had been 'entertaining and exceedingly good-humoured'. He could not say the same of Erskine's wife and daughter, whom he described as '*stickish*'. From the other side of the aisle, Canning admired the acuity of understanding of Granville's brother, Lord Gower, as he attended to the conversation with great care and tactfully conveyed his judgement of the opinions expressed without actually speaking. The normally taciturn Dundas delighted him when loquacious, but the earl of Warwick's younger brother, Charles Francis Greville, Canning labelled as 'an eternal talker, and though a sensible, by no means an entertaining one, seemed very much disposed to have more than his share of the conversation'. His letters suggest that Pitt's all-male 'cabinet dinners' were not only convivial affairs but also facilitated communication of both strategy and favour. In early February 1795, after Pitt thwarted his determination to speak against Charles Grey's peace motion, Canning fumed: 'So angry was I—that I felt very little disposition to go home with Pitt to supper—when he asked me. I did go, however, as did Jenkinson—and we supped and sat till it was full time to betake ourselves to our night's rest.' The following June, he lamented that the dinners had fallen by the wayside, to Pitt's detriment.[79]

Granville also showed a susceptibility to Pitt's charm. He told his mother that he felt more comfortable at Holwood than at Dropmore, the foreign secretary William Wyndham Grenville's residence. On an occasion soon afterwards when he, Pitt, and Canning dined *en trio* at Holwood, he marvelled at the minister's agreeableness, range of conversation and lack of reserve, concluding that Pitt joked 'as if he were exactly of our age'. Granville's inamorata, Lady Bessborough, a stalwart in the Whig camp, mocked him for his hero worship by conveying Frances Russell, fifth Duke of Bedford's praises of Pitt's eloquence:

> he thought Mr. Pitt plain in his person, but towards the close of an interesting speech that he look'd beautiful; and that he had so little Idea of the possibility of any *woman* hearing or seeing him at such a time without being in love with him, that if women were admitted to the H. of Commons, and the D. of Bedford was very much in love with any one, he would make it an absolute point with her always to go out whenever Mr. Pitt got up to speak. There's for you. When did you ever say half as much for your friend? It has made me die to hear him.[80]

All sarcasm aside, Pitt had proved himself a magisterial speaker in the House and a seductive host at Holwood.

Canning, for all his discernment, indulged in the breaches of decorum he derided in others but got away with it. Lady Stafford had been a great fan of his in 1794, but at the end of 1798 she observed tartly to Granville: 'Were I Mr. Canning's near Relation, I would venture to advise him on one Subject which creates many Enemies—I mean that of talking in a contemptible Way of those whom he does not like, calling them Fools, &c., &c. He is so very good temper'd that I should think you might venture to Hint it to him, but I fear you have caught a little of it yourself, and therefore may not perceive the Disadvantage of this Habit.'[81] Canning suffered the same maiden-speech agonies described by Elliot and Windham, but his personal support network allowed him to slough off the considerable criticism that his manner and style attracted. Pitt received him at home, talked to him for hours, shared the king's speech and other documents with him, answered his questions and made sure to prepare him completely for his first appearance in the House on 21 January 1794 for a session that stretched from four o'clock in the afternoon to five in the morning. Canning's friends awakened him later that morning with various inquiries, whereupon he confessed that he might have an opportunity to speak that day, so they set off for the Gallery ahead of him. He steeled himself and eventually 'walked up the House and made my bow, and took my seat just above Pitt, as bold as a lion'. The House, however, was empty after the late hour of the last debate.[82] Meanwhile, the opposition press had noted his presence and used a theatre metaphor to describe expectations of his performance and so insinuate his connection to Sheridan, which enhanced the anticipatory tension.

On 31 January, with Pitt just below him whispering advice and his friends all around, Canning overcame 'not fear—it was tumult' and delivered his maiden speech. He afterwards expressed frustration with Charles Grey for concluding the opposition's case with an argument too narrow for Canning to sink his teeth into, forcing him to attack Fox instead, which he tried to do as decently as possible, not only because Canning admired him, but because he did not want to be the young upstart showing disrespect to an elder statesman. He noted that the opposition behaved civilly (though Fox did not leave off his usual practice of talking over ministerial speakers) except for Grey, on whom he vowed revenge. Canning conveyed the eroticism of the maiden speech:

The thoughts of the great game that I was playing, that I had staked my *all*, and must win or lose through life, by the event of this night—anger too, and indignation against the person who was playing his anticks to perplex me—all conspired at once. I made one effort, regained my breath—drew myself up as undauntedly as I could. The House supported me nobly—and I got triumphantly to the end. During the latter part of my speech—I know no pleasure (*sensual* pleasure I had almost said) equal to that which I experienced. I had complete possession of all that I meant to say, and of myself, and I saw my way clear before me. The House was with me to a degree that was most comfortably assuring and delightful. I ventured to look boldly round me and before me and on each side, and met good-natured, chearing countenances—and there were Pitt and Dundas—as I was afterwards informed by those who saw them in front, with their countenances smirking and glittering, rubbing their hands and beating time to the sentences and nodding to each other—and it was during this period that Dundas exclaimed in the way that I told you yesterday. 'By God, this will do'. All this, as you may suppose, was rapture to me—

Canning felt secure enough to relate the postmortems with humour. He had spoken too rapidly and gestured with such extravagance that on a couple of occasions Pitt and Dundas had been obliged to duck. Like Elliot, he assessed every reaction greedily.[83] His obvious infatuation with Pitt enhanced his confidence and energy to the extent that, by the end of the year, his familiarity with the minister, memorialized by the much-heralded placing of his hand upon Pitt's shoulder in the House, had ignited gossip. The dean of Christ Church as well as his old school friend John Parker, Lord Boringdon, later Earl of Morley, both apprized him of this, which sparked a lengthy, emotionally charged self-justification to the Leighs: 'I know indeed that I have, with people whom I like, old or young, great or small, something of a *caressing* manner (I think I must call it so, for I do not recollect any other word to express it).' He argued that, despite Pitt's reputation for aloofness, 'he is in fact a very hearty, *salutation-giving, shake-handy* sort of person'. He nonetheless concluded: 'But if it be wrong, it must be altered.'[84]

In some ways, the alliances, rivalries and intrigues characteristic of the court had simply spilled out of the palace into the ever-expanding geographical areas where political activity took place, leaving politicians to navigate continually shifting boundaries between the personal and the political. Canning invariably assessed the veracity of reputations when he met people for the first time. When first introduced to him, Loughborough told Canning he wanted to be better acquainted so he would be sending him an invitation 'to eat a bit of mutton with him'. Canning noted: 'He is a great *rogue* I believe—but that is none of my business—and so I will go with all my heart, and eat his bit of mutton, when he pleases.'[85] Although none of his business, he had felt compelled to mention this to the Leighs. In early 1795, he had Boringdon on the carpet for voting with the government in public but criticizing Pitt in private. Canning told Boringdon that it was not fair either to Pitt or 'to *your own character*, for see what people must think of it'. He explained that in public life a man had to be consistent in his consideration of either measures or men in determining his course of conduct. The former, almost an impossible course, required great firmness and judgement, as well as a secure seat in parliament and an independent fortune. The latter demanded trust in the judgement and integrity of one's leader and fidelity to one's profession of friendship to him in private as well as in public.[86]

Tom Pelham did some soul-searching regarding his political and personal relations. Directly involved in the morass of the Hastings prosecution and the further acrimony that disagreement over France brought, he first sided with Fox and then began drifting Burke-wards in summer 1793. After attending church on Christmas Day that year, he took up Machiavelli's account of the trial of Horatius for the murder of his sister, which led him to contemplate the possible results of the Hastings trial in the Lords and in public opinion. As he considered the danger of pardoning a man for crimes because the good of his public service outweighed their evils, Pelham ruminated on the peril in which political office placed personal character. He decided:

Public & private morality are I think in most instances the same here. I think there is a difference & it is owing to the object to which the Principle of Morality is applicable; being different rewards & punishments are made for the sake of example, & relate to ye execution or breach of public duties—Ambition will lead a man to the greatest acts in ye service of his Country, but if his exertions give him an exemption from Punishment for crimes he is no longer upon a footing with his fellow creatures & the superiority he has acquired will not diminish the Ambitions that influenced his original conduct but on ye contrary give it fresh Vigour & he will be tempted to assume a Power inconsistent with ye liberties of this country.

This brings us back full circle to *Cato's Letters*, quoted at the beginning of Chapter 2, which contended that excessive power, not private vices, turned men into tyrants. Pelham went on to contrast the obligations of public service with those of friendship, given that:

> in private life the intercourse of mutual services is different in it's object & in it's effect, the consciousness of our own infirmities & a well tempered mind will make us forgive offences where we have received benefits. [I]n friendship the pleasure in performing services & in receiving them is mutual & equal; I feel no remorse or diminution of independence in receiving continued & replicated obligations from my Friend, & I am never tired or feel any superiority over him in consequence of any services I can render him—in y[e] common Intercourse with men I feel an [internal?] desperation to serve them & to receive services, but as in our state of imperfection it is impossible to render or receive equal services from all y[e] world, there will be a difference in mutual good offices, & in that difference originates Friendships which are hardened affections.

Pelham then reasoned that, in the event of injury, past services rendered would figure in both cases, but the degree of injury felt as well as the chance for reconciliation would be dependent on different principles in public and private.[87] It would seem that the affective bonds associated with political alliances, so freely expressed in the earlier era, now belonged to private life. We must remember, though, that Pelham had been disappointed in his political career and in love.

The importance of friendship, camaraderie and emotional support among politicians appears to have intensified over the course of the century in tandem with public hostility to love between men and to loveless, mercenary aristocratic marriages that facilitated a small number of families maintaining a stranglehold on political power. Paul Ludwig captures the change in sensibilities in his study of eros in Greek thought. His description of the political rhetoric of the ancients does not seem so far removed from that of the first half of the eighteenth century:

> Much classical thought, explicitly and implicitly, based its notions of eros on purely formal resemblances among sexual desire, love, and ambition as well as higher aspirations such as patriotism and cosmopolitanism. Common features in the psychological responses to each of these passions led orators, poets, and philosophers to conclude that said passions were

differing manifestations of a single, underlying eros. They were then able to place the apparently diverse passions on a continuum with one another, so that the logical progression, for example, from sexual license to tyranny or from citizen lovers to loving the city, could seem unproblematic to them. Eros therefore provided them with a bridge, missing in modern thought, between the private and public spheres.

The Greeks, moreover, 'were keenly aware that people often perform acts of service in the hopes of winning favor in the eyes of their beloved'.[88] Hence the attention politicians of the earlier era gave to the personality, personal attractiveness and accomplishments of their cohorts. The Wilkes and Liberty movement rendered such relations suspect by associating them with Stuart corruption and aristocratic effeminacy.

Political eros, however, did not cease; it persisted in the shadows, unperceived or unacknowledged, as Canning's letters illustrate. Domestic virtue might have been the rage rhetorically, but in reality, for politicians, upholding rigid standards of marital fidelity could be just as damning as extramarital excesses. Domestic devotion was admirable as long as it did not render a man a boring homebody. Sexual irregularities were tolerable as long as they did not affect a man's physical and emotional accessibility to other members of his party. As politicians' letters and diaries show, MPs depended on each other's availability for approbation and support as they did battle in parliament. A man's ability to manage relations with women to his best advantage—that is, while maintaining flexibility and independence—became an index of his political prowess and value. A closer comparison of politicians' courtships, marriages and mistresses during the 1730s and 1790s alongside the rhetoric generated by the royal weddings of these eras will further demonstrate the persistence of the courtier ethos in an era of idealized conjugality.

CHAPTER FOUR

Court, Courtship and Domestic Virtue

The hereditary principle allowed the monarch's sexual body to be a legitimate object of public scrutiny. Interest in the Stuarts' sexuality, however, strayed beyond a concern for the dynasty's propagation and survival when these monarchs' personal desires gave royal favourites untoward access to their persons, power and influence. Sexual metaphor in political discourse reached its zenith during the reign of Charles II. Broadside doggerel graphically depicted the royal prick, imagined in substantial dimensions, symbolizing a court ruled by pleasure and, thus, raping the nation, or rendered impotent by continual engulfment.[1] Drawing parallels between a monarch's regnal style and his or her sexual proclivities did not cease after the Revolution of 1688–89, so the extension of this analogy to characterize politicians in, or vying for, power that we have seen in previous chapters should come as no surprise. Nor should the sexual subtexts that persisted in perceptions of proper and improper exercise of power, as well as of relations among political actors.[2] Although most political brokering now occurred outside the royal palace and the Hanoverians did not dominate patronage of the arts, fashion, manners and mores in the way that the Tudors and early Stuarts had done, the elite continued to pay court and the monarchy still influenced society and culture, albeit indirectly. No longer holding sway as the arbiter of elite taste, the royal court became a public arena for articulating and debating societal values, particularly during ceremonial occasions, via the press. A survey of royal marriages, births and intrigues covered in the press during the reigns of George II and George III, juxtaposed with views from behind the scenes in private writings, will show how the idea of domestic virtue became incorporated into politics as well as how fraught with contradiction and paradox this new moral construct was. By the end of the century, affairs of the heart both facilitated valuable communication across party lines and led to dangerous connections, especially when they involved members of the royal family. The pressure to find a suitable love match created new opportunities for politicians to forge personal bonds as they helped one another through the nerve-wracking pre-marital negotiations, but could just as well bring jealousies and estrangements.

Domesticity's very definition and nature have been hotly debated since Lawrence Stone presented his model of companionate marriage born of eighteenth-century affective individualism. Scholars have found evidence of the trends Stone describes occurring much earlier and have disputed his notions of patriarchy, household composition and women's matrimonial experience, among other things.[3] It remains undisputed, however, that a growing interest in the challenges and rewards of achieving wedded bliss took place in didactic literature and fiction, starting with criticism of mercenary matches at the end of the seventeenth century and, by the early nineteenth, blossoming into the ideal of the tender, loving family as a refuge from the bustle of public business. Literary trends, of course, had a nebulous relation to life. Conduct literature presented numerous models of marriage and novels required marital strife or adultery for plot purposes; nonetheless, this literary attention did reflect the time's social pressure to marry. In the closing decades of the seventeenth century, the increasing number of people who remained single attracted concern, with various genres of writing dispensing pity on the 'superannuated virgin' as a victim of the short supply of eligible men. Other publications provoked controversy by contemplating the pleasures of the single life and advocating expansion of women's educational opportunities. By the beginning of the eighteenth century, the sinister figure of the 'old maid' dominated the discursive field because the economic opportunities that emerged between the 1690s and 1700s allowed women to be single by choice when England's involvement in war raised anxieties about the birth rate and encouraged a political and cultural investment in the reproductive nuclear family. Aristocratic women countered with the idea of rational domesticity based on choice, even if it meant choosing not to marry. Nevertheless, bachelors continued to come under fire. The stereotype of the effeminate fop stigmatized men who rejected the now masculinized private domain of domestic responsibility.[4]

Looking specifically at the ruling orders, Judith Schneid Lewis's study of aristocratic families suggests that, in spite of the swelling romanticization of domesticity in poetry, portraiture, fiction and prescriptive literature, a mixture of pragmatism, family interests and emotion dictated women's matrimonial decisions. By mid-century, mutual regard between husband and wife appeared to be the predominant marital aspiration among women of the propertied elite, with the expectation of passionate love within marriage not ascendant for another hundred years.[5] Men, on the other hand, seemed to consider themselves entitled to have it all, but, as we will continue to see, rhetoric often did not accord with reality. Opponents of Lord Hardwicke's 'Act for the better preventing of clandestine Marriages' of 1753, many of whom made fine speeches defending love and freedom of choice (cited by Stone as evidence of affective individualism), had variously run off with heiresses, contracted mercenary marriages, mistreated women or fathered illegitimate children.[6] By the end of the century, the idea that a happy marriage signalled trustworthiness and respectability increased the urgency for politicians to find love as well as an advantageous connection, which was no small feat, as the heartaches of William Windham and Thomas Pelham and the double life of Sir Gilbert Elliot ('Sir Bashful Constant') discussed in the last chapter attest. The experiences of their younger contemporaries examined in this chapter will further demonstrate how courtship in the environs of the court sometimes made politics and passions a volatile mix.

Frederick Lewis, Prince of Wales, son of George II and father of George III, might be seen as a harbinger of the mid-century transition in elite mores from open (for men) marriages of convenience to domestic commitment. Upon his arrival in London from Hanover in 1728, Frederick pursued the pleasures of the town and had his obligatory sexual intrigues, but after he married Augusta of Saxe-Gotha in 1736 he eschewed scandalous activities. The prince threw himself into improving the buildings and grounds of Leicester House as well as the rural properties that the family leased. He collected art, played music and doted upon his ever-growing brood. He could often be seen at public entertainments surrounded by his children. Having had his political ambitions thwarted by parental favouritism of his younger brother, William, Duke of Cumberland, the prince provided a more respectable figurehead than the Pretender for the patriot opposition to Walpole.[7] That Frederick would turn to a nuclear family in response to a lack of parental nurture has a certain irony, or perhaps is simply a hereditary inevitability, considering how the grandson he never knew, George, Prince of Wales, son of the suffocatingly paternal George III, would be incapable of establishing any sort of faithful union within or outside marriage.

George II's mistresses and George III's marital fidelity appear to mark the two kings as products of different eras and moral codes. All the same, upon closer inspection, the approaches that George II and George III took to domesticity turn out to be riddled with paradox. Although he conformed to monarchical and upper-class custom with his unconcealed extramarital relations, the word most often used to describe George II was uxorious, as he was widely perceived to be ruled by his ministers via Queen Caroline.[8] While George III in the latter part of his reign liked to parade Queen Charlotte and their numerous progeny in great shows of familial concord, marital and extramarital scandals involving his siblings had led the king to initiate the Royal Marriages Act in 1772, which required all descendants of George II under the age of twenty-five to have the monarch's permission to marry.[9] Like Hardwicke's Marriage Act, this legislation favoured family interest over individual happiness. George III would make use of it to annul the marriage contracted in Italy between his son Prince Augustus and a pregnant Lady Augusta Murray in 1794, which raised doubts about the reality behind his public image as a benevolent paterfamilias.[10] The king's disapproval of his brothers' marital choices, his ruination of Prince Adolphus's love match with Frederica of Mecklenburg-Strelitz and his failure to yield to the younger princesses' desires to marry all caused unhappiness and disharmony within the family.[11] Additionally, the gambling, drinking and whoring of the elder princes rendered the king's parental authority contemptible. Notwithstanding, fears of the prince of Wales's ascendancy during the Regency Crisis of 1788–89 and his increasingly outrageous behaviour allowed George III to don the mantle of aggrieved father and loyalist writers to downplay instances of paternal ineffectuality or tyranny. In early 1792, *The Times* recklessly declared: 'CHARLES the SECOND said that his *Concubines* were company for any *VIRTUOUS* woman in his dominions. Thank God that is not the case with any of the branches of the present Royal Family. They all take example by their sovereign, and discountenance the introduction of any demirep, let her rank or situation be ever so high, into a society of fashion, elegance, and honour.'[12] As it became impossible for *The Times* to continue pretending this were true, the activities of the demireps who abounded in the princes' circles would provide occasions for this and other papers to debate the meaning of proper relations in family life within political society.

Hence, by the end of the century, the rival courts, with their warring personae so vividly depicted in the press, made for a host of moral contradictions. Public and private discussions of royal marriages and births in the 1730s and 1790s reflect both the changes in attitudes towards matrimony that took place over the course of the century and all the paradoxes that the ideal of domestic virtue engendered. As I will show, similar scenarios during these two decades played out in divergent ways and stimulated disparate public discourses. The two eras featured marriages of the princesses royal—Anne in 1734 and Charlotte in 1797—after uncertainties and uncomfortable delays, to foreign princes considered physically hideous. The endemic battles between the Hanoverian kings and their heirs apparent flared during the negotiations of separate establishments for the princes of Wales upon the marriages of Frederick in 1736 and George in 1795. The circumstances surrounding the arrival in the world of the princes' first-born daughters, in 1737 and 1796, respectively, occasioned further rifts between royal households. Finally, these two princes of Wales shared mistresses with politicians to very different effect. Frederick's embrace of connubial bliss contained the damage done to his political set; George's chronic fickleness would result in exchanges of women that would wreak havoc in both opposition and ministerial circles.[13] Yet, ironically, politicians at the beginning of the nineteenth century who took pleasure in home life and who left flirting and roistering behind them with their youth, as the attainment of domestic virtue demanded, would suffer similar detriments to reputation as had earlier homebodies.

Changing journalistic practices as well as literary and artistic trends over the course of the eighteenth century shaped the presentation of these events and in consequence the monarchy's public image. Newspapers of the 1730s featured editorials that read like moral, historical or literary essays; they employed abstraction and analogies to comment on the tendencies of current trends and the behaviour of politicians. The hard-news items appeared in short paragraphs with only oblique editorial comment. Some papers provided regular and, on particular occasions, detailed accounts of the activities of George II and royal family members, but written usually in a formal, detached manner. In contrast to the preceding decades, the journalistic style of the 1790s can best be described as gossipy: it performed moral evaluations as it invaded the intimate areas of royal, noble, genteel and common lives alike. At a time when the cult of sensibility was falling into disrepute, newspapers embraced it in their coverage of the upper echelons of society. The trend towards humanizing royalty and contemplating royal character in newspapers had a parallel development in visual satire. Eirwen Nicholson cautions scholars against ignoring the continued importance of symbols, emblems and icons in political prints by treating the genre of caricature that developed in the latter part of the eighteenth century as inherently superior to earlier styles. At the same time, she acknowledges the way that caricature created personas. She points out how such portrayals could compliment as well as deprecate; indeed, being worthy of caricature, of however unflattering a kind, indicated one had achieved a particular status in the World.[14]

The Domestic Dramas of Royal Weddings and Births

The press did refer to the 'royal family' during George II's reign, but the construction did not yet have the resonance it would acquire in the latter part of George III's tenure when the personalities of its members developed a more vivid existence in print culture, discursive and visual, with their appearances and sentiments regularly characterized. Representations of Princess Anne's marriage to William IV of Orange and Princess Charlotte's to Frederick William Charles of Württemberg epitomize this depictive transformation. Anne's presence throughout the proceedings seemed more iconic than human; any tears shed for her departure from family and home-land never made it into the papers. Coverage of Charlotte's nuptials, in contrast, can be encapsulated by the loyalist *True Briton*'s declaration about her weeping sisters: 'We cannot omit taking notice of the exquisite sensibility displayed by the PRINCESSES.'[15]

Anne's wedding presented more opportunity for drama and pathos, but the papers did not pursue these, as they had different preoccupations. Upon the prince of Orange's arrival in London in November 1733, he developed a dangerous fever, delaying the ceremony until the following March. Newspapers contained daily reports of his convalescence, his regimen while taking the waters at Bath, and all the sightseeing, assemblies, dinners, balls and other diversions the hospitable English provided for his amusement. Poor Anne's moment as a bride became lost amid the ministerial papers' genuflections to her groom's membership of the family that had liberated Britain in 1688–89 and the match's potential for securing the Protestant succession. Opposition-favouring papers had an interest in touting the prince of Orange's popularity in implicit contrast to feelings about George II and Queen Caroline.[16] Indeed, the queen's birthday that year became more about the prince's celebration of it while visiting Oxford, 'as the Behaviour of his Highness has filled every Mouth here with Applause: His Highness has won the Hearts of the whole University, his Modesty and Learning gained them as a sage and venerable Body; his Wit and Sprightliness charmed them separately'.[17] Press coverage reached a crescendo after the reception he received at Bristol, which, with other aspects of his tour, filled columns in the newspapers of 2 March 1734. A thousand

'Gentlemen of Distinction' on horseback and in coaches met the prince several miles out of town. Two or three hundred weavers (accounts varied) with orange cockades in their hats and wool-combers wearing Holland shirts and orange wool caps or 'sort of Wigs' processed on the common, as did the local regiment of foot. Guns fired, bells rang and people shouted their acclamations in a town resplendent with decorations for the occasion. The mayor and corporation sponsored a splendid dinner and ball, which the prince opened with a minuet with a sheriff's lady 'and was pleased to dance three several Times in the utmost Perfection'.[18]

Only a hint of the underlying political tensions came from a local paper, *Read's Weekly Journal or British Gazette*. This noted that the celebrations gave 'all possible Demonstrations of Respect to the present Royal Family, as well as a graceful Remembrance of our once Glorious Deliverer'. In addition, however, *Read's* described the prince as being 'harangued by our Town-Clerk, in a short, but pathetic Speech, which his Highness answered with a Sweetness of Temper peculiar to himself'. The *Universal Spectator, and Weekly Journal* printed the clerk's speech, which indeed frothily congratulated the prince on the recovery of his health, praised the blessings that sprang from the illustrious House of Orange, and anticipated that 'an Alliance between our Royal Family and the House of Nassau, will become the delightful Theme of Poets and Historians, and the silent Pleasure of all such who are not happily endued with Talents to express the many prosperous Events naturally to flow from so agreeable a Conjuncture'. It declined to print the prince's 'extremely obliging' speech in reply, 'lest the Delicacy of the Expression should be injur'd by the Misrepresentation', suggesting a concern that the prince's words might be open to interpretations calculated to further partisan ends. Accounts of the tour published on 2 March did not offer much more of a sense of the prince's physical presence than the *London Journal's* report that he, 'throughout the Divine Service, charm'd every one by his pious and devout Behaviour. In short, adds our Correspondent at Bath, his Highness's Demeanour during his seven weeks stay here has been one continued Scene of Affability, Generosity, and Humanity to all Degrees of Persons that have either waited on him, or come to Town to see him.' Even this was more character analysis than the press usually extended to the royal family. The *Craftsman*, although it gave the story only a half-column, observed that the prince took leave of Bristol 'in the most tender and affecting Manner'.

The newspapers' coverage belied the consternation caused by the prince's presence. Lord Hervey, the king's sharply observant vice-chamberlain, wrote that his figure, 'besides his being almost a dwarf, was as much deformed as it was possible for a human creature to be; his face was not bad, his countenance was sensible, but his breath more offensive than it is possible for those who have not been offended by it to imagine'. As she was waiting for her turn to meet the prince, the queen explained to Hervey that 'as she thought the King looked upon it as a proper match, and one which, if she could bear his person, he should not dislike', the princess had 'said she was resolved, if it was a monkey, she would marry him'. According to Hervey, throughout the prince's stay the queen persisted in referring to him as the 'monster' while the king, sensible of how personally disliked he and the queen were at this time, resented the public attention that the prince received and treated him shabbily until the marriage took place.[19] While newspaper writers gave no inkling of the malice in the palace, unattributed publications ran with it. A broadside ballad, *The Disappointed Marriage, or An Hue and Cry after an Outlandish Monster*, represented the king and queen as forcing the match upon the princess and the prince as having gone missing:

> Tho' much against the Lady's Will,
> To swallow such a bitter Pill
> But Parents told her that she must
> *Obey* their Dictates, or be curs'd:
> What signifies your Husband's Shape,
> Whether like Monkey or an Ape;
> To marry him we think it fit,
> For tho' deform'd he is a Wit.

In the midst of a grotesque physical description of the prince, the poem worked in an allusion to the king's habit of kicking—customarily his hat—when angry, as well as a crude reference to the real reason for the union, which was to perpetuate the collateral line of the Protestant succession:

> His Body is round, if you regard,
> His A___ sticks out almost a Yard:
> 'Tis mightily handy for a Kick,
> But very limber is his _____.

It concluded:

If you don't find him, this all know,
You'll spoil St. J_____ glitt'ring show.[20]

Similarly, a *roman-à-clef* entitled *A Court Novel: The Secret History of Mama Oello, Princess Royal of Peru* (1733) told the tale of a forced marriage and fabricated a lover for the princess, identified by marginalia in the British Library's copy as Lord Carmichael, an army captain. Anne's biographer finds no corroborating evidence and points out that, if the princess had committed any indiscretion, Lord Hervey certainly would have observed it. The work seemed more an attack on Sir Robert Walpole and the Dutch alliance. Hostile references to Anne appeared elsewhere in connection with her support of Handel, her former music master, which aligned her with the court against Prince Frederick and the opposition, patrons of the Italian opera. Suzanne Aspden argues that the ambiguous allegorical resonances in the opera performances as well as the symbols on ladies' fans commemorating the nuptials reflected public puzzlement over the match because of the royal family's failure to communicate its purpose effectively.[21]

Newspaper accounts of the wedding lavished more attention on the princess royal's dress than her behaviour and focused on the magnificent appearances of the company although, according to Lord Hervey, Anne's 'mother and sisters were under so much undisguised and unaffected concern the whole time, that the procession to the chapel, and the scene there, looked more like the mournful pomp of a sacrifice than the joyful celebration of a marriage, and put one rather in mind of an Iphigenia leading to the altar than of a bride'. Nor did the papers' accounts of the ceremony attending the new couple's retirement to their bedchamber mention the spectacle of the prince of Orange in his nightdress, which, unlike his wedding costume, accentuated rather than disguised his physical irregularities. Instead, they dwelled on the rich fabrics of their undress and the exquisite lace adorning the bed.[22] Likewise, the papers did not consider newsworthy the copious tears that the royal family shed upon the couple's departure in April, but felt compelled to report that all but Lady Southwell suffered seasickness during the Channel crossing. Hervey claimed that the queen 'never ceased crying for three days. But after three weeks (excepting post-days) Her Royal Highness seemed as much forgotten as if she had been buried three years.'[23] The ministerial *London Journal*, apparently wishing to endow her with an ambassadorial role, exaggerated the raptures with which the faction-ridden political milieu of The Hague greeted the new princess of Orange and reflected the snobbery with which the British regarded the Dutch, observing 'her Highness paying a due Regard to those of all Degrees that approach her; and as her Palace Doors are always open the Burghers and their Wives go and admire her whenever they please'.[24] In sum, press coverage of the wedding stressed its political and down-played its personal aspects.

The narrative would have run very differently fifty years later; today, Anne might well be beatified as the martyred patron saint of boomerang children. In its 27 April 1734 account of her departure, the *Universal Spectator, and Weekly Journal* added that 'we hear' the prince planned to join Prince Eugene's campaign, during which time the princess would return to England. On 6 July, it announced Anne's resumption of her place at court as well as the news that she was with child. The princess at long last achieved a personal identity in the press. This paper issued regular assurances of her pregnancy's progress, and by autumn Anne was attracting the same attention that her husband had enjoyed: 'Her Royal Highness the Princess of Orange bore the Fatigues of her Journey to Colchester on Monday last, and back the next Day to Kensington, as well as could possibly be expected, but did not hunt the next Morning with their Majesties. Her Royal Highness's Journey in the two Days was about 100 measur'd Miles.'[25] Also on that day the *Universal Spectator* dispelled rumours that the prince of Orange would be coming to England and reported the splendid appearance of 'the Nobility, Quality, and Gentry' at court for the princess's birthday. It noted that the queen's midwife would be accompanying the princess back to her adopted country but that she had further postponed her return upon learning that the prince's departure from Germany would be delayed. In contrast, the *London Journal* now offered comparatively muted and less detailed accounts of the princess's doings, and, although it gave regular reports of her good health, never mentioned her pregnancy directly.

Despite her efforts to gain attention and respect, and the obvious reluctance with which she departed, the newspapers doggedly stuck to the princess of Orange's diplomatic role. After the king's birthday on 30 October, she set out for the coast and the *Universal Spectator* enumerated the ever-changing arrangements for her passage in response to bad weather in the Channel and concerns for her delicate state. It gave extensive coverage of the joyful receptions she received in Colchester, Harwich and finally Dover, where she 'gain'd the Love and Esteem of all the people there by her Affability and engaging behaviour'. Prior to this, she threw a grand dinner featuring a sumptuous array of rich food and fine wine at the Three

Cups Inn for the mayor, aldermen and corporation of Harwich. Townspeople levelled paths and removed stiles to accommodate her morning walks. The papers boasted that, once the route of her passage had been altered, the king of France himself penned a letter to George II thanking him for the honour bestowed by allowing his daughter to land at Calais.[26] Notwithstanding her reluctance to leave England, at Calais, '[t]he Meeting of their Highnesses was extremely tender and affecting; and as it seem'd to give the highest Pleasure to themselves, furnish'd no small Satisfaction to all about them'. The princess royal's manner towards her consort after the honeymoon and in their correspondence while apart reveals that the arrangement had become a love match.[27] Once the couple took up residence abroad, press interest in them dwindled. A fire at their house at The Hague made the news, and reports of the pregnancy's progress appeared in the *Universal Spectator*. By the time of the queen's birthday in March, rumours flew questioning the princess's condition, and in mid-April came the stark official proclamation that Anne had not been with child after all.[28]

The fuss made over the prince and princess of Orange suggests a segment of the public was desirous of an affable, accessible royal family. That Anne would have, judging by her husband's letters to his mother, a hysterical pregnancy underscores the pressure she must have felt to fulfil one of the match's main purposes: guaranteeing the Protestant line of succession. When she did conceive and carry a daughter to term in 1736, the English male midwife had to sacrifice the infant to save Anne's life. On 18 December, the *Universal Spectator* reported that 'after a long and dangerous Labour' the new princess had died at birth. It added: 'Her Royal Highness is as well as can be expected in her Condition.' Three years later, Anne endured the stillbirth of another girl. Not until February 1743 did she achieve the successful delivery of Princess Carolina; in March 1748 there followed the future William V. Meanwhile, the Anglo-Dutch alliance had not delivered any of its anticipated political benefits. George II might have bestowed a hundred guineas upon the messenger who brought news of the new male heir, but Anne's dying act would be to fight against an English match for her daughter by forcing through approval of a marriage contract with Prince Charles Christian of Nassau-Weilbourg.[29] As for her former admirers in England, within a few months after the news broke that she was not carrying a child, hopes for the Protestant succession shifted to the union between the prince of Wales and Augusta of Saxe-Gotha, 'a most beautiful Princess', the *Universal Spectator* gushed, about to depart for England with a 'handsome Retinue'. Perhaps more aptly named the *Universal Speculator*, it reported the wedding date as having been set for 29 October 1735, the day preceding the king's birthday. The marriage treaty would not actually be signed until the following April.[30]

In contrast, during the betrothal of the next princess royal in 1797, the press made ribald jokes about the dynastic aspect of the match and treated Princess Charlotte as if she were a local village girl rather than a diplomatic asset. Changes in journalistic practice and in the country's condition caused similar events to attract different coverage. Very unlike the peaceful, prosperous 1730s, Britain from the mid–1790s suffered the burdens of war and economic hardship. Additionally, this would be the third royal wedding of the decade. Frederick, Duke of York had wed Princess Frederica of Prussia in 1791. George, Prince of Wales had married Princess Caroline of Brunswick in 1795, fathered a daughter and continued to despise his wife openly. At this juncture, however, nobody could have dreamt that George III and Queen Charlotte, who enjoyed such extravagant fecundity (as Frederick and Augusta had before them), would produce children so reproductively challenged with respect to providing legitimate offspring. In 1797, the press was looking for sources of optimism, particularly the ultra-loyalist *True Briton* and *The Times*, champion of William Pitt the Younger's ministry. The opposition press, here represented by the *Morning Post*, in which the prince of Wales had apparently reinvested, and the *Morning Chronicle*, a stout supporter of Charles James Fox and his party, looked for opportunities to showcase the failings of ministerial policy, but sometimes got sucked up into the atmosphere of hope and sentimental domestic tenderness.[31] Concurrently, though, newspapers now ventured boldly into personal territory where before only anonymous pamphlets and visual satires had dared tread.

Like Anne, Princess Charlotte wed a prince of odd physical proportions. When the match with the prince of Württemberg hit the press in the autumn of 1796, the *Morning Chronicle*, after chastising the other papers for misidentifying him, provided a family history and then came out and said it: 'He is corpulent, but handsome in his person, and extremely active.'[32] *The Times* reported that, even before his arrival in spring 1797, the prince seemed aware of 'the license of our Print Shops'. On the boat journey over, he joked to some English gentlemen that, from what he had heard, he was already on exhibition. The paper added: 'His Serene Highness is, in truth, a most excessively corpulent man, so much so, that his servants in assisting him to put on his *pelice*, are obliged to walk quite round him to put it from one shoulder over the other.'[33] Visual satirists had a field day with the prince's dimensions and family resemblances. On 24 October 1796, James Gillray had published *For Improving the Breed* (*BMC* 8827), a full-body profile of the prince showing him displayed like some prize ram, bull or boar. Given the limited pool of candidates, making a royal match had much in common with the process of breeding rare livestock, notwithstanding the enchantment of its elaborate ceremonial and the press's romanticizing of the occasion. While Gillray mercilessly caricatured the king, queen, princes and politicians, he tended to represent the princesses as fair captives and as more beautiful than they were generally regarded to be. In satirical prints and newspapers, George III's daughters overwhelmingly appear virtuous and modest. The breeding witticism, however, rapidly deteriorated. Gillray's next portrayal of the prince, in April, showed him laden with medals and kissing the full-figured princess's cheek (obscuring her face), which involved leaning in at an acute angle to compensate for his big belly. The pun in the caption suggested the question some might have been asking—how could a man so proportioned actually breed?—as well as the irony of this problem occurring in a time of dearth:

Heav'n grant their Happiness complete
And may they make both Ends to meet;
in these hard times.

In another depiction of the couple's introduction, Richard Newton drew a servant in the background brandishing a saw and raising the question directly: 'Egad they did well to order a piece to be cut out of the Table or he never could have reached his Dinner, and how he will reach her, God only knows. I suppose he has some German Method a rare Ram this to mend the Breed.' In both of these prints, the princess royal looks comely, albeit uncharacteristically bold in the latter; with one hand on her hip and the other raised, she exclaims: 'Lord what a Porpoise Pho!!!'—a small whale of the Phocaenidae family (fig. 7).[34] Along the same lines, after the wedding night, the *Morning Post* quipped cryptically on the question of whether or not the marriage had been consummated but then followed up with the double entendre: 'The PRINCE of WIRTEMBURG has been ridiculed on account of his being *lusty*, but we understand his FAIR BRIDE likes him the more for that reason.'[35]

One might argue that such treatment showed a lack of respect for, and degraded, royalty, but, by making fun of royal personages in the same way that they mocked others, artists and writers also turned them into flesh-and-blood human beings.[36] That George III allowed himself and his family to be caricatured showed off his good nature and carried the implication that he felt secure enough in his people's affection not to consider such lampoons a threatening affront. Artists did occasionally step over the line. Gillray's ill-considered, ghastly representation of the queen in a print, in which he actually intended to lampoon Henry Fuseli's illustrations of Milton, provoked an outcry from the palace. Although derogatory anti-monarchical prints did appear, for the most part mainstream artists issued laughter-producing burlesques, worlds apart from the graphic sexual renderings of Marie Antoinette and the French court that appeared in the run-up to the revolution.[37] In the early eighteenth century, the depictions offered by writers and artists reflected a sense of royal personages as stiff, emblematic figures. Take, for instance, what at the time constituted a racy picture of George II with his mistress, Amalie Sophie Marianne von Wallmoden, made countess of Yarmouth, which appeared in December 1738, a year after Queen Caroline's death (fig. 8).[38] Wallmoden, seated in a chair next to the king on his throne, is hoisting his right leg over her lap with her right hand and reaching over his shoulder with her left. A bottle, two glasses and a plate of sausages (presumably German) lie next to her on a table, which also contains a scrap of paper that reads 'The Black Goat', suggestive of a satanic coupling. The biblical verses quoted in the caption were the wards of a harlot inveigling a man. Anyone well-versed in scripture would know that the man went 'as an ox goeth to the slaughter' (Proverbs 7:22). In the king's left hand carelessly dangles the sceptre. Symbols of the late queen dominate the scene: her portrait hanging above their heads behind them, a suit of mourning clothes on the wall abutting the table and, at their feet, the king's hat and gloves, a pug chewing a mourning hatband, and two pamphlets, *A Whimwam New Come Over* and *Cabinet of Love*. Precisely what the king is doing with his right hand is not clear; likewise the facial expressions of the pair are enigmatic. They look posed, not natural, in comparison to the lively, expressive depictions of royalty in the prints published in the 1790s. Changes in journalism and print culture turned members of the royal family and their circle into distinct personalities with feelings and failings.

Also similar to Anne's betrothal, an awkward interval ensued after the groom's arrival in England, this time not as a result of illness but owing to the king's reluctance to let his daughter go, which delayed the formal preparations. Like the prince of Orange, the prince of Württemberg was packed off on tour, supposedly incognito out of respect for the court, but in fact closely observed. This time the press took the opportunity to score more direct political points. The ministerial papers represented him awed by the riches and prosperity of England while the opposition press lamented the state in which he found the country.[39] This princess royal had much more of an affective presence in the newspapers that crossed party lines. In February, readers of both the loyalist *True Briton* and the radical *Telegraph* learned that she had embroidered her own white muslin wedding dress with gold flowers.[40] *The Times*, Pitt's champion, catalogued virtually every shiver, tear and significant look displayed at the nuptials:

> Her ROYAL HIGHNESS, on her entrance trembled very much, and appeared greatly affected throughout the whole of the ceremony; and so indeed did all the ROYAL FAMILY, particularly the Princess ELIZABETH. The QUEEN had evidently been weeping before she came to the Chapel, and the KING and Duke of CLARENCE frequently wiped away the tear of affection during the ceremony, which was performed by the Archbishop of CANTERBURY, assisted by the Bishop of LONDON.
>
> The KING was so much affected when he gave away the Bride, that he laid hold of the wrong hand, but instantly corrected himself.
>
> Both the Bride and Bridegroom went through the ceremony with the utmost correctness and solemnity.
>
> The BRIDE looked extremely well; indeed, it was generally remarked that her Royal Highness never appeared to so much advantage; and his Serene Highness paid the most affectionate attention to her; his eyes being never drawn from her during the whole time they were in the Chapel, but by his necessary attention to the ceremony.[41]

The *True Briton* observed Princess Mary's particular distress and the duchess of York solicitously providing her with a handkerchief. The newlyweds did not depart with great fanfare, as had the prince and princess of Orange; Württemberg did not have the same cachet. The paper corrected its report of the previous day that the king had ridden out with them: they said their goodbyes days before her actual departure: 'The interview, it is said, was very affecting, and His MAJESTY, in particular, was strongly agitated by the approaching separation from an amiable and accomplished daughter.' Although it only carried an abbreviated account of the wedding, the opposition paper the *Morning Post* covered the tearful goodbye between father and daughter, and noted that the spectators who watched her bid adieu to her servants and board the carriage that would bear her away cried too.[42] Domesticity, not dynastic aspirations, dominated.

In view of the ultimate consequences of the Orange match, the focus on family feelings, not fortunes, should not be surprising. Gillray's sharp eye captured Princess Anne's unhappy legacy. His indecorous portrayal of the Württemberg procession to the bridal chamber has George III hidden behind a column as if to indicate the father of the bride's reluctant participation. The princess royal looks at her capacious new husband demurely from behind her fan; she and her sisters as usual escape caricature. Visible in the company, though, is the bulbous face of Anne's son, William V, with eyes closed, apparently insensate. Isaac Cruikshank's even less decorous version of the scene renders him as a sleeping cupid atop a barrel of Hollands (Dutch gin) stationed next to the door of the bridal chamber, an allusion to a Dutch anti-stadholder print of 1782 that depicted him as Bacchus on a barrel, a representation that had deeply offended the prince (fig. 9). A Dutch pamphlet that year even alleged that he had not sprung from the loins of William IV and called Anne a Jezebel. William V and his family had fled from the invading French army and been exiled in England since 30 January 1795. Albeit a weak leader, William IV had been a devoted husband who went out of his way to help Anne recover from her disastrous pregnancies. Nonetheless, after sacrificing her love of London's vibrant cultural life to endure the tedium of Leeuwarden for the sake of preserving the stadholderate for the House of Orange-Nassau, having her son's ineptitude bring him to England must have had Anne spinning in her grave.[43]

As was the case in reporting the nuptials of their sisters, for the weddings of the princes of Wales the press emphasized diplomatic and dynastic issues in the 1730s and familial affections in the 1790s. The *Universal Spectator, and Weekly Journal* reported in painstaking detail Lord De La Warr's activities at the court of Gotha in negotiating the marriage treaty, who would fill the positions in the new household, the procedures and retinue for Princess Augusta's trip to England, and the ceremonies in preparation for her presentation at St James's. Augusta arrived at Lambeth at a quarter past one to cheering crowds and boarded the king's barge to Whitehall, where the prince awaited her at the garden door: 'upon her sinking to her Knee to kiss his Hand, he affectionately rais'd her up, and twice saluted her.' Taken upstairs to the royal apartments, she repeated this ritual with the rest of the family.[44] The papers gave little sense of any personal affect. The *Daily Gazetteer*, which had superseded the *London Journal* as the pre-eminent ministerial paper, only observed: 'Her Highness has very beautiful Features, a fine Complexion; and appears with a very majestick and becoming Air, that gives a Lustre to her high Birth and other Accomplishments of Person and Mind.' It reported her appearing 'extremely well pleased' at the sight of the people who greeted her, and the prince of Wales 'extremely well pleased' with her conversation.[45] Just as Walpole liked to remind the nation of the Jacobite threat at every opportunity, the *Daily Gazette* stressed the union's importance to the succession: 'This happy Event must give the most sensible Joy to a People who are tenderly concerned in every Circumstance of his Life and Fortunes as the amiable Qualities which we have experienced in his *Royal Highness* engage our Wishes, that the Comfort of his high Dignity may equally take of his Virtues; and the *Protestant Succession* itself depending on this Alliance, our Religion, our Liberties, the present Age, and late Posterity, have the highest Advantage from the personal Merit of the Illustrious Bride.' It went on to underscore the significance of the princess's Protestant lineage: 'HER *ROYAL HIGHNESS* is descended from that ancient SAXON Race, whence the Nations of *Britain* and *Germany* were people as from common Ancestors; and descended as she is from the *Founders* of the Liberties of *England*, from her shall descend the *Preservers* of those Liberties to all succeeding Times.'[46]

In further illustration of changing sensibilities, the personality of Princess Caroline of Brunswick, daughter of George III's sister Augusta, burst forth from the papers. The *Morning Post* reported: 'Her Royal Highness is most sprightly and playful in her manners. On being presented to His Majesty, after kneeling, and being raised, she took the King by the two arms, with the most winning familiarity; and after eyeing him all round said, "You are very like my dear Mama!"—The King laughed heartily.' The *Morning Chronicle* also carried this anecdote, as well as an account of a similar display during a walk in the Queen's House gardens: 'Her Highness broke from the conductor who was leading her with the usual respectful ceremony, and hooking the King under the arm, said with a smile, "You shall be my beau and show me all the charms of the place." The King was enchanted with a familiarity so new to him. From these slight traits the people may form some idea of the princess, whose character is so essential to their future happiness.'[47] These stories, coming from opposition papers, were perhaps intended to reveal the prince of Wales's predicament: saddled with a wife lacking any sense of decorum who was being egged-on by a father-in-law who refused to conduct himself with kingly dignity. Prince George's undisguised contempt for Princess Caroline lost him public sympathy, nonetheless. On the very day before, the *Morning Chronicle*

1. *The C___t Shittle-Cock*, 1742. Satirical prints in the early eighteenth century used symbols to convey character. George II's habit of kicking his hat in anger became emblematic of his irascible nature. The sexual innuendos of Sir Robert Walpole's daughter and the king's mistress seem incongruous among stiffly posed figures displaying elaborate court dress and little emotion.

2. James Gillray, *The Fall of Wolsey of the Woolsack*, 24 May 1792. Caricature turned political figures into personas. George's hurried speech with its signature 'What! What! What!' and his energetic informality feature in prints throughout the 1790s. Pitt's attenuated figure, particularly in the breeches, suggests effeminacy, a holdover from rumours in the 1780s about his sexuality, and his complexion reflects his excessive drinking.

3. *The Festival of the Golden Rump*, 19 March 1737. George II's kicking and his practice of turning his back on, or 'rumping', those who displeased him give birth to a new version of the biblical Golden Calf. Walpole and Queen Caroline have erected a false idol to promote unnatural submission to his Walpole's domination.

4. James Gillray, *Bandelures*, 28 February 1791. As George, Prince of Wales's set routinely traded mistresses, his secret marriage to the Catholic widow, Maria Fitzherbert, is likened to the acquisition of a new plaything that he would tire of quickly. Some saw Richard Brinsley Sheridan's friendship to the outlaw couple as opportunistic. On the mantelpiece, the bust of Claudius brings to mind his scheming third wife Messalina. The figure of Bacchus on a barrel and the horseracing design above the extravagantly blazing hearth indicate other sources of the prince's distraction, along with his new French toy.

5. James Gillray, *God Save the King.—in a Bumper. or—an Evening Scene, three times a Week at Wimbledon*, 27 May 1795. Although insinuations about Pitt's lack of interest in women faded after the 1784 election, his all-male 'cabinet dinners' and regular drinking sessions with Henry Dundas promoted gossip. Dundas sits firmly behind his dining room table, however, holding his pipe aloft and away from his boy Billy, who disports himself upon the table.

6. James Gillray, *Cincinnatus in Retirement: Falsely Supposed to Represent <u>Jeusit-Pad</u>' Driven Back to his Native Potatoes*, 23 August 1782. Edmund Burke's Irish Catholic roots and his dour devotion to matters of principle brought out anti-Catholic stereotypes of corruption, oppression and poverty.

7. Richard Newton, *The First Interview, or an Envoy from Yarmony to Improve the Breed*, 19 April 1797. The marriage of Charlotte, the Princess Royal to Prince Frederick William Charles of Würtemberg generated excitement over his immense proportions. Although, as usual, escaping caricature—indeed, Charlotte looks more like a fairytale princess—the ribald comments about the match departs from the customary representation of George III's daughters as innocent, sweet and rather insipid.

8. *Solomon in His Glory*, 19 December 1738. George II and his mistress, Amalie Sophia Marianne von Wallmoden, Countess of Yarmouth, get frisky in a stilted manner, while relics of mourning his late queen and reigning over Britain are cast aside.

9. Isaac Cruickshank, *The Wedding Night*, 20 May 1797. An echo of the wedding of Anne, the Princess Royal in 1734 comes in the form of the sleeping Cupid with the face of her son, William V, the Dutch stadholder in exile. Princess Charlotte affects modesty with her fan while Queen Charlotte brandishes a bowl of 'cock broth' as the procession moves toward the bed in the next room, resembling less a solemn royal ceremony than the old country custom of bedding the bride.

10. James Gillray, *The Presentation—or—The Wise Men's Offering*, 9 Jan. 1796. As the obsequiousness of Prince George's cronies, Charles James Fox and Sheridan indicate, the birth of Princess Charlotte gave Caroline, Princess of Wales leverage against her errant husband, who affects jollity as he arrives at the christening dishevelled, drunk and late.

11. *Frederick Prince of Wales and Princess Augusta of Saxe Gotha*, 25 April 1736. The betrothal of Frederick, Prince of Wales to Augusta of Saxe-Gotha involved discarding his mistress, Anne Vane and the illegitimate he recognized as his although little Fitzfrederick might have been sired by John, Lord Hervey or William Stanhope, Earl of Harrington. Walpole sits next to the empty throne disgruntled, contemplating how the Prince's enhanced status and independent household would strengthen the opposition's base.

12. Isaac Cruickshank, *A Scene in the Gamester*, 8 February 1792. The marriage of Frederick, Duke of York to Princess Frederica of Prussia fed the fantasy that her self-sacrifice, virtue and love would help him overcome his addition to gambling.

13. Isaac Cruickshank, *Getting the Length of the Duchess's Foot*, 25 November 1791. The appearance of a new royal personage stimulated competition among the fashionable set. The public prints fixated on the new duchess's petite stature and tiny feet as if they were a sign of her superior virtue, in contrast to the excesses of ample aristocratic ladies. Her favouring flat shoes had cobblers working overtime so courtiers could follow the trend.

14. Isaac Cruickshank, *Voluntary Subscriptions*, 16 January 1798. Opponents of the war against France suspected that Pitt and Dundas trumped up the invasion scare to extort higher taxes for the places and pensions that maintained their grip on power. George III's failure to set an example by contributing immediately to Pitt's voluntary fund for the war effort raised questions about the indebtedness of the king, the nation and the people.

15. Isaac Cruickshank, *The Family Party or Prince Bladduds Man Traps*, 11 May 1799. George, Prince of Wales and Frederick, Duke of York became notorious at Bath for their gambling routs and roistering with the Gubbins sisters, who here seem to be taking advantage of royal lust to cheat at cards.

16. James Sayers, *Citizen Bardolph Refused Admittance at Prince Hal's*, 17 March 1794. Big Sam the doorman at Carlton House declares the house loyal and denies admission to Sheridan, who sports a French revolutionary cockade. Prince George temporarily abandoned the opposition in order to have his debts paid via his marriage settlement. The prince's treatment of his old comrade would damage his reputation after Sheridan died miserably impoverished in 1816.

decried his new opera box, which allowed occupants to sit incognito: 'Even in foreign Theatres, where luxury distains to pay respect to decorum, the [sic] *loges* grilles do not obtrude themselves in the centre of the Theatre. They shelter the devotees to pleasure in corners.' Papers of all complexions were less concerned with securing the Protestant succession than with securing the roistering, spendthrift prince of Wales in domestic serenity.

As I have detailed elsewhere, the ministerial press dogged Prince George with lightly veiled references to his suspected marriage to the Roman Catholic Maria Fitzherbert and indignant observations of his mistress Frances, Countess of Jersey's behaviour as Caroline's first lady of the bedchamber. Until the autumn following Princess Charlotte's birth, in January 1796, by which time the Waleses' separation had become impossible to ignore, the papers relentlessly reminded the prince of his marital duties and grasped at any sign of reconciliation. In retaliation, the *Morning Post* commenced a campaign of attack against Caroline for fomenting discord between the prince and his royal parents, as well as for besmirching his reputation with her weeping in public and other flummery. Concurrently, the press presented Frederick, Duke of York, the king's favourite, as a domestic paragon, although he and his consort, Frederica of Prussia, aside from keeping up appearances in public, barely saw one another in private and remained childless. In another paradoxical twist, William, Duke of Clarence, who set up house at Bushy Park with the actress Dorothea Jordan and who would remain with her for twenty years and raise ten Fitzclarences, endured continual ridicule in the 1790s. George III and his supporters attempted to build a model of domestic virtue suited to the middle and lower ranks where marital choice, cooperation, coordinated labour, fidelity and thrift were all vital to survival. Royalty, however, kept company with the upper echelons of society, where innumerable contingencies narrowed marital choices, propriety constrained courtship, husbands and wives had sufficient resources to live separate lives, and a heady mix of temptations, financial privilege and leisure encouraged extramarital unions and adultery, which sometimes brought legal action and public scandal.[48] If anything, the royal family demonstrated how difficult it was (although not impossible—plenty of aristocrats and gentry enjoyed harmonious, even loving marriages) to achieve perfect domestic happiness within the bounds of ruling-class decorum.

George III's family's visible tangle of fraught relations made the royal court a public forum for testing moral standards. Although his sons brought embarrassing details of private life into the public sphere, the interest these accounts stimulated could be beneficial to George III's image. The birth of

Princess Charlotte allowed him to shine warmly as a doting grandpapa in contrast to the reaction of his son, who, among other things, acted churlishly in response to the City of London's address of congratulations.[49] Gillray conveyed the entwined political and personal dimensions with a print featuring a hideously rendered Princess Caroline proffering the new babe face down in her christening gown like a sack of potatoes (fig. 10).[50] Poignantly, the infant reaches out to touch the hand of her father who stands in the doorway unsteadily, dishevelled and squiffy, legs akimbo, arms open in a gesture of 'Here I am', flanked by his lackey Michael Angelo Taylor bearing aloft a cradle emblazoned with the prince of Wales's insignia. Alongside Caroline, Charles James Fox and Richard Brinsley Sheridan, ever alert to the line of succession, bend over to kiss the new princess's buttocks. Evocative images of the Waleses' estrangement flooded the press—the servants in crimson liveries that Mrs Fitzherbert continued to parade in public, the letters between the princess of Wales and her mother allegedly intercepted by Lady Jersey, and the mystery of a jewel box found locked when 'a Great Personage' was dressing for the king's birthday at court.[51] At least two pamphlets reprinted selections of these newspaper stories, purportedly not to spread scandal but, as one claimed, to expose 'the thoughtless individuals, who, for amusement, sport with the refined feelings of Personages of the first rank'. The other, a shorter set of excerpts, wished to 'commiserate the situation of a female stranger consigned to the affections of an honourable people', to see British princesses treated well abroad and to voice concern for the credit of a possible future king. In its conclusion, the compiler presented the foregoing newspaper paragraphs as a plot to undermine the tranquillity of the royal family and lower it in public opinion, obviously the first steps towards subverting the constitution and peace of England. The pamphlet further pointed out that the royal family, like any other in private life, had internal disagreements, but that no other family had to endure rival newspapers making provocative accusations against its members to foment further distrust.[52]

The vividly rendered personalities in these stories encouraged readers to believe that they knew the disputants' characters and to pass judgement on them. As the press reported (having first undoubtedly helped to instigate such a reaction), ordinary people participated in the domestic fracas by shouting and hissing at Lady Jersey when she appeared in public, as well as by gathering outside the palace nursery window to cheer the princess of Wales when in view, babe in arms. Theatre audiences also became involved by showing their support or disapprobation when the characters in the real-life drama came in to take their seats. Lord and Lady Jersey published correspondence they thought would clear some of the allegations, only to have their pamphlet redacted in the *Oracle* in such a way as to produce the opposite effect. Earlier, the *Telegraph* had observed in disgust how the saga served as a distraction from real problems: 'According to this journalist, the people of England, after having kept up their spirits, through all the calamities of the present most ruinous and unfortunate war, all on a sudden are plunged into misery by a family dispute at Carlton-house!' The paper wondered whether this indicated a level of slavishness comparable to France at the height of absolute monarchy.[53] More to the point for one of a republican bent, or merely a proponent of constitutional reform, this politicization of a personal dispute within the royal family might seem a slide back to Stuart subjugation.

The return to a personalization of politics only came about after the real threat of civil war and Catholic conquest abated. Whereas relations were more profoundly fractured in George II's family, few details made it into the newspapers, so the intestinal battles never became the foundation for popular demonstrations or a larger cause. The spectre of potentially trea-sonable Jacobitism acted as a deterrent to popular movements forming around disgruntled royal personages. The dynastic struggle actually taking place went unreported in the press. Regarding the princess of Orange's return to England, Horace Walpole claimed that she 'invented a thousand excuses for loitering here, & for some time pretended she was breeding, when she was not' because she thought that the queen, having fallen ill, might die '& hoped to stay & govern the King. The Q. was too sagacious not to understand this, & never forgave her Daughter.' Lady Suffolk, one of the king's earlier mistresses, told Walpole that after the coronation, when the queen complained of fatigue, the princess exclaimed: 'Fatigue to be crowned! I would die tomorrow, to be crowned today.' Walpole noted that, when the queen did die, the princess would have returned had not his uncle Horace received an order to prevent her from doing so, which contributed to the great aversion she developed to her father at the end of her life. Hervey backed up the last story, explaining that the king had little patience for anyone who had caused him as much trouble as she had during her stay. Like Walpole, he discerned extreme pride and ambition in the princess royal, and to underline his point trotted out examples of her speaking imprudently about the king's faults, particularly his temper, when she bore the brunt of it less than did others. Having Anne's betrothal arranged before that of Prince Frederick, Hervey averred, exacerbated the quarrels between them.[54]

Greater dramas ensued that did not become topics of public interest in the same way that similar happenings would in the 1790s. The incident that definitively severed Frederick from the rest of the royal family was his defiance of the king's command that Princess Augusta have her lying-in at Hampton Court. So determined was he that the birth of his first child would take place away from his royal parents, upon finding Augusta in labour shortly after dining publicly with them at Hampton Court, Frederick spirited her away to St James's in spite of her distress; her waters broke as attendants helped her to the carriage. Newspaper readers would find no clue of anything untoward in the decision to subject the princess to the arduous coach ride or have any inkling of the queen's fury at being informed of the labour too late to witness the birth. If not privy to court gossip, one could learn more about the dispute from pamphlets issued from both sides that selectively translated and printed the letters that flew back and forth between the two households in the aftermath of the episode. Hervey included copies in his memoirs, in addition to a parody of the prince's enquiries after the queen's health that Hervey had penned for her amusement. Hervey refused to give the queen a copy with the disingenuous claim that he would burn the original later.[55] Sir Robert Walpole considered an official separation of the courts advantageous as it removed any ambiguity with respect to the prince's opposition to the king. The lord chancellor, Philip Yorke, Earl of Hardwicke, however, thought the arrangement appalling, particularly for the further damage it could do to familial relations, and wondered how it could be explained to foreign courts. He described an emotional interview with Frederick, during which Hardwicke vowed to do all he could to bring about a reconciliation, and ending with the prince embracing him and kissing his cheek in appreciation, leaving the lord chancellor on the verge of tears. In the case he made to Walpole, Hardwicke reasoned that the king would have to take the drastic measure of assuming custody of the prince's children to put a stop to the alleged pernicious influences of the prince's friends. To the queen he pointed out that if the king died, she, the duke of Cumberland and the four unmarried princesses would be at the new sovereign's mercy. Hardwicke had the mortification of watching Walpole twist his arguments to support the position opposite to the one he had advocated. On 12 September 1737, the prince and his family vacated St James's Palace and moved to Kew. Notice was given that anyone who paid them court would be forbidden the king and queen's presence.[56] Again, one can imagine the feeding frenzy this would have occasioned in the press had it occurred later in the century.

Sex and the Single (or Married) Politician

Hervey's memoirs are a testament to the dangers of mixing sexual or deep emotional bonds with politics, not just in the extravagant character assassination of Frederick that their falling-out inspired, but also in the representation of the jealousies provoked by Hervey's close affiliation with the queen. As seen above in Chapter 2, Frederick's sharing of a mistress with Hervey left him vulnerable to the courtier's spiteful machinations. That the prince claimed paternity of Ann Vane's child, christened Cornwall Fitzfrederick, despite the fact that Vane had been involved with Lord Harrington as well as Hervey, allowed Hervey to nurture Queen Caroline's suspicion of a design to hide the prince's inability to father children.[57] A print illustrating Frederick's union with Augusta focused on the party-political rather than the dynastic questions the prince's liaisons raised. It has Sir Robert Walpole, seated in a chair next to an empty throne, regarding the happy couple with head in hand in an attitude of exasperation. Vane sits distraught in the back of the room, a little manikin Fitzfrederick standing at her knee (fig. 11).[58] Everybody knew that anything the prince did to improve his status fortified the opposition to Walpole. The references to Walpole as the 'Pimp' in the verses beneath accuse him of going so far as to put Vane in the prince's path to trip him up.

Hervey thought that Walpole even felt threatened by the courtier's increasing confidence with the queen. During the letter war with the prince, the queen fell ill and Hervey boasted that 'on this occasion she first broke through the etiquette of the Court, by seeing Lord Hervey in her bed. But as she was confined to it for several days, she said it was too much to be in pain and ennuyer herself for want of company besides; and as she was too old to have the honour of being talked of for it, she would let Lord Hervey come in, and accordingly had him in her bedchamber almost the whole day, during the time of her confinement.' Whether it was the queen's indiscretion (as he asserted), or Hervey's bragging, their growing intimacy raised misgivings in Walpole, whom Hervey took the opportunity to acknowledge as his benefactor, protector, master and teacher. Reflecting the centrality of personal feelings in this political altercation, of all the lies that the prince allegedly spread about him, Hervey mentioned two: that he had had an intrigue with the princess royal, and that, from the time they had met, Hervey had endeavoured to poison the prince's mind against his family.[59] A recent analysis of the relationship between Hervey and Frederick argues convincingly that Vane was not the divisive issue between them. The prince made the decision to end their intimacy because of Hervey's alliance with Walpole, his closeness to the royal family and the suspicions about the nature of his relations with men that the public altercation with William Pulteney raised. Frederick wished to build an independent identity as a supporter of opposition principles and as a dynastic progenitor.[60] The crowd was not involved in his pre-marital scandals or post-marital alterca- tions with the king and queen, as it would be in the 1790s with Prince George's affairs. Gossip about Frederick appeared in scurrilous verse, highly allegorical *romans-à-clef* and, most extraordinarily, in a ballad opera, all of which gave Vane the starring role. Newspapers, meanwhile, contained nothing more suggestive than the report that, on the prince's birthday in 1735, Vane had a splendid entertainment for upwards of twenty 'Ladies of Quality' at Grosvenor Street, which included a fine concert and elegant supper.[61] Hardwicke's dire scenarios did not materialize. The queen died on 20 November 1737, two months after the separation of courts, and Frederick suffered his untimely demise on 20 March 1751.

Newspapers during George III's reign could dramatize the royal fam- ily's divisions now that the dynasty was on a firmer footing. Because the king and queen based their moral authority on domestic probity, writers also felt themselves justified in publicizing any lapses. Most significantly, politicians began to receive the same degree of scrutiny. Their marriages and extramarital liaisons had varying political consequences, which muddled the morals that the press drew from each union. Paradoxically, sharing mistresses appeared easier in a more forbidding moral climate— such behaviour could be glorified as an act of solidarity against oppression. Scorning both the fashion for domestic virtue and the heightened level of surveillance in the newspapers after mid-century, George, Prince of Wales, Fox, George James Cholmondeley, 4th Earl (later Marquis) of Cholmondeley (after serving as the prince's chamberlain) and various ancillaries performed odd sexual quadrilles with the actress Mary ('Perdita') Robinson, the courtesan Elizabeth Armistead (née Cane), the notorious divorcée Grace Dalrymple Elliott ('Dally the Tall'), and miscellaneous demireps and stray married women during the 1770s and 1780s.[62] The prince fell for Perdita the first time he saw her perform on stage at the end of 1779. By early 1781, his attention had shifted to Mrs Armistead, who quickly grew impatient among the crowd of his other inamoratas and went to France, whence Mrs Elliott happened to be returning. On the rebound from Cholmondeley (known variously in the scandal sheets as 'the Athletic Peer', 'Lord Tallboy' and 'the Whimsical Lover'), Elliott had pursued a liaison with the duc de Chartres (later duc d'Orléans and self-styled Philippe-Égalité of the French Revolution), a friend of the prince of Wales. Gossips chattered that the affair between the prince and Dally lasted barely an hour. Although she had renewed her involvement with Cholmondeley at this time, the prince acknowledged as his the daughter she delivered on 30 March 1782, probably with Cholmondeley's complicity.

Unlike Frederick, who appeared to claim an illegitimate child to support his masculinity, George did so to support a friendship. Georgiana Augusta Frederica Elliott would receive the prince's financial support but be raised by Cholmondeley and, from 1791, also by his wife, the former Georgiana Charlotte Bertie, daughter of the third duke of Ancaster and Kesteven, along with his daughter by a mysterious 'Madam St Albans', together with their legitimate children. Cholmondeley also had his turns with Armistead and Perdita. The latter fought off the advances of Chartres while in France, but welcomed the attentions of Fox back in London. The on-again, off-again romance of Cholmondeley and Elliott attracted much attention in the press because of the pair's striking good looks, extravagance in entertainments and dress, and rumoured sexual voracity. The Whimsical Lover had achieved fame for the magnificence of his manly parts, commemorated in *The Torpedo: A Poem to the Electric Eel* (1777), which with mock flattery represented him as the worst sort of libertine. As detailed in the previous chapter, Cholmondeley attracted the ire of William Windham for trifling with a young innocent, and of Sir Gilbert Elliot for ostentatious display of marital affection. In spite of all the bad press, this trading of women between the prince and the Foxites evidently built bonds rather than competition and tension among these three men and most of the hangers-on who participated in the serial couplings. Cholmondeley's reputation obviously did not harm his marriage prospects and his landing of Miss Bertie so impressed his uncle, Horace Walpole, that he made him heir to Houghton. Fox settled down too, albeit less respectably because his status and fortune enabled him to do so. He became attached to Mrs Armistead in the mid-1780s and secretly married her in 1795. The prince, however, remained a loose cannon. Further demonstrating the strength of personal connections in politics, after Fox died in 1806, Prince George's drift towards his father's conservative politics accelerated, having originated in his alarm over the violence in revolutionary France.[63]

The newspapers' fixation on Cholmondeley's ascent (or descent) into uxoriousness best illustrates the moral contradictions that the mixing of personal and political lives generated and the coexistence of old and new attitudes towards conjugality. The *Public Advertiser* of 12 April 1791 announced sardonically: 'The Subscription Concert was not given last Saturday night, on account of the alterations making in Cholmondeley House for the marriage of the Noble Earl, and the fashionable world were reduced to sheer gaming to pass off the dullness of the night.' The papers found whimsical the concurrent betrothal of Lord Cardigan and made mordant intimations regarding the desirability of the brides or perhaps the married state in general for the fashionable set. In the words of *The Times* on the 20th: 'The conversation of the polite circles runs, at this moment upon nothing but the wedding cloathes prepared for the future Lady CHOLMONDELEY.—They comprehend a profusion of dresses in all the expence of taste and elegance:—But the prevailing fashions of veils is rather unexpectedly applied—for one of them is actually attached to the wedding night-cap. To what use the veil of a night-cap can be applied, Lord CHOLMONDELEY will, hereafter we doubt not, inform his friends.—As of Lord CARDIGAN he talks of nothing less than iron-masks.' After the ceremonies, the *World* proclaimed on the 25th: 'This day Lord CHOLMONDELEY and Lord Cardigan start for the *Flitch of Bacon*'—a reference to the prize customarily given to rustic couples as a reward for a year of marital fidelity, so depicted in the eponymous play. The *Gazetteer and New Daily Advertiser* noted both marriages, and in another column observed: 'Lord CHOLMONDELEY, when he was lately at Bath, was frequently *en famille* with his mother. The old Lady admonished him to be prudent in his use of the *good things* of this world, upon the maxim that "a little at a time lasts the longer!"' The transformation from rakishness to respectability attracted much raillery. On 10 May, the *Morning Herald* punned: 'Lord CHOLMONDELEY having now a more *bewitching stake* to play for, than *punting at Faro*, is no longer an active partner in the *Bank* in St. James's-street; he shares, however, in the *comforts* of both games—as a *sleeping partner*.' The Athletic Peer also had renown as one of the founders of the faro bank (maintaining the gambling house's pot) at Brooks's.

Newspapers performed virtually the old customs of bedding the bride and invading the bridal chamber the morning after. They continued to dog the newlyweds after the pair decamped to the Continent. According to the *Morning Post and Daily Advertiser* of 29 April: 'Lady CHOLMONDELEY has had enquiries innumerable after her health since a recent event—Her Answer has been rather *oracular*;—she says—"*Great* Bodies move *slowly*!"' This paper and others reported on 6 May that the couple would remain a full year in France. The *World* made the scurrilous observation: 'Lord and

Lady CHOLMONDELEY are at present at the *Hague*, from whence they are shortly to proceed to *Spa* by way of *Brussels*. There is no doubt but the report of Lady CHOLMONDELEY's increasing situation may be a physical certainty; we hope, however, it is not yet demonstratively oracular.' Hinting at a pre-marital conception placed the new Lady Cholmondeley on a par with the demireps with whom her husband used to run. These papers continued to keep tabs on their whereabouts. Finally, the *General Evening Post* and other papers announced that, on 17 January (a full nine months after the wedding), Lady Cholmondeley was delivered of a son, Lord Malpas. On 13 February, the *Gazetteer and New Daily Advertiser* observed: 'Lady CHOLMONDELEY, since her *accouchement*, has drove a good deal through the streets of Paris, and her equipage, not much noticed in London, excited considerable admiration there.' The Whimsical Lover embraced married respectability. His countess became one of the princess of Wales's ladies-in-waiting, so the couple had the unenviable task of running angry messages back and forth between the warring Waleses, with the prince and princess entrenched in their separate apartments at Carlton House.[64] Perhaps the ridiculous spectacle of the prince's aversion to his consort inspired Cholmondeley to maintain his new-found domestic virtue.

While some inter-party intrigues in the prince's set appeared to foster camaraderie among members of the group, others created friction. One cross-party liaison in particular spawned conflict. While on the Grand Tour in 1794, Granville Leveson Gower, a younger son of the marquis and marchioness of Stafford, fervent Pittites, met Henrietta Ponsonby, Viscountess Duncannon, later Countess of Bessborough, who, with her sister Georgiana Cavendish, Duchess of Devonshire, had campaigned for Fox against Pitt in the infamous 1784 election. The diary of Lady Elizabeth Webster, who would meet Henry Richard Vassall Fox 3rd Baron Holland at this time, and after a messy divorce marry him, documents the hotbed of competitive flirtation the southern clime inspired in the Whig peers and gentry and those drawn into their orbit. Lady Webster had a brief attraction to Lord Granville before settling on Holland as her ticket out of a bad marriage, and Granville competed with Charles George Beauclerk for the attentions of Bessborough. The countess, however, did not yield to Granville completely until 1799. A decade earlier, her husband had almost sought a divorce after catching her in a compromising situation with Sheridan. By the turn of the century, the Bessboroughs had three grown sons and a daughter, and no longer shared a bed, which, along with paying off her debts, freed Henrietta. Bessborough and Granville had a daughter and son on the wrong side of the blanket in 1800 and 1802, respectively. Granville raised them as his wards with the legitimate offspring he had with Bessborough's niece, Lady Harriet Cavendish, after their marriage in 1809.[65] The liaison sparked considerable hostility in the prince of Wales and several Foxites towards Granville. The reason, perhaps, had less to do with party than with Bessborough rebuffing the prince and playing a double game with the others. Along the same lines, James Adair later told Sheridan's biographer Thomas Moore that the prince's dislike of Charles, Lord Grey came primarily from blaming Grey's affair with the duchess of Devonshire for his own lack of success with her.[66]

In her letters to Granville, a close friend of the Pittite George Canning, Bessborough represented herself fending off a number of Foxites, some of whom poured particular scorn upon Granville. She described to her lover how Sheridan confronted her in her opera box in March 1802, telling her that if she had any pride left she should fly from Granville, whom he characterized as 'all falsehood and treachery'. The following August, after eluding Sheridan by taking refuge in her room and then scurrying out to her awaiting carriage, she reflected on the ferocity of his and Sir John Townshend's attentions. She had complained of Townshend's persecution back in August 1799, and at the end of 1800 she reported to Granville 'a violent attack on you, chiefly, I think, for being handsome'. Although Granville married Bessborough's niece with her contrivance, others were quick to assume his betrayal. Bessborough received a visit from the prince of Wales immediately after the wedding announcement during which he launched a lengthy tirade against Granville's inconstancies, made an attempt upon her person, and resorted to tears and entreaties when she resisted him. The prince's offer (in addition to dropping his two current mistresses) to make Canning prime minister in exchange for her cooperation indicates why the fact of a Foxite peeress consorting with a young Canningite might have a deleterious effect beyond exciting personal jealousy. The offer had Bessborough flummoxed, as she and Canning distrusted and disliked one another and had only reached a détente for the sake of Granville. She observed of the prince's elliptical speeches: 'always Mr. Canning à tout bout de change, and whenever he mention'd him it was in the tenderest accent and attempting some liberty, that really, G., had not my heart been breaking I might have laugh'd out at the comicality of having the Pope [her nickname for Canning] so coupled and so made use of—and then that immense, grotesque figure flouncing about half on the couch, half on the ground.' The prince spectacularly wore out what at the onset had already been a reluctant welcome. He and Bessborough hammered out some terms of friendship over the course of two hours, and for two hours more he further fatigued her with stories about her former lover and Princess Galitzen dating from Granville's diplomatic mission to St Petersburg in 1807. Bessborough's account of the encounter's termination must be quoted for its bizarre reversal: 'The Prince ended by saying he was afraid he had not spoken properly to you. I said certainly not, and that he owed you some excuse. He said he would make it up the next time you met, or perhaps write.' Sheridan, as would be expected, followed hot on the prince's heels with questions about the new relations between Bessborough, her niece and Granville. Bessborough easily distracted him by shifting discussion to the splintered Whig party and the rising prospects of Canning.[67]

The rise and fall of Sheridan's fortunes epitomize how a politician's management of his personal affairs affected his public reputation and prospects. Little did he and Bessborough know that the second Mrs Sheridan, the former Hester Ogle, dubbed Hecca, had taken Granville into her confidence in 1807. Sheridan's financial fecklessness, excessive drinking and renewed pursuit of Bessborough, whom Hecca assumed mocked and lied to her, all conspired to place her in the consoling arms of Lord Grey, which ended badly. Lord Holland later quipped to Moore that Grey hated Sheridan for the odd reason that he had intrigued with Hecca.[68] The disorder of the Sheridan marriage reversed the usual trajectories of betrayal, jealousy and resentment. Hecca would probably have been surprised to hear that Bessborough had rebuked Grey so severely for his treatment of her that he threw himself at her feet and sobbed. Meanwhile, two years earlier, Sheridan had gone off the deep end with jealousy of Bessborough's liaison with Granville and sent obscene anonymous letters to her and female members of her family, which for some time alienated him from Devonshire House and the Foxites.[69] That Sheridan's inability to control his wife or his passions, in addition to his finances and his drinking, contributed to his ruin has a certain poignancy considering how the circumstances of his first marriage to Elizabeth Linley, a singer of great beauty and renown, had gained him an entrée into the circles of the beau monde and helped launch his political career. One of his recent biographers argues that, by fighting two duels to defend Linley's honour, eloping with her to France and, once officially married in England in 1773, taking her off the stage, Sheridan attained the status of a gentleman. He reinforced his social standing by pursuing extramarital affairs with the grandes dames of the Whig party, first Frances Crewe and then Bessborough, which his wife accepted, knowing how these liaisons benefited them. In turn, he tolerated her affair with Sir Edward Fitzgerald in a gentlemanly fashion, although it ended tragically with the pregnancy that hastened her demise. John Watkins, albeit a rabidly hostile biographer, reminds us of Sheridan's audacity. He quotes Samuel Johnson's remark to James Boswell that a gentleman would 'be disgraced by having his wife sing publicly for hire', for the purpose of disagreeing with it: 'The interdiction was totally unexpected by her friends, who considered it as an act of severity and insult on the part of a man who could neither boast of pedigree, nor property.' Watkins cites a satire published during the party struggles of 1784 that echoes these sentiments and represents Sheridan as a political adventurer.[70] Sheridan would never have achieved the success he did without his immense talent as a playwright, orator and wit. Nonetheless, his marriages and extramarital affairs crucially shaped his reputation and connections, and thus his political influence.

Mistresses and marriages had variable effects on the relations among politicians. The perilous process of conceiving a passion or an interest in a woman who might be a suitable match, initiating courtship and undertaking matrimony could produce a human drama that fostered bonding among politicians—and might include royalty. Robert Banks Jenkinson, the future prime minister and 2nd earl of Liverpool, fell 'most devoutely in love', as Canning put it, with Lady Louisa Hervey in the winter of 1793. The following spring, he made Canning his sole confidant and gave 'regular intelligence of his progress' from April until Canning left town for summer, 'for Jenkinson never writes when he can possibly help it'. Upon returning to town in November, Canning learned that the pair had decided that Lady Louisa should first broach the match with her father, the infamously capricious 4th earl of Bristol and bishop of Derry, who thereupon surprised them with the warmth of his approval. They had not, however, anticipated that Jenkinson's father, Lord Hawkesbury, would take umbrage at his son having kept him uninformed for so long, particularly since he had suffered the indignity of having heard rumours of the attachment and had dismissed them. By this time, others had been let into the secret. Canning told his aunt and uncle that he had learned the particulars from Lady Malmesbury while dining tête-à-tête. Hawkesbury further objected to the lack of fortune and the 'connection', although Lady Louisa herself had the 'highest character'. Lord Bristol offered a £10,000 dowry to no avail. Hawkesbury also professed a long-held and ardent wish that his son would not marry until the age of thirty. Jenkinson's woe eventually spilled out of the confines of his immediate circle of family and friends to expand into a humanitarian cause among the highest echelons of government, particularly Henry Dundas and his wife, Jane, as the latter was an intimate of Lady Louisa. After Canning had dispatched Sir Ralph Payne to talk some sense into Hawkesbury without success, Dundas summoned Canning to dine and stay the night at Wimbledon in late December. During their postprandial conversation, Dundas informed him that he had 'talked much upon the subject' with Pitt and they were both in warm favour of the match, but 'that there was little hope of Ld. H. being softened by entreaty and submission, but that if Jenkinson hoped to gain the point, it must be by vigour and determination'. Canning agreed.[71] The personal interest that Pitt and Dundas took in the matter is striking, given the stressful political contention of the moment. Several of Canning's friends were wavering in their support of Pitt's prosecution of the war and Canning acted as whipper-in because 'it would be a heartbreaking thing to have our young set split, the very first parliamentary campaign that we meet'.[72]

The camaraderie that developed while relieving an associate of his bachelorhood proved short-lived in this case. Poor Jenkinson's dilemma showed his vulnerability but only temporarily smoothed over the irritating intellectually self-confident manner that Hawkesbury's grooming and connections had imparted. Granville, one of Canning's vacillators, had observed to his mother, Lady Stafford, at the end of 1791: 'there were some traits in his character I heard from different people (Strathaven among others) which inclined me not to look so favourably with regard to him as before, and his excessive importance (unless one is prejudiced in his favour) becomes very disgusting'.[73] The friendship between Canning and Jenkinson had an edge to it, forged as it was in the competitive atmosphere of the Christ Church debating club.[74] Canning's support of the marriage helped heal the rift that had formed between them after a practical joke had misfired: a send-up of Jenkinson's enthusiasm for raising recruits in his new role as colonial in the militia that in effect ridiculed his tendency towards self-importance. The well-attended caper reduced Jenkinson to tears—he was inconsolable for two hours in spite of Lady Malmesbury's ministrations. For his part, when Canning learned of the pain he had caused, he too bawled like a child, earning a rebuke from his informant not to make himself a fool as well.[75]

The 'vigour and determination' that Pitt and Dundas had prescribed to bring about the match only temporarily remedied the bruised egos suffered

all round. With their blessings, Jenkinson resolved to inform his father
that his 'health and spirits' would not allow further attendance in parliament. Although this got Hawkesbury's attention, he remained adamant.
Canning, the Dundases, Pitt and others, after further deliberation, determined that Jenkinson should proceed with the marriage without his
father's consent, a step he dreaded. Various members of the Hervey clan
and others weighed in as well. By late January 1795, a call to the House to
vote on Grey's motion for peace had Jenkinson hamstrung between his
political and personal duties. Hawkesbury continued implacable, and by
early February, with much help from his friends, Jenkinson began planning an elopement. On the 21st, Canning learned of a *deus ex machina*:
George III had stepped in to have a quiet word with Hawkesbury.
Although the wedding of 25 March represented a triumph, Jenkinson's
nerves made him unbearable company. After all the time and emotion
invested, Canning's first dinner with the newlyweds in April left him
apprehensive that marriage had changed his old associate, an impression
reinforced when he dined with them again a month later. He was disappointed in his expectation that Jenkinson's house would become the centre
of sociability for the old Christ Church crowd, now 'the pleasantest set of
young men in London'. Canning did not blame the new Mrs Jenkinson;
rather, he sensed it was her desire that they entertain more extensively, but
her husband 'is so little comfortable with all his old friends'. He could only
conclude: 'marriage does give men odd turns, to be sure'.[76]

Canning's own marriage in July 1800 would indeed give a few odd turns.
In a letter written to Granville on 22 August 1799 to answer his 'enquiry as
to the state in which the business now stands', Canning revealed the
number of people involved in the process of his falling for Miss Joan Scott,
daughter of General and Lady Mary Scott of Bacomie, and navigating the
path to matrimony. The epistle went into elaborate detail to give the necessary background, he explained, to the letter from Granville's sister, Lady
Susan Ryder, who had been acting as go-between, that Canning was
forwarding for Granville to interpret. Canning assured Granville that
sharing Lady Susan's letter did not constitute a breach of confidence, but
'for obvious reasons' Granville should not mention to his sister that he had
read it. One wonders whether the forwarded letter also served as an oblique
explanation of the pragmatic rationale for not bringing Granville into
his confidence sooner. Canning had written to his friend early on during
his stay at Walmer with the Dundases and their other guests, before he
was cognizant of any emotional sentiments to another party except some

ineffable feelings: 'vanity perhaps, and romance, and a certain lively and tender and grateful interest (but not love)'. Canning described the gradual process by which he became conscious of this particular guest. When he learned her name from Lady Susan, he connected it with a string of rejected suitors and thus determined to remain aloof so that his reputation should not suffer by rumour of a similar link. Dundas, perhaps sensing love in the air, contrived to have them both remain beyond their scheduled departure day, when the other guests took their leave. Canning, however, intimidated by Miss Scott's £100,000 fortune, bolted the following day, congratulating himself heartily until he saw Lady Susan that evening and unwittingly confessed his feelings. The role of Granville's sister as intermediary became critical to the business. Canning next went to Holwood for advice from Pitt, who 'answered with a suddenness and appearance of certainty which surprised' him that he had observed Miss Scott's attention and his protégé's avoidance 'and a great deal more such observation as you perhaps would not expect him to have made'. Considering the rumours that flew about his own relationship with Pitt, this qualification seems disingenuous. Canning finally came to ask Granville for advice on a particular passage in Lady Susan's report in which Miss Scott revealed that Canning was not as she expected. Pitt thought that her prejudice stemmed from their running joke with Lady Jane Dundas that involved Canning 'quizzing' her husband to force him into a witty conversational style with which he was not comfortable. Although this seemed logical, Canning feared she had heard Charles Greville's gossip castigating him as satirical, ill-natured and insolent, of which Granville had apprized him on a prior occasion. Canning sought Granville's advice as he reviewed the qualities Miss Scott was said to desire in a husband, the possibility that her fortune might place him in the untenable position of being 'the creature of my wife's', and his prospects for advancement in government. He reported that the Dundases now stayed at Holwood and asked Granville how he could proceed with delicacy, as Dundas was her guardian. Canning reiterated his instruction not to let Lady Susan know that he had consulted Granville, and begged for an answer by return of post. The letter concluded with a lamentation of Canning's potentially ruinous entanglement elsewhere, which had gone further than he had previously admitted. The success of his 'present views', he believed, 'will be the most effectual remedy to all the danger'.[77]

The episode brings to the fore the intimacies that complicated and added a frisson to political relationships. Pitt's nervous behaviour at Canning's wedding generated comment at the time and an awkward explanation by his biographer. The inability to characterize Pitt's sexuality presents a perfect example of how inadequate our modern sexual taxonomies are for describing eighteenth-century intimacies, a point I have argued in more detail elsewhere.[78] Whether or not their relationship was physical, beyond the affectionate touching that observers noted and Canning acknowledged, is of no consequence. More important is the emotional tug between the two men and how it affected others, as evinced by Canning's need to reassure Granville on 30 August: 'Pitt is almost all that you could be to me, with the addition of as much of a father as a person so little above one's own age can feel or shew.' This letter reveals that Canning had eschewed Lady Susan's advice and returned to Walmer in the absence of the Dundases and Pitt, but with Lady Susan's husband, Sir Dudley Ryder, drawn in as an actor in this theatre of courtship. He had also ascertained that it was indeed Greville's gossip that was at the root of the ill impression. Tellingly, Canning reflected: 'It is done away with, I think, and I even doubt whether its previous existence has done mischief. No reason, however, for not revenging.' Did any clear line exist between the personal and the political? On 10 September, Canning was writing to Granville about an unexpected roadblock: a letter from the foreign secretary, Lord Grenville, requesting his service abroad, which Pitt thought he should not decline. Canning professed himself unequal to the task and begged his friend to accompany him unofficially on the mission to enhance its efficacy and speed. He wrote that the hope of Granville's companionship had transformed the plan from a burdensome distraction to an opportunity for Canning to level 'the extreme inequality which subsists between me and Miss S. in point of worldly consideration and importance'. Canning repeatedly pleaded for Granville's understanding of his feelings, considering his 'habit of opening my whole heart to you'. He closed: 'Write to me immediately, and return Ld G.'s letter.'[79]

Personal intimacies had political ramifications. Canning's level of trust in Granville is striking in light of the latter's liaison with Bessborough. Granville apparently only half kept Canning's confidence, judging by Bessborough's enquiries in November after hearing gossip from Lady Holland that gave her a turn: 'she had almost persuaded me that Mr. Canning's married *love* was Ly. Malmesbury[.] Was it? She knows the violent secret of Miss Scott; she would not tell me how; but it would be too ridiculous if, after all your injunctions to me, you had told her!'[80] Canning in fact had been courting even greater scandal. He and other Tory ministers had been making merry at Blackheath with Princess Caroline in order to secure influence over Princess Charlotte should she suddenly become regent or queen. Just as roistering with the prince in the 1780s and 1790s had compromised the Whigs, the Tories lost some of their dignity by their association with the princess. Elliot, now Earl Minto, left accounts of the jolly japes Caroline would initiate after dinner, which would last into the wee hours during the summer of 1799. Even Pitt and Dundas participated in these games, which included the former being inveigled to kiss a bust of the queen of Prussia and the latter to descend to one knee and kiss the hand of Miss Emma Crewe. Elliot found Dundas's behaviour the most puzzling: 'he squeezed the Princess's hand in the tenderest manner possible, called her angel repeatedly, and said he hoped no one but himself would know how much he loved her. What can the old thing mean?'[81]

Caroline's attempts to reach out for personal comfort had uncomfortable but short-lived political consequences. She acted with the greatest impropriety with her guests, often picking out favourites and manoeuvring them into a private room or a long ramble in the garden to flirt and make confidences, for the most part innocently—except in the case of Canning. Caroline's biographer speculates that the two probably refrained from sexual intercourse after Lord Malmesbury's reiterations to Caroline that such activity constituted high treason, but that some physical intimacy took place. While Caroline gracefully stepped aside for Canning's marriage, their continued friendship would place him in an awkward situation when her estranged husband inherited the throne. At the beginning of the so-called Delicate Investigation of 1806–07, Canning's name had appeared among a list of men alleged to have had adulterous relations with her. Hence, when confronted by Caroline's champions while trying to divorce her in 1820, George IV directed his particular wrath upon Canning.[82] This could also have been additional fallout from George's frustrated attempts to make Bessborough bend to his will: her resistance a product of her attachment to Granville, Canning's friend. Appositionally, Canning won his way into the new king's confidence in 1822 by creating a new position—under-secretary of state—for Lord Henry, the husband of George's latest mistress, as well as discreetly finding a new foreign post for Lady Conyngham's former lover after he returned from abroad and dangerous sparks flew between them.[83]

It also seems fitting that after all the disruption and disappointment that Jenkinson's marriage had caused earlier, he should be head of government as Lord Liverpool when Canning's romantic folly became an issue. Moreover, Canning's concern about becoming the creature of his wife had been well placed, if only in respect to appearances. Moore attended a dinner party the couple hosted in 1821 and had the reports he had heard of Mrs Canning's temper confirmed when a dispute arose and her husband quickly backed down. Later that year, while dining with Lord and Lady Holland, Moore learned that Mrs Canning's 'impatience' with her husband's 'frequent infidelities' had produced an irreconcilable rift between them.[84] Canning's modern biographers, however, cite correspondence between the couple that demonstrates not only enduring mutual devotion, but also that Canning sought his wife's advice and that she took a keen interest in his career. Assessing the negative remarks other women made about the Cannings, P.J.V. Rolo concludes that this domestic devotion made him behave obtusely when women wanted his attention, which produced spiteful reactions. Other biographers observe how political spouses such as Lady Holland resented Canning for the way he had advanced via his political friendships. In her study of women's participation in politics, Judith S. Lewis points to passages from Canning's letter-journal disparaging women and to Lady Bessborough's perception of his scorning her opinions as evidence of his misogyny.[85] Bearing in mind the number of times we have seen Canning offending men in this and the previous chapter, his words and behaviour seem more indicative of general arrogance and self-absorption. That the same man who criticized his friend Jenkinson for not wishing his marital home to be a party venue for his bachelor friends would become so wrapped up in an exclusive domesticity is yet another rich irony to contemplate in considering the impact of domesticity in politics.

Models of familial virtue had a chequered history over the course of the eighteenth century. Although George II and George III endorsed very different codes of domestic decorum, their behaviours had similarly deleterious effects. After the deaths of Frederick Lewis and his sister Anne's consort, William IV of Orange, in 1751, and their youngest sister, twenty-seven-year-old Louisa, Queen of Denmark at the end of 1752, George II whined to Horace Walpole that, although he found his children annoying when young, he had eventually grown to love them like any father, but, alas, too late. The king's regret probably resulted from the fact that his uncharacteristically affectionate condolence letters offering assistance to Anne (who, now she was at the helm of the Dutch government, could be useful as a daughter) failed to elicit the desired response.[86] George III's excessive yet conditional love for his children and his obsession with preserving their morals manifested in a harsh, controlling possessiveness, which they resented and resisted when they could. Perhaps reflecting the changing fashion in child-rearing from teaching self-discipline to building self-esteem, the most recent biographies of George IV have abandoned the traditional view of him as a selfish wastrel by focusing on his good qualities and contributions to culture, society and, controversially in E.A. Smith's work, the monarchy as an institution. They attribute George IV's vices to the bad parenting of George III and Queen Charlotte.[87] Notwithstanding evidence to the contrary, the contemporary press projected the image of a happy family occasionally disrupted by errant sons falling into bad company.

Domesticity and anti-domesticity operated in multifarious ways in high political circles. Lewis's work, as well as that of Elaine Chalus, amply demonstrate how friendship and female sociability kept channels of communication open and allowed discreet negotiation across party lines. Chalus notes how women disguised their participation in politics by presenting it as part of their familial role: advancing the careers of their husbands or looking out for the family interest. Yet, as Lewis details, by the early nineteenth century these activities had become associated with 'old corruption' and had to be conducted with more discretion.[88]

Regardless of its lacking a basis in the actual experience of the majority of the ruling elite's most prominent figures, the domestic idyll did have a discursive impact. In political propaganda, concern shifted from sodomitical corruption to female chastity. This was not due to a domestic revolution, however, but rather to the seemingly opposite yet intimately related increase in heterosociability and close male bonding in party politics. Rhetoric changed but particular types of behaviour remained constant. In spite of growing condemnation of extramarital liaisons and sharper scrutiny by newspapers, politicians' shared intrigues could forge lifelong allegiances, particularly when one man took care of another's cast-off mistress or raised his illegitimate child. At the same time, rivalry for women could spark jealousies that had political repercussions, but so could a politician's isolation in marital fidelity and domesticity. A man's clubbability and his willingness to accommodate the disruptive desires of his friends remained essential to political success. Pitt the Younger compensated for his renowned lack of interest in romantic or sexual intrigues for himself by hosting convivial dinners and taking an interest, and even assisting, in the courtships and betrothals of others. Fox, although publicly castigated for his fast lifestyle, inspired unimaginable loyalty in the men with whom he gambled and whored.

Lady Bessborough deserves the last word on the subject. In 1798, she became absorbed in *The Life and Administration of Sir Robert Walpole* by A.W. Coxe, just published. The 'one continued series of intrigues, cabal, petty ambition, selfishness and party fury' fascinated and disgusted her all at once. As she told Granville: 'I see all times, all parties, were the same, all Ministers and all Oppositions actuated by the same little motives in half their measures, so we must not complain so bitterly of the present age. There are very few people I reckon quite sincere and well principled, but there are *some*.'[89] As we shall see, adding money to the mix presented further challenges to sincerity and principles.

CHAPTER FIVE

The Ethics of Fashion, Spending, Credit and Debt

In a monarchy, as in marriage and family life, disagreements over money can bring on a whole world of grief. Although the contestation caused by cash-strapped Stuart kings raising revenue without parliamentary consent, which helped launch the British Isles into civil war in 1642, finally had resolution in the Civil List Act of 1698, bickering over royal finances did not cease. E.A. Reitan has pointed out that, while the civil list was only a small part of the total governmental budget, it continued to be a touchy issue because it brought several constitutional principles into conflict: the independence of the crown, parliamentary control over finance and ministerial responsibility. Reitan argues that Edmund Burke's Economical Reform Bill, which passed in a watered-down form in 1782, had the opposite effect from what he had intended. In spite of Burke's assurances to the contrary, allowing parliamentary interference with civil-list accounts undermined the independence of the crown in favour of parliamentary supremacy. Even worse, by 1802 the civil list ran a debt of almost £900,000, so the act had not reduced royal profusion and influence as promised.[1] As had been the case in earlier initiatives for oeconomy at court, the need to keep up a suitable appearance of splendour and to reward faithful supporters outweighed the dangers of indebtedness. The crown's moral dilemma reflected the difficult ethical choices eighteenth-century Britons faced in maintaining personal as well as national credit. No longer the sole arbiter of fashion, the monarchy could easily become its victim.

Members of the royal family could spend as they wished because merchants extended them unlimited credit, confident that parliament would ultimately be forced to pay outstanding crown debts. The precedent had been set in Anne's reign.[2] Additionally, unpaid royal commissions could sometimes be compensated for by the volume of additional orders they generated. Manufacturers in the latter part of the eighteenth century began giving gifts to members of the royal family and the aristocracy in order to promote their wares. In some respects, monarchs had greater financial latitude than they had had in the bad old days of shaking down subjects with forced gifts and loans and the abuse of purveyance, wardship and ship money. Hence, the enhanced parliamentary (and, thus, public) scrutiny of the monarchy's expenditure opened up a new arena for discussing not only the problem of governmental corruption through the use of places, pensions and sinecures, but also the consequences of the ever-increasing expansion of trade, commerce, consumption and colonization, and the excesses of the fashionable world. The intricate and often incongruous moral, political and economic objectives influencing the royal family's personal income, spending and credit also operated and wreaked havoc on the estates of politicians as well as on the system of national finance.

The rise of a consumer society, the luxury debate and the commercialization of politics, so strongly associated with the eighteenth century thanks to the influence of the Habermasian model of the bourgeois public sphere, had strong roots in the seventeenth.[3] Similarly, criticism of George II and George III as skinflints came out of the same set of conflicting principles as the vilification of the Stuarts as spendthrifts. Monarchs had to keep up a splendid appearance and promote national prosperity while simultaneously setting a good example for the upper echelons of society to emulate. James I incited much censure with his lavish spending on favourites, particularly the Scots who followed him across the border. Critics of the regime disparaged his courtiers' lavish dress for its effeminate luxury. Concurrently, they poured derision on the king's protective, not fashionable, quilted doublets and pleated breeches, worn until threadbare, as evidence of his cowardice and moral laxity. James's criticisms of against foreign fashions, inescapable in the clothing of the ruling elite at the time, appeared hypocritical.[4] Yet reports of the king's shabbiness seem at odds with royal wardrobe accounts. In demonstrating how habits of conspicuous display set by the palace helped impoverish many an aristocratic family, Lawrence Stone notes that even the parsimonious Queen Elizabeth tended to excess in her self-adornment and to capriciousness in setting fashion. 'As for King James, over a period of five years from 1608 to 1613 he bought a new cloak every month, a new waistcoat every three weeks, a new suit every ten days, a new pair of stockings, boots, and garters every four or five days, and a new pair of gloves every day. Silks alone were costing the

King and Queen over £10,000 a year, and the wardrobe expense altogether was running at over £25,000 as early as 1610.[5] Either James's enemies perceived a slackness about his person notwithstanding his appearance or he immediately gave away new items of clothing as tokens of his personal affection. James viewed his unlimited bounty as essential for maintaining the reciprocal relations of loyalty and duty between sovereign and subjects, and justified this to all who would listen with classical writings extolling the patronage-clientage system. The king's ability to dispense rewards and gifts as he chose reflected his godlike qualities; he should not be subjected to the common exigencies of money. Linda Levy Peck presents the defence of this position encapsulated in Robert Cecil, Earl of Salisbury's declaration in parliament: 'For a King not to be bountiful were a fault.' When James I began selling offices and titles, however, the splendorous tradition of gift-giving became sullied in the mire of the marketplace. Bounty now looked more like bribery.[6]

James did demonstrate sensitivity to commerce's importance in England's economy, particularly the trade in morally suspect luxuries. He sought to reduce imports by promoting domestic production of silk, glass, crystal, tapestry and other sumptuous goods through patents of monopoly. Yet, again, scandal overshadowed any economic benefits that the king's attention bestowed after he granted his favourites the power to broker these patents. The plan also involved importing to England foreigners skilled in these manufactures and developing silk cultivation in Virginia, which James hoped would displace the tobacco he personally abhorred. Although the resulting availability of rich clothing to a broader segment of the populace raised alarms against the corrupting effects of expensive fashions in both England and the Massachusetts Bay Colony, the manufacture, import and trade of luxury goods did not abate, even during the Civil Wars and Interregnum. Puritans, although they favoured domestically produced, modestly cut, drably coloured, unadorned clothing, likewise appreciated high-quality workmanship and fabric, and would pay handsomely for it. Whereas they had objected to court fashion's starched collars and saffron yellow dye on the principle that these practices wasted foodstuffs on vanity, they saw nothing wrong with trimming collars and cuffs with lace. And they certainly did not object to amassing wealth through commerce, even in tobacco.[7]

Royal stinginess attracted derision well before George II's neglect of British belletrists and George III's untoward attention to his vegetable gardens and dairy. Attempts at personal economy at court invariably brought ridicule and resistance. Charles II had a Parisian tailor prepare an appropriate wardrobe for his re-entry into England and restoration to the throne in May 1660, and even persuaded the man to set up shop in London. Nonetheless, two years later, Samuel Pepys recorded in his diary that he saw the king wearing an unfashionable suit in public.[8] After the ravages of the plague of 1665 and Great Fire of 1666, Charles resolved to set fashions that would promote the domestic economy and teach the nobility thrift. His introduction of the 'Persian vest' established the three-piece suit—coat, waistcoat and breeches—as standard formal attire for men, in spite of Louis XIV immediately ridiculing the style by kitting out his footmen in waistcoats. The suit nonetheless failed to curb sartorial extravagance. While Charles championed English woollens in his everyday dress and in pitches to foreign ambassadors, court ceremonies required the sensible new ensemble to be made brilliant with expensive foreign materials and trimmings. The association of sober dress with masculine independence and virtue would not be forged in male fashion until the late eighteenth century.[9] Luxury had become well entrenched. As Peck observes: 'English society as a whole used new as well as traditional luxury goods to make relationships of patron and client, master and servant, and good neighbors through gift exchange. Men and women knowingly used luxury goods to display status, to create social ties, to gain favor, to rein-force memory, and to worship. The "demoralization" of luxury was well under way in the early seventeenth century.'[10] After the Restoration, moreover, playhouses, public pleasure gardens (the first was at Vauxhall) and shopping galleries began rivalling royal palaces and gardens as venues for fashionable display.[11] Nevertheless, luxury continued to cause disquietude among various segments of the public.

Although the Stuart reputation for profligacy endured, the issue of access to markets as well as excess in spending contributed to the ouster of the Catholic branch of this dynasty. James II reduced the number of places in the royal household by roughly a third and presided over a moral, culturally refined and cost-effective court.[12] A recent study of the Revolution of 1688–89 stresses the economic policies that helped provoke resistance against him. James subscribed to the Tory model of political economy based on the idea that wealth lay in land. He followed Louis XIV's methods of centralization and bureaucracy-building as he maintained the East India and Royal Africa Companies' monopolies in pursuance of imperial territorial expansion. Whigs, in contrast, recognized the value of human labour and therefore advocated support of domestic manufactures

through building a banking system based on the Dutch model of investment and credit as the foundation for commercial expansion.[13] After
1688–89, tensions between landed and moneyed interests became a strong
feature of the political landscape as industry and commercial agriculture
grew alongside development of a system of government finance, which
together helped build an economy capable of sustaining wars in defence of
trade and, in time, colonies.[14] Debate in the 1690s over the best way of
achieving a favourable balance of trade had merchants clamouring for a free
market, while the landed and manufacturing interests backed governmental regulation of foreign imports. Ironically, the mercantilist policy that
would prevail did not have the support of merchants. The recognition of
the role that broadening domestic demand could play in stimulating
industry, posing the first challenge to traditional associations of consumption with wasteful spending on luxuries by the rich, would suffer a temporary setback with the controversies sparked by Bernard Mandeville's *Fable
of the Bees* in 1714.[15] Later, Adam Smith and his fellow Scots, who
combined political economy and moral philosophy to more significant
effect, pointed out the injustice of depriving workers of the ability to
consume the goods they produced.[16]

The ongoing duel between the Christian association of frugality with
virtue and the tradition of royal patronage and splendour made it difficult
for monarchs to strike the right balance of self-discipline and largesse. As
each sovereign had an individual style and faced different circumstances,
setting down consistent principles and practices regulating luxury at court
proved impossible. Whatever the monarch did would be wrong in one way
or another. Appearances, moreover, often deceived. Notwithstanding the
Dutch court's habits of thrift, William and Mary presided over a shock-
ingly extravagant household in England owing to the restoration of offices
abolished by James II, ambitious building projects and lack of effective
supervision. The dual monarchs at first used ritualistic display to reinforce
their legitimacy but, although both took care to dress with elegance,
neither showed any inclination to set fashion trends. The queen, however,
had a weakness for diamonds that left her in debt to her jeweller and to
others from whom she borrowed to buy new ornaments.[17] Mary had a bit
of her uncle Charles's sense of fun, and gleefully reinstated drawing-
rooms, card parties, dances and plays at court. When William returned
from campaigning in Ireland in 1690 to learn that in his absence his
consort had attended a politically sensitive performance at a playhouse and
visited shops run by women of morally suspect reputation, he castigated

her behaviour both in private and in public. Queen Anne followed the former regime's policy of responsible management and respectable conduct in the royal household. Physical infirmities undermined her efforts at reviving regal ceremonial grandeur in spite of her strong sense of style and enjoyment of personal adornment. From 1710, court dress became a subset of high fashion because of its insistence on the archaic, with men weighed down by gold embroidery and decorative swords and women encumbered by hoops and long trains.[18] By pushing regal finery outside mainstream fashion and giving it an aura of tradition, monarchs and courtiers could be presented as performing a duty rather than indulging in vanity, and thus be forgiven the expense. Yet such display also gave a platform to critics, who could make an issue of its cost or the impression it created in order to comment on Britain's economic or diplomatic status.

The accession of the Hanoverian dynasty coincided with a rapid expansion of the newspaper press, so appearances at court broadened in significance over the course of the century as the papers provided increasingly detailed descriptions of royal rituals and their participants for a steadily growing readership. In addition, as the royal families became progressively larger, so did the number of celebratory occasions. The reinstatement of magnificent spectacle at court came in fits and starts as contradictory expectations continued to complicate royal expenditure and tastes. George I arrived in London with an irregular ménage that required discretion. He had divorced his adulterous consort, left her back in Hanover under house arrest and had in tow his devoted mistress, Melusine von der Schulenberg, whom he forthwith dubbed duchess of Kendal. George's efforts to guard his privacy at court brought criticism of his lack of accessibility and rumours regarding what he might be concealing. The palace at Herrenhausen, however, remained the locus of his personal extravagance, paid for with Hanoverian revenues. Still, in the same way that the Prussian monarchy was turning against the baroque grandeur of Louis XIV, George I scaled back his father's plans for renovating the palace and dispensed with its more elaborate entertainments. Unlike Prussia, though, this change was less voluntary than necessary, as a result of Hanover's war-depleted treasury. In England, George, Melusine, their unacknowledged daughters (officially her nieces), his illegitimate half-sister, Sophia Charlotte von Kielmansegg (née von Platen), and other intimates preferred visiting the estates of ministers and courtiers to admire their architecture, painting collections and gardens as well as attending masquerades, concerts and plays in London. George did host grand receptions on his birthday, New

Year's Day and Twelfth Night, and entertained opulently when necessary to win adherents and to countermand the popularity of the more convivial prince and princess of Wales. But, for the most part, the king dressed plainly, disliked ritual and formality, and made little effort to promote British fashion or luxury goods. Nevertheless, after all the care that the late Stuarts took to set fashion for ceremonial occasions in ways advantageous to national interests, and the competition among attendees to make a splendid appearance, the great wardrobe remained the department most difficult to control and most susceptible to overcharging and waste, in spite of the efforts of the Treasury.[19] The extravagance of this court lay with George I's significant increase in the number of household servants.[20]

George I's heir, on the other hand, had a reputation for vanity because of his dapper appearance. With his favourite son, William, Duke of Cumberland, George II oversaw the designing of elaborate military uniforms that allowed rank and regiment to be identifiable at a glance. Queen Caroline, in contrast, had a subdued approach to self-adornment. She tried to set limits on the expense of clothing for ceremonial occasions by personal example and, as much as possible, patronized English dressmakers and materials. In return for all her care that court expenditure should promote British interests, she endured scornful remarks regarding the effects that excesses of the table had on her person. Frederick, Prince of Wales enjoyed fashion and manifested the Hanoverian fascination with military dress by sporting a hunting costume of patriotic blue trimmed with red collar and cuffs and gold buttons and braid, which his partisans adopted in his support. In the late 1770s, his son George III took this as his template for a new court dress, the so-called 'Windsor uniform', which marked who was in favour, reinforced order and discipline in the royal household, paid tribute to the military and permitted civilians to share in its glory. The women's version of this dress faded quickly, but Queen Charlotte continued to draw scorn as a stickler for anti-quated rules governing female fashion. Somewhat paradoxically, she also attracted criticism for appearing bedecked in an excess of diamonds during formal events. When George, Prince of Wales became old enough to rebel against his parents' dull court, he embraced dandyism and extravagance and, with his unrequited desire for military glory, would parade about in a series of elegantly cut uniforms of various designations. The replacement of the *habit habillé*, or *habit à la française*, with a national uniform based on military dress or the *frac* (frock), the riding coat, as appropriate attire at court was under way in most other European courts but, significantly, not at Versailles. In the latter part of the eighteenth century, the rulers that historians would later christen the 'enlightened absolutists' inclined towards informality, simplicity, and less waste and pomp at court.[21] As will be shown in due course, the economic impact of war put pressure on both Georges to support manufacturers of domestic luxuries; nonetheless, sumptuousness of decorations or dress sometimes raised hackles.

The sartorial dilemmas facing royal personages reflected a broader social conundrum. Scholars have offered various theories to explain the growth of consumption in the eighteenth century and the ultimate triumph of capitalism, given the middling sort's puritan roots. While they disagree on the role and relative participation of the different classes of society in the consumer revolution, a small sample of these studies captures the range of discourses regarding expenditure. Albert O. Hirschman has extended Max Weber's model of the Protestant work ethic to eighteenth-century economic thought. He describes how philosophers challenged the Christian policy of repression of the passions—schematized in the seven deadly sins—with the theory of countervailing passions, which involved rechristening acquisitiveness as an interest that could moderate pride, lust, envy, gluttony, anger and sloth. In other words, valorizing the desire to improve one's material condition inspired moderation of the disorderly appetites. Colin Campbell thinks the process entailed not the rational management of the passions but rather an evolution of religious and emotional practices. The puritan belief that melancholic and self-confident dispositions were signs of grace gave way to the cult of sensibility, which considered the capacity for all feelings as evidence of a person's moral grounding. Emotional sensitivity could be demonstrated in reactions to artistic works, particularly in the appreciation of beauty, making good taste a sign of virtue. Campbell points out that puritans had no objection to pleasure as long as it served a higher purpose, most notably in sexual gratification's role in procreation. Similarly, costly adornments and furnishings could be defended as an aesthetic exercise in self-betterment. By contrast, the aristocratic ethos, he argues, mixed stoicism, nonchalance, honour and pride, resulting in standards of taste designed to reinforce a lofty status: a studied carelessness rather than thoughtful construction of a moral self. Woodruff D. Smith, on the other hand, sees more of a connection between the fashionable consumption of the commercial classes and aristocratic principles of gentility. He identifies a bourgeois narrative vindicating expenditure on luxuries to achieve gentility based on a practical notion of respectability that put a premium on cleanliness, comfort and health.[22] In each of these models, virtually any spending decision could be an occasion for moral expression.

Scholars who have focused on the actual behaviour of different social groupings find that these moral performances did not come easily. The discourses of self-justification for consumption did not establish clear rules regarding the proper degree of luxury to which one should aspire. Leonore Davidoff and Catherine Hall present the middle class caught between religious admonitions against worldliness and the need to demonstrate moral worth with the trappings of success. One strategy for supporting a particular degree of material indulgence involved distancing oneself from aristocratic mores, which social commentary and imaginative literature stereotyped as licentious and wasteful, although a landed family, in fact, had to practise good estate management and could just as easily be ruined by a profligate son. Margaret R. Hunt sums up another aspect of this position's paradoxical nature:

> For if wayward youths epitomized the dangers of emulation, they were also walking proof of its wide appeal. In this hierarchical, status-oriented society, there were real advantages to acquiring an air of gentility. Middling people who served (or aspired to serve) a high-class clientele profited from a familiarity with the latter's ways and tastes. And those who wished to be thought prosperous and credit-worthy by their peers might, up to a point, adopt genteel patterns of consumption (wearing better clothes, acquiring another servant, attending balls, etc.), for these were universally associated with wealth. Nor were the middling immune to the appeal of gracious living for its own sake: luxury was routinely condemned in the eighteenth century, but ostentatious asceticism was not an alternative many championed.

Ultimately, it came down to finding the proper balance between prudence and show.[23] A closer look at the practices of the fashionable elite—the *bon ton*, the beau monde—also challenges the rhetorical polarization of aristocratic and middling mores. As Hannah Grieg shows, great wealth and status did not automatically confer an entrée into fashionable circles. Nor did the elite throw money around frivolously, but rather made careful calculations in the selection of even the minutest details of furnishings and dress. Fashionable women and men inspected the latest improvements that their peers made to their townhouses and landed estates, and scrutinized the trimmings and jewels they wore to court. Achieving a becoming splendour on ceremonial occasions involved considerable anxiety and expense, with the court continuing to be a key site for reinforcing one's place in society or competing for advancement. Hannah Smith observes that, on the eve of such events, rumours flew regarding what courtiers would wear. Members of particular coteries arranged to view one another's ensembles ahead of time.[24]

The landed classes did not sit idly by and allow merchants and traders to colonize the moral high ground with their claims that upstanding principles regulated expenditure and display. The upper ranks guarded their position by establishing their own manners and standards of taste. Social parvenus drew ridicule from all sides. James Raven has demonstrated how the word 'vulgar' evolved from referring to the lower classes of society, or something ordinary, to connoting bad taste; specifically, behaving or dressing in ways inappropriate to one's station. Contemporary literature began using the word to condemn ostentation lacking refinement, delicacy, elegance or manners. While economic thinkers discussed the value of promoting new consumer industries, popular literature continued to tout the dangers of luxury and to caricature trading families who aped their betters. As the century progressed, however, novelists and periodical writers shifted the blame for moral corruption. They first targeted business families who grew fat on peddling luxuries and irresponsibly spent their gains on frivolities. Next, they became preoccupied with the dangerous temptations that the metropolis offered. Finally, writers focused on the follies of members of the ton who were of indeterminate class: personifications of fashion itself.[25] Indeed, the commercialization of fashion undermined traditional distinctions of rank. In setting fashion, royal and aristocratic appearances now competed with a proliferation of fashion dolls, ladies' magazines containing fashion commentary and plates, shop-window displays and advertisements. Celebrated singers and thespians became trendsetters inside and outside the theatre. Nonetheless, warnings of fashion's pitfalls persisted in very socially specific terms.[26] Much of the difficulty in finding the proper level of royal munificence came from the monarch's ambiguous social status: hovering above the hierarchy of ranks but associated at various times with the ethos of one group or another. In the same way that royal families had trouble realizing the domestic ideal of literature, the proper balance within the various models of moral restraint, sensible taste and regal grandeur often proved elusive.

The Incivilities of the Civil List

Unlike other wealthy social sets, royalty had the civil list cramping its style, which somewhat distorted the discourse on living within one's means or in a way suitable to one's station. One feature that all of the civil-list settlements had in common was their inadequacy; at first because the revenues set aside for their funding fell short of their target, and later because the sum settled at the beginning of each reign could not pay all the necessary salaries, pensions and tradesmen's bills. Parliament granted both William III and Anne £700,000 per annum but the customs, excise, Post Office and hereditary revenues designated to provide this sum came nowhere near the mark. At the end of Anne's reign, parliament sponsored a lottery to pay off her debts. George I received the same allocation, but his ministers successfully pressed for guarantees in light of past arrears and the added expense of his children, notably the £100,000 per annum bequeathed to George, Prince of Wales. Nonetheless, the civil list continued to run on a deficit. When George II ascended the throne, Sir Robert Walpole successfully moved to raise the civil list to £800,000 per annum as well as to allow the king any surpluses on the funds, which would yield an average of £823,000 per annum and in the last year of his reign £876,000. By denying as long as he could the sums due to the prince of Wales, the king had even more money at his disposal. Prince Frederick proclaimed that, when king, he would return to the settlement made on his beloved grandfather. Fulfilment of this promise would fall to his son. George III foolhardily gave up the revenue surpluses despite being faced with the immediate expense of his coronation, wedding and provisions for his five siblings, as well as planning for his future progeny, who would number fifteen, with all but three living into adulthood. George III had to apply to parliament in 1769 for relief from debts of £513,000. When the civil list became encumbered in debt again in 1777, parliament increased it to £900,000: an act of futility.[27]

Opposition politicians did not lay siege to the civil list for swaddling these kings and their families in a corrupting luxuriousness but rather for shrouding the monarchs' discretionary spending in secrecy. Notwithstanding, they were not above deploying anti-luxury discourse when convenient, although this could be risky with the reputedly penny-pinching first three Georges. William Shippen, Tory and Jacobite, the only MP to oppose Walpole's augmentation plan of late June 1727, would, the following September, publish his speech in a twenty-three-page pamphlet, which did not reach its real target until page fourteen—'that bottomless Gulf of Secret Service', the words being set in bold Old English typeface for emphasis. Thereafter, the word 'secret' received this treatment repeatedly. Also leaping from the pages in this font were the opposition's monetary tropes:

'Bubbles', 'the hired Slaves, and the corrupt Instruments of a Profuse, and Vain-glorious Administration', 'The Sinking Fund', the 'National Debt' and 'Exorbitant Taxes'. In a lengthy attack on the published version of the speech, 'Britannus' of the *London Journal* interpreted Shippen's 'ingenious [typographical] Device' as a way to ensure 'that his Admirers may have due Notice of his design to be witty, and not fail to laugh when the Jest comes'.[28] The MP showed no sign of levity; ethical argument dominated the first half of his speech. He described the House of Commons as being entrusted to uphold a *'Rule of Frugality'* and extolled in detail the visible honourable and charitable causes that had contributed to Queen Anne's debt. These he contrasted with George I magnifying the threat of a Swedish invasion to extort parliamentary grants and making empty promises to retrench his expenses. Although Shippen stated that he had reason to believe that the king pocketed considerable profits in the sale of captured Spanish vessels, the civil list remained over £600,000 in debt: 'If so, surely there must have been a *most egregious Neglect of Duty*, to say no worse; there must have been *a Strange Spirit of Extravagance* somewhere, or *such Immense Sums* could never have been so soon, so insensibly *squandered away*.' Addressing Walpole's justification for his motion, Shippen drew attention to sources of disunity within the royal family as he speculated that the increased expense of the queen's establishment should be offset by the prince receiving a financial settlement much inferior to that of his father when prince of Wales. Sardonically, he noted: *'many Personal, many Particular Expences* in *the late Reign*, especially *those for frequent Journies to* Hanover, will be discontinued, and entirely cease'.[29] As we will see, Walpole's hacks reported on the individual expenditures made by members of the royal family in a way that subtly undercut such insinuations.

Arguments over the civil list tended to flip back and forth and therefore blur the distinction between the issues of supporting the dignity of the crown and of allowing the king's revenues to influence the composition of the House of Commons. At this juncture, Britannus of the *London Journal* dismissed as irrelevant Shippen's aspersions on George I's financial machinations and his encomiums on Anne's oeconomy. He alleged that the MP published the speech months after delivering it in an attempt to render Walpole's measure 'odious to the People' and belittled Shippen as a failed poet turned orator. He thought it laughable that Shippen should want surplus revenues directed to the sinking fund, not the civil list, considering that he had been denouncing the sinking fund since its inception. Britannus skirted the issue of secrecy and focused on Shippen's representation of frugality as a virtue: 'But does it therefore follow that the Dignity of the Royal House shou'd lose its Lustre, at a Time when the Wealth and Splendour of the *British* Subject has attain'd its Meridian Glory, and seems to insult the Poverty of its Neighbours?'[30] Somehow, the crown had to achieve the precise degree of splendour that would be at once reflective of the country's international consequence and economic condition, and conducive to maintaining constitutional balance.

Similarly, Burke's Economical Reform Bill of 1780 rested on the claim that crown influence had increased, while its opponents countered that 'the revenue of the Crown had remained stationary, or nearly so, while that of the people had increased tenfold since the revolution, and consequently rendered the people more independent'.[31] Nonetheless, begrudging the king his income could too easily be construed as disloyalty or be ridiculed as small-minded. John Wolcot, who, as Peter Pindar, made a good living satirizing George III, captured the first impression of the Economical Reform Bill that probably sprang to the public mind. In a mock-heroic poem inspired by a royal order to have the kitchen staff's heads shaved for reasons of hygiene, he compared the king's disgust at finding a louse in his soup to the sensation he experienced when he caught sight of Charles James Fox. In addition:

Not with more horror did his eye-balls work
Convulsive on the patriotic Burke,
When guilty of economy, the *crime!*
Edmund wide wander'd from the *true sublime*,
And, cat-like, watchful of the flesh and fish,
Cribb'd from the R_y_l table many a dish—
Saw ev'ry slice of bread and butter cut,
Every apple told, and number'd ev'ry nut;
And gaug'd (compos'd upon no sneaking scale)
The Monarch's belly like a cask of ale;
Convinc'd that, in his scheme of state-salvation,
To *starve** the PALACE, was to *save* the NATION.

The asterisk directed the reader to a footnote explaining that, after an excessive liberality with apples dispensed to the royal children, the Board of Green Cloth had refused the king any more. Keeping to the custom of mocking George's stinginess, the story concluded with him giving a page sixpence for two pennies' worth of pippins and expecting change.[32] Until the future George IV came of age and exceeded any establishment set for him in an orgy of self-indulgence, frugality in the palace or attempts to impose it attracted satirists because the idea that appearances at court reflected a country's prosperity and strength had become entrenched.

Also contributing to the difficulty of trimming the civil list, a good share of politicians, their dependants and their friends had become hope-lessly caught up in the competition for a share in the royal bounty.[33] William Pulteney's career in opposition epitomizes the manifold traps that places and pensions, as well as the shifting personal and political identities of royalty, laid. In one of his salvos against Walpole's financial policies published in 1729, Pulteney challenged the belief that the state of public credit indicated prosperity, likening this to a man estimating his wealth according to the mortgages and debts upon his estate. He warned:

> A Luxurious and *extravagant* Way of living in any country, is very seldom a Mark of its being, or at least, an Omen of its continuing in a flourishing Condition; for though *Riches* first introduced *Luxury*, yet the Histories of all Ages assure us, that *Poverty* follows close upon the Heels of it; and in our present Circumstances, nothing but the most rigorous Frugality can preserve us from the Ruin that seems to threaten us. It is to be hoped, therefore, that neither *Laws, Encouragement*, nor *Example* will be wanting to put a Stop to this prevailing and most destructive Vice, for our Constitution and Liberties must otherwise be soon sacri-ficed to a Vogue of unrestrained *Extravagance* and *Profusion* which will always meet with Connivance and Encouragement from Men of *arbi-trary Principles* and *Designs*, who know how successful it hath been in destroying the Freedom of other Nations, and that Men must be first made *poor*, before they will tamely submit to the Yoke of *Slavery*.

Here, he also made the same connections between national prosperity and the people's independence as, paradoxically, the pro-ministerial opponents of the Economical Reform Bill would do in 1780. Pulteney went on to lament that many were misled by the prospect of obtaining court favour when a proportionally small number actually received it. Besides, a £500 place did little to offset the expense of office, neglect of one's business and loss of independence. He declared that the only hope would be a 'Revival of our ancient *Frugality*, and an Abatement of all immoderate Expences, both *Publick* and *Private* [. . .] as the Royal Example, in his Majesty's prudent Management of his *private Affairs*, seems to recommend the same

Oeconomy to the whole nation'.[34] While Pulteney did practise what he preached in the (some would say, avaricious) management of his own estate, in the prior reign he had energetically solicited the office of cofferer to the household, but once obtained thought it insufficient to his dignity. This and other perceived slights received from Walpole had provoked Pulteney into blocking the motion to pay off the civil-list debts in April 1725 with a demand that its accounts first be laid before parliament. Walpole would speak of the king's expenditures only in general terms, except for the £5,000 needed to pension off Lord Godolphin to free up the post of cofferer for Pulteney. In spite of this nettling, Pulteney did not back down until George I himself reportedly asked him whether he intended to prevent the king from being an honest man who pays '*his butcher, his baker, and other honest tradesmen?*' This rebellion put an end to Pulteney's tenure as cofferer. The following February he launched an investigation into the national debt, an issue with which he could harass Walpole without appearing to be rifling through royal pockets. By 1731, Pulteney found himself fending off innuendos made by pro-Walpole writers regarding the sources and scope of his own personal estate.[35] Burke too would endure hostile scrutiny when his debts drove him to accept a pension when he retired from parliament in 1794. Not only did this seem an act of hypocrisy; for his enemies, it also supported the rumours of Burke having received a secret annuity since he began supporting the Pitt administration.[36]

Following the Money

Newspapers of all political stripes accounted for the king's and his family's whereabouts and activities: attending church services, holding levees, dining in public, reviewing military regiments, paying visits, patronizing the arts, hosting galas to celebrate royal anniversaries and birthdays, enjoying the chase and other pastimes. They noted visible civil-list expenditure as if in a reminder to everybody that the royal family's income came from the people and the monarchy invested in elaborate decorations, clothing and jewels for the public benefit. The *Craftsman* admired the sword made for George II in honour of his daughter's nuptials: 'It is the finest Piece of Work of the Kind that has been seen in England, and the Hilt set with Diamonds to the Value of 10.000 l.'[37] During this reign, acts of largesse attracted notice. A week after reporting Prince Frederick's travel incognito from Hanover and arrival in England aboard a Dutch vessel, another opposition paper detailed the bounty lavished upon the crew:

His Royal Highness has order'd 100 Guineas to the Mate of the Packet
Boat that brought him over, and 5 Guineas to each of the Sailors; and
likewise recommended the Mate for Preferment, the Captain not going
that Voyage to Holland, being ashore with his Family at Harwich.
When the Packet was hired, the Mate was not acquainted with the
Quality of his Passenger, but soon suspected him to be the Electoral
Prince of Hanover, from a Picture he had of his Royal Highness at
Home, compar'd with some Circumstances he observ'd in the Voyage,
and therefore gave several Orders to the Mariners to be more careful in
the Discharge of their Duty. And on Monday last the Mate attended at
St. James's, when besides the 100 Guineas order'd him, his Royal
Highness presented him with a Gold Medal of great Value.[38]

The following month, the politically neutral *Universal Spectator* relayed
news of the prince ordering a hundred guineas for the poor of St Martin-
in-the-Fields parish.[39] Reports of spontaneous expressions of generosity
and gratitude also issued from King George's camp. For example, while
taking the air in Hampstead, the royal family had eight guineas distributed
to the brick- and haymakers labouring in the field.[40] At the time of her
wedding arrangements, the princess royal made a gift of five guineas to the
gentleman of the Life Guards who returned the gold snuffbox she had
dropped during a stag hunt.[41] Acts of royal largesse helped preserve some
of the monarchy's mystique in the post-Divine Right era.

In response, the opposition press could undermine the sense of benevolence underlying donations by hinting at their inadequacy: 'His Majesty
having given 500 l. toward Rebuilding the Ancient Chapel at Kingston
upon Thames; which fell down in March last and killed several Persons.
Monday a Committee of that Corporation met at the Castle Inn to
consider of Means for Augmenting his Majesty's said Bounty.'[42] Eventually,
members of the royal family found it more practical to be discreet in their
giving so as not to be overwhelmed with petitions. George III continued
to press coins into the hands of the distressed when he encountered them,
Queen Charlotte used intermediaries to distribute money to needy families, and royal tours did not cease being occasions for giving relief to
debtors and grants to local charities. Now most royal benevolence went to
philanthropic associations, which had been displacing traditional forms of
almsgiving. Complete accounts do not exist of the royal family's expenditure on charity, but George III and George IV appear to have given similar
amounts. Revealingly, the sum represented about a quarter of George III's

personal income but only a fraction of what his son laid out on clothes and furnishings. Likewise, while George IV's daughter had been schooled in the virtues of generosity by her grandmother, her wardrobe expenditure far exceeded her gifts to the poor. Frank Prochaska contends that royal endorsements, personal appearances at charitable events and the consequent pressure on the elite to make donations could be as valuable as an actual monetary contribution from a member of the royal family when raising funds for a cause.[43] Therein lay one of the moral justifications of the time for the demanding fashion requirements for admission to court galas: the luxurious self-adornment of courtiers involved expenditure that stimulated domestic ingenuity.

Celebrations of royal anniversaries and birthdays brought the largest number of observations on visible outlay in diaries, letters and the press because of the emphasis on rich dress and extravagant display as a show of loyalty and the problems as well as the benefits attending these efforts. Lord Hervey observed wearily, albeit wittily, to the duke of Richmond:

> You will think me most incomparably dull for not having picked up anything worth relating from the occurrences of a Birthday, but one Birthday is so like another, that excepting the colours of people's clothes, your Grace may tell yourself the history of the day full as well as anybody that made a part of it. The Spanish Ambassadress was there dressed in the English fashion, and stared at in the English fashion; for wherever she turned there was a ring of spectators, whisperers and laughers, which put me (who am concerned for the reputation of England) as much out of countenance as did her.[44]

While members of this milieu seemed to acknowledge the absurdity of the exercise, all felt compelled to participate.

An account of the ill-conceived celebrations at Bath of George II's first birthday as king had produced a similar gleeful censoriousness in, ironically, Hervey's nemesis, the *Craftsman*. The paper began with a winking preamble:

> Tho' we have hitherto avoided printing those Accounts which have been brought us of the publick Rejoycings in the several Parts of these Kingdoms, on the Day of their Majesties Coronation or the King's Birth-Day; yet we hope it will not be esteemed a Mark of the least Disaffection in us, since we do assure our Readers that our only Reason

was that we might not tire their Ears with endless Repetitions of the same thing; but the following being the most remarkable Piece of Loyalty, we hope we need make no other Excuse for giving it a Place in our paper, than by declaring that we are not paid for inser[t]ing it.

It reported bells rung at four in the morning, a bonfire lit, and an ox set to roast 'with a Quantity of Liquor, and Huzza's to his Majesty's Health'. At six, drums summoned the volunteers to arms. At eight, 160 assembled at the house of their colonel, a local jeweller. Around ten they commenced marching after lifting many glasses of brandy in toast. The *Craftsman* listed every extravagant element of finery on display. By noon, they had marched through most of the town accompanied by a band, sword-bearers and morris dancers, finally assembling at the market place to fire a volley and drink wine bumpers, throwing the glasses over their heads (an activity pursued in other parts of the town as well), and to listen to their captain recite loyalist verse. The eight men who donated the roasting ox cut into its flesh to stuff it with silver coins and gemstones. At two in the afternoon, they placed the ox on a twelve-foot-long, six-foot-wide serving dish made for the occasion to serve at the Market House, 'but the Stuffing made the Mob so furious, that they flung themselves over the Heads of the Officers into the Dish, and stood over their Shoes in Gravy, and one was *stuffed* into the Belly of the Ox, and almost stifled with Heat and Fat. The Grease flew about to that Degree which made the Officers quit the Table, or all their Cloaths must have been spoiled.' They remained until three, marched back to the colonel's until four, and at five participated in the illuminations and drank more toasts, with the festivities lasting until eleven.[45] The paper reported that the officers resolved to observe the king's birthday and coronation day in the same manner every year; however, I have found nothing of the kind in subsequent years. A local paper unfriendly to the ministry, *Farley's Bristol News-Paper*, ran a similar story on the same day as the *Craftsman*.[46] Drunkenness and chaos likely featured in many celebrations of this kind, but the sordid details did not usually make their way into the London papers. The *Craftsman*, facing increasing accusations of disloyalty to the king, found it more politic to refrain from such coverage in future.

Royal celebrations gave the opposition press other ways to lobby its positions on financial issues. For the queen's birthday in 1730, the *Craftsman* admired the visible expenditure, noting that 'his Majesty had on a very rich suit, the Buttons on his coat being of Diamonds, every one worth, as is said, 200 l.' It then went on to detail how 'a Cavalcade of about 100 Wool-combers march'd in Procession from Bishopgate-street to St. James's in their shirts, with long Woollen Caps of several Colours'. George and Caroline came to the window to hear the leader's speech 'expressing the Thanks of their Body for the Encouragement already given to the Woollen Manufacture, and entreating the Continuance of their Majesties Favour, in order to promote the Welfare of the Community, and to redress the Grievances they yet labour under'.[47] The queen's birthday occasioned new clothes for royal household guards and servants, a boon to manufacturers and tradesmen.[48] The Spitalfields weavers showed their true gratitude and respect in 1731, however, by spreading the rumour that the queen had died in the night, which caused their stocks of crepe and black clothes to sell out in four hours.[49] Perhaps this insensitive opportunism was due to the king not sharing the queen's interest in English craftsmanship. The prince of Wales scored points by making the cause his own. Upon receiving gushing praises from the lord mayor of London when presented with the key to the City at the end of 1736, Frederick responded with a speech extolling the importance of commerce and vowing to promote it.[50] After the courts separated, the opposition press made sure its readers knew Prince Frederick was the true friend to domestic industry. In 1738, the papers declared: 'We hear that the Prince and Princess of Wales gave orders before His Majesty's birthday to all gentlemen and ladies belonging to them not to wear any cloathes or trimmings not of English Manufacture.'[51] Prince Frederick and Princess Augusta continued to lavish attention on the commercial sector. They toured Bath and Bristol where guildsmen carrying emblems of the different trades paraded in their honour, in contrast to the military reviews that featured when George had visited as prince of Wales in 1718. In a quirk of fate, the later visits had a less pacific outcome as the mercantile interest pressed for war against Spain and helped oust Walpole. Nevertheless, championing commerce was not a posture temporarily assumed for political gain. After the Peace of Aix-la-Chapelle when French goods glutted the market, the prince and princess of Wales wore English-made fashions and insisted that all visitors to their court follow suit. Frederick, Augusta and the two elder princesses even went so far as to pay a call on the homes of Spitalfields weavers in 1750 to compliment and encourage their work.[52]

Courtiers, on the other hand, did not necessarily appreciate the idea that royal galas should be an occasion for promoting domestic industry. Lord Hervey bubbled with excitement over a friend sending 'cloathes from

France for the Birthday' which he feared, correctly, would not arrive on time.[53] The opposition press lay in wait, ready to pounce. Quoting an ad from a silk-mercer who 'had the honour to serve most of the Quality upon their last Birth-day suits' and would be continuing this service in a great warehouse at St James's, the *Craftsman* observed: '*As the Design of* this Undertaking *is to relieve the nobility and Gentry of both Sexes, from the Impositions of* common Mercers, *and the vulgar Frippery of our* own Manufacture, *we doubt not that the* Beaumonde *will give it all suitable Encouragement.*' Two years later, after it admired the king's red velvet suit, observed the queen to be wearing more jewels than ever known before, and adjudged the countess of Suffolk and Count Ughi as making the grandest appearance of the company, the *Craftsman* mentioned that a great quantity of rich velvets from France for ladies in anticipation of the birthday had been seized at the Customs House at Dover. The paper reported that, shortly before the king's birthday in 1735, a raid at a house near Leicester Fields yielded a considerable quantity of smuggled gold and silver laces, brocades and embroidered handkerchiefs, waistcoats and aprons. Each offence carried a fine of £100. Earlier that year, the *London Evening Post* had reminded readers of this penalty when it heard tell that 'several French Taylors and others are very busy in procuring great Quantities of Gold and Silver Lace from France, against the Queen's Birthday, notwithstanding its Prohibition', and praised the efforts of Customs commissioners.[54]

Smuggling finery was not the only pecuniary crime that court galas attracted. Count Ughi, so admired at the king's birthday in 1731, turned out to be an adventurer by the name of Eugenio Mecenati, a godson of the duke of Parma, who, it was rumoured, had met Jacobites in Portugal who recruited him to their cause. Ughi gained entry into high society by admiring the Austrian ambassador's coach horses and purchasing them on the spot for twice their value, cultivating the ambassador's friendship, and winning invitations to all the best receptions, dinners and balls with his elegance and wit. César de Saussure appropriated gossip about Ughi into his travel letters on London and spun the story into a morality tale. Saussure wrote that people thought the worst when Ughi disappeared three months after his arrival, leaving £3,000 in debts, until an advertisement in the papers gave directions to creditors for receiving repayment that re-established his credit. Ughi reappeared months later with an air of mystery about his secret mission and true identity. He re-established a fine residence, gave concerts and lavish galas where he showered ladies with expensive gifts, almost married the duchess of Buckingham, and suddenly had Walpole ordering him out of the country. The £6,000 in debts he left behind this time remained unpaid. Hence, Saussure concluded, do not always take people at their word.[55] Allowing anyone who was suitably dressed into the palace provided further lessons on the dangers of false appearances. Indeed, at court celebrations of the king's fifty-fourth birthday in 1737, a thief 'dressed like a gentleman' unsuccessfully tried to make off with a lady's gold watch.[56]

Nevertheless, the court at St James's remained the government's moral platform. George II's absences brought accusations that he neglected his British subjects, so court papers attempted to present his ceremonial shows while away in Hanover as beneficial to the power and status of Britain. For example, the *London Journal* announced on 31 May 1735 that the king had arrived in Hanover the preceding Sunday, described his journey and catalogued the greetings he received from the prince of Orange, Horatio Walpole (brother of Sir Robert) and other worthies. News that he had skipped the planned ceremony with the merchants of Utrecht might have assured those who feared him becoming involved in his son-in-law's political struggles. Others, however, might have seen this as indicative of the king's indifference towards trade, considering the hit that London businesses took when fewer people went to court in his absence. On 7 June, the *London Journal* further reported the king had been reviewing the troops of the electorate and had not yet enjoyed the entertainments of the city. Readers learned that at court in Herrenhausen he had been filling vacant posts; appearing at nightly galas, plays or assemblies; and supping with the nobility. On the 21st, the paper assured Britons:

We learn from Hanover, that his Majesty din'd on Wednesday last week, for the first time, at his Palace in that City, and went afterwards to see a Play acted in the great Theatre, which is reckoned one of the largest and finest in Europe. The Concourse of People on this Occasion may be imagin'd.

His Majesty seems extremely fond of the young Prince of Hesse Cassel, who is arrived at Hanover with his Father. He appear'd with the King at the Reviews which were made last week, and had an Adjunct-General to attend him by his Majesty's Order, and conduct him through the Battalions. The Troops perform'd their Evolutions and Exercises with such a surprising Dexterity, that his Majesty declared in the Field, that next to his British Soldiers he never saw a finer Body of Men, nor better Order and Discipline.

George II's life seemed happier, more sociable, and filled with greater pomp and circumstance in Hanover, where Madame Wallmoden became his mistress that year. Moreover, the king found it a sturdier platform from which to conduct diplomatic negotiations, accompanied as he was there just by supportive British ministers and aided by trusty Hanoverian servants. After Queen Caroline's death at the end of 1737, the relocation of Wallmoden to London only kept him in England until war drew him back to the court that agreed with his tastes and provided greater freedom of manoeuvre. Courtiers in the electorate appeared more appreciative of him than their British counterparts. During the months when George was not present, they would assemble every Sunday at the Leine palace, bow to his portrait sitting propped up on a chair, and perform all the rituals of the drawing room: modest conversation, a splendid dinner and then cards (or needlework for the ladies).[57] Although George III never set foot in his electorate, a similar ameliorative story appeared when his favourite son's misbehaviour abroad brought censure. During Frederick, Duke of York's campaign in the Netherlands in winter 1793–94, tales of wine, whores and high living at camp reached London. *The Times* counteracted these by detailing the duke's celebration of the queen's birthday with a ball for six hundred guests at the town hall in Ghent, concluding: 'The entertainment was suitable to the occasion, and the phlegmatic Flemmons were astonished at British munificence.'[58] With the succession of wars that commenced in 1739, impressing foreigners became a major justification for royal splendour.

During George III's reign, the meanings attached to royal display would become more pronounced and the principles of expenditure more contentious as newspaper coverage and personal and public indebtedness all swelled. While he and Queen Charlotte dedicated themselves to maintaining decency, decorum and frugality at court, they also aspired to achieving an appropriate degree of splendour on ceremonial occasions. Just as his father, Prince Frederick, had done, George made a point of patronizing domestic clothiers. After the resolution of the Regency Crisis of 1788–89, some papers devoted one to two pages to describing the festivities on the king's and queen's birthdays as well as the cut, colour, fabric and trimmings worn by each notable lady and gentleman present and any new equipages that rolled up to the palace. Often, though, the eminently fashionable prince of Wales stole the show and gathered accolades in spite of the immensity of the debts he ran up with his expensive tastes and passion for horseracing. On the queen's first birthday after the king's recovery, the descriptions of the sartorial displays of father and son reflected their discordant ways and consequent unease:

His MAJESTY

Wore a suit of scarlet cloth, enriched with a splendid embroidery of gold, the pattern a column formed of stars of gold, entwined with beautiful wreaths of laurel, and the whole, as we informed the World yesterday, was entirely of English manufacture. The Loup, Star and George which his MAJESTY wore, were of brilliants.

The PRINCE *of* WALES

Had on a most superb and beautiful cut velvet coat, the ground of which was dark; it is striped with green, the front and all the seams were very richly covered with a broad embroidery of silver, on point lace, inter-mixed with foil stones, &c. The pattern is of a variety of flower and palm leaves, raised and worked in a most beautiful manner. His ROYAL HIGHNESS wore a shoulder-knot of brilliants, his Star George, &c. were also of brilliants; the breeches the same as the coat; the waistcoat of rich silver and white tissue, embroidered in a most superb manner, with silver and stones.

This dress surpasses any thing of the kind we ever beheld, and is an additional proof of what the WORLD acknowledges, the superior taste and elegance of HIS ROYAL HIGHNESS the PRINCE OF WALES.[59]

The king's adornment in a laurel-wreath pattern symbolized his victory in the Regency Crisis while the prince's palm leaves suggested a peace offering after his patricidal behaviour.[60] The *World and Fashionable Advertiser* went on to pronounce the prince the best-dressed man at the drawing room, followed closely by the similarly habited 'Duke of Orleans'. Drawing attention to the connection between the two men might have been a sly jab at the prince. Not yet Philippe-Égalité the revolutionary, the duc d'Orléans nonetheless had a reputation for dissipation and rakishness. The account observed the 'tears of sensibility' that dropped from the eyes of the princesses as it stressed how the celebrations acknowledged the 'exalted Virtue' of the queen, which 'placed her above the envious attacks of all but an abandoned, prostituted, disappointed, and degraded Opposition'. It noted the number of foreign nobility present and speculated that the brilliance and elegance at court must have given them 'a high opinion of the grandeur of this country'. With the king's support of English fashion, it was now the ministerial press that mocked the aristocrats who patronized French tailors. At the queen's birthday two years later, *The Times* claimed that many who had ordered their suits from France had been disappointed with their quality. It pointed out that giving English manufacturers hope for future sales would encourage speculation and increase the variety of styles available for lower prices. 'But prejudices require the aid of time to limp away.'[61] Once Britain and France went to war in 1793, appearing in French finery became indefensible and debates over the degree of splendour suitable for wartime turned into political fodder.

The significance accorded to the prince of Wales's dress by newspapers best illustrates how political interests, emotional resonances and the strength of appearances overwhelmed rationality and introduced wild inconsistencies into the debates over proper spending and indebtedness. No sooner did the prince reach his majority in 1780 than he applied to his father for £5,000 to quietly pension off a discarded mistress. In 1783, the £62,000 per annum establishment settled upon him included a supplement of £30,000 to settle tradesmen's bills. In 1787, after he and the duke of York attempted to negotiate foreign loans, parliament granted the prince further princely sums to pay off his creditors and complete the renovations of Carlton House. By 1795, he owed an additional £650,000. Payment of these debts occasioned public controversy.[62] Ministerial and opposition papers alike praised the prince's elegance in some contexts and voiced qualms about its cost in others. In 1791, he appeared at the queen's birthday wearing a diamond sword surpassing anything ever made before; newspapers on both sides gushed, as they totted up the £80,000 in diamonds he sported.[63] In the prince's camp, the *Morning Post* pushed this further, declaring that a foreigner would have found the event insipid and gloomy had it not been for the presence of the prince. 'Yet this splendour and taste which have rescued and elevated the national character, has actually been the theme of illiberal remark!—such are the effects produced by the combination of rancour and venality.' At the end of the year it enthused over the prince's new state carriage, the most magnificent coach ever built, with the carving and painting alone costing £1,000 and with a body so high it took a six-foot-tall man to open its doors. Next to it, the empress of Russia's triumphal car 'sinks into mere mechanism': 'All the attendants' liveries and hats are upon the same splendid Scale of Princely magnificence and unbound liberality.'[64] Much like the modern shopaholic, the press took pleasure in the luscious items of expenditure, only to cry in dismay when the bills came in.

The newspapers' cavalier attitude towards criminal activity around the palace was another reflection of the ambiguity of its moral terrain. The prince's extraordinary brilliance became the target of exceptionally audacious thieves. Royal events had continued to be a haven for pickpockets in borrowed finery. Indeed, in anticipating the festivities for the queen's birthday in 1791, *The Times* warned that 'the light-fingered gentry will make a tolerable strong show this day' and advised leaving valuables at home. At this event the following year, 'genteely dressed' men gained admission to court, but attracted the suspicion of one of the prince's gentlemen. Nonetheless, in the crush, one miscreant got close enough to the prince for a violent grab that almost broke off the diamond-encrusted hilt of the celebrated sword.[65] In the ensuing days, *The Times*, no friend to the prince, made merry with the incident: 'The attempt on the PRINCE was truly en *Militaire—to take him* OFF *his Guard* and a *brilliant* business it would have been—To the *Pickpocket Gentleman*.' The paper quipped that the prince was clearly not a convert to the revolutionary doctrine of the rights of man judging by 'the vast profusion of armorial decorations' on his new coach. Two days later, it speculated that the thief, in contrast, must have subscribed to French principles and believed in equality of riches.[66] At the same time, in its reports on court fashion on the king's and queen's birthdays that year, *The Times* celebrated the prince as 'the best-dressed Gentleman at Court'.[67] Court spectacles placed on display the pleasures and dangers of wealth and extravagance, and to some degree opened up discussion about the foundational principles of British identity.

Alarmed by the escalating violence of the French Revolution and hemmed in by his mounting debts, the prince tried to make friendly overtures to his disapproving father.[68] As he broke away from his old friends, the pro-French Foxite Whigs, the prince signalled his support for joining the hostilities against France as well as his aspirations to military glory by appearing at his mother's birthday in 'a General's uniform suit, with his diamond star and epaulet'. That spring, the ultra-loyalist *Sun* voiced pleasure when the prince was spotted in Hyde Park wearing the Windsor uniform, 'a change which he may be assured it rejoices all good subjects to see'.[69] The Foxite *Morning Chronicle*, which earlier had attacked Treasury newspapers for criticizing the princely debts that came from 'the ill-managed expence natural to the sanguine disposition, and to the generosity of youth' and had argued that the arts received the best lustre from the crown, ridiculed the prince's sartorial shift. On the king's birthday in 1793, the paper observed that 'the PRINCE was in the light uniform of which he is lately so fond, and which the Ladies say but ill accords with the increasing rotundity of his figure'.[70] *The Times*, on the other hand, praised the prince's colonelcy in the Light Dragoons insofar as it was able as it reported the regiment's march from Egham and Staines to Windsor to take garrison duty: 'The officers and soldiers being in their full uniform, made a very brilliant appearance. This being his Royal Highness's first entry into that place, in his military capacity, the bells at both churches were rung on the occasion.' After his exertions he went to dine with his parents at the castle.[71] Deprived of any real power or function, the prince became the sum of his outward appearances, which received praise or censure depending on his current political alliance.

Playing soldier only ran up more tradesmen's bills, so in 1795 George resorted to a precipitous marriage in order to have parliament settle his debts and grant him a larger annual income. When it became apparent that marriage had not reformed him and he was drifting back to his friends in opposition, *The Times* snubbed the prince and declared his consort 'the best-dressed Lady at Court' on the queen's birthday in 1797. The following month, the paper took note of his new bob wig and questioned whether the old arbiter of elegance could make the style fashionable. If readers had not caught the paper's drift, it made its derision plainer a few days later, describing the wig as 'the most gallant compliment ever paid to a MISTRESS. The attempt of the lover is to look as old as the object of his affections.' The *Sun* assured readers of the prince's practicality by claiming that he did not cut his hair (perhaps to distance him from republicanism) but wore the bob because his hair was thinning and he wished to keep his head warm. The *Morning Chronicle*, better disposed towards the prince now that he was taking a Whiggish stance towards Irish policy, offered that the light curls of the wig made him more resemble his father.[72] Tom Nairn's analysis of how the press in 1977 treated glimpses of the present prince of Wales's balding pate as flashes of some fascinating secret is useful here. He points out that something as mundane as a comb-over became fetishized when the mystique of monarchy, with its 'dialectic of the normal and the (utterly) extra-ordinary', insinuated a bevy of implications.[73] As I have detailed elsewhere, George's debts provoked great public outrage but the remedy of having a future king reduce his establishment and live like a private gentleman seemed to some a concession to republican principles.[74] Even when war brought further privation to the unprivileged masses of society, newspapers, except for the stalwart radical press, still supported this larger-than-life figure of magnificent style as if therein lay reassurances of future prosperity and strength. When the prince failed at his designated role or in support of the interests the papers championed, they sniped at his imperfections—weaknesses that perhaps represented Britons' anxieties as they battled revolutionary France.

Royal Oeconomy and National Interests

The financial settlements and festivities that accompanied the royal weddings of the 1730s and 1790s show the difficulty of reaching a desirable equilibrium of prudence and largesse as well as the multifaceted meanings of money within a family. Comparing these two decades further illustrates how the culture of the market complicated court splendour. Display took on an increasing number of meanings and commerce's naturalization of credit gave royal grandeur a potential limitlessness that some saw as the bastion of British superiority and others predicted would bring national ruin. Additionally, royal nuptials paraded the stark financial interests underlying matrimony prettied up in rich emblematic embroidery, silver and gold brocade, diamonds, pearls, silk and lace. The subtleties underlying the dominant characterizations of George II as downright mean and George III as merely parsimonious become clear when we examine how the progeny of each made their way to the altar. Royal household management showcased how complicated the principles of oeconomy had become.

George II manipulated money in attempts to assert his power and status that often had the opposite effect to the one desired. The offhand manner in which he requested an £80,000 marriage portion for his daughter in 1733 inadvertently drew attention to the uneasy relations between the civil list and the national debt. The request appeared as a clause in an application for £500,000 from the sinking fund for multiple appropriations, including £100,000 for distressed persons emigrating to Georgia. While not actually opposing the bill, the earl of Chesterfield and other anti-ministerial lords decried the indecency of throwing the illustrious princess in with charitable appeals. Others jumped in to question the propriety of raiding the sinking fund, which led to a debate over the relative tax burden of the landed and commercial interests, and the expectations of creditors. A motion for restricting future use of the funds for current service, however, saw defeat.[75] Meanwhile, the king became less dismissive towards his future son-in-law after he showered the princess royal with £30,000 in jewels, including a magnificent diamond necklace of twenty-two large stones. While courtiers assessed the scale and value of the diamonds and pearls proffered, the newspapers endowed the prince of Orange's gifts to Princess Anne with dynastic significance as well. The *Universal Spectator* observed 'an exceedingly fine Pearl Necklace of very great Value, which belong'd to the late queen Mary, Consort to King William the Third'. The *Weekly Register* reported 'a curious Pearl Necklace, with a Solitaire, and a Pair of Diamond Ear-Rings to the Values of 3000l. made by Mr. Syrrack in *York-Building*, Jeweller', and published a copy of Princess Mary's will as if to remind readers that Charles I's eldest daughter was William III's mother: 'As the Publick remembers very little of the Princess, and as her wishes in this Piece for the Prosperity of her son, and his country's Good, as well as the great Benefit to his Friends and Allies, were so remarkably answered by that Prince; and more especially as the Family of *Orange*, takes up the Attention and Discourse of every *Englishman*, we thought we could not insert a Piece more acceptable to the Curious at this Time.'[76] Hence, William could be seen to be both honouring the families' shared heritage and patronizing British tradesmen. He attended to charity as well. After his convalescence in Bath, he made a gift of a 'handsome sum' for the mayor to distribute to the poor.[77]

Not to be outdone, the king had the French chapel at St James's adorned in crimson velvet, taffeta and gold roses. Precious tapestries suffered depredation when installed to enhance the chapel's grandeur. Builders cut through the gardens in the construction of a covered gallery between the king's apartment and the chapel to accommodate close to four thousand guests. Although the queen insisted that Anne's trousseau be made in England, the blue silk of the wedding gown came from France. George managed to outshine the prince in dress. As the courtier, Mary Delany, observed: 'The Prince of Orange was in a gold stuff embroidered in silver; it looked rich but not showy. The King was in a gold stuff which made much more show, with diamond buttons to his coat; his star and George shown most gloriously.' Lord Hervey opined that had the king loved his daughter more than show he would have given her the money instead; when the newlyweds departed in April, he noted that the king 'gave her a thousand kisses and a shower of tears, but not one guinea'. George had presented his favourite daughter with diamond earrings almost as an afterthought. More materially, delayed payment of her jointure caused the couple financial embarrassment. The exquisite diamond necklace did not appear again, most likely being broken up and sold to pay off the enormous debts the prince of Orange had incurred with the increased credit line that the gamble of his courtship had brought him.[78] Although Lord Hervey's personal resentments certainly coloured his account of George II and his family, others shared his impression of the king's love of money. As his most recent biographer has shown, George was capable of great acts of generosity but not of the kind that attracted notice.[79] The metaphor that Hervey used later while contemplating the significance of trifles in the history of princes has poignancy in the context of this marriage: 'The intrigues of Courts and private families are still the same game, and played with the same cards, the disparity in the skill of the gamesters in each equally great; there are excellently good and execrably bad, and the only difference is their playing more or less deep, whilst the cutting and shuffling, the dealing and the playing, is still the same whether the stakes be halfpence or millions.'[80] Newspapers had happily totted up the riches on display: the white satin dress with gold embroidery that the princess royal wore for the ceremony had diamond buttons costing £300 each, the 'Counterpane to the Bed was Lace of an exceedingly great Value' and, upon their departure, the king presented the prince and princess of Orange with 'his set of fine dun horses'.[81] The visible exchanges of costly gifts and the efforts of all to create a magnificent appearance masked the pettiness within the palace and made onlookers, domestic and foreign, more willing to invest in the dynasty's future.

The ill will between the king and his heir apparent could not so easily be covered over. George tried to use money to control Frederick and came off the worse for it. Hervey claimed that nobody liked the civil-list settlement but only Shippen had sufficient indifference towards gaining royal favour to oppose it. The prince's £100,000 sounded a refrain throughout Hervey's memoirs from the time of Frederick's arrival from Hanover in 1728 when the king, wishing to prevent his son becoming a threat, kept him on a short allowance. This slight only made the prince more susceptible to the opposition. Hervey averred that even he and others friendly to the king and queen thought the prince had insufficient funds, but George and Caroline refused to heed their warnings. Meanwhile, the prince's friends offered loans and his debts mounted. The king persisted in denying his son the same income that he had enjoyed as prince of Wales even with Frederick's marriage in April 1736, the arrangements for which the king hurried in order to return to Hanover by 29 May as he had promised Madame Wallmoden he would do.[82] The opposition embarrassed the king in parliament by using the address of congratulations on the nuptials as an opportunity to praise the prince's virtues with warmth and the king's paternal feelings with lightly veiled sarcasm.[83]

Press coverage of the wedding contained the usual assessments of splendour and dress, with little notice taken of the king, who had obviously not made the same effort as he had for his daughter. The ministerial *Daily Gazetteer* proclaimed national standing preserved with its observation: 'Most of the ladies were dressed in rich white Silks finely embroidered, and adorned with so many Brilliants, and other Jewels, that they far surpassed the Lustre and Splendor of the Court of Vienna at the Marriage of the Duke of Lorraine with the Emperor's Eldest Daughter, according to the accounts we received from thence.' The neutral *Universal Spectator* reminded readers of the prince's commitment to promoting commerce: ' 'Tis assur'd that most of the rich Clothes were the Manufacture of England; and it must be acknowledged, in Honour of our own Artists, that the few which were French did not come up to these in Richness, Goodness, or Fancy, as may be seen by the Clothes worn by the Royal Family, which are all of the British Manufacture.' It also revealed the prince's injudicious scheme to win popularity: 'the Prince of Wales had procur'd 400l. in shillings and sixpences, to have thrown among the Populace at Greenwich; but his Royal Highness made acquainted with the ill Consequences that might attend such a Distribution, with Regard to the Lives and Limbs of the People, receded from his generous Purpose.'[84] Still, Frederick seemed the good egg.

Public opinion of the king deteriorated further as he dawdled in Hanover and missed the celebrations for his birthday. When he finally started the journey back to England, storms brought more delays, breaks in communication and speculation on George's demise as the prince continued to court popular acclaim. Even Walpole began worrying about the queen being stripped of all her income should her son ascend the throne. Riding the tide of popularity which continued even after George's return, Frederick remained unmoved by the various emissaries sent to impress on him the dire prediction that royal family disunity would encourage the Jacobites, and he took the dispute over his £100,000 to parliament. In a double irony, Pulteney, after all his fine words against extravagance and luxury, reluctantly introduced the motion in the Commons, and Hervey, after all his animus towards Pulteney and Frederick, thought he made a good case. The king won the majority of votes in both Houses thanks to bribery and threats, whereupon the Lords in the minority issued a protest that became incorporated into the pamphlet literature published by the prince's friends.[85]

Indicative of the moral flexibility of political combatants, Chesterfield and the second wave of anti-Walpole writers behind *Common Sense; or The Englishman's Journal* crowned miserliness the reigning vice. On 5 March

1737, the lead editorial quoted a book containing reflections on the various forms of avarice, how the vice contaminated individuals who colluded in it and how it could combine with other moral failings such as vanity to bring great harm. 'It is not at all to be wondered at that the World in general should agree to hate Persons of this Character, for an avaricious Man can neither be a good Father, a good Husband, a good Master, a good Servant, a good Friend, a good Prince, or a good Subject; no Virtue can enter into that Heart that is once possessed by Avarice; nay, what shews Avarice in the most odious Light is, that avaricious People are not only hated by others, but they hate one another.' Lest it be thought that this hatred would prevent an avaricious prince or minister from hurting subjects, the piece warned that they had subtle methods of encroaching on liberties. In contrast, Queen Elizabeth, 'personally frugal and publicly generous at the same time', did not hoard money or have ministers versed in the tricks of stockjobbers. On 2 April, in decrying ministers' raids on the sinking fund and suggesting that the king could easily invest £300,000 to £400,000 of the civil list in the fund to help reduce taxes, *Common Sense* noted that hoarding away such sums would hurt trade and further impoverish the poor. It also speculated on the damage that would ensue should an avaricious prince who had lost the affections of his people send hoarded specie to a foreign bank and leave Britain with paper, adding ambiguously: 'I know what I shall be told, that his present Majesty's known Contempt of Money, is Security enough against all these Fears; I shall agree with all that can be said of the Generosity of both their Majesties.' The paper kept up its criticism of George II's bloated civil list and, when convenient, decried the luxuries of the rich.[86] On 25 March 1738, it congratulated the prince for not adding to the people's tax burdens.

By the time Frederick's grandchildren reached marriageable age, the system of public credit had gained in complexity. Britain had raised funds for three major wars, lost the American colonies and, in spite of all the dire predictions, eluded bankruptcy. Nevertheless, anxiety about the national debt persisted.[87] The intergenerational conflict within the royal family continued but with a new dynamic. In contrast to his grandfather, George III appeared devoted to his children. Yet beneath the façade of the benevolent paterfamilias lurked the same or an even a greater impulse to control them. The extremes of George III's parsimony and his sons' profligacy, combined with the fickleness of political alliances, made attitudes towards royal spending even more fraught with contradictions.

The nuptials of George's favourite, Frederick, Duke of York, with Princess Frederica of Prussia took place in 1791, between the king's jubilant recovery and the commencement of war with revolutionary France, so the press could celebrate the magnificence of the occasion in a relatively untroubled economy. When the marriage negotiations and first wedding ceremony took place in Berlin in the spring, *The Times* made no secret of the need for settling the duke's debts and persisted with strong hints that he should give up the faro table, tennis and horseracing, particularly considering that his new duchess abhorred gambling. It told an anecdote of her enquiring into the expense of the English turf and receiving the reply from an unnamed courtier that it consumed more in a day than would give bread to ten thousand people in a year.[88] With mistaken optimism, Isaac Cruikshank's print has the duke shamed into penitence by a loving wife offering her jewels to pay off his debts (fig. 12).[89] At the time of the English wedding ceremony in the autumn, *The Times* reported that Frederica had a settlement of only £13,000, a bequest from her grandfather, but for the occasion the king ordered a profusion of jewels and clothes, with the latter requiring alterations to suit English taste. The *Morning Post* declared that the event set the season's fashions and noted the influence of the prince of Wales as well as his order of a £9,000 diamond stomacher for his new sister-in-law.[90] Visual satirists seized upon rumours that the new duchess had brought £300,000 with her, and represented the royal family and the duke's creditors grasping at the incoming moneybags and the queen offering the duchess her cheap trinkets in exchange for the hard cash.[91] News of the duchess's preference for flat heels had shoemakers scrambling to accommodate female courtiers. Cruikshank caricatured fashion's slavishness with tonish ladies trying to fit into the duchess's dress and shoes. Meanwhile, the notorious gamester Lady Archer is shown unsuccessfully trying to inveigle the diminutive duchess into a dice game (fig. 13).[92] Concurrently, the papers either observed, or projected upon her, her awestruck reactions to court spectacle as well as casting her as the representative foreign observer to British greatness as she underwent the process of becoming a trendsetting member of the royal family, which gave her dichotomous identities on top of her moral role as vanquisher of chance.[93]

Accounts of the prince of Wales's marriage exhibited even more contradictions and strain in a year of wartime privations and harvest failure alongside the debate over who would pay his £630,000 in debts. Traditional conceptions of royal munificence did not sit well with the need for princely retrenchments. Ironically, one of the few grand efforts that George II had made for an extravagant show in London would be used to reflect badly on his grandson. Regarding the readying of the Chapel Royal, *The Times*

observed that the exiled stadtholder and his family would be accommo-
dated in a private closet normally used by foreign ministers and a new box
by the altar would be fitted up for the royal family. It lamented that the
chapel's size did not make for a grand appearance: 'It will fall far short of
what took place at the marriage of the Prince and Princess of ORANGE,
which was performed in the German [formerly the French] Chapel
and for which very magnificent preparations were made.' The *Morning
Chronicle* carried the same story the following day.[94] The ultra-loyalist *Sun*
could take pleasure in the exquisite wines on order (Tokay d'Espagna at
twenty-four guineas per dozen) and the elegant preparations that 'do
honour to the taste and liberality of the Prince' but would only say that the
princess's wedding dress and jewels were 'superb beyond description',
avoiding the usual thrilling intakes of breath over the monetary value of
adornments and gifts.[95] The opposition papers batted around rumours
regarding the prince's purchase of Madame du Barry's jewels as well as a
£15,000 or £30,000 headdress for the princess: sums, some observed, that
could be better applied in relieving the starving poor. In response, *The
Times* took special note of a superb cornet of diamonds made for the princess to wear on the occasion and afterwards be kept in the Tower. The
paper cryptically described her dress as 'the most costly that could be
made', which, given the controversy over the prince's spending, could have
implied that it came within budget rather than that it could not have been
more sumptuous.[96] To diffuse the ill will of the debt debate, ministerial
and loyalist papers expressed relief regarding the new unity within the
royal family, a development they suggested was worth celebrating with
some indulgence after the Regency Crisis had exposed the country to
instability and the rise of Jacobinism had brought new dangers.

Economic conditions only worsened by the time of the princess royal's
betrothal two years later, but the press could hardly take issue with this
captive of the court, innocent of scandal and debt, who wore muslin, not
French silk, which she decorated herself.[97] Yet discrepancies surfaced
regarding the precise amount of her settlement, which at £80,000 must
have seemed profligate in the current economic circumstances. As detailed
in the last chapter, caricatures of the wedding procession have Pitt bearing
a moneybag inscribed with that sum (fig. 9). The *Morning Chronicle*,
which enjoyed berating *The Times* for elevating Pitt at the expense of the
king, observed ingenuously: 'A Courtly Print chose yesterday a very
singular topic for the adulation of the King on the occasion of the nuptials
of the PRINCESS ROYAL. Referring to the marriage of the daughter of

KING JAMES I—the common ancestor of the present bride-groom and bride, the writer says with a sneer, that King James, though his private coffers were low, *paid* his daughter's *portion* out of *his own pocket*; whereas his present Majesty who is a pattern of laudable oeconomy, successfully *transfers* the payment to the *people!*'[98] The opposition press also pounced on *The Times* for representing the prince of Württemberg's tour of the country (undertaken as the palace scrambled to finish its preparations) as properly providing him with a view of England's thriving manufactures, business institutions and prosperity. It pointed out that he was two years late for such an exhibition and instead had him witnessing mutinous fleets, declining trade and the death of public credit.[99] These criticisms would undoubtedly have been much stronger had observers not had personal sympathy for the princess.

Everyone was aware that the king, not just his sons, had been running up debts. Sometimes the papers made an issue of this, whereas at other times they found it prudent to forget the bleak economic picture. Back in 6 February 1796, while reporting on ministers floating new loans, the *Morning Chronicle* had observed that it would not be surprised to hear of a request to pay off arrears in the civil list. Reminiscent of the anti-Walpole era, it asserted that money that should have been applied to servants' salaries and tradesmen's bills had been diverted to emigrants and expeditions to the French coast. As we saw in Chapter 4, the press was happy to facilitate the royal family sharing with its subjects the touching moments of the princess royal's wedding and departure. After its snide comments about the dismal economy at the time of the nuptials, the *Morning Post* on 15 May 1797 turned around and gave a rapturous description of the entire royal family out in carriages, making a grand appearance with numerous footmen and outriders: a beautiful sight, it noted, enjoyed by a great number of spectators in the fine weather on a market day. Money spent visibly by the royal family, particularly when it stimulated domestic commerce, was preferable to sums channelled into clandestine political intrigues.

Royal birthdays in the later 1790s, however, provided fodder for opponents of the war and of the Pitt administration as the numbers in attendance decreased and most gentlemen who did attend appeared in military uniform. The *Morning Chronicle* declared on 19 January 1797: 'These are not times of the indulgence of magnificent expence.' On the same date in 1798, the paper appeared to reverse its position by lamenting that for the past several years the court had not been as crowded or brilliant as was warranted for the queen's birthday, to the detriment of all classes dependent on the luxuries of fashion. *The Times* that day assured its readers that the thin crowd was due to a quarter of the usual attendees being at Bath, 'which was never known to be so full of gay company', as a consequence of parliament not sitting. The government-sponsored *Sun* chose to focus on the presentation of forty scholars from Christ's Hospital patronized by the king: 'They had their new cloathing, and bore in their hands the several emblems of their Academical Studies. HIS MAJESTY received them graciously, and ordered the usual benefactions.' The newly radicalized *Morning Post and Gazetteer* (no longer '*Fashionable World*') was having none of it: 'as it was a mere day of ceremony, the appearance of yesterday will convince the Royal FAMILY how fruitless it is to attempt to draw forth grandeur and gaiety at a season when poverty and dejection prevail'. The paper explained that the poor showing was not due to the unpopularity of the queen, but rather to high taxes and the unfortunate state of affairs brought on by a 'corrupt and desperate Administration'. Nevertheless, its account of the queen's birthday got swept up in the occasion and it evaluated critically individual performances on the dance floor, including those by Prince William, who seemed to think himself the Adonis of the room, and by Princess Elizabeth, who ignored her sisters' reproofs that her garter had come down and finished her dance. Similarly, on the king's next birthday, *The Times* carped about the prince of Wales's absence, the thinness of the company, the 'indolence of the young of fashion' who did not participate in the minuet, and the haste with which servants snuffed the candles after the king and queen had departed. *The Times* and the *Morning Chronicle* had on occasion in the early 1790s complained about the old-fashioned court dress and the over-crowding and heat in the too-small space inhibiting dancers and detracting from the splendour. To now level criticisms about breaches of decorum and sparse attendance in wartime showed the papers torn between seasonable retrenchments and a desire for grand appearances at court.[100]

Pitt's voluntary contributions scheme of 1798 brought George III's income and expenditure under closer scrutiny. The awkward question of whether the king would lead by example brought to the fore the odd position in which the civil list and its tendency towards indebtedness placed him. Cruikshank published a print on 16 January showing Dundas and Pitt in cahoots, with the former sounding the invasion alarm next to a subscription book revealing the funds going to places and pensions. The king, just visible in profile behind an open door, protests: 'cant afford it I tell you cant afford it, always some new fangled nonsense or another, I wish you would let us be at Peace and Quietness'. At the door, decorated with scenes from British military defeats, a man clutching petitions from the boroughs, signifiying the protests against war and taxation, offers to prick and bleed him again while Pitt shushes him and whispers that he should come back later (fig. 14).[101] The newspapers' war of words illustrates how they fancied themselves to be both moral arbiters and the clarions of public opinion. The day after Cruikshank's print appeared, the *Morning Post* announced that the books left at the banks to receive military subscriptions remained empty: 'Some persons assert that it is owing to the reluctance of *one certain individual,* not to subscribe a farthing. They say that every means have been used to induce him to come forward but without effect: hints privately and personally, hints publicly in the newspapers; squibs and hints of all sorts have been given; *but he is determined not to take the hint.'* The following day the paper asserted the unconstitutionality of supposing the king possessed any money other than his annual allowance from the people. On the 24th, it attacked *The Times* for what it called 'malignant insinuations', which it quoted extensively and thus helped to spread: 'The agents of the ministerial junto shew they can calumniate the Sovereign as readily as they can traduce Mr Fox, whenever he declines concurring in their schemes of avarice and ambition.' The *Morning Post* asserted that *The Times* treated the king as if he were a Jacobin and observed the offending paragraphs did not appear in the *True Briton* because the Treasury controlled that paper directly. How, it inquired, could the king fund the war when the civil list was five quarters in arrears?

Within a few days news had spread that George had contributed £20,000 out of the Privy Purse, but the controversy did not end. *The Times* felt it incumbent to explain that the £65,000 Privy Purse represented a small portion of the civil list, which the king received in monthly instalments from the Exchequer 'and out of which he is known to pay many benevolent gratuities'. The paper asserted that his contribution constituted a third of his disposable annual income, a suspicious mathematical error given the *Morning Post*'s allegations. The *Sun* put the Privy Purse at £60,000 and explained that the rest of the civil-list expenditure had been appropriated by law to support public service. While this paper discounted rumours that the king had other sources of income, *The Times* made a less convincing disclaimer: 'In respect to the reports in general circulation of the KING's wealth in the English or Foreign Funds, we must plead ignorance; though we have been assured from the most respectable quarters, that such reports are destitute of foundation.' The *Morning Post* rejoined that *The Times* had given the impression that its libels had extorted the royal contribution and 'precluded his MAJESTY from the gracious appearance of paternal Benevolence'. The paper had placed the king in a situation in which he could not subscribe with dignity or decline without the odium of parsimony and insensitivity to public need.[102] Although clearly a bit of opposition posturing to embarrass the Pitt administration, this damned-if-he-did-damned-if-he-didn't position nonetheless captured the predicament in which the whole royal family often found itself in relation to spending.

The court mirrored the various anxieties about money that came with the growing wealth of the commercial classes, broader access to finery and imagined spread of aristocratic vice trumpeted in popular literature.[103] These concerns intermingled with suspicions born of partisan political interests. Dutiful, frugal and pious Queen Charlotte had her public image compromised by a love of gemstones and pearls. Whereas Queen Caroline had processed to George II's coronation adorned in brilliants loaned by jewellers from one end of town and by ladies of quality from the other, Charlotte had arrived in London with an impressive array of her own which was immediately augmented by her bridegroom. The queen's jewels attracted comment on royal birthdays, either celebrated as a mark of British brilliance or castigated as an unseemly display in hard economic times. After the lamentations over poor appearances at court in 1798, for the king's birthday in 1799 both ministerial and opposition papers gushed that the diamond ensembles on the queen and the princess of Wales surpassed anything ever seen before.[104] At the same time, the collection of costly gems exacerbated George and Charlotte's reputation as hoarders, particularly as this form of wealth had become associated with morally suspect fortunes brought back from India. When the queen wore a profusion of jewels on celebratory occasions, it made some people wonder how many more had been secreted away. Charlotte's acceptance of gifts from nawabs presented by East India Company officials in the 1780s gave critics of the government the opportunity to speculate on the link between the palace and corrupt practices in the colonies. This idea gained traction in the early stages of the trial of Warren Hastings. Remarks on the queen's attraction to brilliants continued to be a way of keeping alive rumours of hoarded riches conveyed to Hanover. In 1794, for example, the *Morning Post* sniped: 'Lady MANNERS wore jewels at the last Birth-day Ball, which cost £5000 and belonged formerly to the Queen of France. It was observed, that our most gracious QUEEN and Madame SCHWELLENBERG, cast a very feeling look at these precious ornaments.'[105] Comments such as this could not but feed worries about riches funnelled into the 'Secret Service' funds.

Gambling became another ethically ambiguous area for the monarchy as the moral climate underwent its inevitable dialectical shifts. The first two Georges hosted Twelfth Night galas that featured Hazard, a game of chance played with dice, but with royal winnings conspicuously donated to various charitable causes. Newspapers accordingly celebrated the sparkling company as they listed wins, losses and beneficiaries, and gave accounts of the spectators present.[106] George and Charlotte, however, dispensed with this custom in their efforts to elevate the moral tone at court. Not surprisingly, games of chance proliferated outside the palace and charges of hypocrisy mounted. At the end of 1796, as it reported the series of raids on gaming houses in poorer neighbourhoods, the radical *Telegraph* pointed out that, in contrast, the faro banks in elegant residences carried on unmolested although all venues had the same potential for bringing young men to ruin. In its characteristic sardonic tone, the *Morning Post* a few years earlier had declared that it would be 'too great an insult' to compare the queen's sixpenny whist to the routs of female gamblers.[107]

More seriously, the whole British government stood morally compromised by its reliance on public lotteries to raise revenue. The first of these had taken place, in spite of a reluctant populace, during Elizabeth's reign to finance the repair of havens and harbours.[108] Inevitably, whenever a bill concerning lotteries came before the House, at least one member felt compelled to decry the whole system of government-sponsored gambling. The ethical ambiguity inherent in the connection between stockjobbing and games of chance came to the fore in the May 1733 debate over a motion for a million-pound lottery to compensate investors defrauded by the Charitable Corporation, an investment established to raise funds for the relief of the industrious poor. Some MPs objected to protecting speculators in stock, who they thought should be treated like any other gamester. Others pointed to the injustice of innocent wives and daughters suffering in consequence of the seductiveness of the scheme. George Heathcote raised a fundamental moral question: had the spirit of charity reached such a low ebb as to necessitate lotteries? In answer, Sir William Wyndham gave substance to the *Telegraph*'s later suspicion that a double standard regarding gambling existed along class lines: 'Every lottery, public or private, is a public nuisance, because it makes a great many poor unthinking people ruin themselves by venturing more money in that way than their circumstances can admit of; and as all lotteries are a sort of gaming-tables, they give great encouragement to idleness and extravagance, by buoying up weak people with the hopes of getting riches in another way than by industry and frugality, which is the only way of getting riches that ought to be encouraged by a wise people.' Notwithstanding the voicing of such scruples, a majority agreed to a £500,000 lottery.[109]

The monarchy could not but be swept up in consumer culture and the profitable vices of London life. By the 1790s, newspaper accounts of royal birthdays not only performed an assessment of the participants' richness of dress and adornments, but also measured the splendour of the buildings that had been decorated and illuminated, including those of the royal family's tradesmen and the gaming houses. The papers also praised royal patronage, most notably when it saved Birmingham manufacturers from ruin by rejecting the French fad of shoelaces and helping to bring back into fashion buckles and ornamental metal buttons as well as promoting newly styled shoe latchets.[110] Royal involvement in commerce manifested more often in other ways. Andrew C. Thompson argues that the accidents that marred George II's grand celebration of the 1749 Peace of Aachen in Green Park, in contrast to the success and profitability of the rehearsal of Handel's music at Vauxhall Gardens five days earlier, did not necessarily signify an eclipse of the court by the London commercial world given the large audience that the official ceremony attracted. Furthermore, the court commemorated the peace with other activities as well, elements of which saw replication in the provinces. In support of the same point, Hannah Smith has detailed how the first two Georges inspired commissions of loyalist art, with portraits reproduced in engravings and commemorative pottery for wider consumption.[111] In the 1760s, Josiah Wedgewood began his lucrative marketing campaign by presenting Queen Charlotte first with a dazzling gold and green tea set, and then a creamware dinner service that she permitted him to christen 'Queen's Ware', which imparted a commercially favourable aura of exclusivity. He continued to design crockery for the queen and prominent aristocrats and gentry, first displayed in his showrooms and then reproduced for eager buyers.[112]

Although the court no longer dominated patronage, it still had considerable market cachet. As Craig Muldrew has demonstrated, 'contractually negotiated credit relationships made all over the social scale' created bonds of obligation and trust across class lines.[113] Participation in the consumer economy gave the appearance that the royal family shared in these bonds but such involvement also exposed it to fashion's moral dangers. The consequences would be most visible in the dilemmas faced by those on the perimeter of political power.

CHAPTER SIX

Views from the Peripheries of the Political World

The importance that politicians and journalists gave to personal character, when mixed with enduring court traditions, the practical demands of party organization and the pressures of changing cultural trends, produced moral inconsistencies and paradoxes. The hereditary succession kept familial duty at a premium and the monarchy's unremitting symbolic value preserved the need to maintain variable degrees of splendour in the palace. Yet the royal family had to adapt to changing societal attitudes and economic conditions that called into question the rectitude of strong paternal power and the value of luxurious display. The idealization of domestic fidelity and oeconomy also encroached upon a political milieu accustomed to leaving wives and children in the country while party allies pursued masculine conviviality in London. The nature of court life, with its rivalries and intrigues, unwittingly encouraged personally competitive party and extra-parliamentary political activities that rendered admirable, and rewarded a rakish, clubbability. In order to appreciate fully the ramifications of this meeting of continuities and changes we must next examine the perspectives of individuals close to those in power but inhabiting the peripheries of the political arena. Public and private writings of former courtiers as well as accounts of the plight of political wives document the ill effects of the personalization of politics in a constitutional monarchy. At the same time, the private observations of people who never held place but who attended court and events where politicians and royalty were present reveal the false sense of intimacy that this culture and literary fashion combined to fabricate. These writings also illustrate how impressions of personal character and individual circumstance figured in the calculation of ethical judgements.

Lady Mary Wortley Montagu, intimate of Lord Hervey and partisan of Sir Robert Walpole, contested Lord Chesterfield's conception of political acumen, which, as we have seen, deemed that the statesman needed to master his susceptibility to the fair sex along with his love of lucre. In *Common Sense; or The Englishman's Journal*, Chesterfield and his associates provocatively expounded on the corollaries to this ethos.[1] The paper's treatment of women and Walpole would, in December 1737, launch Montagu into journalism anonymously, using a male persona. The title of her paper, *The Nonsense of Common-Sense*, left no doubt as to its target.[2]

From its inception, *Common Sense* constructed a model of frivolous womanhood as a foil to the eminently rational male politician. Alluding to Queen Common-Sense from Henry Fielding's play *Pasquin*, Chesterfield, in the first issue of 5 February 1737, quipped: 'The Fair Sex in general (Queen excepted) are infinitely above plain downright Common Sense; sprightly Fancy, and shining Irregularities are their Favourites, in which despairing to satisfy, tho' desirous to please them, I have, in order to be of some Use to them, stipulated with my Stationer, that my Paper shall be of the properest Sort for pinning up their Hair; as the new *French* Fashion is very favourable to me in this Particular, I flatter myself, they will not disdain to have some Common Sense about their Heads at so easy a Rate.' In Chesterfield's worldview, women were not only incapable of comprehending rational discourse, they were also susceptible to foreign corruption. His leader of the 26th began with observations from the ancients on dress being a reflection of character, segued into an argument for women dressing appropriately to their rank and then quickly degenerated into categorizing women by appearance—the handsome, the pretty and the genteel—which became redundant once they reached a certain age, at which time they should fade from the public gaze. Chesterfield went on to identify another category of women, the ugly, who should know who they were by the absence of 'very warm Addresses and Applications' and 'who may more properly be called a Third Sex, than a Part of the Fair one, should publickly renounce all Thoughts of their Persons, and turn their Minds another Way; they should endeavour to be honest good-humour'd Gentlemen, they may amuse themselves with Field sports, and a cheerful Glass; and if they could get into parliament, I should, for my own part, have no Objection to it'. The piece also condemned effeminate men susceptible to 'the rage of foreign Fopperies, by which some considerable Sum of ready Money is annually exported out of the Kingdom for Things which ought not to be suffered to be imported even *gratis*'. As the earl supported an illegitimate son and the Frenchwoman who bore him, his remarks seem a bit hypocritical.[3]

Chesterfield wanted to confine women to the domestic realm well before the ideology of separate spheres became fully articulated in the nineteenth century.[4] In September, he resumed his ridicule of men and women who violated what he considered to be the essential character of each gender. He explained that women's vanity and weakness confined them to a limited sphere, whereas 'Man's Province is universal, and comprehends every Thing, from the Culture of the Earth, to the Government of it; Men only become Coxcombs, by assuming particular Characters for which they are particularly unfit'. In due course he made clear that he was referring to the sort of man that ladies disparaged as a 'cotquean', who 'invades a certain Female Detail, which is unquestionably their Prerogative'. He then presented examples of the different types of pretentious women, the most frivolous of all being the sort who deluded herself about her own frivolity by holding back from the general conversation and confining her whispers to some poor man of the company, to whom she condemned others of her sex for their trifling when she herself was the biggest trifler. Chesterfield referred to ancient histories that revealed their famous heroines to be hermaphrodites and posited that this would account for the masculine qualities of more recent exceptional women, most notably Elizabeth of England and Christina of Sweden. He proclaimed that every woman who overstepped the boundaries of her sex should acknowledge that she belonged to 'this Epicene species' and be listed in the parish register as a hermaphrodite so as to 'not confound Politicks, perplex Metaphysics, and darken Mysteries'.[5]

The earl could well have been thinking of Montagu. Feminist scholars have wrestled with the harsh observations regarding others of her sex that she made in various venues. As I have discussed elsewhere, she rebelled against the predominant effeminate model of womanhood, engaged in much gender play in letters, essays and poems, and had a particular affinity with intellectual man-loving men such as Hervey and the *philosophe* Francesco Algarotti.[6] Sandra Sherman argues conversely that 'Montagu's apparent anti-feminism does not reflect bouts of gender disaffection', yet characterizes her rhetorical strategy as 'a gambit, instrumental to a unisex view of politics that requires each sex to act responsibly', which suggests that Montagu at the very least had a disaffection with prevailing *constructs* of gender. Sherman perceptively notes the crucial difference between Montagu's criticisms of her own sex in *The Nonsense of Common-Sense* and in other writings, and the Restoration satires on women that they echoed: Montagu expressed confidence in every woman's ability to calculate her own self-interest in line with the greater good and to reform her ways accordingly. Montagu presented women's foibles not as a female issue but as something concerning the polity as a whole.[7] Chesterfield's essays in *Common Sense* followed the tradition of the misogynistic texts that Sherman characterizes as representing women as incorrigible. An examination of Montagu's positions in *Nonsense* juxtaposed with those in *Common Sense* further demonstrates how issues of money and sex extended beyond gender relations: they lay at the heart of the hypocrisies that characterized political culture.

Montagu's challenges to Chesterfield's pronouncements on self-adornment exposed inconsistent moral arguments reminiscent of those stemming from the royal family members' sartorial dilemmas as they dressed to maintain majestic appearances and tradition while needing to be mindful of the economic impact of their fashion choices. In his essay of 26 February referred to above, observing dress to be the main preoccupation of the fair, Chesterfield declared:

> I am far from objecting to the Magnificence of Apparel, in those whose Rank and Fortune justify and allow it; on the contrary, it is a useful Piece of Luxury, by which the Poor and the Industrious are enabled to live, at the Expence of the Rich and the Idle. I would no more have a Woman of Quality dress'd in Doggerel, than a Farmer's Wife in Heroicks. But I do hereby notify to the profuse Wives of Industrious Tradesmen, and honest Yeomen, that all they get by dressing above themselves is the Envy and Hatred of their Inferiors and their Equals, with the Contempt and Ridicule of their Superiors.

This placed him in the middle ground of the luxury debate: believing that the elite's magnificence aided the poor, but not going as far as Mandeville in seeing social emulation as a spur to innovation and industry.[8] Yet, when Queen Caroline died that November, Chesterfield wrote to one of his collaborators in *Common Sense*: 'Pray what do those peers, who are neither paid for voting nor mourning, intend to do with regard to this silly Order of Council for putting coaches and servants in mourning?' He deemed it 'indecent to comply' after so many deserving this mark of reverence had not received it because of the Order of 1728 that cut back on public mourning due to its detriment to silk manufacturers. He put off deciding on compliance until he returned to London, which he claimed to be anxious to do in order to escape the regimen at Bath. Nonetheless, he remained there, professedly for his wife's health, where he fulminated further against the order, which he compared to 'an *arrêt de par le Roi* in France to overturn all the rights of blood, friendship, and regard, for any but the sacred persons of the Royal Family, to whom alone to be sure, they are due, but here, in my opinion, it is *yet* a meanness to do it [. . . .] I am sorry it did not occur to my Lord President to propose the Deification of her late Majesty, and that the bishops should be ordered to perform the ceremony of her apotheosis in the true pagan manner.'[9] As Chesterfield resented the queen for her role in promoting Walpole's long tenure, the extra trouble and expense caused by her death added personal insult to political injury.

Montagu showcased the damage that such reasoning wrought. The first issue of *Nonsense*, published on 16 December 1737, addressed the protests against the expanded mourning regulations. Adopting a male guise, Montagu extolled the practical benefits of supporting domestic woollen manufacturers and claimed that the regulations brought relief to the poor, 'reduced now to a very low Ebb, by the Luxury and ill Taste of the Rich, and the fantastic Mimickry of our Ladies, who are so accustomed to shiver in Silks, that they exclaim at the Hardships of Warmth and Decency'. She castigated the hypocrisy of Chesterfield and his ilk when they argued that their luxuries benefited the economy and the poor, only then to complain when these superfluities incurred additional tariffs: 'No Man is compelled to keep an Equipage; and if there be any *Peer* that cannot *honestly* afford to pay for it, I think he may *honourably* discharge it.' Montagu further shamed those who grumbled over an expense they could easily afford by detailing the oppression suffered by cloth workers at the hands of master tradesmen.[10]

In the next issue of her paper, Montagu connected sartorial ethics to the larger issue of public finance and showed that her professed favouring of morals over politics was not mere Addisonian posturing.[11] In addition to her advocacy of woollen manufacturers, her defence of Sir John Bernard's scheme for cutting the interest on the public funds to 3 per cent, which had been defeated months before, in March, represented a rare instance in which she and her husband, a stalwart foe of Walpole since 1719, agreed on political issues, albeit for different reasons. Other Walpole partisans found merit in Bernard's bill, which tended to attract the support of the landed and resistance from moneyed interests. Each side of the debate presented a different picture of investors and beneficiaries. Aside from disputing Bernard's claims that the measure would reduce taxes and stimulate trade, the pro-Walpole newspapers had pointed out at the time how detrimental a lower return would be to widows and orphans who lived on government securities and to those who would be drawn into luxury and extravagance by borrowing money more cheaply.[12] The *Common Sense* of 25 February 1738 would revive the moribund issue of 3 per cent interest in order to remind retail traders that they depended more on landed gentlemen than people who lived upon the funds. Reducing the interest rate, the paper declared, would allow the lowering of taxes on basics such as soap and candles while creditors would still have enough for necessities without being tempted to 'lay out so much Money in debauching the Wives and Daughters of their industrious Neighbours; in Drunkenness, Pampering, and Gluttony; in Plays, Operas, and Masquerades; or in French Wine, fine Heyssom Tea, Quadrille, and the like Vices and Extravagancies'. *Nonsense* two months before had decried such luxury too—but placed its corrupting influence higher up the social ladder and within ladies' power to stop.

Montagu scoffed at the spectre raised by her husband's side in the debate of shopkeepers investing in the stocks to raise dowries designed to turn their daughters into gentlewomen instead of having them pursue an honest trade that would contribute to national prosperity. The real objects of concern, she averred, were the 'many Ladies of high Birth with the small Fortunes of 5 or £6000 and how can they live upon 2 or 3 *per Cent?*' Montagu answered: 'Very easily: Very agreeably; if they can abandon *Quadrille* and *fine Cloaths*.' She observed that during the current winter, when ladies had been restricted to stuffs and linen, they had enjoyed as many conquests as 'when they shined in *Silks* and *Laces*'.[13] She argued that the greatest beauties had the power to set the fashion: the plainest dress would be considered the most genteel if they wore it. In Chesterfield's worldview, this position would be attributed to the disappointments of a woman who had lost her youth and once-celebrated beauty: back in 1715, Montagu's arresting dress had drawn the admiration of the future George II, to the temporary ire of his consort. Yet her rejection of silks and laces came prior to her loss of face by smallpox, and well before turning a certain age. Temperamentally unsuited to a courtier's life, Montagu did not for long aspire to making a grand appearance at drawing rooms and card parties. She preferred conversation and collaboration with the literary set and, accordingly, penned satirical poems about court society.[14]

In *Nonsense*, Montagu kept her critical eye on Chesterfield's milieu and its self-delusions, which she saw as detrimental to society at large. The fourth number, issued on 10 January 1738 and excerpted in the *London Magazine* that month, voiced approval of monarchs and great ministers having levees to transact their vast range of business efficiently and give access to persons outside their circle who wished to present petitions. Unfortunately, levees had become 'a good Custom turned to a ridiculous Use by Vanity or Ostentation'. Nowadays, Montagu lamented, 'every Creature that has got a great Title, or a great Estate, must have a Levee, whether he has any Business or no; and many who have *great* Titles with *small* Estates have Levees. Not because they have *Business*, but because they have *Creditors*.' Moreover, 'at our modern Levees few but Favourites appear, and most of them come there only to shew their Impudence and Assiduity' by pushing aside modest men of knowledge and virtue who are not members of their set. Even the levees of truly great men had been turned into a useless farce this way. She bade the great 'to take particular Care to make choice of Men of Merit and Character' as their companions and be wary of men who importuned, flattered and courted.[15]

In the sixth number, issued on 24 January 1738, which the *London Magazine* reprinted in full this time, Montagu explained how male vanity spawned misogyny and misery. She began by calling out the *Common Sense* of the 14th for recommending that ladies choose opera over drama to avoid taxing their minds and inflaming their imaginations. In her male guise, she declared: 'Amongst the most universal Errors, I reckon that of treating the weaker Sex with a Contempt which has a very bad Influence on their Conduct. How many of them think it Excuse enough to say, they are Women, to indulge any Folly that comes into their Heads?' Montagu blamed such ignorant notions on the predominance of collegian authors who had little experience or knowledge of the fair sex. Their ridicule or declamations then found an eager audience in coffeehouses, where nine out of ten men blamed women for their disappointments:

> Perhaps his Sister's Fortunes are to turn away with the Money that would be better bestowed at the Groom-Porter's; or an old Mother, good for nothing, keeps a Jointure from a hopeful Son, that wants to make a Settlement on his Mistress; or a handsome young Fellow is plagued with a Wife, that will remain alive, to hinder his running away with a great Fortune, having two or three of them in love with him [. . . .] How many pretty Gentlemen have been unmercifully jilted by pert Hussies, after having curtsied to them at *half a Dozen Operas*; nay permitted themselves to be led out *twice:* Yet after these Encouragements, which amount very near to an Engagement, have refused to read their *Billets-Doux*, and perhaps married other men under their Noses.

Yet, the essayist reasoned, prose and verse scorning women as irrational, ornamental creatures only perpetuated the bad behaviour of which men complained by pronouncing women incapable of change. This view also libelled God's plan of creating woman as man's helpmeet. If Eve in her inexperience 'hearkened to the persuasions of an impertinent Dangler', it must be remembered that 'he succeeded by persuading her that she was not so wise as she should be'. Men brought calamity on themselves by denying women reason. In a subsequent issue of *Nonsense*, Montagu painted a dark picture of the ruling elite enslaved by pride, deceived by flattery, maligned by envy, deprived of real friendship, vulnerable to defamation, limited to the imaginary happiness of wealth, weakened by luxury, sickened by excess, further robbed of health by doctors, apothecaries and surgeons hungry for fees, and, in the end, having their fortunes squandered by foolish, ungrateful children.[16] She had experienced most of these depredations first-hand.

Montagu, however, pushed back against the limitations that court society imposed. She ceased writing *The Nonsense of Common-Sense* in mid-March as she shifted her efforts to escaping England, recklessly pursuing Algarotti and more soberly cultivating Henrietta Louisa Fermor, Countess of Pomfret, one of the ladies of the bedchamber pensioned off after the death of Queen Caroline. In October, Montagu observed Chesterfield again at Bath missing the royal birthday and gloated to her new friend:

> it must be disagreeable to play an under-part in a second-rate theatre. To me that have always been an humble spectator, it appears odd to see so few desirous to quit the stage, though time and infirmities have disabled them from making a tolerable figure there. Our drama is at present carried on by such whimsical management, I am half inclined to think we shall shortly have no plays at all. I begin to be of opinion that the new northern actress has very good sense; she hardly appears at all, and by that conduct almost wears out the disapprobation of the publick.[17]

Her veiled reference in this context to George II's mistress, Madame Wallmoden, sensibly keeping a low profile since her arrival in London, encapsulates Montagu's seeming hypocrisy. She castigated women who became involved publicly in controversies and professed her own indifference to politics while expressing strong political opinions as well as trying to participate in public debate behind the scenes.[18] By couching these opinions in moral terms, she voiced her disillusionment with, and rejection of, politics as currently practised. In the same way that she refused to live within an idea of womanhood that she considered demeaning, she sought to position herself above the knavery, coarseness and malice she saw degrading public discourse.[19]

Admittedly, although Montagu found fault with others for their crudeness and spite, she did once run with the satirists and continued to exercise her wit. Pilloried in print after her friendship with Alexander Pope soured, Montagu's damaged reputation constrained her intolerably and contributed to her decision to go abroad. When she reached Venice, she wrote to Lady Pomfret (now living on the Continent with her family to accommodate their reduced income) extolling the liberty and stimulating company she enjoyed there in contrast to London: 'it is so much the established fashion for every body to live their own way, that nothing is more ridiculous than censuring the actions of another'. The absence of a court, she suggested, allowed variety in conversation and a happier society: 'Here are foreign ministers from all parts of the world, who, as they have no court to employ their hours, are overjoyed to enter into commerce with any stranger of distinction. As I am the only lady here at present, I can assure you I am courted, as if I was the only one in the world.' This sentiment only intensified over time. While inveigling her to visit, Montagu told Pomfret she suspected that 'Venice is more agreeable than Florence, as freedom is more eligible than slavery; and I have an insuperable aversion to courts, or the shadows of them, be they in what shapes they will'.[20] Decades later, when acknowledging to a new correspondent her pleasure at her daughter's happiness at court, Montagu had to add that she herself 'could never endure with tolerable patience the austerities of a court life'. Indeed, Montagu declared, she would rather belong to an order of ascetic medieval nuns than be lady of the bedchamber to any current European queen. She asserted that her view did not come with 'age and disappointment', but was rather a long-standing sentiment, and referred her new friend to the volume of verses written in Constantinople in 1716 and published without her permission in 1720.[21]

Pomfret did not follow Montagu in extolling republicanism, but she did look back at her career as a courtier with a jaundiced eye. Concurrent to her friendship with Montagu blossoming, Pomfret drew closer to a fellow former lady of the bedchamber, Frances Seymour, Duchess of Hertford, whose reaction to viewing a bust of the late queen on the anniversary of her death suggested that the strains of her late position remained with her: 'I could not look upon it without feeling a return of that tender concern which we each experienced this time twelve months, with as much truth as any that were in her service, though possibly with more silence. The recollection was so strongly on my spirits all Sunday and Monday, that I was downright ill, and had, in imagination, much conversation with you on the subject.' Pomfret rejoined that, even without seeing the new likeness, she too had a vision of the queen and was similarly affected.[22] Pomfret confessed how Hertford had once intimidated her with her seniority because of all that had to be left unsaid at court:

> I do not grieve that our friendship did not begin sooner; since I am certain it would have excited the good-nature of a great many people, though they had not cared one farthing for either of us, to have made it their business, by a thousand lies on both sides, to inform us how dangerous a person each was to the other, and how unfit for a friend. Now, though parted, we may in peace communicate our thoughts; we may reason, reflect, and become as much acquainted with each other's hearts as we please; not but I must own that a little verbal converse, now and then, would be a great addition to one's satisfaction.

Hertford too found peace in retirement: 'I believe I shall never again desire to act more in public, unless either the people or myself alter extremely.'[23]

Hertford remained in England, and came to dread going to court. After attending a drawing room to play cards with Princess Amelia, she explained: 'when one has lived so long in the country as to become a stranger to the modes in vogue, one does not immediately enter into a taste for them; at least such is my case; and I cannot discover their charms so easily as a person of more polite genius undoubtedly would do'. Months later, she sent a more candid letter to Pomfret via an officer in the Horse Guards whom she trusted. Having gone to St James's to take leave before departing for the country, she reported: 'To shew you that I have no matters of much importance to employ my eloquence in the drawing-room, the Princess Amelia was reduced to the necessity of asking whether my jewels were new. This question arose either from want of conversation, or else to prove to me how completely she had forgotten all that related to me at the time I served the queen.'[24] In great contrast to her mother, Amelia preferred gambling and equestrian pursuits to belles-lettres. Hertford and Pomfret, like Montagu, both had an intellectual bent; much of their correspondence concerned literature, theatre and the fine arts. Also like Montagu, they resented the prejudices against female learning. Hertford sent Pomfret young Elizabeth

Carter's translations of Algarotti and observed archly: 'I am well informed that she is an admirable Greek and Latin scholar; and writes both these languages, as well as French and Italian, with great elegance. But what adds to the wonder she excites, is, that all the learning has not made her the less reasonable woman, the less dutiful daughter, or the less agreeable and faithful friend.' Pomfret expressed pride regarding Carter's genius and told Hertford of a counterpart in Italy, Laura Bassi of the University of Bologna.[25]

Nonetheless, some of the old court diffidence persisted. Hertford worried that descriptions of her garden would be dull and laughable to Pomfret as she read them amid the magnificence of Italy. Pomfret assured her: 'Is not one thought of your own more valuable than volumes of the designs, the contrivances, or even the exploits, of all the lovers, politicians, and heroes, that fill the scenes of private and of public life in our metropolis of London? And does not one kind expression from a friend, create more pleasing ideas than all the cheats that grandeur can bestow?'[26] Hertford attributed her insecurities to their former milieu: 'There is a style of thinking that the great ladies with whom you and I have been acquainted, do not always enter into; but no matter;—as you very justly observe, their good-natured representations cannot alter the real state of things; and there is an intrinsic value in home-felt peace from a sense of having acted rightly, that all the grandeur and pomp on earth cannot boast.'[27] When Princess Mary married by proxy in May 1740, Hertford decided not to attend the ceremony although she had clothes prepared. She had no curiosity, having seen such things before, and reasoned that other members of her family would make a finer show; she preferred not to contribute to, or be inconvenienced by, the crush. She did pay her respects and extend her felicities the following day, however, and, in spite of herself, like a good courtier, provided Pomfret with a detailed audit of the jewels sent by Friedrich of Hessen-Kassel and other brilliants that Princess Mary had received.[28]

The strength of the bonds formed by common experiences at court prevailed in all three lives, in spite of their different states of mind. Pomfret shared Montagu's writings with Hertford and the two became friends by proxy in spite of one melancholy poem provoking Hertford to advise that Montagu look more to scripture than to Tully.[29] Unlike her friends, Montagu felt unable to escape the accidents of her destiny and professed doubt in the existence of free will.[30] During carnival in Venice she noted to Pomfret the irony of being 'seated by a sovereign prince, after travelling a thousand miles to establish myself in the bosom of a republic, with a design to lose all memory of kings and courts'. She likened this turn of fate to her innocent friendship with an obscure girl unwittingly drawing her into political turmoil, a reference to the speculations regarding the part she had played in Maria Skerrett's affair with, and marriage to, Sir Robert Walpole.[31] Pomfret, on the other hand, did not feel as oppressed by court life but admitted that it had its dangers. After another lament to Hertford that their friendship had not begun earlier, she declared: 'Like actors in a play, in one scene we are to be pleased, in another angry: now struggling under misrepresentation and deceit; then made happy in the enjoyments of this world, or quiet in the grave, where we no more desire them. And all this appears to me very consistent with free will: for each performer may play his part well or ill.' In her next letter to Hertford she averred, however, that one had to remain on one's guard; specifically, that, born with a desire for innocent, pleasing society, she often had found herself grasping at shadows. Pomfret declared friendship to be the noblest sentiment: affection undertaken without a particular end or in quest of sensual gratification, but in itself a comfort that enriched the mind.[32] For all three, the culture of the court did not allow such disinterested affection and meeting of minds.

Although notorious for dissimulation and pretence, the moral posturing of courtiers presents a vivid picture of the slippery ethical terrain they inhabited. Sarah Churchill, Dowager Duchess of Marlborough and former courtier to Queen Anne, who had wielded more political influence in her day than had the other three combined (although she would have vociferously denied it), also looked on as a spectator during her later years.[33] She described herself wrapped in flannel and wheeled about her rooms in a chair, yet her infirm body did not dull her powers of observation or blunt her judgements as she kept John Dalrymple, Earl of Stair informed about doings at court. She took politics personally and internalized opposition rhetoric in her loathing of Walpole and his supporters, characterizing them as 'a sort of People, without any real Friendship or Truth, and mean nothing but their own Interest'.[34] Weighing in on the debate over the reduction of the interest rate, she adjudged that Walpole at first intended the bill to pass but that it had then not been drawn up properly in order to defer it to the next session of parliament and so allow major creditors to sell out. The dowager duchess claimed that the queen had a million of her own money in the fund and suspected another individual had a great deal more. Moreover, the stocks had risen upon defeat of the bill, which further enriched investors. Returning to the topic the following month,

Marlborough continued to wonder what lay behind the wish to take away a quarter of people's incomes under the pretext of reducing the national debt when it only placed more money under Walpole's control. She averred: 'I don't wonder at any thing that the King or Queen does, because they know nothing of the Truth.' Whether out of the morbidness of old age or a tendency towards revenge fantasies, her reports included conjectures on the consequences that would follow each player's death. Here she hypothesized that Walpole would continue to indulge his passions, cognizant that, being older than George and Caroline, he could well die in office, which Marlborough hoped he would do, for the sake of her family, to save them from French slavery. Four months earlier, while relaying information from one of her sources indicating that official statements about the king's health concealed the physicians' prognosis of death within a twelvemonth, she displayed an unwholesome interest in the state of his piles.[35] At court, the political could get invasively personal. Regarding a false newspaper report of Walpole's illness being fatal two years later, she remarked ruefully: 'I think 'tis though a fault to wish any body Dead; but I hope 'tis none to wish he might live to be hang'd.'[36]

Rumours of the queen's demise came to fruition first. When Marlborough learned that Caroline had a rupture rather than the stomach gout as reported, she predicted Walpole's imminent fall and snorted at all the talk about Princess Amelia being enlisted to control the king. Caroline's long-anticipated end sent her into a frenzy of speculation, which she prefaced, pro forma: 'I am nothing but an ignorant, old Woman; but I have seen a great deal of Courts.' Like her friend Lord Chesterfield, Marlborough expostulated at length about the order of mourning, trotted out her knowledge of precedent and human nature in predicting who would follow it or not, and, in discussing what her sources told her about the provisions of the will, declared that the value of the queen's jewels and other assets would never be known. Then she reached the subject that she really wanted to discuss: reports of Lord Hervey's constant presence and favour with the king. In this and subsequent letters, Marlborough vacillated between treating the prospects of Hervey's rise as an absurdity and as a real threat. Although she continued to maintain an intimacy with Hervey's father, the earl of Bristol, the only peer she claimed to have made,[37] she considered Hervey's personal character thoroughly despicable: 'He has certainly Parts, and Wit; but is the most wretched, profligate Man that ever was born, besides ridiculous: A painted face, and not a Tooth in his Head.' Moreover, she continued, six months before the king could not abide him; indeed, 'all the World, except S:ʳ Robert, abhorrs Him'. She would even prefer that Walpole continue in power although she was not 'fond of any absolute Ministers, whatever His Character may be'. Two days later she carried on in this vein, having seen someone who had dined with 'my Lord Fanny' and witnessed a postprandial summons from the king: 'I will now give you an Account of some things concerning His Character, that I believe you don't know. What I am going to say, I am sure is as true as if I had been a Transactor in it my self.' Much of this concerned the 'forward and pert' behaviour of Lady Hervey in both her manners at court and in the financial peculation started in her girlhood by her father that eventually came to benefit her husband. As for Hervey, taking the pension from Walpole involved voting against his principles when he could not avoid attending parliament by feigning sickness. Marlborough claimed that at Hervey's request she had tried to broker a deal whereby Bristol would support his son and allow him to live privately. Here she could not resist a reckless conjecture: 'I did not know at that time the Fact of his having a mind to make His Wife the King's Mistress.' Later in her epistolary narrative she admitted it was her own fancy only that 'Lady Fanny's Wife' would replace the king's mistress, and not in that capacity but only as a diversion with her wit.[38] In keeping with the political elite's mindset, Marlborough saw Hervey's character reflected in the conduct of his wife.

Marlborough tirelessly championed the cause of Frederick, Prince of Wales and saw the superiority of his court displayed by its women. She remarked that Princess Augusta spoke English better than the rest of the family and practised civility towards all, unlike the late queen, who, in spite of her understanding and goodness, said things that offended, which Marlborough blamed on trying to please her consort. She painted a bleak picture of women at court. Agreeing to intercede in a matter on Stair's behalf, the duchess warned it would be in vain: 'For whatever Great Men govern they have more of their own Friends than they can provide for. And since I was Incapable of doing any Good, Civility from a few is all that I have met with. And all that I can ever expect. For women signifie nothing unless they are the Mistress of a Prince or a first Minister. Which I would not be if I were young. And I think there are very few, if any Women, that have Understanding or Impartiality enough to serve well those they really wish to *serve*.'[39] Yet this did not apply to Skerrett's marriage to Walpole, 'Which, tho' some People are pleas'd with, I don't think it of any Consequence, but to her'.[40] In this case, however, Marlborough admitted that she approved of what little she had seen of Skerrett's behaviour and, unlike others, she could understand the match, comparing it to Louis XIV's betrothal to Madame de Maintenon. With further inconsistency, she asserted that a good wife made Walpole no less of a villain. Warming to her analogy in the next missive, she declared: 'His Wedding was Celebrated, as if He had been King of France.' She took a snobbish delight in Horatio Walpole's wife, 'daughter to my Taylor, Lumbar', having the honour of presenting the bride, 'Who is the daughter of a Clerk that sung the Psalms in a church where D:ʳ Sacheverell was'.[41] In another implicit character judgement, after Skerrett's untimely death, she announced Walpole's official recovery from grief on the basis of gossip that he had taken a twenty-five-year-old beauty into his house.[42] Marlborough had also closely monitored the progress of George II's bereavement and derided the unprecedentedly public manner in which he had had Madame Wallmoden presented in the drawing room. Hervey earned a rare accolade from the dowager duchess on this occasion by not being among the great men who participated in this impropriety by rushing to pay their respects.[43]

Having his son as well as his wife at court and an abiding hatred of Walpole, Lord Bristol maintained a virtuous retirement at Ickworth as he fretted over Hervey's ruin at the hands of false friends and Lady Bristol's meddling in elections.[44] Money and marital ties bound him. Upon his son being made Baron Hervey of Ickworth to allow him a seat in the Lords, Bristol reiterated to him:

> that one of my greatest griefs in life have been that you by marrying without a considerable portion shoud stand in need of more than I have been able to do for you, & that I by multiplicity of children, continuation of heavy taxes, & other accidents, have not had wherewithal to shew you how much readyness & pleasure I woud have allowd any share of my estate to have made you as easy & independent as I have always wishd to see you, especially as this last circumstance enables men whose minds are virtuously disposed to make much better figures out of place than those now in any, the whole world is convincd, can or will be sufferd to make.[45]

Corroborating Marlborough's observation of Hervey's strategic absences from parliament, Bristol pressed him to admit the truth: 'that you have been soundly rumpd [that is, he had had George II turn his back on him in the drawing room] for pretending you was sent for by an express from hence that I might see you before I dyed; whereas it seems it has been found out that you had only a mind by your absence at that juncture to avoid being concernd in the Scotch affair, which made his Majesty so very angry with you, that he did not speak to you for several days after you returnd to Court etc.' Bristol presented this alienation of the king's affections as proof of the 'selfish, avaricious, ungrateful temper of those to whose depreciating service you have sacrificed all your times and talents' and drew a parallel to the breach in the relations between king and prince of Wales, for which he blamed that same company.[46] Bristol's cognizance of Hervey's enmeshment with the royal family inspired frantic letters to his son upon Caroline's final illness 'most earnestly to beg of you not to sacrifice your own life by fruit- lessly watching and grieving your self to death for what cannot be amended or prevented by either'.[47] He urged his son and his daughter-in-law to draw together in order to help Hervey fill the void that the queen's death made in his life and reminisced about overcoming his grief over the deaths of his first wife and their eldest son. Bristol also took the opportunity to reiterate his offer to secure his son's independence by giving him his inheritance early.[48] Hervey took no heed. He became Lord Privy Seal in 1740, only to be ejected from court in 1742 after Walpole resigned.

Public Figures Personalized

For a completely different perspective on the early Hanoverian court, we need look no further than the next tier of attendees. Gertrude Savile, as sister of George Savile, baronet and MP, could have been presented at court but her morbid shyness, due to an embarrassing skin condition and emotional alienation from her family, prohibited what she most craved. Nonetheless, she took every opportunity to be in the royal presence at military reviews, at the opera, in the king's gardens at Richmond and at public celebrations. With her profoundly misguided romantic feelings for Chesterfield, of all men, and then Lord William Manners, MP, Savile provides an evocative view from one close to political power and yet so sequestered from influence and intrigue.[49] Miserable in her home life, she followed George II with fervent personal interest. After attending a mili- tary review in Hyde Park on 22 July 1727, she expressed delight at having seen him for the first time since he became king and immediately berated herself: 'Unhappy unaccountable Creature that I am, I have excommuni- cated myself from his presence and must not dare to see him except by accident thus, tho' seeing his Father was, and now him, woud be one of the greatest pleasures I coud have.' Dismayed at the multitudes that flocked to court, which exposed the oddity of her not following suit, she at length contemplated in anguish whether not allowing her to do so was God's punishment for her sins. Self-consciously, she extracted herself from what she called 'this digression' to reiterate her pleasure in the sight of the king and the 'general joy and sattisfaction in every Face', and concern about the ill effect that 'the Mob' with their 'noise, swety Caps and stinking breaths' had upon the king, queen, three princesses and Prince William, and observed, as if the king were her intimate, that he looked pleased but must be 'prodigiously fetegu'd'. She ended the day 'Not Happy'.[50] Later that summer, she prevailed upon her mother to take an excursion to Richmond where they had the good fortune to see the king walking with a great entourage and have him pass near. Savile imagined that he had stopped two or three times to look at their party and felt as she had with his father: 'a warmth of heart, a sort of Cordiall to my Spirits which can calm and please me when I am most out of humour and leave a tincture, a sattisfaction, upon my mind for a long time. Something tells me 'tis right, and I take a sort of pride and self-complacency in being capable of it.' In this moment of reciprocity between subject and sovereign, she noted that he too looked pleased but, 'affraid of being too perticular'; her party departed, to her pain, before he withdrew and she worried about having done wrong. She reasoned that the king might have the same capacity as Queen Elizabeth to read countenances, so 'he would see that tho' I am the rudest of Subjects, that has not paid the appearance of Duty I ought, yet that my heart is much devoted to him, and that he has not a more sensear and zealous Subject'.[51] Indeed, she even attended an opera she disliked with an aunt she hated for a glimpse of the king and queen, 'who come in much more Grandeur than the last King chose to do'.[52] Not exposed to the competitive, backbiting side of the court, Savile could romanticize the scene.

Savile's possessiveness and protectiveness of the king enjoyed the boundlessness of her imagination. She and her mother secured a window for the October coronation in August for ten guineas, which they wound up relinquishing on the eve of the ceremony at a loss of four guineas when her brother obtained seats in Westminster Hall for them. In the days beforehand, they had tried to gain access to the music rehearsals without success and fought the crowds to view the preparations to little satisfaction. Savile became cross with her mother and aunt exposing her to the added expense of viewing the gold canopy, which meant nothing to her.

On the night before the great day, she felt dread; her only motivation for going being 'the shame of not haveing seen it'. In spite of her comparatively privileged seating, Savile carped about the limited view it afforded her of her king, the frivolous elements in the festivities, missteps in the ceremony and the evil portents observed by ill-wishers. She also added to her melancholy by harping on the insufficient recognition given to George I's death.[53] In her end-of-year reckoning for 1727, she noted that the then prince and princess of Wales had honourably shed tears when they received the news, but that few public addresses had expressed due gratitude.[54] When Prince Frederick arrived from Hanover, Savile, impatient to see him, attended her least favourite play where she could only view him from afar, which nonetheless made her glow with affection.[55] She undertook the gruelling business of preparing clothes and having her hair dressed for the first time in ten months to attend Twelfth Night at court. There, she endured the mortification of having to mix socially and what she saw as the mismanagement of the ladies who accompanied her; on her own initiative, she fulfilled her objective of standing near the royal family's table for fifteen minutes. She found the prince agreeable in appearance, described with approval each member of the family, and took note of the courtiers who played Hazard. George II received more personal treatment in her diary. Divining his inner life from his appearance, she sensed that he found the custom a 'disagreeable task' and fretted that he looked tired and had aged ten years since being crowned.[56] After a cousin's bequest helped Savile make peace with her own family, she nonetheless maintained a fierce personal loyalty to the king and wrote about royalty as if they were her own relations. Her heart ached for Princess Mary trapped in a bad marriage, but was warmed by George's tender behaviour after the ungrateful Frederick died. She worried about the toll on the king after the deaths of several other members of his family within a short period of time.[57] When Chesterfield was made secretary of state after his long period of opposition, Savile thought George too forgiving and she blasted her old heartthrob at length for his gambling losses, ingratitude and treachery.[58] Changes in the ministry inevitably inspired disparaging assessments of politicians' true loyalty and service to her dear king.[59]

Observing royalty as if personally intimate with it had become commonplace by George III's reign. The most vivid examples appear in the journals of Caroline Girle Powys, a member of the upper gentry and connoisseur of material culture who made numerous tours of aristocratic estates. In contrast to Savile, she wrote in the self-satisfied tone of one 'too fortunate to live in a continual round, of *what* the polite term pleasure', took a keen interest in national events and recorded them alongside accounts of her warm, loving family, although her father had advised her to perform these exercises in separate books.[60] Intensely royalist, Powys described the universal mourning in response to the death of George II 'from a people by whom he was sincerely beloved', and observed that it was 'astonishing to see the amazing consternation, bustle and confusion an event like this quite unexpectedly made in a metropolis such as London'. She joined a party of twenty-five that paid 120 guineas for a room that afforded an excellent view of the coronation and joined the throngs to see the new sovereign go in state to the House of Lords. Years later, she made the effort 'to see what is rather a difficulty to see at all, The Queens Palace, a House altogether more worth notice than any in Town, from yᵉ variety of curiosities it contains, indeed in itself tis an excellent one, one hardly wonders Sᵗ James was quitted for this where Majesty may reside in *comfort* as well as state, at Sᵗ James, tis Impossible as it now is'.[61] She took a tour of Windsor Castle to inspect the queen's new bed and was pleased to find the castle had been spruced up since her last visit. With the pictures cleaned and new furnishings, it 'looks much more like yᵉ residence of Royalty, than it did some years ago'. Eight years later, she returned to see how the improvements had progressed and, as she had feared during her last visit, the bed's beautiful colour and design had already faded.[62]

Although concerned about the personal comfort and fitting splendour of the royal family, Powys could be critical when appearances at court did not meet her expectations. She attended the queen's birthday in 1772 and admired Charlotte's satin dress trimmed with sable, a present from the empress of Russia, but wrote of the princess of Brunswick, then visiting: 'we need to think her tho' not handsome a good *Figure*, but she is now grown so fatt and plain, that tho' cover'd with Jewels I never saw a woman that look'd more unfashionable'. After the king's recovery in 1789, Powys went to Ranelagh the night after the Spanish ambassador's celebratory fête, as everything had been left for the public to view, which gave flight to her imagination. Likely aided by accounts in the papers, she described the scene as if she had actually observed the royal family enjoying the entertainments. At an assembly at Wargrove, Powys had the opportunity to scrutinize the prince of Wales first-hand. She detailed with approval the ease and good humour with which he sat with the guests, talked to the whole company and danced with excellence, but added: 'what a pity such an accomplish'd young Man, knowing so well how to make himself admired and beloved, can be wanting in Duty to such parents as his'.

However, she predicted that in time he would realize his 'Juvenile Conduct' prejudiced his own future happiness. More sagacious regarding the potential disintegration of home decor than of princely behaviour, a decade later she would be cataloguing with disgust the disreputable company the prince brought to Bath to indulge in high-stakes gambling and dissipation.[63] For those without a first-hand view, Cruikshank imagined the scene at George's Bath lodgings as he entertained a local family: a porcine prince wastefully applies a snuffer halfway down a candle with one hand to darken the room while with the other he gropes Honor Gubbins as her sister Mary slips her a card under the table. The duke of York has put down his cards and turned to the sisters' mother, Mrs Carr, who appears to be distracting him to facilitate the cheating (fig. 15).[64]

Powys's journals also illustrate how the political arena had become one of London's entertainments. In 1788, she prolonged her stay in town into June in order to hear Richard Brinsley Sheridan's long-anticipated speech at the trial of Warren Hastings, who had come to personify every evil perpetrated by the East India Company. Sixteen months earlier, when public interest in his alleged crimes had been flagging, Sheridan's oratorical pyrotechnics in presenting the charge on the maltreatment of the Begums of Oude had revived the prosecution. Edmund Burke, its main promoter, became convinced that generating publicity would be essential to bringing justice to India, no small order considering that the trial would take place over 149 days between 13 February 1788 and 23 April 1795. Like many others, Powys had purchased a ticket to Westminster Hall for a tidy sum to hear Sheridan. Yet her pleasure in being situated 'commodiously' in one of the best front-row seats at a venue 'full of the highest Rank' turned to disappointment. She reflected:

few perhaps would be so honest to give their sentiments so Contrary to the Multitude, but indeed Mr Sheridan answered not my expectations either as to Oratory, Eloquence, or Manner: the latter totally Unpleasing as a continual Thumping upon his desk, and most vehement passion: never surly can be stiled elegance; I had indeed highly raised my Ideas and thought of being in the same pleasing Extacies as I had often experienced, from Garrick or Siddons, he spoke four hours and a quarter; we had been once before that day, when Middleton was examined who could not recollect one Thing that was asked him. The Hall was then very Thin, but on the day of Sheridan's speech the Sight was really magnificently Grand.[65]

Sheridan's dual career as dramatist and politician might have fuelled Powys's anticipation of theatrics; however, even its participants saw the trial as a grand performance. The prior February, when William Windham, one of its managers, espied the novelist and courtier Frances (Fanny) Burney in the Great Chamberlain's Box (her ticket bestowed by the queen), he climbed up to greet her, took in the view and exclaimed: 'What an assembly is this! How striking a *spectacle*! I had not seen half its splendour down there. You have it here to great advantage; you lose some of the Lords, but you gain all the Ladies. You have a very good place here.'[66] Judging by her postmortem, Powys had expected the event to provide the pomp and circumstance that she treasured in court ceremonial on top of the diversions of the playhouse.

As a reluctant courtier and someone who actually socialized with Hastings as well as many of his key antagonists, Burney's accounts of her attendance at Westminster Hall reveal the complex interplay that existed between the personal and the political in judging the character of public figures. Serving as the assistant keeper of the queen's robes from 17 July 1786 to 7 July 1791, during which time she chafed under the authority of the infamous Mrs Schwellenberg, Burney's letter-journals show her taking a firm stand against Hastings's impeachment and trial while trying to maintain civil relations with all involved. In August 1786, at tea in Mrs Schwellenberg's rooms, Colonel Stephen Digby, the queen's new vice-chamberlain, with whom Burney would have an ill-fated flirtation, lamented Marian Hastings's being associated too closely with the queen in the newspapers. Mrs Schwellenberg not only reacted strongly against any criticism of their mistress; she also spluttered and stammered in defence of her long-time friend, the former Anna Maria Apollonia von Imhoff, whose husband had given her a divorce so she could marry Hastings. One of the king's equerries unsuccessfully tried to diffuse her outrage with platitudes, which prompted Burney to declare to the company that she pitied Mrs Hastings and thought her ill-served considering that in Germany a divorce with leave to remarry indicated that no misbehaviour had taken place.[67] Notoriously prudish and largely unsympathetic to Schwellenberg, Burney based her judgement on her own impressions. As she had told her father the previous year, she liked the way Hastings spoke so unreservedly about India when asked, 'yet was never the hero of his own tale'. After an outing with the couple in May 1785, during which he had spoken frankly of his troubles, Burney declared: 'he appears to me to be one of the greatest men now living, as a public character; while, as a private one, his gentleness, candour, soft manners, and openness of disposition, make him one of the most pleasing'. She was struck with how he adored his wife, who seemed to provide recompense for all his tribulations and labours: 'How rare, but how sweet and pleasant, the sight of such unions!' A few weeks after the tempest at tea, she enjoyed an evening at the Hastings' Windsor home, describing him as 'intelligent and very informing' and her as 'lively and very pleasing'. She now pronounced Hastings 'the man most oppressed and injured of modern times'.[68]

After taking her seat at the trial a year and a half later, Burney reflected on the horror of Hastings's humiliating treatment and how ill and pale he now looked: 'I was much affected by the sight of that dreadful harass which was written on his countenance.' She worried that he would see the acquaintances she had among his enemies saluting her. 'Why will any man of principle join any party?' she lamented as she contemplated them. Trying with limited success not to meet their gazes, she studied Hastings and made further interpretations of his mien. She reasoned: 'he looked with a species of indignant contempt towards his accusers, that could not, I think, have been worn had his defence been doubtful'. Although she seemed to enjoy piquing the curiosity of the queen, who sat incognito with the four elder princesses in the duke of Newcastle's box, she fretted about the impression Hastings would receive seeing her with Windham after he came over to talk to her. She had met the statesman twice before and held him in great esteem for his good breeding, brilliant conversation and devotion to her beloved Dr Samuel Johnson in his last illness. During her lengthy exchange with Windham, Burney tried to reconcile the 'young man of fashion' who had demonstrated 'an elevated mind and character' and 'a noble way of thinking' in his care of 'an old, however dignified philosopher', one not of his political party, with the man before her who exulted in what she saw as malign cruelty.[69]

Burney's rendition of their encounter represented her politely yet doggedly questioning Windham's construction of Hastings as a monster. At the beginning of their discussion, they seemed to reach different conclusions based on the same mode of observation. As each processed the shock of the other's stunningly different perceptions of the man's appearance, they began to interrogate each other's method of judging character, further exposing the vexed relation between public and private life. In Hastings's contemptuous air, Windham saw a proud heart and profound ambition. Burney parried by asking rhetorically whether a man defending himself would better serve his cause by looking defeated. She then confessed that she came to the trial predisposed towards the defendant, whereupon Windham, visibly startled, asked her whether she had read the charges or listened to Burke's speeches. She answered in the negative to both. Had she heard Burke, Windham argued, she would see Hastings in a different light: 'There is more cruelty, more oppression, more tyranny, in that little machine, with an arrogance, a self-confidence, unexampled, unheard of.' She replied that those who knew him did not see this. Intrigued, he wished to know more, but when she described Hastings as 'so mild, so gentle, so extremely pleasing in his manners' he made sceptical interjections, forcing her to elaborate that, having met him when he had just returned from India, where he wielded unimaginable power, she had been impressed by how unassuming, diffident and simple he had been in his demeanour. When Windham vowed to convert her to his cause, Burney turned the conversation away from the trial to less controversial topics. After a short time, however, Windham fixed his eyes upon Hastings and declared his countenance unpleasant. Burney again came back with the riposte that, given the circumstances, how could he look otherwise? Windham had recourse to quoting Burke's description of Hastings looking like 'a hungry tiger, ready to howl for his prey'. The question then became at what time Hastings showed his true character. Burney argued that, on the social occasions during which he had imparted to her so much valuable information on the geography, peoples and customs of India in such an entertaining way, he had no motive for hypocrisy. Windham replied: 'there is nothing so winning as gentleness of manners'. Missing his sarcasm, Burney proceeded to the sartorial evidence: 'I was myself so entirely surprised by that mildness, that I remember carrying my admiration of it even to his dress, which was a very plain green coat', made before he went to India: in donning it again, he renounced the splendour of his station there. This inspired Windham to note that Hastings's coat now, whether purple or blue, defied the custom of prisoners wearing black, harking back to the arrogance he had read in his face. Burney's one cold comfort was that Windham 'harboured no personal rancour' against Hastings, being 'wholly ignorant of his character in private and social life'; yet she also wondered about the source of prevailing impressions of his nature as inherently vicious.[70]

In their subsequent verbal jousts at Westminster Hall, which Windham continued to initiate, he dwelled upon the power of Burke's oratory and therein Burney had her answer. While listening to one of Burke's speeches herself, she almost forgot all she knew of Hastings: 'the whirlwind of his eloquence nearly drew me into its vortex'. Windham held forth in broad terms on the nobility of vanquishing corruption in high office for the sake of 'oppressed millions' while Burney kept bringing him back to the victimization of the man at the bar. She remained hopeful that Windham had so much 'liberality and candour' that he would one day regret 'joining a party so violent as a stain to the independence of his character'. Meanwhile, she had done her homework. She informed Windham that, upon reading the late India Bill, she noticed that Windham's speech was the only one that contained no personal invective, which, she prodded him, led her to trust that he would treat Hastings in the same businesslike manner. At that point Windham jocularly accused her of trying 'to skate [him] down'; that is, he explained, use praise to make him redouble his efforts to the point of exhaustion.[71] Neither would give any ground. With gentle teasing, Windham kept trying to make Burney see the absurdity of her notion that a pleasing demeanour precluded a tyrannical heart. Her conviction respecting Hastings's innocence based on her personal observations of his behaviour in private life, although unsound empirically, did not seem all that far out of line in the context of the personalization of politics that had intensified over the century. Burke's committee, after all, had chosen to project all that was wrong with imperial policy in India upon the character of one person. Hastings's eventual acquittal showed the folly of this way of thinking and Burney's instincts to have been correct.

Burney's practice of basing her ethical judgements of public figures on her personal observations would be placed under pressure beyond Windham's quizzing. Burke presented a more daunting moral challenge. She had long revered him and had been thrilled to learn that he was a fan of her novels. Upon seeing him in person for the first time, she gushed to her sister: 'he had just the air, the manner, the appearance, I had prepared myself to look for in him, & there was an evident, a striking superiority in his demeanour, his Eye, his motions, that announced him *no common man*.'[72] Consequently, she could not presume to sway him from his misguided persecution of Hastings. Burney spent much time at the trial heartsick over Burke's misuse of his talents. When they were inadvertently thrown together at Westminster Hall, she tried to remain aloof and coldly polite to convey her disapprobation. Finding herself seated next to him at one of Mrs Crewe's dinners in 1792, she resorted to casuistry in order to allow a resumption of their former ease in one another's company. In a reversal of her mode of judging Hastings, she separated public and private character. She decided that Burke was essentially two people. She wished that her correspondents 'could meet this wonderful Man when he is easy, happy, & with people he cordially likes!—But Politics, even on his own side, must always be excluded: his irritability is so terrible on that Theme that it gives immediately to his Face the Expression of a Man who is going to defend himself from Murderers.'[73] Windham had also offered evidence that any individual could well have a dual nature and that outward appearances could be deceptive. He had been candid with her regarding his anxieties about public speaking, which she probably aggravated by brushing them aside and repeatedly expressing her desire to hear him.[74] When she finally did, Burney was shocked and dismayed by the 'unpleasing and crude quality' of his voice and lack of grace in his manner: these 'by no means seemed to belong to the elegant and high-bred character that had just quitted me'. Years later, when again assailed by the 'palpable tremor and internal struggle' displayed in his public performance, she concluded: 'I can only suppose that by nature he is extremely diffident, and by inclination equally ambitious; and if so, the conflict may last through life.'[75] More disillusionment awaited her at an elaborate public breakfast in 1792 where Burney met Marian Hastings dressed like 'an Indian Princess' and outshining the rest of the company. Stubbornly, in her account of the occasion Burney repeated her earlier judgement of her good breeding and manners, but added a regret that Mrs Hastings's vanity imparted her with 'an indiscretion so peculiarly unsuited to her situation, as to aim always at being the most conspicuous figure wherever she appears'.[76] Perhaps in small consolation, this reinforced her narrative of Hastings betrayed by all around him.

The biases that resulted from Burney's tendency towards personal impressions ruling her judgement come out in her treatment of Sheridan and Fox. Her first meeting with Sheridan and his first wife, the former Elizabeth Linley, had Burney dazzled by their charismatic good looks and apparent happiness. Sheridan's encouragement of her to turn playwright, which ultimately caused her grief—albeit not by his doing—made Burney resentful of his reminders that he awaited her manuscript. From her acquaintance with the castrato singer Pacchierotti, she also knew Sheridan to be inconsiderate to those on his payroll. When he approached her at Westminster Hall in 1788 she took umbrage at his reproaches for ignoring his advice, finding his manner unpleasantly abrupt, and she had no interest in his speeches.[77] Fox, a stranger to her, could easily be dismissed as coming nowhere near the gentlemanly, scholarly genius of Burke. She admitted: 'It may be I am prejudiced by old kindnesses of Mr. Burke, and it may be that the countenance of Mr. Fox may have turned me against him, for it struck me to have a boldness in it quite hard and callous.' Discussing the oratorical styles of the various speakers with Windham, Burney explained that while Burke's excesses seemed unaffected, Fox 'looked all good humour and negligent ease the instant before he began a speech of uninterrupted passion and vehemence, and he wore the same careless and disengaged air the very instant he had finished. A display of talents in which the inward man took so little share could have no powers of persuasion.'[78] On this occasion, Windham talked up the talents of William Pitt, his enemy, to undermine her accusations of party prejudice. She answered that a man of his liberality could never harbour such narrow-minded partisanship for long, thus demonstrating Burkean prophetic powers, as Windham would become Pitt's secretary of state for war in 1794. She did not think this a good fit for her old friend and this time incorrectly predicted that his independent spirit would not allow him to stay for long in the administration; in fact he did not desert Pitt until early 1804. Pitt did not attend the trial and when Burney finally set eyes on him at Weymouth in 1789, she wrote him off: 'his appearance is his least recommendation; it is neither noble nor expressive.'[79]

A comparison of Burney's perceptions with those of Sheridan's sister Betsy shows similar observations given very different interpretations. Predictably, hearing her brother speak at the Hastings trial in May 1789 made Betsy's pulse race and tears come to her eyes. Burke's manner, she thought, took some getting used to, but once one did it was 'impossible not to admire his flow of language and force of imagination'. She disliked Fox's voice but admired his simplicity and clarity, 'and at the same time [he was] so earnest as to force conviction'. Her personal reaction to those men reflected the reputations they had among their Whig colleagues, as discussed in Chapter 3 above. At the end of that trial day, when Burke came over to assist Sheridan's companion, she informed her sister that he 'Irishman-like insisted on the *Young Lady* as he stiled me, taking his other arm, so under the care of this Friend of the Begums I got thro' the croud'.[80] In contrast, her first encounter with Fox in 1786 in a similar crush at a theatre was more like a star-sighting: 'In the croud I had once been edged close to two immense Men one of whom spoke to me very civilly and did what he could to assist me, on coming to our seats I saw the next Box to me and discover'd my corpulent neighbours to be no other than Charles Fox and his Brother. If I had known that circumstance at the time it would have comforted me for a little additional suffocation.' During the 1784 election, she thought 'that Puppy Pitt' unpopular and that Fox had a chance 'but then 'tis great pity he games so deep and loves Women so bad'. After mixing with Fox socially, however, his gambling and womanizing ceased being a detriment; she cherished the time in his company although she could not stand the hours he and her brother kept. She loved his 'plain and unaffected' manner: 'If one did not know he was a great man, the idea one would take up would be merely that he was goodnatured and goodhumoured to the greatest degree.'[81] As for Hastings, Betsy observed from a distance the devotion he showed to his wife but, in contrast to Burney, turned it into a negative quality: 'One looks in vain for any trace of that beauty that could have induced Hastings to purchase her of her former husband.'[82] For Burney and Betsy Sheridan both, personal acquaintance influenced perceptions of character.

Lest it be thought that this was gendered behaviour, it must be observed that Thomas Coutts, the social-climbing banker to the duchess of Devonshire's set, displayed the same tendencies. Accustomed to receiving ingratiating letters from Fox, he became hostile when Pitt ignored his overtures. Also financial adviser to the countess of Chatham, he complained to her in 1791 of the difficulty he had in seeing her brother-in-law. He whined:

> Indeed, I am sorry to say I have found a marked distance and coldness from him to me for a long time, such as I have never met with from any other of my friends, and I am so very unconscious of having deserved it, that I am quite at a loss how to account for it. After my long absence I receive very uncommon attention and kindness from many of the first persons and characters of the times, not only to myself but to my young family; nor can I trace the smallest neglect from any persons besides, which perhaps make it strike me the more.

Pitt eventually condescended to visit him upon the betrothal of one of Coutts's daughters, but apparently failed to display sufficient warmth. Although Coutts did manage to make advantageous matches for his progeny through his connections, his lack of real influence over national finances still irked him. Frustrated with Pitt's foreign policy in 1794, he wrote to a friend from the country that 'walking about here solitary among wild mountains and a dismal country, oppressed with very many ailments myself, and my family depressed and ill with vexations and disappointments, I wish our Princes and Dukes saw something in the same way, as it would at least put them on their guard—and make them act with more common sense than we have seen practiced by them in our times'.[83] The personal could seem political too.

Notwithstanding his legendary aloofness, Pitt attracted admiration beyond the young men who enjoyed his cabinet dinners. Lady Stafford held him up for her son Granville Leveson-Gower to emulate before she and her husband solicited Pitt for a place for him. In 1787, she described a dinner-party dispute over Homer and wished Granville had been present, 'for Mr. Pitt, with the *greatest Diffidence*, in his Manner, shew'd how thoroughly he understood and explain'd the Lines. He was as lively and entertaining as if he had never thought of anything but being it and pleasant in company.' She made a direct connection between his behaviour in private and his sterling character as a leader in a panegyric inspired by the Regency Crisis's resolution:

> Mr. Pitt, popular as he has been for these last five Years, never was in such high Estimation as he now is. His Conduct, his Patience, his Wisdom, his Attachment to our afflicted King, his Love for his Country, his Earnestness to preserve its Rights and to prevent the Constitution being infringed, have all been so conspicuous, that he is admired and adored by all who wish well to Great Britain—indeed, he is a most wonderful Being, for with all the extraordinary Endowments of Judgement, Quickness of Apprehension, ready Wit, Cheerfulness, sound Understanding, perfect good Temper, and unassuming Manners, his Heart is full of Integrity, Truth, and Justice—it is really impossible to tell the Half of his Merits. My dearest Leveson, I hope he will be your Model—and he is so kind, so attentive a Son to his old Mother! Perhaps I may be dead and gone when you come into the World, but I hope and wish you may attach your self to Mr. Pitt, for his Principles, his Intentions are good, and I had rather you were *out of the way of* Preferment with him, than high in Office with those who have neither Religion nor Principle. Remember this, my beloved Leveson: when, never forget that, according to those with whom you associate and connect yourself, you will turn out well or ill.

Although Granville disregarded his mother's repeated cautions against connections with married women of ill repute, Pitt did become his idol—in spite of Lady Stafford risking that her son might sicken of him with her fulsome praises. She herself recognized the latter danger and tried to circumvent it with humour. In reporting a discussion that his father had had with the chancellor respecting the importance of Granville excelling in logic and mathematics at Oxford, she added: 'Mr. Pitt with his wonderful Quickness of Apprehension, with his strong Understanding, with all his Literature, and his honest upright Heart, would not have made the Figure he does had he not applied himself to Mathematicks with the greatest Assiduity. I write so gravely that, à la Mode des jeunes Gens, you will think me a great *Bore*, and wish my poor Letters in the Fire.'[84] Lady Stafford's enthusiasm for Pitt's character continued throughout her son's political career, and Granville ignored the snide comments of Lady Bessborough, the married woman of ill repute who became his mistress as his mother had dreaded. In keeping with the power of the personal in politics, after he met Fox in 1801, Bessborough crowed: 'How glad I am you liked Mr. Fox. I was sure you would, and know he would like you very much if he knew you.'[85] Nonetheless, Granville's allegiance remained with Pitt, even after the latter's resignation over Catholic emancipation.

The increase in personal detail that appeared in political reporting capitalized on the moral justifications of the time for judging character by outward appearance and shows the growing acceptance of the idea that a man's personal life reflected his suitability for public office. The press depicted the manners and exposed the private lives of notable figures, ostensibly so that interested members of the public unable to see their leaders for themselves could make an informed judgement. As the personal observations of those with a ringside seat in the political arena have demonstrated, subjectivity and self-interest significantly shaped interpretations of behaviour and expression. In addition to this, the extravagance and sexual licence that traditionally featured in royal courts collided with the new fads for domesticity and oeconomy to generate a high degree of hypocrisy in public life. Politically engaged women relegated to the sidelines by their sex such as Lady Mary Wortley Montagu and Fanny Burney tried to point out the harm that self-interested ethical posturing could produce, but to limited effect given their lack of substantive political influence. In a world filled with hypocrisy, their interests and resulting prejudices compromised them in ways that politicians were able to slough off.

The Personal Toll on Political Families

Richard Brinsley Sheridan embodied the licentious sexual ethos lurking beneath the fashionable domesticity of the high political elite, as detailed in Chapter 4. His life also dramatized that class's swashbuckling financial mores and the range of consequences that fell especially hard upon women of the family. Familial letters written in his early twenties reveal the manipulative, self-serving approach towards spending, credit, debt and personal character that he retained for the rest of his life. Playing the dutiful son by pretending to study law and forget about Elizabeth Linley after his gallant rescue of her, he grovelled to his father:

> You desired me to write to you from hence an account of what I owed. These are debts of Folly and Extravagance, some of them contracted later than they should have been, tho' to get rid of obligations of a former Date. My resolutions on this hand I can only date from the time I *left Bath*; as there is no inconvenience of a Debt which I have felt more than the necessity sometimes of adding to it. And had I staid there, while I ow'd a sixpence I believe I should have been incapable of fixing myself to new articles.

On the same day he wrote a letter to Betsy, then just fourteen, which began: 'This Letter is wholly entre nous—and your Sister if you will', and gave directions on how to pay a number of tradesmen's bills without his father finding out about some and knowing the details of others that he would include but not itemize in his account. He instructed: 'If anything else occurs I must rely on you and Lissy to do the best for me and let me know the Particulars.' Assuring Betsy he planned 'Prudence and all the Cardinal Virtues', which conveniently did not number Honesty among them, he reiterated: 'You see this is a mere letter of business for you and your Sister: never *shew* my Letters to *any* one. You may just tell my Father you have a letter from me. I shall write to Lissy next Post in a Style.'[86] When one had ambitions above one's station, some role-playing and construction of multiple personas might be required.

Against his father's wishes, Sheridan married Linley and pursued a literary career. Credit continued to be a vehicle for his self-advancement in audacious acts of both borrowing and lending, but ultimately it proved his undoing. The relations and friends that his contemporary biographer Thomas Moore interviewed thought Sheridan's financial machinations more the product of vanity and bad judgement than corrupt design.[87] Optimism, mixed with charm and effrontery, carried him a long way. Using bluff nautical imagery, he assured one Drury Lane Theatre investor in 1798: 'The Pleasure I feel in *every step* made towards *getting out of Debt*, will I know make my attention and parsimony increase with our success. When we *owe* nothing we will talk of a more careless course and letting out a Reef or two.'[88] In practice, Sheridan's optimism usually scuppered his attention as well as his parsimony, and he travelled at full sail until in ill health he could no longer pilot the ship.

While Sheridan might have affected an aristocratic nonchalance in his free style of spending, a cursory perusal of his letters reveals that his perennial robbing of Peter to pay Paul, and usually doing so at the last possible moment or too late, made money a constant preoccupation. It did not help that Drury Lane Theatre had to be rebuilt in the early 1790s or that the grand new edifice burned to the ground in early 1809. His political career too occasioned great expenditure. In soliciting the duke of Bedford's patronage for his son Tom in 1806, Sheridan reminded the noble lord of his thirty-year service to the Whig party and claimed that he had spent £20,000 of his own money in maintaining his parliamentary seat of twenty-six years.[89] His self-defence in a suit raised by Drury Lane Theatre's trustees in 1801 captures what contemporaries referred to as his vanity—what we now would call his sense of entitlement: 'It is a great disadvantage, relatively speaking, to any man, and especially to a very careless and a very sanguine man, to have possessed an uncertain and fluctuating income. That disadvantage is greatly increased, if the person so circumstanced has conceived himself to be in some degree entitled to presume, that by the exertion of his own talents, he may at pleasure increase that income—thereby becoming induced to make promises to himself which he may afterwards fail to fulfil.' He spun this into the beginnings of an adage: 'Occasional excess and frequent unpunctuality will be the natural consequence of such a situation.'[90]

Sheridan's reliance on credit in his day-to-day life, combined with his inability or unwillingness to keep track of receipts, or even to open his mail regularly, meant that he wasted much money in avoidable extravagance and duplicate payments to unscrupulous duns. If he ran out of funds while travelling he would break his journey and stay in expensive lodgings while awaiting a remittance.[91] Although Sheridan approached most aspects of his life like a gambler and had a weakness for reckless gentlemanly wagers, he had little time or inclination for roulette or cards. Nevertheless, he became involved in high-stakes gambling by proxy, turning out his pockets for ladies of the Devonshire House set (who aided his social advancement) when they played too deep, as well as for Eliza, who in eking out some compensation for his infidelities threw off her habits of thrift in pursuit of pleasure.[92] The temptations of the high life pressed in from all sides.

The conventions of credit allowed much risk-taking, while marriage settlements and family helped draw down the stakes. Sheridan's disordered balance sheets made for much suffering in the final years of his life but did not beggar his family after his death, thanks to his second father-in-law, the dean of Winchester, insisting on a marriage settlement that included a trust for his daughter, Hester Jane Ogle. The second Mrs Sheridan—younger, of grander birth and a more luxury-loving disposition—did not do well with the inconveniences of their increasingly unstable finances.[93] The opening of a letter that Sheridan wrote to the Drury Lane Theatre's treasurer in 1801 on the need to tap their friends for desperately needed revenue is reminiscent of his instructions to his sister quoted above: 'I cannot wait to explain why but tho' I am as eager as for Life not to be beat and disgraced in this business I *cannot* leave Mrs. S. to Day nor explain to her my situation.' To a political ally, he described the source of his predicament as 'my dilatory and procrastinating manner in carrying into effect anything to the advantage of my own affairs', a carelessness also connected to his excessive drinking, another source of strain in the marriage. In this letter, however, he gave a more realistic assessment of his likelihood of ever escaping from debt than he had earlier in the message to the Drury Lane investor quoted above: 'It will be the happiest Day of my Life to feel that I am in Debt to no one, or at least that I have no debt for which there is not an adequate and accepted Security.'[94] As long as the appearance of a security existed, credit could buy the finer things in life. For the Sheridans, continually moving house to evade creditors, the façade became compromised. While trying to settle Hester and their son, Charles, in Richmond Park, circa 1806, Sheridan had to intervene when his wife experienced insulting treatment there, such as her servants being denied access to the laundry to wash their shifts and to the orchard to get fruit for the boy. Likewise, in 1809, he implored his theatre's treasurer: 'The fourteen guineas to Shepperd if not paid early in the morning strips Mrs. S of her carriage and plays the devil with my domestic quiet—that therefore pray pay at any rate.'[95] The habit of 'pay[ing] at any rate' as a result of the lack of an 'adequate and accepted Security' became corrosive.

In spite of Sheridan's efforts to maintain his wife in a proper style of living, the indignities of debt became almost too much for her to bear. The long letter he wrote in response to hers proposing a separation illustrates the interplay between political and personal identities with respect to fiduciary worth. Outlining their fiscal history together, he again blamed his 'negligent forgetful and procrastinating habit of mind [. . .] united at the same time with a most unfortunately sanguine temper, and a rash confidence', but faulted her for failing to 'judge of my conduct[,] character and principles upon a larger scale of observation and not from the defects of daily Life which arise from the Failings I acknowledge'. Sheridan set up a contrast between his responsibilities as a public man and the petty concerns of the domestic realm. He insisted that if she truly knew him she would realize that her sufferings did not come from his disregard of her; indeed, although his 'Privations and vexations' were even greater than hers, he bore them happily when they afforded her comfort.[96] He reminded her of his selfless, upstanding conduct in his generous contribution to her marriage settlement, the voluntary promise he had kept not to avail himself of the interest until the stock reached £40,000, and his suggestion of two trustees he knew would meet with her family's approval. In further defence of his character, Sheridan set out in great detail how and why he covered the expenses of his son Tom's political career as well as the debts born of the young man's misadventures. He justified the debts he himself had run up while in office about which she had complained. He listed all sources of his income, of which he claimed Hester had an inflated notion, and laid out their expenses, including her pin money, carriage and servants. In claiming the depth of his habit of self-sacrifice, he declared: 'I am willing to give up for the Present having a servant to myself tho' without dissembling the hardship it will be to me, At my Time of Day, and helpless as I am in this respect, from having been used to have one for nearly forty years.' He presented a plan for paying off her debts, made a wildly optimistic prediction of his future income and, in response to the thanks she had expressed in her letter, reiterated his unwavering commitment to the welfare of her relations. In the event that all this had not moved her, Sheridan drove his case home by meting out a good dose of guilt with ruminations on his illness and mortality followed up with the threat that if they separated he would take 'my Boy with me to some corner of the earth, and be no more heard of till my Death'. He reminded her of the pain wrought when private life became public, enquiring: 'can you hold lightly the becoming the Topic of discussion to a deriding malicious and unsparing society all of whom would find their amusement and many their gratification in such an event'? He doubted that any member of her family would support her claims and bade her contemplate the effect of family schisms on children. He closed by assuming—correctly—that she would pardon him and, in anticipation of this, offered her his forgiveness with his apology.[97]

Even without the scandal of a marital separation Sheridan's deteriorating credit became notorious in his final years. He tried to preserve his dignity in his requests for loans from friends. Several began along the lines: 'You will, perhaps, be surprised at receiving this letter, but not more than I am at writing it, and, perhaps, thro' life no man that has not always stood free from embarrassments has so resolutely and perseveringly stood free from personal obligations as I have done. In making this application you are the second person in the world I ever asked a pecuniary favour from.'[98] Hester resorted to pawning sheets and table linen, and their son suffered from insufficient food and clothing until friends stepped in to help. After he fell out with the prince regent and lost his seat in parliament, Sheridan wound up at least twice in debtor's prison, but friends quickly came to his aid. When he lay dying in 1816, while his wife languished in the next room with the cancer that would eventually kill her, friends prevented bailiffs from confiscating their furniture and from wrapping Sheridan in a blanket and hauling him off to prison. The irony of his self-professed carelessness became clear after his death: his debts were not nearly as extensive as commonly assumed. Charles inherited the entire £40,000 trust upon his mother's death the following year.[99] As his biographer Moore lamented: 'There are many persons in the enjoyment of fair characters in the world, who would be happy to have no deeper encroachment upon the property of others to answer for; and who may well wonder by what unlucky management Sheridan could contrive, to found so extensive a reputation for bad pay upon so small an amount of debt.'[100]

Sheridan's financial dealings became an area of contention in assessments of his legacy, again demonstrating the importance of attitudes towards money and skill in handling it as components of personal character. Alecia (Lissy) Lefanu set about correcting the numerous errors she found in the first memoir of her brother's life that appeared shortly after his death. She took exception to the author, John Watkins, representing Sheridan's prohibition of his wife singing in public as pretentious in a man lacking pedigree, property and the means of supporting a family. After doling out a lesson on the antiquity and respectability of their Irish forebears, Lefanu huffed that her brother had been a member of the Middle Temple at the time of his marriage and certainly would have been called to the Bar had not more exciting prospects emerged; in any event, his second wife was in no distress. She denied that his first wife, Eliza, had co-authored Sheridan's literary pieces or given concerts in private homes for pay: they 'certainly were in straitened circumstances, but he extricated himself by his own exertions'.[101] Sheridan's tangled web of credit compromised the characters of others as well. The degree of squalor in which the Sheridans ended their lives, how much aid they received and who rendered it became points of controversy. When Moore's memoir appeared in 1825, he received a rebuke from Lord Lansdowne on behalf of the Whig gran-dees for listing the mourners at Sheridan's splendid funeral and asking where they were 'but a few weeks before, when their interposition might have saved his heart from breaking,—or when the zeal, now wasted on the grave, might have soothed and comforted the death-bed?'[102]

George IV's reputation suffered the most for his treatment of Sheridan. Already he had a reputation for fickleness in friendship as well as in love. Back in 1794, when Prince George broke with the Whigs in order to have his debts paid, James Sayers had drawn a forlorn Sheridan turned away by Big Sam, the gatekeeper at Carlton House (fig. 16).[103] George insisted that he had sent John Taylor Vaughan with £200 and a promise of more to relieve the Sheridans' distress, only to have the money returned a few days later with a notice from Hester's friends that they had all expenses covered. Moore had expressed scepticism that Vaughan had acted under anything other than his own auspices, which brought critical reviews of his book in Tory journals loyal to George and circulation of a story that prior to Vaughan's mission the prince regent had given Sheridan £4,000 to purchase a seat. Whether this had been a loan or a gift with strings attached remained a matter of debate. Moore could find no evidence of Sheridan ever receiving the money, but felt pressured enough to address the issue in the fifth edition of his *Life of Sheridan* and to say as much. Yet he tried to reconcile this with the claims of the Tory reviewers by suggesting that George's emissary had made some error in the transmission of the money.[104] Moore achieved his goal of pleasing Charles Brinsley Sheridan with the book, so the public acclaim that greeted it and the greater sales than expected appeared as an added bonus.[105]

Whereas Moore had expected the political fallout, he seemed surprised at the emotional impact of Sheridan's history. In explaining his intentions for the book, he made a statement that encapsulates how public lives had taken on the qualities of fictional characters. He told Charles: 'My wish was to leave the same impression on my readers as your father did on those who knew him—namely, a feeling of love towards him in spite of all his irregularities & faults, and this I most anxiously hope I have effected. I had two female hearers crying over the last pages to-day, as if it were a Novel.'[106] As the conventions of fiction writing had influenced the style of reporting on public figures, readers expected to be able to have insight into their true natures in the same way that they could know the characters depicted in imaginative writing.

CHAPTER SEVEN

The Persistence of Casuistry

On Wednesday Morning, about half an Hour after Nine o'Clock, his Majesty, the Prince of Wales, and the Duke, on Horseback, and the Queen, the Princess of Wales, and the Princesses, in their Coaches, attended by a great Concourse of the nobility of both Sexes, Foreign Ministers, and other Persons of Distinction, came into Hyde Park. The Royal Family rode round the Three Regiments of Foot Guards there drawn up, and entered at the Right Wing. His Majesty rode through the several Ranks, and then placing himself in the Front, caused the said Regiments to pass in Review before him. He was pleased to express a great Satisfaction at their Appearance and good Order. They afterwards drew up into a hollow Square and fir'd in Platoons. Soon after One the Royal Family retir'd, and set out for Richmond and Kew.

Common Sense; or The Englishman's Journal, 16 July 1737

[. . .] the PRINCE gave the word of command in the most General-like manner, and the Troops went through their various evolutions with a precision and ability that did honour to those who have had the disciplining of them, and astonished every military man present. The grand charge was one of the finest manoeuvres we have seen. The KING and the DUKE of YORK, who are both excellent judges of military matters, decided that nothing could be better.

[. . .] The KING, who is always good-humoured and Facetious, told the DUCHESS of YORK she ought not to come to a Review in a curricle, unless she was as good a whip as Mrs. ONSLOW. Accordingly, she had her horses taken out during the exercise. The PRINCESS of WALES seemed highly gratified with the encomiums passed on the discipline of the PRINCE's Regiment.

Sun, 17 May 1796

As these representative examples from the eras of Sir Robert Walpole and William Pitt the Younger attest, over the course of fifty years even reports of military reviews, not just celebrations of royal anniversaries, weddings and birthdays, had been turned into human-interest stories. Members of the court came to life in print as distinct personalities. Concurrently, politicians became public personas as party designations evolved from Tory and Whig, to Court and Country, to ministry and opposition, to Rockinghamites, Chathamites, Wilkites, Foxites, Pittites and the like. Men had overwhelmed measures with respect to political identity as the press followed men's private tendencies to judge one another on their personal qualities. Principles remained of central importance in politics, of course, as the disintegration of the Foxite party well demonstrates, but the positions avowed by the Foxites who jumped ship to the Pitt administration likewise show that principles could be tweaked to accommodate changing circumstances. Yet the length of time that it took for Fox's friends to break from him indicates the force of personal connections. Maintaining companionable relationships outside the court and Houses of Parliament facilitated these bonds. Consequently, making a suitable match, conducting strategic extramarital liaisons, and not letting either become a detriment to manly or financial independence increased in importance as politicians built reputations and alliances. Borrowing and lending money, exchanging mistresses, getting drunk with, and helping, one another out of scrapes could forge friendships just as well as assisting in a respectable courtship process. Hence, conforming to the ideal of a sterling personal life as the foundation for a man's capacity for public service involved some old-fashioned hypocrisy and a new form of casuistry.

Politicians and moralists debated the meaning and ethics of various forms of hypocrisy throughout the eighteenth century. Jenny Davidson productively focuses on the strand of this argument concerning manners, particularly 'texts that avow something very like hypocrisy under another name (chivalry, gallantry, politeness, self-restraint)'. Some defenders of hypocrisy, she notes, likened it to habit: 'If hypocrisy simply means playing a part, might not the sufficient repetition of a given action allow the hypocrite a kind of functional sincerity? Regardless of an individual's initial motivation, habit can become second nature in contexts as various as religious observance, oaths of political allegiance, courtesy to a spouse and deference to a superior.'[1] Davidson charts a sea change after the publication of the earl of Chesterfield's letters to his son in 1774, a year after his death, by comparing the outrage sparked by his defence of gallantry to the less rancorous debate that had followed after

David Hume had essentially done the same in essays published some thirty years earlier, roughly when Chesterfield had been writing. Hume represented gallantry as a product of civility. He contrasted the deferential treatment of women, a sign of men's confidence in their own natural superiority, with the violence towards, and slavery of, women found in barbarous nations. After making such a sharp demarcation, however, Hume remained decidedly ambiguous on whether polite intercourse between men and women included adultery. Chesterfield, on the other hand, had blithely advised his son to conduct affairs with married women for personal gain. Although by the 1790s revulsion against Chesterfield had become subsumed in a broader movement against aristocratic privilege, as the present study has shown, in high political circles a species of hypocrisy persisted, whether through force of habit or tradition. The culture of politeness, after all, had evolved from court etiquette.[2]

As Hume's defence of gallantry indicates, favouring social interactions ruled by dissimulation rested on a belief in a natural order of subordination. This assumption came under pressure in the decade of the French Revolution. Most often in the context of challenging the hereditary principle or bemoaning the expense of monarchy, proponents of reform pointed to the vices generated by the many toiling away in poverty to support the luxury of the few, by wealth becoming the standard of merit and by adulatory forms of address supporting artificial distinctions among men.[3] Mary Wollstonecraft drew the most direct connection between monarchy and immorality beyond the world of courtiers. She traced society's progress from barbarism to feudalism to people demanding political rights. She elaborated: 'Thus, as wars, agriculture, commerce, and literature, expand the mind, despots are compelled to make covert corruption hold fast the power which was formerly snatched by open force. And this baneful lurking gangrene is most quickly spread by luxury and superstition, the sure dregs of ambition. The indolent puppet of a court first becomes a luxurious monster, or fastidious sensualist, and then makes the contagion which his unnatural state spread, the instrument of tyranny.' This she evocatively dubbed 'the pestiferous purple'. Elsewhere Wollstonecraft paralleled the situations of women and courtiers, both being 'decked with artificial graces that enable them to exercise a short-lived tyranny. Love, in their bosoms, taking place of every nobler passion, their sole ambition is to be fair, to raise emotion instead of inspiring respect; and this ignoble desire, like the servility in absolute monarchies, destroys all strength of character.'[4] The monarchical tradition, combined with the progressive democratization of politics, facilitated as it was through print culture, perpetuated the seductive legacy of gallantry beckoning just beneath the surface of idealized domestic virtue.

Scholarly investigations into eighteenth-century masculinities, their construction and performance further illuminate the foundations of the ruling elite's inconsistent ethics. In her analysis of the simultaneous condemnation of, and nostalgia for, the figure of the Restoration rake, Erin Mackie draws attention to the broader lack of concern regarding gentlemanly violence: that rape, assault, vandalism and even homicide, when committed by gentlemen, often passed as youthful frolics. She shows how literature of the time purporting to advocate the reformation of manners actually glorified outlaw masculinity and invited imitation. Elite men thus tended to consider themselves exempt from the rules regulating the behaviour of lesser beings when they thought circumstances warranted it. Indeed, men shaped their ethos as they formed associations and won approval from other members of their group. Valérie Capdeville presents the exclusively male spaces of London clubs as the English solution allowing men to enjoy refined conversation without being exposed to the effeminizing tendencies of French polite sociability, which favoured the mixing of the sexes. Samuel Johnson, she argues, coined the word 'clubb-able' as an alternative to the French *sociable* better to capture English practice.[5] The Houses of Parliament formed the ultimate men's club as women by law could not be members, only spectators. In this club, as in royal courts, however, women sometimes pulled strings behind the scenes. Nonetheless, while politicians increasingly attended entertainments and dinners orchestrated by women who took an active interest in politics, they continued to engage in homosocial activities that promoted intimacy and male bonding. Perhaps this reinforced a sense of manly independence thought to be required in exercising political power, free from the distractions and biases of family interest and domestic obligations.

Ultimately, the question of whether or not a political leader's personal finances and domestic life affect his or her ability to govern is moot and really less important than the question of why, with every new exposure of peccadilloes, the press has to reopen the debate only to arrive at the same lack of resolution. In the aptly titled 'The Talk of the Town' section of the *New Yorker*, two regular contributors mulled over the spate of scandals in the US in 2011 and 2012 in ways that attested to the enduring ethical legacy of eighteenth-century Britain. The week after Anthony Weiner's resignation from his seat in congress, Margaret Talbot observed that the feminist dictum of the personal being political no longer served given the growing trend towards compartmentalization in life and guarding of privacy. Affecting a sophisticated indifference to the private lives of politicians did not work either when these revealed, as in this and in Arnold Schwarzenegger's case, a lack of self-control and a tendency to prevaricate, or, with respect to Silvio Berlusconi and Dominique Strauss-Kahn, the possibility of criminality. Talbot lamented: 'It would be useful to have a grand theory to explain these lapses—there are so many, and one feels obliged to think something about them. But you can really only take them case by case, and that's a daunting task.' After revisiting the increasingly intimate details revealed in the press over the past fifty years, she noted the anomaly of current opinion polls showing that a much larger percentage of Americans avow that they would divorce a philandering spouse than would be troubled by a presidential candidate's extramarital affair. She thought that this indicated 'a tacit acceptance that some of the qualities that launch people into public office—self-regard bordering on narcissism, risk-taking—can also launch them into risks of a more personal kind, and that this doesn't inevitably reflect on their ability to govern'. Writing about the David Petraeus affair less than a year and a half later, Adam Gopnik unintentionally illustrated the knotty relation between imaginative and real-life characters. He opened by recalling Philip Roth pronouncing the death of satirical fiction fifty years earlier, a victim to real events inevitably topping anything one could invent. Gopnik framed his essay around the novelist's notion of the human stain (a product of duplicity) and contemplated its potential to spread and engulf. He argued that the lapses of Petraeus, Weiner, Eliot Spitzer and Bill Clinton had less to do with bad judgement than with desire, which never involves 'judicious choice': 'The point of lust, not to put too fine a point on it, is that it lures us to do dumb stuff, and the fact that the dumb stuff gets done is continuing proof of its power.' Gopnik thought the bigger story that week was Roth's retirement from fiction-writing.[6] Like the moral performance of the novel that Laetitia-Matilda Hawkins wrote to gratify a selfish whim, discussed in Chapter 1, public shaming rituals, which include poring over sordid details and speculating on motives, obviously do not act as deterrents, but societies feel compelled to perform them nonetheless to reinforce their ethical ideals.

While Talbot and Gopnik each presented wayward lads roistering about the corridors of power as a product of human nature, my study posits that these tendencies towards daring, intrigue and deceit should be attributed more specifically to the vestiges of court mores, even in the USA. Most significantly, the transition from personal monarchy to press-mediated personalized governance included an evolution in casuistry. The technique of using logical reasoning to resolve cases of conscience, specifically the problem of applying general rules to complex situations that feature a mix of practical and ethical considerations, can be traced back to the ancients. Its usage peaked between 1550 and 1650 as the province of clergymen who counselled parishioners faced with moral dilemmas by determining what divine laws applied best to the particular circumstances. This involved close analysis of real and hypothetical cases to find certainty. Casuistry could ease a tormented conscience and encourage good acts, or it could devolve into sophistry and rationalize indulging one's appetites. Blaise Pascal famously caricatured the practice, giving it lasting associations with Jesuitical laxity: 'King Louis XIV, it was said, would abjure his mistress on Holy Thursday, confess to his Jesuit confessor on Good Friday, take Communion on Easter Sunday, and bring back his mistress on Easter Monday.'[7] Meanwhile, by questioning the legitimacy of long-held values in light of changing conditions in England, puritan casuists had helped justify the execution of Charles I. By the end of the seventeenth century, Anglican divines tended to reject intricate argumentation as dangerous and preach a morality best achieved simply by embracing God and goodness. As Keith Thomas sums it up: 'Instead of thinking of life as made up of a series of discrete problems, each to be solved separately in accordance with the rulebook, theologians were increasingly inclined to place their emphasis upon the formation of an individual's general moral character.'[8] He goes on to observe that casuistry then moved into the secular realm of moral philosophers, political theorists, newspaper advice columnists and novelists.

Essentially, print culture appropriated the role once held by clergy of dispensing ethical judgements. Sometimes the moral arithmetic showed through. The radical *Telegraph*, in its ongoing campaign to expose the immorality of placing the burden of George, Prince of Wales's debts on the public at a time of economic hardship and deprivation, called out the ministerial press for representing his spending, without documentation, as 'the exercise of benevolence in relieving of the indigent—rewarding the virtuous—in raising modest merit to the proper level—and patronizing the arts—and in the encouragement of our manufactures'. The paper invoked good casuistry by prefacing its remarks: 'In speaking of this delicate, but important subject, we have ever felt with what nice precision it was necessary to draw the line between respect to the illustrious party on the one hand, and our paramount duty to the people on the other. Never having indulged in the license of fiction, we have spoken with the boldness of truth. We have no wish to delude—it was our duty to inform the public.' The *Telegraph* reasoned that, based on appearances, until the public saw vouchers that proved actual expenditure, one could as logically conclude 'that for every 10,000l. thus laid out, the national generosity will overlook 50,000l. expended in a manner less meritorious'.[9] This argument was doomed. Even radical papers had been complimenting the prince's splendour and taste on ceremonial occasions, sometimes in order to draw attention to his royal parents' parsimony and dullness, as Chapter 5 details—not surprisingly, bad casuistry prevailed.

A man's character, not just the course of action he should choose, became subject to casuistic reckoning. As Talbot and Gopnik each acknowledged regarding reactions to compromising information disclosed today, whether one initially condemned or doubted the allegations could not but be influenced by one's prior opinion of the accused. When mixed, personal feelings wreaked havoc with principles. In the eighteenth century, animus towards the king plunged politicians into moral dilemmas. Sir Gilbert Elliot's support of the prince of Wales during the Regency Crisis of 1788–89 gave him pangs of conscience. Writing to his wife after the king's recovery, which dashed his party's aspirations, he admitted:

I have indeed fought a battle with myself, as well as I could, to avoid being very savage as to the cause which was to produce such great things for us—I mean the King's horrible distemper. I certainly do not feel any new affection or respect for the King, whom I do not think either better or worse of for being mad. Nothing can appear more preposterous or more disgusting than the violent enthusiasm of humanity and loyalty in those who have so manifest an interest in the subject of their joy. I do not know, on the other hand, whether it is *possible* for us, who have such powerful interests the other way, to feel either the same compassion for the King's misfortunes, or the same satisfaction in his relief, as if we were not concerned in these events. But still I think that, on reflection, we should wish to sacrifice as little of our natural feelings to our interests as we are able, and I would therefore persuade myself that such a horrible calamity to any other person as insanity, is one of those means by which I would not enter into power. And with this reflection I am certainly better reconciled to the present disappointment of these views, and to waiting for their accomplishment till it may happen by the usual means.

The burst of moral clarity and fellow feeling that Elliot experienced by performing a critical self-examination in light of the rules of human decency was short-lived. After describing for Lady Elliot's entertainment the loyalist celebrations in London, he eased his conscience by speculating that he was not alone in his ambivalence: 'It would have been curious to know how many, in the midst of this paroxysm of love for his Majesty, really cared a straw about him.'[10] As we have seen, Elliot would adapt to changing conditions and serve the king's government.

Similar conflicts of personal feeling and principle spilled into public debates. After Edmund Burke's defection from the prince and the Foxites, in the midst of the pamphlet war launched by his *Reflections on the Revolution in France* (1790) and Thomas Paine's response in *Rights of Man* (1791–92), Sir Brooke Boothby, gentleman botanist, poet and promoter of Jean-Jacques Rousseau in England, tried to establish a middle ground between the two antagonists by determining how well their positions on various points of contention held up to constitutional principles. In the process of addressing Burke's justifications for breaking with Charles James Fox in *An Appeal from the New to the Old Whigs* (1792), Boothby dismantled Paine's assertion that adulation of the king promoted slavishness, which, as noted above, became a prominent theme in reformist writings, and Burke's intimations of the regicidal potential in the sentiments of his former party. Boothby began by describing how a king fulfilled his political role by staying within the law; subjects would be 'well disposed to believe that much of the good which they enjoy descends from him who is the fountain of honour and the source of mercy. They are near enough to be warmed and enlightened with his splendour and too far off to discern the spots upon his orb.' Boothby's generic description of kingship implicitly criticized those who saw oppression in traditional forms of reverence as well as those who suspected the worst of subjects who declined to participate in them. Referring to the personal qualities of his hypothetical king, he stipulated that if

> his *natural* constitution leads him to no glaring excesses, if he fulfils with ostensible decency the common offices of life, if he represents with tolerable grace the dignity of his station, I do not say he may be adored though I think it, but I am sure he will hold the hearts and lives and fortunes of his subjects in his hand. To oppose the dangers of the amiable idolatry has always been one among the chief objects of the guardians of the constitution. A watchful and suspicious jealousy of the court is their

peculiar characteristic. In the very virtues of a king or the well-earned popularity of a minister they can find cause of alarm. So that though the whigs are perhaps above all men the most firmly devoted to the constitutional throne, they do not wear upon their external habit those marks of personal attachment to the king, the want of which to vulgar observation is easily made to pass for disloyalty or disaffection.[11]

After Burke's defence of monarchy, Boothby seemed optimistic that others who had expressed contempt towards the king during the Regency Crisis would follow suit if they allowed reason to guide them. Fox, nevertheless, continued to despise George III.

Ironically, Fox's mere presence at court made him suspect among the reform-society members who continued to meet after the trials of their leaders for treason at the end of 1794. According to spy reports, at the 'Temple of Reason and Humanity' in Panton Street, after the attack on the king's coach of 29 October 1795 brought the threat of repressive legislation, they debated 'whether the avowed principles and political conduct of Mr Fox entitled him to the confidence and support of the real friends of liberty'. Demonstrating an awareness of political friendships, debaters mooted whether a politician, even an avowed patriot, could escape corruption as a result of his obligations to the statesmen who facilitated his rise. One speaker observed: 'It is true Mr Fox last week opposed the Address to the King but did he not the next Day go up with another Address to the King and attend his Levee among the other courtly Caterpillars of the Day?' Another drew laughter and applause by rejoining sardonically: 'Mr Fox went up with the Address to congratulate his Majesty upon his fortunate escape from Assassination, and it was to his honor that he did so, for it proved, that altho' Mr Fox has been cruelly treated; altho he has been deprived of that Power which his Situation and Abilities entitle him to expect, he feels no personal resentment against the King, and would be sorry that he should lose his life by the Knife, or the Bullet of an Assassin.' The spy recorded a low turnout during the third discussion of this question when the show of hands favoured Fox, but noted that the chair, John Gale Jones, declared against him.[12] That these extra-parliamentary activists would spend time assessing the character of a politician in the midst of strategizing against potential restrictions to their activities, which came into force in December with what became known as Pitt's Two Acts against treasonable and seditious practices and seditious meetings, attests to the persistence of the vision of politics as a personal battle between

Fox and Pitt. Moreover, they appeared to believe that through analysing appearances they could determine what Fox really thought and felt, which in truth was unknowable and of little use.

Two scholars who became aware of the practice of casuistry while studying the structure of the abortion debate in the US contend that it can be useful in resolving contentious ethical issues if it means taking seriously both 'the concrete circumstances of actual cases, and the specific maxims that people invoke in facing moral dilemmas'.[13] As long as the focus remains on the character of the speaker rather than the rationality of the argument, however, political debates will be moral performances, not sincere efforts to perform good casuistry.

Notes

Chapter 1

1. A common theme in political prints: see, for example, H.W., *The Angelic Child Presented to the _____ [Queen] of Golconda*, 10 Feb. 1791, a satire on the marriage between Lord Ducie and Mrs Child, a rich widow. It depicted Queen Charlotte attempting to trade a rattle of coral and bells for one dangling moneybags held by Child (represented by a woman in child's dress). The queen's keeper of the robes, Mrs Schwellenberg, urges: 'Tell her there is a monstrous fine Diamond in every Bell.' *Catalogue of Prints and Drawings in the British Museum: Division I: Political and Personal Satires*, ed. Frederic George Stephens, Edward Hawkins and M. Dorothy George, 11 vols (London: British Museum Publications, 1870–1954) (hereafter *BMC*), 4826. Similarly, James Gillray, *An Angel, Gliding on a Sun-Beam into Paradise*, 11 Oct. 1791, *BMC* 7906, has Schwellenberg laden with moneybags borne headlong to Hanover.
2. Linda Colley, *Britons: Forging a Nation* (New Haven and London: Yale University Press, 1992), ch. 5; John Barrell, *The Spirit of Despotism: Invasions of Privacy in the 1790s* (Oxford: Oxford University Press, 2006), ch. 3; Marilyn Morris, *The British Monarch and the French Revolution* (New Haven and London: Yale University Press, 1998). See also Vincent Carretta, *George III and the Satirists from Hogarth to Byron* (Athens and London: University of Georgia Press, 1990). For a critique of the various models of monarchy, see David M. Craig, 'The Crowned Republic? Monarchy and Anti-Monarchy in Britain, 1760–1901', *Historical Journal* 46/1 (2003): 167–85.
3. See H.T. Dickinson, 'The Eighteenth-Century Debate on the Sovereignty of Parliament', *Transactions of the Royal Historical Society*, Fifth Series 26 (1976): 189–210.
4. For the use of 'oeconomy' to designate household management, see Karen Harvey, *The Little Republic: Masculinity and Domestic Authority in Eighteenth-Century Britain* (Oxford: Oxford University Press, 2012).
5. Jeremy Bentham, *Handbook of Political Fallacies*, ed. Harold A. Larrabee (Baltimore: The Johns Hopkins University Press, 1952), pp. 221–22.
6. Paul Langford, 'Politics and Manners from Sir Robert Walpole to Sir Robert Peel', *Proceedings of the British Academy* 94 (1997): 103–25.
7. Gordon J. Schochet, *Patriarchalism in Political Thought: The Authoritarian Family and Political Speculation and Attitudes, Especially in Seventeenth-Century England* (Oxford: Basil Blackwell, 1975); Daniela Gobetti, *Private and Public: Individuals, Households, and Body Politic in Locke and Hutcheson* (New York and London: Routledge, 1992). For a longer view of the problem, see Constance Jordan, 'The Household and the State: Transformations in the Representation of an Analogy from Aristotle to James I', *Modern Language Quarterly* 54/3 (1993): 307–26.

8. Marie Mulvey Roberts, 'Pleasures Engendered by Gender: Homosociablity and the Club', in Roy Porter and Marie Mulvey Roberts, eds, *Pleasure in the Eighteenth Century* (New York: New York University Press, 1996), p. 54; Valérie Capdeville, 'Gender at Stake: The Role of Eighteenth-Century London Clubs in Shaping a New Model of English Masculinity', *Culture, Society & Masculinities* 4/1 (2012): 24.

9. For the debate among historians over the nature and performance of 'hegemonic masculinity' and the tension between domesticity and homosociability, see John Tosh, 'The Old Adam and the New Man: Emerging Themes in the History of English Masculinities 1750–1850', in Tim Hitchcock and Michèle Cohn, eds, *English Masculinities 1660–1800* (London and New York: Longman, 1999), pp. 225, 228–30.

10. See Christopher J. Berry, *The Idea of Luxury: A Conceptual and Historical Investigation* (Cambridge: Cambridge University Press, 1994); Maxine Berg and Elizabeth Eger, *Luxury in the Eighteenth Century: Debates, Desires and Delectable Goods* (Basingstoke: Palgrave Macmillan, 2003).

11. G.J. Barker-Benfield, *The Culture of Sensibility: Sex and Society in Eighteenth-Century Britain* (Chicago and London: University of Chicago Press, 1992); Colin Campbell, *The Romantic Ethic and the Spirit of Modern Capitalism* (Oxford: Basil Blackwell, 1987); Jules Lubbock, *The Tyranny of Taste: The Politics of Architecture and Design in Britain, 1550–1960* (New Haven and London: Yale University Press, 1995).

12. Harriet Blodgett, *Centuries of Female Days: English Women's Private Diaries* (New Brunswick, NJ: Rutgers University Press, 1988), p. 21; Richard Wendorf, *The Elements of Life: Biography and Portrait-Painting in Stuart and Georgian England* (Oxford: Clarendon Press, 1990), pp. 152–58.

13. Michael Mascuch, *Origins of the Individualist Self: Autobiography and Self-Identity in England 1591–1791* (Stanford: Stanford University Press, 1996), pp. 99–100; Felicity Nussbaum, *The Autobiographical Subject: Gender and Ideology in Eighteenth-Century England* (Baltimore and London: Johns Hopkins University Press, 1989), pp. xii–xiii. See also Patricia Meyer Spacks, *Imagining a Self: Autobiography and the Novel in Eighteenth-Century England* (Cambridge, MA: Harvard University Press, 1976).

14. Laetitia-Matilda Hawkins, *Memoirs, Anecdotes, Facts, and Opinions, Collected and Preserved*, 2 vols (London: Longman, Hurst, Rees, Orme, Brown, and Green; C. and J. Rivington, 1824), 1:156. For a different reading of this passage, see Norma Clarke, *Dr Johnson's Women* (London: Hambledon, 2000), p. 211.

15. Patricia Meyer Spacks, *Gossip* (Chicago: University of Chicago Press, [1985], 1986), p. 22; David A. Brewer, *The Afterlife of Character, 1726–1825* (Philadelphia: University of Pennsylvania Press, 2005), pp. 14, 21.

16. See Dror Wahrman, 'National Society, Communal Culture: An Argument about the Recent Historiography of Eighteenth-Century Britain', *Social History* 17 (1992): 43–72.

17. 13 March 1739 N.S., *Correspondence between Frances, Countess of Hertford (Afterward Duchess of Somerset) and Henrietta Louisa, Countess of Pomfret, between the Years 1738 and 1741*, ed. William Bingley, 3 vols (London: Richard Phillips, 1805), 1:75–76.

18. Edward Gibbon, *The Autobiographies of Edward Gibbon Printed Verbatim from Hitherto Unpublished Manuscripts with an Introduction by the Earl of Sheffield*, ed. John Murray (New York: Fred de Fau & Co. Publishers, 1907), pp. 91, 297; [Thomas Green], *Extracts from the Diary of a Lover of Literature* (Ipswich: John Raw, 1810), p. 28.

19. Elizabeth Montagu to Sarah Scott, 1 Nov. 1765, Huntington Library MO 5832. I am indebted to Betty Schellenberg for bringing this letter to my attention.

20. Kate Retford, *The Art of Domestic Life: Family Portraiture in Eighteenth-Century England* (New Haven and London: Yale University Press, 2006); Desmond Shawe-Taylor, *The Georgians: Eighteenth-Century Portraiture and Society* (London: Barre & Jenkins, 1990).

21. For the commercialization of erotica that led to the designation of pornographic material, see Lynn Hunt, ed., *The Invention of Pornography: Obscenity and the Origins of Modernity, 1500–1800* (New York: Zone Books, 1993). See also Marilyn Morris,

'Marital Litigation and English Tabloid Journalism: Crim. Con. in *The Bon Ton* (1791–1796)', *British Journal for Eighteenth-Century Studies* 28 (2005): 33–54.

22. Misty G. Anderson, *Female Playwrights and Eighteenth-Century Comedy: Negotiating Marriage on the London Stage* (New York: Palgrave, 2002); Lisa A. Freeman, *Character's Theater: Genre and Identity on the Eighteenth-Century English Stage* (Philadelphia: University of Pennsylvania Press, 2002); L.W. Conolly, *The Censorship of English Drama 1737–1824* (San Marino, CA: The Huntington Library, 1976).

23. The conflicting representations of matrimonial and illicit relations in portraiture, theatre, litigation, scandal sheets and personal writings will be the subject of my next book.

24. Vincent Carretta, *The Snarling Muse: Verbal and Visual Political Satire from Pope to Churchill* (Philadelphia: University of Pennsylvania Press, 1983), chs 2 and 6; Eirwen E.C. Nicholson, 'English Political Prints and Pictorial Political Argument *c*.1640–*c*.1832: A Study in Historiography and Methodology' (Ph.D. diss., University of Edinburgh, 1994), ch. 5. Tamara L. Hunt's survey of caricature prints notes a new interest in the private life of the royal family occurring in the 1780s: *Defining John Bull: Political Caricature and National Identity in Late Georgian England* (Aldershot, UK, and Burlington, VT: Ashgate, 2003), p. 232.

25. *BMC* 2451 and 8096.

26. David Kuchta, *The Three-Piece Suit and Modern Masculinity: England 1550–1850* (Berkeley: University of California Press, 2002), p. 52. See also John Brewer, *The Pleasures of the Imagination: English Culture in the Eighteenth Century* (New York: Farrar, Straus, Giroux, 1997), ch. 1.

27. Michael McKeon, *The Secret History of Domesticity: Public, Private, and the Division of Knowledge* (Baltimore: The Johns Hopkins University Press, 2005), chs 3, 10–15.

28. Jürgen Habermas's *Strukturwandel der Öffentlichkeit* (1962) appeared in translation as *The Structural Transformation of the Public Sphere: An Inquiry into a Category of Bourgeois Society*, trans. Thomas Burger with the assistance of Frederick Lawrence (Cambridge, MA: MIT Press, 1989; paperback edn, 1991), pp. 5–14, quotation on p. 7.

29. Ibid., pp. 200–1.

30. Dena Goodman, 'Public Sphere and Private Life: Toward a Synthesis of Current Historiographical Approaches to the Old Regime', *History and Theory* 31/1 (1992): 1–20. See also Dario Castiglione and Lesley Sharpe, eds, *Shifting the Boundaries: Transformation of the Languages of Public and Private in the Eighteenth Century* (Exeter: University of Exeter Press, 1995).

31. John Brewer, 'Commercialization and Politics', in Neil McKendrick, John Brewer, and J.H. Plumb, eds, *The Birth of a Consumer Society: The Commercialization of Eighteenth-Century England* (Bloomington: Indiana University Press, 1982), ch. 5; Nicholas Rogers, *Whigs and Cities: Popular Politics in the Age of Walpole and Pitt* (Oxford: Clarendon Press, 1989); Frank O'Gorman, *Voters, Patrons, and Parties: The Unreformed Electorate of Hanoverian England, 1734–1832* (Oxford: Clarendon Press, 1989); Kathleen Wilson, *The Sense of the People: Politics, Culture and Imperialism in England, 1715–1785* (Cambridge: Cambridge University Press, 1995).

32. Barrell, *Spirit of Despotism*, pp. 95, 246.

33. H.T. Dickinson, *Liberty and Property: Political Ideology in Eighteenth-Century Britain* (London: Methuen, 1977), p. 5.

34. Hannah Smith, *Georgian Monarchy: Politics and Culture 1714–1760* (Cambridge: Cambridge University Press, 2006); Clarissa Campbell Orr, 'New Perspective on Hanoverian Britain', *Historical Journal* 52/2 (2009): 513–29; Andrew C. Thompson, *George II King and Elector* (New Haven and London: Yale University Press, 2011).

35. Colley, *Britons*, pp. 199–206. Christine Gerrard, *The Patriot Opposition to Walpole: Politics, Poetry, and National Myth, 1725–1742* (Oxford: Clarendon Press, 1994), pp. 192–93, thinks that Colley overstates her case, but can cite only a few instances of the early Hanoverian kings sponsoring widely observed court splendour and admits

their overall failures at effective image management. Yet I do agree with her larger argument that the rival court of Frederick, Prince of Wales helped to preserve the glamour of monarchy: pp. 46–67, 194–98.

36. Morris, *British Monarchy*, p. 27.
37. Anna Clark, *Scandal: The Sexual Politics of the British Constitution* (Princeton and Oxford: Princeton University Press, 2004), p. 5. For her dismissal of Habermas, see p. 225, n. 6.
38. Historians of eighteenth-century France find this as well: see Jeffrey Merrick, 'Sexual Politics and Public Order in Late Eighteenth-Century France: The *Mémoirs secrèts* and the *Correspondence secrète*', *Journal of the History of Sexuality* 1/1 (1990): 68–84, and Sara Maza, *Private Lives and Public Affairs: The Causes Célèbres of Prerevolutionary France* (Berkeley: University of California Press, 1993).
39. John B. Thompson, *Political Scandal: Power and Visibility in the Media Age* (Cambridge: Polity Press, 2000), p. 345 (italicized in original).
40. S. Elizabeth Bird, 'What a Story! Understanding the Audience for Scandal', in James Lull and Stephen Hinerman, eds, *Media Scandals: Morality and Desire in the Popular Culture Marketplace* (New York: Columbia University Press, 1997), p. 102. See also Thompson, *Political Scandal*, pp. 270–71, and Bruce E. Gronbeck, 'Character, Celebrity, and Sexual Innuendo in the Mass-Mediated Presidency', in Lull and Hinerman, *Media Scandals*, pp. 125–35.
41. Richard Sennett, *The Fall of Public Man* (New York: Alfred A. Knopf, 1977), pp. 4–5.
42. Ibid., pp. 99–106, 150–53, 265, quotation on p. 99. Although they present more balanced assessments of the impact of politicians' lives being under intense media scrutiny, studies of political scandals do entertain the dangerous possibility of character overshadowing competence, and celebrity and likeability becoming marks of competence or morality. See Thompson, *Political Scandal*, p. 255, and Gronbeck, 'Character, Celebrity, and Sexual Innuendo', pp. 122–42.
43. Jürgen Habermas, 'Further Reflections on the Public Sphere', in Craig Calhoun, ed., *Habermas and the Public Sphere* (Cambridge, MA, and London: MIT Press, 1992), p. 426.
44. Barker-Benfield, *Culture of Sensibility*; John K. Sheriff, *The Good-Natured Man: The Evolution of a Moral Idea* (University, AL: University of Alabama Press, 1982).
45. Several contributors to Calhoun, *Habermas* address the problem of multiple publics and the interplay of the political establishment. See especially Nancy Fraser, 'Rethinking the Public Sphere: A Contribution to the Critique of Actually Existing Democracy', pp. 109–42, on the 'strong publics' produced by sovereign parliaments (p. 134), and Keith Michael Baker, 'Defining the Public Sphere in Eighteenth-Century France: Variations on a Theme by Habermas', pp. 181–211, on the absolutist strain in the French Enlightenment in contrast to the Rousseauean republicanism that Habermas stresses (pp. 192–93). Geoff Eley, 'Nations, Publics, and Political Cultures: Placing Habermas in the Nineteenth Century', pp. 289–339, productively suggests the application of Antonio Gramsci's idea of hegemony to sort out the problematic relation between the state and the public sphere (pp. 321–25). Habermas himself, in his 'Further Reflections', pp. 421–61, concedes that in his presentation of the liberal public sphere he was 'not careful enough in distinguishing between an ideal type and the very context from which it was constructed' (p. 463). For the independence, vitality and political consciousness of the plebeian public sphere, see Nicholas Rogers, *Crowds, Culture and Politics in Georgian Britain* (Oxford: Clarendon Press, 1998).
46. J.L. Austin, *How to Do Things with Words* (Cambridge, MA: Harvard University Press, 1962), pp. 2–3.
47. C. Wright Mills, *The Sociological Imagination* (Oxford: Oxford University Press, [1959], 2000), p. 5.
48. Elaine Chalus, 'Women, Electoral Privilege and Practice in the Eighteenth Century', in Kathryn Gleadle and Sara Richardson, eds, *Women in British Politics, 1760–1860:*

The Power of the Petticoat (Basingstoke and London: Macmillan, and New York: St. Martin's Press, 2000), pp. 19–20. For the wide scope of extra-parliamentary political activities pursued in London and the provinces, see Wilson, *Sense of the People*.

49. Chalus, 'Women, Electoral Privilege and Practice', p. 21.

50. Elaine Chalus, *Elite Women in English Political Life, c.1754–1790* (Oxford: Clarendon Press, 2005), ch. 3; Steve Pincus, '"Coffee Politicians Does Create": Coffeehouses and Restoration Political Culture', *Journal of Modern History* 67/4 (1995): 807–34.

51. Clark, *Scandal*, p. 3; Thompson, *Political Scandal*, p. 159. For sex and money as central themes in gossip because of the part that all three play in power relations, see Spacks, *Gossip*, pp. 68–69.

52. J.G.A. Pocock, *Virtue, Commerce, and History: Essays on Political Thought and History, Chiefly in the Eighteenth Century* (Cambridge: Cambridge University Press, 1985), *The Machiavellian Moment: Florentine Political Thought and the Atlantic Republican Tradition* (Princeton: Princeton University Press, 1975), and *Politics, Language and Time: Essays on Political Thought and History* (New York: Atheneum, 1973). McKeon argues that capitalist ideology had a far greater impact than civic humanism on moral discourse from the mid-seventeenth century: *Secret History*, pp. 24–26. For a more nuanced treatment of political virtue and the republican tradition than Pocock's, see Shelley Burtt, *Virtue Transformed: Political Argument in England, 1688–1740* (Cambridge: Cambridge University Press, 1992).

53. Edward G. Andrew, *Conscience and its Critics: Protestant Conscience, Enlightenment Reason, and Modern* Subjectivity (Toronto: University of Toronto Press, 2001); James Tully, 'Governing Conduct', and Margaret Sampson, 'Laxity and Liberty in Seventeenth-Century English Political Thought', in Edmund Leites, ed., *Conscience and Casuistry in Early Modern Europe* (Cambridge: Cambridge University Press, 1988), pp. 12–71, 72–118; G.A. Starr, *Defoe and Casuistry* (Princeton: Princeton University Press, 1971).

Chapter 2

1. Tony Claydon, *William III and the Godly Revolution* (Cambridge: Cambridge University Press, 1996), pp. 57, 63, 92–100, 111–20; Faramerz Dabhoiwala, 'Sex and Societies for Moral Reform, 1688–1800', *Journal of British Studies* 46 (2007): 300–1.

2. Daniel Defoe, *Reformation of Manners* (1702), ll: 216–25, in Frank H. Ellis, ed., *Poems on Affairs of State: Augustan Satirical Verse, 1660–1714*, 7 vols (New Haven and London: Yale University Press, 1963–75), 6: 408–9.

3. Maximillian E. Novak, *Daniel Defoe: Master of Fictions. His Life and Ideas* (Oxford: Oxford University Press, 2001), pp. 171–72, 185–86, 190–98, 360–64.

4. John Timbs, *Clubs and Club Life in London* (London: Chatto & Windus, 1872; republished by Gale, 1962), pp. 13–21, 47–53.

5. Richmond P. Bond, *The Tatler: The Making of a Literary Journal* (Cambridge, MA: Harvard University Press, 1971), pp. 4, 44–46, 60–68, 73–83; *Tatler*, ed. Donald F. Bond, 3 vols (Oxford: Clarendon Press, 1987), 3: 33–34; *Guardian*, ed. John Calhoun Stephens (Lexington: University Press of Kentucky, 1982), 28 April, 12 May 1713, pp. 166–68, 209–10; Delarivier Manley, *The New Atalantis*, ed. Rosalind Ballaster (London and New York: Penguin Books, 1991), pp. 101–5.

6. Paula Backscheider, *Daniel Defoe: His Life* (Baltimore and London: The Johns Hopkins University Press, 1989), pp. 259–60, 328–32.

7. Novak, *Daniel Defoe*, pp. 370–71.

8. Bertrand A. Goldgar, *The Curse of Party: Swift's Relations with Addison and Steele* (Lincoln: University of Nebraska Press, 1961), pp. 11–18.

9. Joseph Addison, *The Freeholder*, ed. James Leheny (Oxford: Clarendon Press, 1979), 24 Feb. 1716, pp. 118–19.

10. [Jonathan Swift], *A Short Character of Thomas Earl of Wharton* (1711), in *The Prose Works of Jonathan Swift*, ed. Temple Scott, 12 vols (London: G. Bell and Sons, 1897–1908), 5: 10. Swift penned this work in December 1710.

11. Barry Coward, *The Stuart Age: England 1603–1714*, 2nd edn (London and New York: Longman, 1994), pp. 401, 423.

12. For this common strategy, see C.R. Kropf, 'Libel and Satire in the Eighteenth Century', *Eighteenth-Century Studies* 8/2 (1974–75): 153–68.

13. Swift, *Prose Works*, 9: 100. See [Daniel Defoe], *A Short Narrative of the Life and Actions of His Grace, John, D. of Marlborough* (1711), Augustan Reprint Society no. 168, intro. Paula Backsheider (Los Angeles: William Andrews Clark Memorial Library, 1974); Francis Harris, *A Passion for Government: The Life of Sarah, Duchess of Marlborough* (Oxford: Clarendon Press, 1991), pp. 114–15, 142–65, 175, 183–84.

14. Bernard Mandeville, *The Fable of the Bees; or Private Vices, Public Benefits*, ed. F.B. Kaye, 2 vols (Indianapolis: The Liberty Fund, 1924). This work had elicited little notice when first published in 1714, but then caused a major scandal in 1729 when it was reissued with the more explicit *Essay on Charity, and Charity-Schools*. My account of the Mandeville scandal in this paragraph is indebted to this edition's 'Commentary Critical, Historical, and Explanatory' and to M.M. Goldsmith, *Private Vices, Public Benefits: Bernard Mandeville's Social and Political Thought* (Cambridge: Cambridge University Press, 1985).

15. Goldsmith, *Private Vices*, p. 40.

16. Mandeville, *Fable of the Bees*, p. 322 (p. 387 in the original pagination of the 1733 edition).

17. Ibid., p. 323 (pp. 388–89).

18. J.A.W. Gunn, *Beyond Liberty and Property: The Process of Self-Recognition in Eighteenth-Century Political Thought* (Kingston and Montreal: McGill-Queen's University Press, 1983), ch. 7.

19. John Carswell, *The South Sea Bubble* (Stanford: Stanford University Press, 1960), p. 73; for the methods and reach of the bribery, see pp. 115–16, 125–30, 160–61.

20. J.H. Plumb, *Sir Robert Walpole: The Making of a Statesman*, 2 vols (London: Cresset Press, 1956), 1: 243–380.

21. For William III's relations with Hans Willem Bentinck, Earl of Portland and Arnauld Joost van Keppel, Earl of Abermarle, and Anne's relations with Sarah Churchill, Duchess of Marlborough and Abigail (Hill) Masham, see Ruth Herman, 'Dark Deeds at Night', in Chris Mounsey and Caroline Gonda, eds, *Queer People: Negotiations and Expressions of Homosexuality, 1700–1800* (Lewisburg: Bucknell University Press, 2007), pp. 195–209.

22. Rictor Norton, *Mother Clap's Molly House: The Gay Subculture in England 1700–1830* (London: GMP, 1992), p. 52.

23. Scholars have disagreed over precisely what political tradition the work represents—constitutionalist, ecclesiological, Machiavelian/neo-Harringtonian, selfish-individualistic, innovative republican, or natural-rights Whiggism: Ian Higgins, 'Remarks on *Cato's Letters*', in David Womersley, ed., *'Cultures of Whiggism': New Essays on English Literature and Culture in the Long Eighteenth Century* (Newark: University of Delaware Press, 2005), pp. 127–46.

24. John Trenchard and Thomas Gordon, *Cato's Letters; or Essays on Liberty, Civil and Religious, and Other Important Subjects*, ed. Ronald Hamowy (Indianapolis: Liberty Fund, 1995), 10 June 1721, p. 231.

25. Ibid., 15 April 1721, p. 180.

26. Ibid., 13 May 1721, pp. 207, 211. For the Hell-Fire Club of 1721, see Evelyn Lord, *The Hell-Fire Clubs: Sex, Satanism and Secret Sins* (New Haven and London: Yale University Press, 2008), pp. 51–57.

27. This passage is quoted in Norton, *Mother Clap's*, p. 41, Cameron McFarlane, *The Sodomite in Fiction and Satire 1660–1750* (New York: Columbia University Press,

NOTES to pp. 35–40

1997), p. 102, and Ruth Herman, 'Enigmatic Gender in Delarivier Manley's *New Atalantis*', in Chris Mounsey, ed., *Presenting Gender: Changing Sex in Early-Modern Culture* (Lewisburg: Bucknell University Press, 2001), p. 215. I have drawn the information in this paragraph on Sunderland's life and the writings of Gordon and Manley from these studies.

28. For the text of *Love-Letters*, see *Journal of Homosexuality* 19/2 (1990): 11–46.
29. McFarlane, *Sodomite*, p. 107.
30. G.S. Rousseau, 'The Pursuit of Homosexuality in the Eighteenth Century: "Utterly Confused Category" and/or Rich Repository?', in Robert Maccubbin, ed., *'Tis Nature's Fault: Unregulated Sexuality in the Enlightenment* (Cambridge: Cambridge University Press, 1987), pp. 132–68; Alan Bray, 'Homosexuality and the Signs of Male Friendship in Elizabethan England', in Jonathan Goldberg, ed., *Queering the Renaissance* (Durham: Duke University Press, 1994), p. 41.
31. Trenchard and Gordon, *Cato's Letters*, 29 April 1721, p. 196.
32. *Tracts and Pamphlets by Richard Steele*, ed. Rae Blanchard (New York: Octagon Books, 1967; orig. pub. The Johns Hopkins University Press, 1944), pp. 465–66, 471; G.S. Rousseau, 'An Introduction to the *Love-Letters*: Circumstances of Publication, Context, and Cultural Commentary', *Journal of Homosexuality* 19/2 (1990): 72–77, quotation on p. 76.
33. Simon Targett, 'Government and Ideology during the Age of Whig Supremacy: The Political Argument of Sir Robert Walpole's Newspaper Propagandists', *Historical Journal* 37/2 (1994): 289–317.
34. Simon Varey, '*The Craftsman*', in J.A. Downie and Thomas N. Corns, eds, *Telling People What to Think: Early Eighteenth-Century Periodicals from 'The Review' to 'The Rambler'* (London: Frank Cass, 1993), pp. 58–77; Michael Harris, *London Newspapers in the Age of Walpole: A Study of the Origins of the Modern English Press* (Rutherford, NJ: Fairleigh Dickinson University Press, 1987), p. 114.
35. Robert Halsband, *Lord Hervey Eighteenth-Century Courtier* (New York and Oxford: Oxford University Press, 1974), p. 50.
36. For the larger context of the confrontation, see Alexander Pettit, *Illusory Consensus: Bolingbroke and the Polemical Response to Walpole, 1730–1737* (Newark: University of Delaware Press, 1997), ch. 2.
37. John, Lord Hervey, *To the Patrons of the* Craftsman (1731), and William Yonge, *Sedition and Defamation Display'd* (1731), ed. Alexander Pettit (New York: AMS Press, 1997), p. ii.
38. Ibid., pp. iii–iv.
39. William Pulteney, *A Proper Reply to a Late Scurrilous Libel; Intitled*, Sedition and Defamation Display'd (1731), ed. H.T. Dickinson (New York: AMS Press, 1998), pp. 3–4, 37n.
40. Ibid., p. 5.
41. See Norton, *Mother Clap's*; Randolph Trumbach, 'The Birth of the Queen: Sodomy and the Emergence of Gender Equality in Modern Culture', in Martin Duberman, Martha Vicinus and George Chauncey, Jr., eds, *Hidden from History: Reclaiming the Gay and Lesbian Past* (New York: Meridian/Penguin, 1989), pp. 129–40. For a contemporary depiction of the language, manners and antics rumoured to take place in molly houses, see Ned Ward, *The History of the London Clubs* (1709), excerpted in Ian McCormick, ed., *Secret Sexualities: A Sourcebook of 17th and 18th Century Writing* (New York and London: Routledge, 1997), pp. 131–34.
42. The *Craftsman* portrayed Walpole 'as Volpone, Catiline, Sejanus, Wolsey, Macheath, Menzikoff, Joseph Blake (a cut-throat known as "Blueskin") and Blake's fellow gangster, Jonathan Wild. Walpole also appeared in this paper as a strolling actor, buffoon, Harlequin, theatre manager, embezzler, bird of prey, Leviathan, Satan, steward (a hated stereotype akin to the rent collector of other eras), coachman, quack doctor, alchemist, blunderer, conjurer, gamester, gourmand, projector, and confidence trickster.' Varey, '*The Craftsman*', pp. 67–68.

43. Pulteney, *A Proper Reply*, p. 27. Pulteney did speculate that Hervey might have had the direct help of Walpole or his brother Horatio (p. 10).

44. Arend H. Huussen, Jr., 'Sodomy in the Dutch Republic during the Eighteenth Century', in Duberman et al., eds, *Hidden from History*, pp. 141–49.

45. Pulteney to Swift, 9 Feb. 1731, *The Correspondence of Jonathan Swift*, ed. Harold Williams, 5 vols (Oxford: Clarendon Press, 1963–65), 4: 439. Quoted in Dickinson's introduction to Pulteney, *A Proper Reply*, p. xviii. Pulteney made the same point on p. 25 of the pamphlet. Yonge, *Sedition and Defamation Display'd* argued that political satire long had been directed at party principles but, in the case of the present opposition, 'a fatal Necessity has driven them into a Method, which I am persuaded many of them dislike in their Hearts; and they are forced by personal Abuse, and private Scandal, to justify their differing, not only from their former Friends, but from their own former Conduct and Behaviour' (p. 47).

46. Halsband, *Lord Hervey*, pp. 77, 86–87.

47. Pulteney, *A Proper Reply*, pp. 6–7.

48. John, Lord Hervey, *Some Materials towards Memoirs of the Reign of King George the Second*, ed. Romney Sedgwick, 3 vols (New York: AMS Press, 1970; orig. publ. 1931), 1: 106, 107.

49. Yonge, *Sedition and Defamation Display'd*, p. 25.

50. Pulteney, *A Proper Reply*, p. 29.

51. Harriette Andreadis, *Sappho in Early Modern England: Female Same-Sex Literary Erotics 1550–1714* (Chicago and London: University of Chicago Press, 2001), pp. 173–74; Emma Donoghue, *Passions between Women: British Lesbian Culture 1688–1801* (New York: HarperPerennial, 1993), p. 162.

52. Jill Campbell, 'Politics and Sexuality in Portraits of John, Lord Hervey', *Word and Image* 6 (1990): 281.

53. BMC 2327; see also *Idol Worship; or, The Way to Preferment* (1740), BMC 2447, depicting a colossal Walpole under the Treasury arch, breeches lowered and bent over to receive the kisses of sycophants. More scatological, William Dent's *Public Credit, or The State Idol* (3 June 1791), BMC 7872, has Pitt in Walpole's place farting 'SURPLUS' upon members of the opposition. See Vic Gattrell, *City of Laughter: Sex and Satire in Eighteenth-Century London* (New York: Walker and Co., 2006), p. 182.

54. [William Arnall?], *Remarks on the* Craftsman's *Vindication of his Two Honble Patrons, in his Paper of May 22. 1731* (London: J. Peele, 1731), pp. 9–10, 59. For evidence of Arnall's authorship, see Alexander Pettit, 'Propaganda, Public Relations, and the Remarks on the Craftsman's Vindication of his Two Hon[oura]ble Patrons, in his Paper of May 22, 1731', *Huntington Library Quarterly* 57 (1994): 45–59.

55. [William Pulteney], *An Answer to One Part of a Late Infamous Libel, Intitled, Remarks on the Craftsman's Vindication of his Two Honourable Patrons; In Which the Character and Conduct of Mr. P. Is Fully Vindicated* (London: R. Francklin, 1731), pp. 52, 60.

56. William Coxe, *Memoirs of the Life and Administration of Sir Robert Walpole, Earl of Orford*, new edn, 4 vols (London: Longman, Hurst, Rees, Orme, and Brown, 1816), 3: 42–46.

57. This was in the dedication to Walpole in *Mr. Steele's Apology for Himself and his Writings Occasioned by his Expulsion from the House of Commons* (published by Burleigh, 22 Oct. 1714), reprinted in *The Correspondence of Richard Steele*, ed. Rae Blanchard (London: Humphrey Milford for Oxford University Press, 1941), pp. 489–94. Steele wrote of his advocate: 'A long Course of suffering for your Zeal in an honest Cause, has gained you the Character of an *open honest English Gentleman*, with the Capacity which takes off the Imputation of Weakness from Simplicity of Manners, and adds the Dignity of Knowledge to the Beauty of Innocence' (p. 492). That same year, ironically, Steele dedicated the second volume of the *Guardian* to Pulteney with a glowing assessment of his character. Blanchard notes that, having paid his respects to the elder statesmen of the Whig party in the *Tatler* and *Spectator*, Steele turned to the younger opposition Whigs. Steel addressed Pulteney as a man of merit and a friend,

a gentleman at the pinnacle of literary taste in whom literature would find nothing to correct but much to praise: 'Affability, Complacency, and Generosity of heart, which are natural to You.' The dedication lauded Pulteney's service to his country: 'Zeal for the Publick Good is the Characteristick of a Man of Honour, and a Gentleman, and must take place of Pleasures, Profits, and all other private Gratifications.' Steele closed by declaring the justice of his 'Reputation of a Man of Sense, a good Citizen, and agreeable Companion, a disinterested Friend, and an unbiassed Patriot'. As Blanchard's editorial note observes: 'This dedication obviously is not clear-cut and pointed in setting forth Pulteney's private and public virtues'; Steele probably simply wished his literary journal to be associated with a premier parliamentary orator and writer (pp. 476–78).

58. *The Free Briton. To Be Continued Weekly. By Francis Walsingham of the Inner Temple, Esq.*, 19 Aug. 1731. Walsingham was William Arnall's pseudonym: Harris, *London Newspapers*, pp. 102–3.

59. Hervey, *Some Materials*, 1: 1.

60. Ibid., 2: 622. See also 2: 364–65 (1734), where he anticipated the reaction of readers after he had gone, and drew upon Tacitus to explain Walpole's policy and defended his method of examining individuals 'with such curious eyes as virtuosos in microscopes examine flies and emmets'.

61. Reed Browning emphasizes the influence of Tacitus and Machiavelli on Hervey: *Political and Constitutional Ideas of the Court Whigs* (Baton Rouge: Louisiana State University Press, 1982), pp. 35–66.

62. Andrew Wallace-Hadrill, *Suetonius* (New Haven and London: Yale University Press, 1983), pp. 8–10, 23, 143, 171; Ronald Mellor, *Tacitus* (New York and London: Routledge, 1993), pp. 47–51, 88–89.

63. Hervey, *Some Materials*, 1: 7–9.

64. Wallace-Hadrill, *Suetonius*, p. 175.

65. Catherine Edwards, *The Politics of Immorality in Ancient Rome* (Cambridge: Cambridge University Press, 1993), pp. 5, 46–47; Mellor, *Tacitus*, p. 84.

66. Hervey, *Some Materials*, 1: 2–3, 2: 362.

67. Ibid., 1: 103–4.

68. Hervey went on to explain why these two things were impossible: 'In the first place because a Minister only answers for what he can do, the adherent for what he will do. And in the next place it is the interest of a solicitor to power to pretend to be deceived, because it is his interest not to break off his solicitation, and to make even the false profession he has received a pretence to renew it; whereas it is the interest of power to catch at any indirect dealing or shuffling conduct in a solicitor to justify either a denial or a delay in granting what is asked.' Ibid., 1: 108.

69. Ibid., 1: 104–8, quotation on pp. 104–5.

70. Ibid., 1: 19.

71. Ibid., 1: 107–8.

72. Ibid., 3: 773–74.

73. Ibid., 2: 284–85.

74. Ibid., 1: 86. Hervey did relate unkind things that Queen Caroline said about the liaison, which reflected upon her blindness to her own flaws (2: 421), and noted occasions when Walpole should have been attending to business rather than retiring to the country with Molly Skerret (1: 294, 2: 633–34).

75. Ibid., 2: 285.

76. Philip Dormer Stanhope, fourth Earl of Chesterfield, *Characters 1778, 1845*, with intro. by Alan T. McKenzie, The Augustan Reprint Society, Publication Numbers 259–60, William Andrews Clark Memorial Library, University of California, Los Angeles (Pasadena: The Castle Press, 1990), p. 32.

77. Of George I he observed: 'Lazy and inactive even in his pleasures, which were therefore lowly sensual.' He passed most of his time with his mistress, the duchess of Kendal,

who 'was very little above an idiot'. George II 'had no favourites, and indeed no friends, having none of that expansion of heart, none of those amiable, connecting talents, which are necessary for both. This, together with the sterility of his conversation, made him prefer the company of women, with whom he rather sauntered away than enjoyed his leisure hours. He was addicted to women, but chiefly to such as required little attention and less pay. He never had but two avowed mistresses of rank, the countesses of Suffolk and Yarmouth. The former, though he passed half his time with her, had no degree of influence, and but a small one of profit; the latter, being taken after the death of the queen, had more of both, but no extravagance of either.' Ibid., pp. 1, 5–6.

78. Ibid., p. 27.
79. Ibid., pp. 4, 31, 45, 55.
80. Ibid., p. 12.
81. Hervey, *Some Materials*, p. 16.
82. Chesterfield, *Characters*, p. 21.
83. Hervey, *Some Materials*, pp. 80, 86–87, quotation on p. 86; Chesterfield, *Characters*, p. 12.
84. McKenzie introduction, Chesterfield, *Characters*, p. iv.
85. Hervey, *Some Materials*, 1: 72; Samuel Shellabarger, *Lord Chesterfield* (London: Macmillan, 1935), p. 41. The letter was dated 27 March.
86. Horace Walpole, *Memoirs of the Reign of King George the Second*, ed. John Brooke, 3 vols (New Haven and London: Yale University Press, 1985), 1: 36.
87. Alexander Pope, *The First Satire on the Second Book of Horace* (1733), l. 6, and *Epistle to Dr. Arbuthnot* (1735), ll. 305–7, 325–26, in *Imitations of Horace. With an Epistle to Dr. Arbuthnot and the Epilogue to the Satires, The Twickenham Edition of the Poems of Alexander Pope*, ed. John Butt (London: Methuen, 1936), vol. 4, pp. 5, 117–19.
88. Edwards, *Politics of Immorality*, p. 48. As she observes: 'Adulterers were villains, but glamorous ones.' The pages of Hervey's memoirs spanning from May 1730 to summer 1732, the period covering his friendship with Prince Frederick and its demise, were ripped out in the original and the copy inherited by his grandson: Hervey, *Some Materials*, 1: 119; Halsband, *Lord Hervey*, p. 130. Frederick's recent biographer catalogues Hervey's misrepresentations of the prince's personal relationships, in this instance claiming that Hervey pimped Vane to ensnare him: Frances Vivian, *A Life of Frederick, Prince of Wales, 1707–1751: A Connoisseur of the Arts*, ed. Roger White (Lewiston, NY: The Edwin Mellon Press, 2006), pp. 190–98.
89. Hervey, *Some Materials*, 2: 477–79.
90. Ibid., 2: 479–83, quotation on p. 481.
91. Ibid., 1: 35–36.
92. Ibid., 1: 71, 279, 280.
93. For an assessment of Chesterfield's political principles, see Shellabarger, *Lord Chesterfield*, pp. 154–69.
94. *The Letters of Philip Dormer Stanhope, 4th Earl of Chesterfield*, ed. Bonamy Dobrée, 6 vols (New York: AMS Press, 1932), 2: 490–91. He published this opinion in *Old England*, 5 Feb. 1743: Shellabarger, *Lord Chesterfield*, p. 167, n. 1.
95. To George Lyttelton, 6 June 1741, Dobrée, *Letters of Chesterfield*, 2: 456.
96. 20 Sept. 1739, ibid., 2: 378.
97. See Maynard Mack, *The Garden and the City: Retirement and Politics in the Later Poetry of Pope 1731–1743* (Toronto: University of Toronto Press, 1969).
98. Michael C. McGee, '"Not Men, But Measures": The Origins and Import of an Ideological Principle', *Quarterly Journal of Speech*, 64 (1978): 141–54. See also I.G. Doolittle, 'A First-Hand Account of the Commons Debate on the Removal of Sir Robert Walpole, 13 February 1741', *Historical Research*, 53/127 (May 1980): 125–40.
99. David Hume, 'Essay VIII: Of Parties in General', in *Essays Moral, Political, and Literary*, ed. Eugene F. Miller (Indianapolis: Liberty Classics, 1985), pp. 56–57.
100. Ibid., p. 63.

NOTES to pp. 60–64   229

Chapter 3

1. Karen Harvey, 'The History of Masculinity, circa 1650–1800', *Journal of British Studies* 44/2 (2005): 296–311; Tim Hitchcock and Michèle Cohen, *English Masculinities 1660–1800* (London and New York: Longman, 1999); Dror Wahrman, '*Percy's* Prologue: From Gender Play to Gender Panic in Eighteenth-Century England', *Past and Present* 159 (1998): 113–60; Linda Colley, *Britons: Forging the Nation* (New Haven and London: Yale University Press, 1992), chs 4–5; Paul Langford, *Public Life and the Propertied Englishman 1689–1798* (Oxford: Clarendon Press, 1991), ch. 8.
2. Corinna Michelle Wagner, The Politics of Private Life: Propaganda, Morality and the Family, 1789–1820 (PhD diss., University of York, 2006).
3. Gillian Russell, *Women, Sociability and Theatre in Georgian London* (Cambridge: Cambridge University Press, 2007); see also John Brewer, 'Commercialization and Politics', in Neil McKendrick, John Brewer and J.H. Plumb, eds, *The Birth of a Consumer Society: The Commercialization of Eighteenth-Century England* (London: Europa, 1982), pp. 197–262.
4. Paul Langford, 'Politics and Manners from Sir Robert Walpole to Sir Robert Peel', *Proceedings of the British Academy* 94 (1997): 103–25, quotation on p. 119.
5. See Nancy Armstrong, *Desire and Domestic Fiction: A Political History of the Novel* (Oxford: Oxford University Press, 1987); Christopher Flint, *Family Fictions: Narrative and Domestic Relations in Britain, 1688–1798* (Stanford: Stanford University Press, 1998); Eve Tavor Bannet, *The Domestic Revolution: Enlightenment Feminisms and the Novel* (Baltimore and London: The Johns Hopkins University Press, 2000); Chris Roulston, *Narrating Marriage in Eighteenth-Century England and France* (Farnham: Ashgate, 2010).
6. Thomas A. King, *The Gendering of Men, 1600–1750. Volume 1: The English Phallus* (Madison: University of Wisconsin Press, 2004); Rictor Norton, *Mother Clap's Molly House: The Gay Subculture in England 1700–1830* (London: GMP Publishers, 1992), ch. 11.
7. For an able rebuttal of Peter Mandler's allegations that revisiting the role of families, interests and influence in politics constitutes some sort of neo-Namierism, see Elaine Chalus, *Elite Women in English Political Life, c.1754–1790* (Oxford: Clarendon Press, 2005), p. 10.
8. For similar imagery used in Restoration propaganda, see Harold Weber, *Paper Bullets: Print and Kingship under Charles II* (Lexington: University Press of Kentucky, 1996); Rachel Weil, 'Sometimes a Scepter Is Only a Scepter: Pornography and Politics in Restoration England', in Lynn Hunt, ed., *The Invention of Pornography: Obscenity and the Origins of Modernity* (New York: Zone Books, 1993), pp. 124–53.
9. Jason M. Kelly, *The Society of Dilettanti: Archaeology and Identity in the British Enlightenment* (New Haven and London: Yale University Press, 2009), pp. 77–88.
10. Anna Clark, *Scandal: The Sexual Politics of the British Constitution* (Princeton and Oxford: Princeton University Press, 2004), ch. 2; John Sainsbury, *John Wilkes: The Lives of a Libertine* (Aldershot, Hants, and Burlington, VT: Ashgate, 2006).
11. Philip Dormer Stanhope, 4th Earl of Chesterfield, *Characters 1778, 1845*, with intro. by Alan T. McKenzie, The Augustan Reprint Society, Publication Numbers 259–60, William Andrews Clark Memorial Library, University of California, Los Angeles (Pasadena: The Castle Press, 1990), p. 470. (This is one of four additional characters reproduced in facsimile from Lord Mahon's 1845 edition of Chesterfield's letters, volume 2.)
12. Ibid., pp. 471, 480.
13. Ibid., p. 474.
14. *The Memoirs and Speeches of James, 2nd Earl Waldegrave, 1742–1763*, ed. J.C.D. Clark (Cambridge: Cambridge University Press, 1988), p. 229.
15. Horace Walpole, *Memoirs of the Reign of King George the Third*, ed. G.F. Russell Barker, 4 vols (London: Lawrence and Bullen; New York: G.P. Putnam's Sons, 1894), 1: 212.

16. Horace Walpole, *Memoirs of the Reign of King George the Second*, ed. John Brooke, 3 vols (New Haven and London: Yale University Press, 1985), 2: 151, n. 2.

17. John L. Bullion, 'The Origins and Significance of Gossip about Princess Augusta and Lord Bute, 1755–1756', *Studies in Eighteenth-Century Culture* 21 (1991): 245–65; Patricia Meyer Spacks, *Gossip* (Chicago: University of Chicago Press, 1985).

18. Hannah Smith, 'The Court in England, 1714–1760: A Declining Political Institution?', *History* 90/297 (2005): 23–41, quotation on p. 33.

19. John Brewer, 'The Misfortunes of Lord Bute: A Case-Study in Eighteenth-Century Political Argument and Public Opinion', *Historical Journal* 16/1 (1973): 3–43.

20. Jason M. Kelly, 'Riots, Revelries, and Rumor: Libertinism and Masculine Association in Enlightenment London', *Journal of British Studies* 45/4 (2006): 759–95, quotation on p. 790.

21. John Brewer, *A Sentimental Murder: Love and Madness in the Eighteenth Century* (New York: Farrar, Straus and Giroux, 2004); Cindy McCreery, 'Keeping Up with the *Bon Ton*: The *Tête-à-Tête* Series in the *Town and Country Magazine*', in Hannah Barker and Elaine Chalus, eds, *Gender in Eighteenth-Century England: Roles, Representations and Responsibilities* (London: Longman, 1997), pp. 206–29; Donna T. Andrew, '"Adultery à-la-Mode": Privilege, the Law and Attitudes to Adultery 1770–1809', *History* 82 (1997): 5–23.

22. Lawrence Stone, *Broken Lives: Separation and Divorce in England 1660–1857* (Oxford: Oxford University Press, 1993), p. 139. My account of the Grafton marriage and divorce in this paragraph draws upon ch. 7 of this study.

23. 24 April 1769, *The Letters of Junius*, ed. John Cannon (Oxford: Clarendon Press, 1978), p. 67.

24. 22 June 1769, ibid., pp. 78–79. See also pp. 68–69: in this letter of 30 May 1769, Junius also commented on the lack of virtue in Grafton's pedigree.

25. 30 May, 22 June, 12 June 1769, ibid., pp. 70–71, 79, 76.

26. Walpole, *Memoirs of George the Second*, 1: 1, 2.

27. Horace Walpole, *Memoirs and Portraits*, ed. Matthew Hodgart (New York: Macmillian, 1963), pp. 210–12, quotation on p. 211.

28. 7 Oct. 1769, *Letters of Junius*, p. 130; Chesterfield, *Characters*, p. 12. Linguists note that the most common source for metaphors of shame in American speech today is the state of undress: Zoltán Kövecses, *Metaphor and Emotion: Language, Culture, and Body in Human Feeling* (Cambridge: Cambridge University Press, 2000), pp. 32–33.

29. 19 Sept., 7, 13 Oct. 1769, *Letters of Junius*, pp. 117–18, 130, 134–35.

30. To Charles O'Hara, [11 April 1768], *The Correspondence of Edmund Burke*, ed. Thomas W. Copeland, 10 vols (Cambridge: Cambridge University Press; Chicago: University of Chicago Press, 1958–78), 1: 349.

31. Edmund Burke, *Thoughts on the Cause of the Present Discontents* (1770), in *The Writings and Speeches of Edmund Burke*, ed. Paul Langford, 9 vols (Oxford: Clarendon Press, 1981–91), 2: 318, 319.

32. John Brewer, *Party Ideology and Popular Politics at the Accession of George III* (Cambridge: Cambridge University Press, 1976), pp. 14–15, 23, 47, 56–57.

33. Burke, *Present Discontents*, pp. 276, 314–15, 316.

34. Jeremy Black, *George III: America's Last King* (New Haven and London: Yale University Press, 2006), pp. 95–97, 239–40, 247–63; see also Nigel Aston and Clarissa Campbell Orr, eds, *An Enlightenment Statesman in Whig Britain: Lord Shelburne in Context, 1737–1805* (Woodbridge, Suffolk: Boydell Press, 2011).

35. L.G. Mitchell, *Charles James Fox* (Oxford: Oxford University Press, 1992), pp. 70, 71. See also his *Charles James Fox and the Disintegration of the Whig Party 1782–1794* (Oxford: Oxford University Press, 1971). I have drawn the information in this and the following two paragraphs from these works.

36. *Albion*, 25/2 (1993): 328.

37. James Gillray, *Bandelures*, 28 Feb. 1791, *BMC* 7829.

38. Judith S. Lewis, *Sacred to Female Patriotism: Gender, Class, and Politics in Late Georgian Britain* (New York: Routledge, 2003), pp. 135–38, 140–42.
39. Mitchell, *Fox*, p. 75.
40. John Ehrman, *The Younger Pitt*, 3 vols (London: Constable, and Stanford: Stanford University Press, 1969–96), 1: 108–9, 3: 69–70, 92–97. For his part, Ehrman does not know what to make of Pitt's sexuality. See also J. Holland Rose, *William Pitt and National Revival* (London: G. Bell and Sons, 1911), pp. 285–86; Miles Johnson and A.D. Harvey, 'Political Verse in Late Georgian Britain: Poems Referring to William Pitt the Younger (1759–1806)', *British Library Journal* (2004): 5–6.
41. John Barrell, *Imagining the King's Death: Figurative Treason, Fantasies of Regicide 1793–1796* (Oxford: Oxford University Press, 2000), p. 653.
42. British Library, *Place Collection*, set 38, vol. 3, fo. 180.
43. *BMC* 8651.
44. See, for example, James Gillray, *Cincinnatus in Retirement: Falsely Supposed to Represent Jesuit-Pad' Driven Back to his Native Potatoes*, 23 Aug. 1782, *BMC* 6026.
45. Isaac Kramnick, *The Rage of Edmund Burke: Portrait of an Ambivalent Conservative* (New York: Basic Books, 1977), p. 84; Katherine O'Donnell, '"Dear Dicky," "Dear Dick," "Dear Friend," "Dear Shackleton": Edmund Burke's Love for Richard Shackleton', *SEL: Studies in English Literature* 46/3 (2006): 619–40; Nicholas K. Robinson, *Edmund Burke: A Life in Caricature* (New Haven: Yale University Press, 1996); Corinna Wagner, 'Loyalist Propaganda and the Scandalous Life of Tom Paine: "Hypocritical Monster!"', *British Journal for Eighteenth-Century Studies* 28 (2005): 97–115.
46. Joanna Innes, 'Politics and Morals: The Reformation of Manners Movement in Later Eighteenth-Century England', in Eckhart Hellmuth, ed., *The Transformation of Political Culture: England and Germany in the Late Eighteenth Century* (Oxford: Oxford University Press, 1990), pp. 57–118.
47. Stella Tillyard, *Aristocrats: Caroline, Emily, Louisa, and Sarah Lennox 1740–1832* (New York: Farrar, Straus and Giroux, 1994), p. xx.
48. 17 Nov. 1754, *The Letters of Philip Dormer Stanhope, 4th Earl of Chesterfield*, ed. Bonamy Dobrée, 6 vols (New York: AMS Press, 1932), 5: 2165.
49. *Life and Letters of Sir Gilbert Elliot, First Earl of Minto from 1751 to 1806*, ed. by his great-niece the Countess of Minto, 3 vols (London: Longmans, Green, and Co., 1874), 1: 175, 178. Chesterfield gave the same assurances to his son, who experienced the same sort of halt: Chesterfield, *Letters*, 5: 2165–66.
50. Minto, *Life and Letters*, 1: 176–77. (Elliots' emphasis.)
51. Ibid., 1: 218–19.
52. To Lady Elliot, 13 Dec. 1787; to Mrs Philip Francis, 20 April 1787, Burke, *Correspondence*, 5: 368–69, 326–27.
53. Minto, *Life and Letters*, 1: 181, 184–86.
54. Ibid., 1: 144–45, 136–38, quotation on p. 137.
55. Ibid., 1: 212–15.
56. See, for example, his vexation and self-criticism in accounts of 18 April 1785, 2 June 1786, 2 Feb., 5 June, 6 July 1789, 16 April 1790, 31 May 1791, 2 April 1792 in *The Diary of the Right Hon. William Windham 1784 to 1810*, ed. Mrs Henry Baring (London: Longman's, Green, and Co., 1866), pp. 51, 78, 162, 178, 180, 193–94, 228.
57. Ibid., pp. 77, 245.
58. Ibid., p. 265; James Boswell, *Life of Johnson*, ed. R.W. Chapman (Oxford: Oxford University Press World's Classics Paperback, 1980), p. 1219.
59. Minto, *Life and Letters*, 1: 174–75. When Elliot was a guest at Beaconsfield in the autumn of 1788 and Burke was helping him revise his speech for publication, he joked about growing fat with all the others in 'meals, conversation, and sauntering walks': 1: 226.
60. To William Windham, 14 Oct. 1784; to James Boswell, 8 April 1788, Burke, *Correspondence*, 5: 177, 386–87.

61. Nathaniel William Wraxall, *Historical Memoirs of My Own Time*, 2 vols (London: T. Cadell and W. Davies, 1815), 2: 37–38.

62. Walpole, *Memoirs and Portraits*, p. 239; Mitchell, *Fox*, p. 97; M.J. Levy, *The Mistresses of George IV* (London: Peter Owen, 1996), pp. 28–29.

63. Minto, *Life and Letters*, 1: 224–25, 237, 257–58.

64. *Memoirs of Sir Philip Francis K.C.B. with Correspondence and Journals*, ed. Joseph Parkes and Herman Merivale, 2 vols (London: Longmans, Green, and Co., 1867), 2: 460–61; for Fox's secession, see 2: 304–14.

65. John Cannon, 'Francis, Sir Philip (1740–1818)', *Oxford Dictionary of National Biography* (Oxford University Press, 2004), http://www.oxforddnb.com/view/article/10077, accessed 29 Dec. 2008.

66. See especially Minto, *Life and Letters*, 1: 144–49, 296.

67. Ibid., 2: 5–6; *The Journal of Elizabeth Lady Holland (1791–1811)*, ed. Earl of Ilchester, 2 vols (London: Longman's Green, and Co., 1908), 1: 119; R.G. Thorne, *The History of Parliament: The House of Commons 1790–1820*, 5 vols (London: The History of Parliament Trust, Secker & Warburg, 1986), 3: 696.

68. D.R. Fisher, 'Pelham, Thomas, Second Earl of Chichester (1756–1826)', *Oxford Dictionary of National Biography* (Oxford University Press, 2004), http://www. oxforddnb.com/view/article/21799, accessed 11 Dec. 2007; see entries for 25 Feb. 1793 and 24 Jan. 1794 in Diary of Thomas Pelham, Earl of Chichester, BL Add. MS 33,630, fo. 36 and 33,631, fo. 7.

69. Quoted in Mitchell, *Fox*, p. 96.

70. *The Windham Papers: The Life and Correspondence of the Rt. Hon William Windham 1750–1810 [. . .] with an Introduction by the Rt. Hon. The Earl of Rosebury*, 2 vols (Boston: Small, Maynard & Co., 1913), 1: 75–80, quotation on pp. 77–78.

71. Ibid., pp. 62–63; *The Correspondence of the Right Honourable Sir John Sinclair, Bart.*, 2 vols (London: Henry Colburn and Richard Bentley, 1831), 1: 142–44; Michael Fry, *The Dundas Despotism* (Edinburgh: Edinburgh University Press, 1992), pp. 22, 48, 60, 156–57. The story has the additional twist of Dundas dropping his courtship of the poet Lady Anne Lindsay in 1792 because of her unreturned favour of Windham.

72. *Diary of Windham*, p. 205.

73. Wraxall, *Memoirs*, 2: 490–92; compare this to 2: 470–72.

74. Ibid., 2: 474–75, quotation on p. 474.

75. *The Letter-Journal of George Canning, 1793–1795*, ed. Peter Jupp, Camden Fourth Series, vol. 41 (London: Royal Historical Society, 1991), pp. 1–7, 66; Lord Granville Leveson Gower (First Earl Granville), *Private Correspondence 1781 to 1821*, ed. Castalia Countess Granville, 2 vols (London: John Murray, 1916), 1: 79. For a broader look at bipartisan sociability and its importance to political life, see Lewis, *Sacred to Female Patriotism*, ch. 3.

76. *Letter-Journal of Canning*, pp. 25, 139; for his first dinner at Pitt's, see pp. 28–30; for his illness and dietary resolutions, see pp. 67–77.

77. Ibid., pp. 278–79, 287.

78. See his dismay at finding himself all dressed up with no place to go when debate was cancelled due to lack of a quorum on 19 June 1794, ibid., p. 128.

79. Ibid., pp. 116, 153–54, 202, 278.

80. Leveson Gower, *Private Correspondence*, 1: 169, 170, 177–78.

81. Ibid., 1: 228.

82. *Letter-Journal of Canning*, pp. 46–47, quotation on p. 47.

83. Ibid., pp. 47–60, quotations on pp. 56, 58.

84. Ibid., p. 169.

85. Ibid., p. 82.

86. Ibid., pp. 184–88, quotation on p. 186.

87. Diary of Thomas Pelham, Earl of Chichester, BL Add. MS 33629, fos 34–36. For his political positions, see Burke, *Correspondence*, 5: 371, 6: 452, 7: 30, 414.

88. Paul W. Ludwig, *Eros and Polis: Desire and Community in Greek Political Theory* (Cambridge: Cambridge University Press, 2002), pp. 1–2, 5.

Chapter 4

1. Michael B. Young, *King James I and the History of Homosexuality* (New York: New York University Press, 2000); Harold Weber, *Paper Bullets: Print and Kingship under Charles II* (Lexington: University Press of Kentucky, 1996); Rachel Weil, 'Sometimes a Scepter Is Only a Scepter: Pornography and Politics in Restoration England', in Lynn Hunt, ed., *The Invention of Pornography: Obscenity and the Origins of Modernity* (New York: Zone Books, 1993), pp. 124–53; Rachel Weil, *Political Passions: Gender, the Family and Political Argument in England, 1680–1714* (Manchester: Manchester University Press, 1999).

2. Thomas A. King productively investigates this legacy of the Stuart court, which he calls 'residual pederasty', in early eighteenth-century representations of political relations: *The Gendering of Men, 1600–1750. Volume 1: The English Phallus* (Madison: University of Wisconsin Press, 2004).

3. Lawrence Stone, *The Family, Sex and Marriage in England 1500–1800* (New York: Harper and Row, 1977). See, for example, Randolph Trumbach, *The Rise of the Egalitarian Family* (New York: Academic Press, 1978); Lois G. Schwoerer, 'Seventeenth-Century English Women Engraved in Stone?', *Albion* 16/4 (1984): 389–403; Susan Moller Okin, 'Women and the Making of the Sentimental Family', *Philosophy and Public Affairs* 11/1 (1981): 65–88; Alan Macfarlane, *Marriage and Love in England: Modes of Reproduction 1300–1840* (Oxford: Basil Blackwell, 1986). Scholarship on domesticity has moved on to debating the significance of social class, the ideology of separate spheres and the dynamics of female subordination. For a useful overview of the various points of controversy, see the introduction to the revised edition of Leonore Davidoff and Catherine Hall, *Family Fortunes: Men and Women of the English Middle Class, 1780–1850* (London and New York: Routledge, 2002) and R.W. Connell and James W. Messerschmidt, 'Hegemonic Masculinity: Rethinking the Concept', *Gender and Society* 19/6 (2005): 829–59.

4. Chris Roulston, *Narrating Marriage in Eighteenth-Century England and France* (Farnham: Ashgate, 2010); Amy M. Froide, *Never Married: Singlewomen in Early Modern England* (Oxford: Oxford University Press, 2005), pp. 164–81, 218, *passim*; Irene Q. Brown, 'Domesticity, Feminism, and Friendship: Female Aristocratic Culture and Marriage in England, 1660–1760', *Journal of Family History* 7 (1982): 406–24; King, *Gendering of Men*.

5. Judith Schneid Lewis, *In the Family Way: Childbearing in the British Aristocracy, 1760–1860* (New Brunswick, NJ: Rutgers University Press, 1986).

6. David Lemmings, 'Marriage and the Law in the Eighteenth Century: Hardwicke's Marriage Act of 1753', *Historical Journal* 39/2 (1996): 339–60.

7. Stella Tillyard, *A Royal Affair: George III and his Scandalous Siblings* (New York: Random House, 2006), pp. 7–10, 14–16. For details of Frederick's household and patronage, see Frances Vivian, *A Life of Frederick, Prince of Wales, 1707–1751: A Connoisseur of the Arts*, ed. Roger White (Lewiston, NY: The Edwin Mellon Press, 2006).

8. George II's reputation as an ineffectual king has been disputed by John B. Owen, 'George II Reconsidered', in Anne Whiteman, J.S. Bromley and P.G.M. Dickson, eds, *Statesmen, Scholars and Merchants: Essays in Eighteenth-Century History Presented to Dame Lucy Sutherland* (Oxford: Clarendon Press, 1973), pp. 113–34, and Jeremy Black, 'George II Reconsidered', *Mitteilungen des Österreichischen Staatsarchivs* 35 (1982): 35–56.

9. Tillyard, *Royal Affair*, pp. 170–73.

10. Marilyn Morris, 'The Royal Family and Family Values in Late Eighteenth-Century England', *Journal of Family History* 21/4 (1996): 519–32, esp. p. 529.

11. Jeremy Black, *George III: America's Last King* (New Haven and London: Yale University Press, 2006), p. 160; see also Morris Marples, *Six Royal Sisters, Daughters of George III* (London: Michael Joseph, 1969).
12. *The Times*, 7 Feb. 1792.
13. For the classic exposition on this phenomenon in its broader context, see Gayle Rubin, 'The Traffic in Women: Notes on the "Political Economy" of Sex', in Rayna R. Reiler, ed., *Toward an Anthropology of Women* (London and New York: Monthly Review Press, 1975), pp. 157–210.
14. Eirwen E.C. Nicholson, 'English Political Prints and Pictorial Political Argument, *c.*1640–*c.*1832: A Study in Historiography and Methodology', PhD. diss., University of Edinburgh, 1994, pp. 322–24.
15. *True Briton*, 19 May 1797.
16. Of the available papers of this era that I consulted, the *Universal Spectator, and Weekly Journal* prided itself on its London news and contained the most extensive reporting on the royal family. It attempted neutrality during the 1730s but had become more aligned with the opposition by the 1740s. The *Weekly Register or Universal Journal* appeared to print many of the same stories, but in an abbreviated form. The ministerial *London Journal* also contained more regular and detailed reports on the royal family than the other papers I read extensively: *Common Sense*, the *Craftsman, Daily Gazetteer, Fog's Weekly Journal, Grub Street Journal, Nonsense of Common Sense* and *Old Common Sense*. For the political connections, circulations and contents of these papers, see Michael Harris, *London Newspapers in the Age of Walpole: A Study of the Origins of the Modern English Press* (Rutherford, NJ: Fairleigh Dickinson University Press, 1987).
17. *Universal Spectator, and Weekly Journal*, 9 March 1734.
18. *Universal Spectator, and Weekly Journal, Weekly Register or Universal Journal, London Journal*, 2 March 1734.
19. John, Lord Hervey, *Some Materials towards Memoirs of the Reign of King George the Second*, ed. Romney Sedgwick, 3 vols (New York: AMS Press, 1970; orig. publ. 1931), 1: 194, 281–83. Horace Walpole corroborated Hervey's version of events by questioning Lady Suffolk and others at court. He thought the queen and the princesses aside from the princess royal 'extravagant' in their open aversion to his person: 'I myself saw him the first Day when he came to Somerset House; I have seen many worse figures; His face was good. His Back very high, but covered with very long curled hair; his breast projected, he had little waste, his legs & thighs very long & lean; his hands were extremely long & scraggy.' Unlike Hervey, he noted saltier gossip regarding the wedding's delay: 'for some time; I had always heard, it was, that a string was to be cut before He cd consummate. Ly S. as decently as she cd. intimated that he had a bad distemper; but it was so wrapped up, I am not sure this was what she meant' (meaning Lady Suffolk spoke in polite euphemisms): Horace Walpole's Book of Materials, Sept. 1759, MS49.2615, fos 96–97, Lewis Walpole Library, Yale University. More generously inclined, the courtier Mary Granville Pendarves, later Delany, observed that the prince of Orange danced well in spite of his shape: Mary Delany, *Autobiography and Correspondence of Mary Granville, Mrs. Delany: With Interesting Reminiscences of King George III and Queen Charlotte*, ed. Lady Llanover, 6 vols (London: Richard Bentley, 1861–62), 1: 437.
20. Anon., *The Disappointed Marriage, or An Hue and Cry after an Outlandish Monster* (London: S. Gardiner, 1733). The missing word is James's, a reference to the royal palace.
21. Veronica P.M. Baker-Smith, *A Life of Anne of Hanover, Princess Royal* (Leiden: E.J. Brill, 1995), pp. 44–45; Suzanne Aspden, 'Ariadne's Clew: Politics, Allegory, and Opera in London (1734)', *The Musical Quarterly* 85/4 (2001): 735–70. I wish to thank Thomas McGeary for bringing this article to my attention.
22. Hervey, *Some Materials*, 1: 271; *Universal Spectator, and Weekly Journal*, 16 and 23 March 1734; *London Journal*, 16 March 1734.

23. *Universal Spectator, and Weekly Journal* and *Weekly Register or Universal Journal*, 4 May 1734; Hervey, *Some Materials*, 1: 289.

24. *London Journal*, 6 July 1734; Baker-Smith, *Life of Anne*, pp. 50–53.

25. *Universal Spectator, and Weekly Journal*, 26 Oct. 1734.

26. Ibid., 9, 16, 23, 30 Nov. 1734; quotation from 30 Nov. The *London Journal* of the 23rd also carried the story of Louis XV's letter.

27. *Universal Spectator, and Weekly Journal*, 7 Dec. 1734. The *London Journal*'s report did not mention this affecting reunion. For what occurred behind the scenes, see Baker-Smith, *Life of Anne*, pp. 48, 53, 55–56.

28. *Universal Spectator, and Weekly Journal*, 4, 25 Jan., 1 Feb., 8 March, 19 April 1735.

29. Baker-Smith, *Life of Anne*, pp. 57–58, 63–64, 77, 86, 107, 176–79.

30. *Universal Spectator, and Weekly Journal*, 23 Aug. 1735, 10 April 1736.

31. *The Times*, 31 Jan. 1797, declared: 'It is reported that a Gentleman of Rank has a second time purchased a scurrilous newspaper.' With tongue in cheek, it disputed the rumour, 'for though we know of many married people who disagree, yet it never came within our knowledge to hear of a man to suffer his wife's honour, which is so connected to his own, to be reflected on to gratify the envy of an antiquated mistress'. The *Morning Post* obviously became the prince of Wales's champion. For example, on 25 March 1797, in response to a story in *The Times* that he had withdrawn his support from the administration, the *Post* declared: 'We congratulate the PRINCE and the Country upon such an auspicious event; for, surely, there never was a Gentleman so vilely treated by those he condescended to support in compliment to his Father, whether we consider their private slanders or their public attacks, through the medium of certain Treasury Newspapers.' On 9 August, the *Post*, in attacking ministerial libels against the prince, purported to be surprised 'when we see the *Morning Chronicle*, a Paper affecting to be *in the confidence of* the *Opposition*, daily fanning the flame!'

32. *Morning Chronicle*, 14 Sept. 1796.

33. *The Times*, 12 April 1797. The *Morning Post* the following day reported that the prince's valet had to pull up one coat sleeve and then walk a considerable distance to repeat the operation with the other.

34. James Gillray, *Le Baiser A La Wirtembourg*, 15 April 1797, BMC 9006; Richard Newton, *The First Interview, or An Envoy from Yarmony to Improve the Breed*, 19 April 1797, BMC 9007. A print attributed to Temple West emphasized the resemblance between the prince and George III and his sons: *A Draft of* Sweet-Wirt, *from the* Princes Head *on the Road to London*, 21 April 1797, BMC 9008.

35. 'The answer to a very kind message sent by the Marquis of SALISBURY the morning after the marriage of the Prince and Princess of WIRTEMBURG was, "that the PRINCE was as well as would be expected, and HER ROYAL HIGHNESS *much the same!*"': *Morning Post*, 20 May 1797.

36. For an opposing view, see Diana Donald, *The Age of Caricature: Satirical Prints in the Reign of George III* (New Haven and London: Yale University Press, 1996), pp. 146–47. In response to the evidence she presents in support of this position—that the prints angered members of the Association for Preserving Liberty and Property against Republicans and Levellers—I must counter that their meeting minutes and correspondence demonstrate that they saw sedition everywhere. Raising alarm justified the association's existence and sense of self-importance.

37. James Gillray, *Sin, Death, and the Devil*, vide Milton, 9 June 1792, BMC 8105; [Joseph Grego], *The Works of James Gillray, the Caricaturist; with a History of His Life and Times*, ed. Thomas Wright (London: Chatto & Windus, 1873), pp. 147–48; Lynn Hunt, ed., *Eroticism and the Body Politic* (Baltimore: The Johns Hopkins University Press, 1991). For republican prints that attack rather than burlesque George III, see Anon., *Farmer Looby Manuring the Land*, c.1794, BMC 8515, and Anon., *Plan of Mud Island*, c.1794, BMC 8515. For a print that does not spare the princesses, see Richard Newton, *Psalm Singing at the Chapel* **** *[Royal]*, 17 May 1792, BMC 8089.

38. Anon., *Solomon in his Glory*, 19 Dec. 1738, *BMC* 2348.
39. For details, see Marilyn Morris, *The British Monarchy and the French Revolution* (New Haven and London: Yale University Press, 1998), p. 146.
40. *True Briton*, 11 Feb. 1797; *Telegraph*, 13 Feb. 1797.
41. *The Times*, 19 April 1797.
42. *True Briton*, 19 April, 4, 5 June 1797; *Morning Post*, 19 April, 3 June 1797.
43. James Gillray, *The Bridal Night*, 18 May 1797, *BMC* 9014. Isaac Cruikshank, *The Wedding Night*, 20 May 1797, *BMC* 9015. For the republican pamphlets of 1782, see Herbert H. Rowan, *The Princes of Orange: The Stadholders in the Dutch Republic* (Cambridge: Cambridge University Press, 1988), pp. 212–13; for Anne's efforts to preserve the stadholderate after William IV's death and William V's disastrous leadership, see ibid., ch. 10.
44. *Universal Spectator, and Weekly Journal*, 1 May 1736; see also 3, 10, 17, 24 April.
45. *Daily Gazetteer*, 27 April 1736.
46. Ibid., 30 April 1736.
47. *Morning Post*, 13 April 1795; *Morning Chronicle*, 11 April 1795.
48. Morris, 'Royal Family and Family Values'.
49. Morris, *British Monarchy*, pp. 167–73; *Sun*, 14, 29 May 1796.
50. James Gillray, *The Presentation—or—The Wise Men's Offering*, 9 Jan. 1796, *BMC* 8779.
51. *Telegraph*, 31 May 1796; *Sun*, 27 May 1796; *True Briton*, 7 June 1796.
52. Anon., *A Review with Suitable Remarks and Reflections, of the Astonishing Misrepresentations and Gross Contradictions Which Have Been Circulated in All the Daily Presses Relative to a Late Domestic Fracas in a Family of the First Rank; And Which Has Been Fortunately Succeeded by a Perfect Reconciliation: Together with Most Curious Particulars, Which Have Been Inserted in Various Papers since the Reconciliation* (London: By Author, 1796), p. 6; Anon., *Observations on the Various Accounts of a Late Family Difference in High Life, Now Happily Adjusted to the Satisfaction of All Parties Concerned* (London: R. Faulder, 1796), pp. 1, 41–44.
53. *Oracle and Public Advertiser*, 20 July 1796; *Telegraph*, 2 July 1796.
54. Hervey, *Some Materials*, 1: 195, 273, 276–77, 3: 902; Walpole, Book of Materials, fos 97, 116.
55. A painstakingly detailed account of the pregnancy, birth, christening, quarrels and separation of the courts can be found in Hervey, *Some Materials*, 3: 756–857; compare *Daily Gazetteer*, 3 Aug. 1737; *Common Sense, or The Englishman's Journal*, 6 Aug. 1737; *Universal Spectator, and Weekly Journal*, 6 Aug. 1737; see, for example, *Letters in the Original, with Translations and Messages, That Passed between the King, Queen, Prince, and Princess of Wales, on Occasion of the Birth of the Young Princess* (London: J. Roberts, 1737).
56. Philip C. Yorke, *The Life and Correspondence of Philip Yorke, Earl of Hardwicke Lord High Chancellor of Great Britain*, 3 vols (Cambridge: Cambridge University Press, 1913), 1: 170–82.
57. Hervey, *Some Materials*, 2: 614–18.
58. Anon., *Frederick Prince of Wales and Princess Augusta of Saxe Gotha*, 25 April 1736, *BMC* 2270.
59. Hervey, *Some Materials*, 3: 804, 809–10, 775. Elsewhere I have argued that Hervey's relationship with the queen was the most important in his life: 'Transgendered Perspectives on Premodern Sexualities', *SEL*, 46/3 (2006): 585–600.
60. Hannah Smith and Stephen Taylor, 'Hephastion and Alexander: Lord Hervey, Frederick, Prince of Wales, and the Royal Favourite in England in the 1730s', *English Historical Review* 124/507 (2009): 283–312.
61. Anon., *The Christening. A Satirical Poem. In Which Are Contain'd the Humorous Transactions, Speeches, and Behaviour of the Guests Who Were Present at the Ceremony and Entertainment* (London: W. James, 1732); Anon., *The Fair Concubine: or, The Secret*

History of the Beautiful Vanella, 2nd edn (London, 1732); [James Miller], *Vanelia; or, The Amours of the Great. An Opera. As It Is Acted by a Private Company near* St. James's (London: E. Rayner, 1732); Anon., *Tell-Tale Cupids Lately Discover'd in the Eyes of a Certain Court Lady, Now Displac'd. With Faithful Memoirs of the Amours and Intrigues of the Countess Matilda, from her First Coming to Court, to the Time of her Being Displac'd* (London: P. Monger, 1735); Anon., *Authentick Memoirs of the Unfortunate Vanella, a Roman Lady, from her Birth to her Sickness* (London: T. Reynolds, 1736); Anon., *The Forsaken Fair. An Epistle from Calista in her Late Illness at Bath, to Lothario on his Approaching Nuptials* (London: B. Dickson. 1736); *Universal Spectator, and Weekly Journal*, 25 Jan. 1735.

62. Material for this paragraph and the next is drawn from Jo Manning, *My Lady Scandalous: The Amazing Life and Outrageous Times of Grace Dalrymple Elliott, Royal Courtesan* (New York: Simon and Shuster, 2005), pp. 111–13, 128–33, 144–56, 171–73, 181–83, 191–93, and M.J. Levy, *The Mistresses of King George IV* (London and Chester Springs: Peter Owen, 1996).

63. E.A. Smith, *George IV* (New Haven and London: Yale University Press, 1999), p. 65.

64. Flora Fraser, *The Unruly Queen* (New York: Alfred A. Knopf, 1996), pp. 74, 81–84.

65. *The Journal of Elizabeth Lady Holland (1791–1811)*, ed. Earl of Ilchester, 2 vols (London: Longman's Green, and Co., 1908), 1: 121–22; *The Letters of Richard Brinsley Sheridan*, ed. Cecil Price, 3 vols (Oxford: Clarendon Press, 1966), 1: 207–8; Arthur Calder-Marshall, *The Two Duchesses* (New York: Harper & Row, Publishers, 1978), pp. 123–24, 131–32, 161–63.

66. *The Journal of Thomas Moore*, ed. Wilfred S. Dowden, 6 vols (Newark: University of Delaware Press, 1984), 1 May 1819, 1: 170.

67. Lord Granville Leveson-Gower (1st Earl Granville), *Private Correspondence 1781 to 1821*, ed. Castalia Countess Granville, 2 vols (London: John Murray, 1916), 1: 334 (quotation), 352, 250, 286 (quotation); 2: 349–50 (quotations), 353.

68. Linda Kelly, *Richard Brinsley Sheridan: A Life* (London: Pimlico, 1998 [1997]), pp. 249–51; *Journal of Thomas Moore*, 1: 61.

69. Fintan O'Toole, *A Traitor's Kiss: The Life of Richard Brinsley Sheridan, 1751–1816* (New York: Farrar, Straus and Giroux, 1998 [1997]), pp. 386–95.

70. Ibid., pp. 84–87, 141–43, 264–72; John Watkins, *Memoirs of the Public and Private Life of the Right Honorable R.B. Sheridan, with a Particular Account of his Family and Connexions*, 2 vols, 2nd edn (London: Henry Colburn, 1817), 1: 195, 308.

71. *The Letter-Journal of George Canning, 1793–1795*, ed. Peter Jupp, Camden Fourth Series, vol. 41 (London: Royal Historical Society, 1991), pp. 164–67, 169–70.

72. Ibid., p. 168. I apologize for using a fox-hunting metaphor given Canning's dislike of the sport.

73. Granville, *Private Correspondence*, 1: 35. Lady Stafford had voiced her reservations about Jenkinson after observing his behaviour while at home from Oxford in 1787: ibid., 1: 8.

74. Norman Gash, *Lord Liverpool: The Life and Political Career of Robert Banks Jenkinson, Second Earl of Liverpool, 1770–1828* (Cambridge, MA: Harvard University Press, 1984), pp. 14–15.

75. *Letter-Journal of Canning*, pp. 109–16, 123–24.

76. Ibid., pp. 178–79, 183, 191, 193–94, 199–200, 210, 228–29, 239–40, 253.

77. Granville, *Private Correspondence*, 1: 250–55.

78. John Ehrman, *The Younger Pitt*, 3 vols (London: Constable, and Stanford: Stanford University Press, 1969–96), 3: 94–97; Marilyn Morris, 'Transgendered Perspectives on Premodern Sexualities', *Studies in English Literature* 46 (summer 2006): 585–600.

79. Granville, *Private Correspondence*, 1: 256–59, quotations on pp. 256, 259.

80. Ibid., 1:274.

81. Minto, *Life and Letters*, 3: 61.

82. Fraser, *Unruly Queen*, pp. 123–25, 164, 381–82.

83. Cynthia Campbell, *The Most Polished Gentleman: George IV and the Women in his Life* (London: Kudos Books, 1995), pp. 280–81.

84. *Journal of Thomas Moore*, 2: 423, 462.

85. P.J.V. Rolo, *George Canning: Three Biographical Studies* (London: Macmillan, 1965), pp. 40–45; Dorothy Marshall, *The Rise of George Canning* (London: Longmans, Green & Co., 1938), pp. 206–7; Wendy Hindle, *George Canning* (New York: St. Martin's Press, 1974), p. 79; Judith Lewis, *Sacred to Female Patriotism: Gender, Class, and Politics in Late Georgian Britain* (New York and London: Routledge, 2003), pp. 148, 168–69.

86. Baker-Smith, *Life of Anne*, p. 138.

87. Smith, *George IV*, pp. ix–x, 3–12, ch. 20; Campbell, *Most Polished Gentleman*, pp. vi, 15–17; Saul David, *The Prince of Wales and the Making of the Regency* (New York: Little, Brown and Company and Atlantic Monthly Press, 1998), pp. 5–31. David even presents as fact the far-fetched tale that George III secretly married and had children with the Quaker Hannah Lightfoot, in order to represent him as a hypocrite with respect to his son's marriage to Maria Fitzherbert (pp. 33–34). For further rehabilitations of George IV's image at George III's expense, see Steven Parissien, *George IV: Inspiration of the Regency* (New York: St. Martin's Press, 2001) and Tom Ambrose, *Prinny and his Pals: George IV and his Remarkable Gift of Friendship* (London and Chester Springs, PA: Peter Owen Publishers, 2009).

88. Elaine Chalus, *Elite Women in English Political Life c.1754–1798* (Oxford: Clarendon Press, 2005), p. 26; Lewis, *Sacred to Female Patriotism*, pp. 118–25.

89. Granville, *Private Correspondence*, 1: 208.

Chapter 5

1. E.A. Reitan, 'The Civil List in Eighteenth-Century British Politics: Parliamentary Supremacy versus the Independence of the Crown', *Historical Journal* 9/3 (1966): 318–37. For early Stuart financial conflicts, see Barry Coward, *The Stuart Age: England 1603–1714*, 2nd edn (London and New York: Longman, 1994), pp. 138–49, 160–69.

2. J.C. Sainty and R.O. Bucholz, *Officials of the Royal Household 1660–1837*, 2 vols (London: University of London, 1997–98), 1: lxv–lxvi.

3. Linda Levy Peck, *Consuming Splendor: Society and Culture in Seventeenth-Century England* (New York: Cambridge University Press, 2005), p. 352. For a pre-Habermasian argument for consumerism's origins in the eighteenth century, see Neil McKendrick, 'The Consumer Revolution of Eighteenth-Century England', in Neil McKendrick, John Brewer and J.H. Plumb, eds, *The Birth of a Consumer Society: The Commercialization of Eighteenth-Century England* (Bloomington: Indiana University Press, 1982), pp. 9–33. Of course, one could trace moralists' association of vanity with self-adornment back to the advent of Christianity, and concern about foreign luxuries to Henry VIII's reign: Aileen Ribeiro, *Dress and Morality* (Oxford: Berg, 2003 [1986]).

4. Valerie Cumming, *Royal Dress: The Image and Reality 1580 to the Present Day* (New York: Holmes and Meier, 1989), p. 18.

5. Lawrence Stone, *The Crisis of the Aristocracy 1558–1641* (Oxford: Clarendon Press, 1965), p. 563.

6. Linda Levy Peck, *Court Patronage and Corruption in Early Stuart England* (Boston: Unwin Hyman, 1990), pp. 12–20, quotation on p. 13.

7. Peck, *Consuming Splendor*, chs 2 and 6; Leora Auslander, *Cultural Revolutions: Everyday Life and Politics in Britain, North America, and France* (Berkeley and Los Angeles: University of California Press, 2009), pp. 59–63.

8. Cumming, *Royal Dress*, p. 31; Woodruff D. Smith, *Consumption and the Making of Respectability 1660–1800* (New York and London: Routledge, 2002), p. 36.

9. Cumming, *Royal Dress*, pp. 31–33; David Kuchta, *The Three-Piece Suit and Modern Masculinity in England 1550–1850* (Berkeley: University of California Press, 2002).

10. Peck, *Consuming Splendor*, p. 347.
11. William B. Boulton, *The Amusements of Old London*, 2 vols (London: John C. Nimmo, 1901), 1: 207–12, 2: 2–10; Claire Walsh, 'Social Meaning and Social Space in the Shopping Galleries of Early Modern London', in John Benson and Laura Ugolini, eds, *A Nation of Shopkeepers: Five Centuries of British Retailing* (London and New York: I.B. Tauris, 2003), pp. 52–79.
12. R.O. Bucholz, *The Augustan Court: Queen Anne and the Decline of Court Culture* (Stanford: Stanford University Press, 1993), pp. 23–26.
13. Steve Pincus, *1688: The First Modern Revolution* (New Haven and London: Yale University Press, 2009), ch. 12.
14. John Brewer, *The Sinews of Power: War, Money and the English State, 1688–1783* (New York: Alfred A. Knopf, 1989).
15. Joyce Oldham Appleby, *Economic Thought and Ideology in Seventeenth-Century England* (Princeton: Princeton University Press, 1978).
16. Istvan Hont and Michael Ignatieff, 'Needs and Justice in the *Wealth of Nations*: An Introductory Essay', in Istvan Hont and Michael Ignatieff, eds, *Wealth and Virtue: The Shaping of Political Economy in the Scottish Enlightenment* (Cambridge: Cambridge University Press, 1983), pp. 1–44.
17. Bucholz, *Augustan Court*, pp. 26–27; Cumming, *Royal Dress*, p. 37.
18. Bucholz, *Augustan Court*, pp. 31–32, 239–41.
19. Ragnhild Hatton, *George I, Elector and King* (Cambridge, MA: Harvard University Press, 1978), pp. 97–99, 132–34, 203–5; J.M. Beattie, *The English Court in the Reign of George I* (Cambridge: Cambridge University Press, 1967), pp. 11–14, 55, 123–26, 257–62; Hannah Smith, *Georgian Monarchy: Politics and Culture, 1714–1716* (Cambridge: Cambridge University Press, 2006), pp. 62–69.
20. Sainty and Bucholz, *Officials of the Royal Household*, 1: lxvi.
21. Cumming, *Royal Dress*, pp. 52–53, 55, 68–69, 72–73, 86, 88; Philip Mansel, 'Monarchy, Uniform and the Rise of the *Frac* 1760–1830', *Past and Present* 96 (1982): 103–32.
22. Albert O. Hirschman, *The Passions and the Interests: Political Arguments for Capitalism before its Triumph* (Princeton: Princeton University Press, 1977); Colin Campbell, *The Romantic Ethic and the Spirit of Modern Capitalism* (Oxford: Basil Blackwell, 1987); Smith, *Consumption*; Woodruff D. Smith, *Consumption and the Making of Respectability* (New York, Routledge, 2002)
23. Leonore Davidoff and Catherine Hall, *Family Fortunes: Men and Women of the English Middle Class, 1780–1850* (Chicago: University of Chicago Press, 1991), p. 360; Margaret R. Hunt, *The Middling Sort: Commerce, Gender, and the Family in England 1680–1780* (Berkeley: University of California Press, 1996), pp. 46–53, quotation on p. 50; see also Dror Wahrman, *Imagining the Middle Class: The Political Representation of Class in Britain, c.1780–1840* (Cambridge: Cambridge University Press, 1995).
24. Hannah Grieg, 'Leading the Fashion: The Material Culture of London's *Beau Monde*', in John Styles and Amanda Vickery, eds, *Gender, Taste, and Material Culture in Britain and North America 1700–1830* (New Haven and London: Yale University Press, 2006), pp. 293–313; Smith, *Georgian Monarchy*, pp. 224–26. See also Anne Buck, *Dress in Eighteenth-Century England* (New York: Holmes & Meier Publishers, 1979), pp. 13–33.
25. James Raven, *Judging New Wealth: Popular Publishing and Responses to Commerce in England, 1750–1800* (Oxford: Clarendon Press, 1992), chs 7–8.
26. McKendrick, 'The Commercialization of Fashion', pp. 34–99; Buck, *Dress*, p. 25.
27. Beattie, *English Court*, pp. 106–18; John Brooke, *King George III* (New York: McGraw Hill, 1972), pp. 203–4; Reitan, 'Civil List', pp. 323–24. The expansion of the royal household during the reigns of the first three Georges contributed to the debt: Sainty and Bucholz, *Officials of the Royal Household*, pp. lxvi–lxxix.
28. *A Speech against Sir R—— W——'s Proposal for Increasing the Civil List Revenue: As it Was Spoken in the House of Commons, July 3. 1727. By W—— S—p—n, Esq*, 2nd edn

(London: J. Watson [1727]); *London Journal*, 30 Sept. 1727; *Cobbett's Parliamentary History of England from the Norman Conquest, in 1066, to the Year 1803*, 36 vols (London, 1811), 8: 599–605.

29. *Speech against Sir R—— W——'s Proposal*, quotations on pp. 6, 16, 9.
30. *London Journal*, 30 Sept. 1727.
31. Speech of William Adam in John Almon, *The Parliamentary Register* (London, 1780), 18: 133, cited in Ian R. Christie, 'Economical Reform and "The Influence of the Crown", 1780', *Cambridge Historical Journal* 12/2 (1956): 148. Christie points out that neither side produced any hard statistical evidence; moreover, while the war increased the opportunity for influence through military patronage and contracts, the number of placemen in the Commons and the number of seats controlled by the Treasury had declined since 1761: pp. 144–54.
32. Peter Pindar [John Wolcot], *The Lousiad: An Heroi-Comic Poem*, 7th edn (London: G. Kearsley, 1787 [1785]), pp. 8–9.
33. For the psychological power of places and pensions, see Reitan, 'Civil List', pp. 322–23.
34. [William Pulteney], *Some Considerations on the National Debts, the Sinking Fund, and the State of Publick Credit: In a Letter to a Friend in the Country* (London: R. Francklin, 1729), pp. 81–85, quotations on pp. 83–84, 85.
35. William Coxe, *Memoirs of the Life and Administration of Sir Robert Walpole, Earl of Orford*, new edn, 4 vols (London: Longman, Hurst, Rees, Orme, and Brown, 1816 [1798]), 3: 27, 31–38, quotation on p. 34; [William Pulteney], *An Answer to One Part of a Late Infamous Libel, Intitled, Remarks on the Craftsman's Vindication of his Two Honourable Patrons; In Which the Character and Conduct of Mr. P. Is Fully Vindicated* (London: R. Francklin, 1731), pp. 34, 38.
36. Steven Blakemore, *Intertextual War: Edmund Burke and the French Revolution in the Writings of Mary Wollstonecraft, Thomas Paine, and James Mackintosh* (Cranbury, NJ: Fairleigh Dickinson University Press, 1997), ch. 4.
37. *Craftsman*, 9 March 1734.
38. *Fog's Weekly Journal*, 14 Dec. 1728.
39. *Universal Spectator, and Weekly Journal*, 25 Jan. 1729.
40. *London Journal*, 20 July 1734.
41. Ibid., 29 Sept. 1733.
42. *Fog's Weekly Journal*, 3 April 1731.
43. Frank Prochaska, *Royal Bounty: The Making of a Welfare Monarchy* (New Haven and London: Yale University Press, 1995), pp. 4–7, 12, 15–16, 18–19, 21, 39–43.
44. 31 Oct. 1732, *Lord Hervey and his Friends 1726–38*, ed. Earl of Ilchester (London: John Murray, 1950), pp. 144–45.
45. *Craftsman*, 11 Nov. 1727.
46. Quoted in Benjamin Boyce, *The Benevolent Man: A Life of Ralph Allen of Bath* (Cambridge: Harvard University Press, 1967), p. 36. The story made its way across the Atlantic the following year, appearing in the *New York Gazette*, 29 Jan. 1728, and cited as the first reference to an ox roast in Thomas F. DeVoe, *The Market Assistant* (New York: Hurd and Houghton, 1867), pp. 33–34.
47. *Craftsman*, 7 March 1730.
48. See, for example, the *Craftsman*, 2 Feb. 1728, for the new uniforms that three regiments of foot guards would receive for the queen's birthday, and 1 Jan. 1732, for the prince of Wales fitting out a fine new barge and kitting out twelve watermen and a coxswain in new clothes in honour of his mother's birthday.
49. Lord Hervey to Stephen Fox, 2 Oct. 1731, *Lord Hervey and his Friends*, p. 100.
50. Veronica Baker-Smith, *Royal Discord: The Family of George II* (London: Athena Press, 2008), p. 87.
51. *Craftsman*, and with slight variants in *Common Sense; or The Englishman's Journal*, 18 Nov. 1738.

52. Christine Gerrard, 'Queens-in-Waiting: Caroline of Anspach and Augusta of Saxe-Gotha as Princesses of Wales', in Clarissa Campbell Orr, ed., *Queenship in Britain 1660–1837* (Manchester and New York: Manchester University Press, 2002), pp. 154–56. See the glowing account of the prince's reception at Cirencester and Bath in *Common Sense; or The Englishman's Journal*, 28 Oct. 1738.

53. To Stephen Fox, 23, 28 Oct. 1731, *Lord Hervey and his Friends*, pp. 105 (quotation), 106.

54. *Craftsman*, 22 Nov. 1729, 6 Nov. 1731, 11 Oct. 1735; *London Evening Post*, 8 Feb. 1735.

55. Lowell Lindgren, 'The Three Great Noises "Fatal to the interests of Bononcini"', *Musical Quarterly* 61/4 (1975): 574–78, 583; César de Saussure, *A Foreign View of England in the Reigns of George I and George II*, trans. and ed. Madame van Muyden (London: John Murray, 1902), pp. 330–35. *Fog's Weekly Journal* on 13 March 1731 identified Ughi thus: 'they say [he] is an Italian, and suppos'd to be a Prince come to see our Court incognity', when it reported the purchase of Count Kinski's horses for £1,000.

56. *Daily Gazetteer*, 2 Nov. 1737.

57. See Andrew C. Thompson, *George II King and Elector* (New Haven and London: Yale University Press, 2011), pp. 86–90, 113, 197–204.

58. *The Times*, 3 Feb. 1794. Caricaturists had a field day with the scandalous reports from the front: James Gillray, *Fatigues of the Campaign in Flanders*, 20 May 1793, BMC 8327; Isaac Cruikshank, *Preparing for Action or An English Man of War Engaging Two Dutch Doggers*, 9 June 1793, BMC 8329, and *The Wet Party or The Bogs of Flanders*, 7 Dec. 1793, BMC 8351.

59. *World and Fashionable Advertiser*, 19 Jan. 1790.

60. For the various ways clothes conveyed political meanings at court, see Hannah Grieg, 'Dressing for Court: Sartorial Politics and Fashion News in the Age of Mary Delany', in Mark Laird and Alicia Weisberg-Roberts, eds, *Mrs. Delany and her Circle* (New Haven and London: Yale University Press), pp. 80–93.

61. *The Times*, 19 Jan. 1792.

62. For details of the prince of Wales's debts and the debates over their payment, see Marilyn Morris, 'Princely Debt, Public Credit, and Commercial Values in Late Georgian Britain', *Journal of British Studies* 43 (2004): 339–65.

63. *The Times*, 19 Jan., 6 June 1791; *Morning Post*, 13, 20 Jan. 1791.

64. *Morning Post*, 31 Jan. 1791, 30 Dec. 1791.

65. *The Times*, 18 Jan. 1791, 21 Jan. 1791; second quotation from *Morning Chronicle*, 20 Jan. 1792.

66. *The Times*, 23, 25 Jan. 1792.

67. *The Times*, 19 Jan., 5 June 1792.

68. See E.A. Smith, *George IV* (New Haven and London: Yale University Press, 1999), pp. 62–69.

69. *The Times*, 19 Jan. 1793; *Sun*, 30 March 1793.

70. *Morning Chronicle*, 16 Nov. 1792, 5 June 1793.

71. *The Times*, 13 Nov. 1794.

72. *The Times*, 3 Feb., 9 Feb (quotation) 1797; *Sun*, 6, 7 Feb. 1797; *Morning Chronicle*, 7 Feb. 1797. For the prince's interest in Ireland, see Smith, *George IV*, pp. 82–85.

73. Tom Nairn, *The Enchanted Glass: Britain and its Monarchy* (London: Hutchinson Radius, 1988), pp. 25–29, quotation on p. 27.

74. Morris, 'Princely Debt'.

75. *Cobbett's Parliamentary History*, 9: 119–39. Readers could find edited versions of parliamentary debates in the *Gentleman's Magazine* and the *London Magazine*.

76. John, Lord Hervey, *Some Materials towards Memoirs of the Reign of King George the Second*, ed. Romney Sedgwick, 3 vols (New York, AMS Press, 1970; orig. publ. 1931), 1: 266; Mary Delany, *Autobiography and Correspondence of Mary Granville, Mrs. Delany: With Interesting Reminiscences of King George III and Queen Charlotte*, ed.

Lady Llanover, 6 vols (London: Richard Bentley, 1861–62), 1: 432; *Universal Spectator*, and *Weekly Register or Universal Journal*, 5 Jan. 1734.

77. *Universal Spectator*, 16 March 1734.
78. Baker-Smith, *Royal Discord*, pp. 66–68, 79–80, Delany, *Autobiography*, 1: 437; Hervey, *Memoirs*, 1: 271, 289.
79. Nigel Aston, 'The Court of George II: Lord Berkeley of Stratton's Perspective', *Court Historian* 13 (2008): 181; Thompson, *George II*, 7–8, 64, 291–92.
80. Hervey, *Memoirs*, 2: 623.
81. *London Journal*, 16 March 1734; *Universal Spectator*, 23 March, 4 May 1734.
82. Hervey, *Memoirs*, 1: 34–35, 95–96, 234–35; 2: 507, 549, 554–55.
83. *Cobbett's Parliamentary History*, 9: 1220–25.
84. *Daily Gazetteer*, 29 April 1736; *Universal Spectator*, 1 May 1736. For other examples of the prince's charitable impulses, even when in debt, see Frances Vivian, *A Life of Frederick, Prince of Wales, 1707–1751: A Connoisseur of the Arts*, ed. Roger White (Lewiston, NY: The Edwin Mellon Press, 2006), pp. 178, 228–29, 284–85.
85. Hervey, *Memoirs*, 2: 624–28; 3: 665–67, 682–705; [William Pulteney], *A Letter from a Member of Parliament to his Friend in the Country, upon the Motion to Address His Majesty to Settle 100,000 l. per Annum on His Royal Highness the Prince of Wales, &c. In Which the Antient and Modern State of the Civil List, and the Allowance to the Heir Apparent, or Presumptive of the Crown, Are Particularly Consider'd* (London: H. Haines, 1737).
86. *Common Sense; or The Englishman's Journal*, 30 April, 18 June 1737, 11, 25 Feb., 18 March 1738, 15 Dec. 1739.
87. For the broader debate about public credit, see E.L. Hargreaves, *The National Debt* (London: Frank Cass, 1930, reprinted New York: Augustus M. Kelley, 1966).
88. *The Times*, 15 June, 18 Nov. 1791. For the duke's gambling debts, see 22 Nov.
89. Isaac Cruikshank, *A Scene in the Gamester*, 8 Feb. 1792, *BMC* 8062.
90. *The Times*, 19, 24 Nov. 1791; *Morning Post*, 14 Aug. 1791.
91. See William Dent, *The Recruiting Officer, or, A Matrimonial Trip to the Continet [sic]*, 27 Sept. 1791, *BMC* 7903; James Gillray, *The Soldier's Return;—or—Rare News for Old England*, 14 Nov. 1791, *BMC* 7916; Isaac Cruikshank, *The Triumphal Entry of 100,000 [Crown]s or the Lucky Hit for E-O T-O P-O HO. And All the Rest of the O's*, 20 Nov. 1791, *BMC* 7914.
92. *Morning Post*, 22 Nov. 1791; Isaac Cruikshank, *Getting the Length of the Duchess's Foot*, 25 Nov. 1791, *BMC* 7921; see also William Dent, *The York (Shoe) Warehouse*, 16 Jan. 1792, *BMC* 8056.
93. See, for example, the hyperbolic account of the royal family attending Covent Garden Theatre, stressing their apparent happiness, the king's role as father to them and to his people, the particular attention that her new family and the audience paid to the new duchess, and the richness of her jewels and dress of silver tissue: *World*, 29 Dec. 1791.
94. *The Times*, 18 March 1795; *Morning Chronicle*, 19 March 1795.
95. *Sun*, 24 March, 7 April 1795.
96. *Morning Post*, 1 Jan., 24 Feb., 16 March, 17 April 1795; *Morning Chronicle*, 18 March 1795; *The Times*, 9 April 1795.
97. *True Briton*, 11 Feb. 1797; *Telegraph*, 13 Feb. 1797.
98. *The Times*, 12 April 1797, reported the dowry as £100,000. James Gillray, *The Bridal Night*, 18 May 1797, *BMC* 9014; *Morning Chronicle*, 19 May 1797.
99. *The Times*, 15, 18 April 1797; *Morning Chronicle*, 17, 20 April 1797; *Morning Post*, 19, 20, 26 April 1797.
100. *The Times*, 5 June 1798, 5 June 1793; *Morning Chronicle*, 17 Jan. 1792, 20 Jan. 1795.
101. Isaac Cruikshank, *Voluntary Subscriptions*, 16 Jan. 1798, *BMC* 9157.
102. *The Times* and the *Sun*, 27 Jan. 1798; *Morning Post*, 28 Jan. 1798.

103. Raven, *Judging New Wealth*, ch. 9.
104. Hervey, *Memoirs*, 1: 66; *The Times*, 5, 6 June 1799; *Morning Post*, 5 June 1799.
105. Marcia Pointon, 'Intriguing Jewellery: Royal Bodes and Luxurious Consumption', *Textual Practice* 11/3 (1997): 493–516; *Morning Post*, 28 Jan. 1794.
106. See, for example, the accounts in the *Original Weekly Journal*, 4–11 Jan. 1718; *Evening Post*, 8–10 Jan. 1723; *Daily Journal*, 16 Jan. 1725; *London Journal*, 7 Jan. 1727; *Weekly Journal, or Saturday's Post*, 11 Jan. 1727; *Daily Gazetteer*, 8 Jan. 1736.
107. *Telegraph*, 6, 14 Dec. 1796; *Morning Post*, 7 Jan. 1791.
108. David Dean, 'Elizabeth's Lottery: Political Culture and State Formation in Early Modern England', *Journal of British Studies* 50/3 (2011): 587–611.
109. *Cobbett's Parliamentary History*, 9: 68–76, quotation in cols 72–73; for details of the fraud, see 8: 861–62. For the continuation of state lotteries in spite of various objections until 1826, see John Ashton, *A History of English Lotteries* (London: Leadenhall Press, 1893).
110. Morris, *British Monarchy*, p. 151; see *The Times* and *Morning Chronicle*, 20 Jan. 1794.
111. Thompson, *George II*, pp. 187–91; Smith, *Georgian Monarchy*, pp. 138–42.
112. Neil McKendrick, 'Josiah Wedgwood and the Commercialization of the Potteries', in McKendrick et al., *Birth of a Consumer Society*, pp. 100–45.
113. Craig Muldrew, *The Economy of Obligation: The Culture of Credit and Social Relations in Early Modern England* (New York: St. Martin's Press, 1998), p. 97.

Chapter 6

1. For the attributions to Chesterfield, see Thomas Lockwood, 'The Life and Death of *Common Sense*', in J.A. Downie and Thomas N. Corns, eds, *Telling People What to Think: Early Eighteenth-Century Periodicals from 'The Review' to 'The Rambler'* (London: Frank Cass, 1993), p. 92, n. 10. Quotations from Chesterfield's leaders are from *Common Sense; or The Englishman's Journal. Being a Collection of Letters, Political, Humorous, and Moral; Publish'd Weekly under That Title, for the First Year* (London: J. Purer and G. Hawkins, 1738).
2. Lady Mary Wortley Montagu, *The Nonsense of Common-Sense 1737–1738*, ed. Robert Halsband (Evanston: Northwestern University, 1947).
3. While ambassador at The Hague, Chesterfield met Elizabeth du Bouchet, a governess, who gave birth to their son on 2 May 1732: Samuel Shellabarger, *Lord Chesterfield* (London, Macmillan, 1935), pp. 142–44.
4. See Amanda Vickery, 'Golden Age to Separate Spheres? A Review of the Categories and Chronology of English Women's History', *Historical Journal* 36/2 (1993): 383–414.
5. *Common Sense*, 10 Sept. 1737; on the 3rd, Chesterfield had quoted from La Rouchefcauld's writings to support his categorizations of male and female affectations, pretensions and hypocrisies.
6. Marilyn Morris, 'Transgendered Perspectives on Premodern Sexualities', *SEL* 43/3 (2006): 585–600.
7. Sandra Sherman, 'Instructing the "Empire of Beauty": Lady Mary Wortley Montagu and the Politics of Female Rationality', *South Atlantic Review* 60/4 (1995): 1–25, quotations on pp. 9, 1.
8. Bernard Mandeville, *The Fable of the Bees; or Private Vices, Public Benefits*, ed. F.B. Kaye, 2 vols (Indianapolis: The Liberty Fund, 1924), 1: 124–32 (pp. 125–39 in 1733 edn).
9. Chesterfield to George Lyttelton, 28 Nov., 12 Dec. 1737, *The Letters of Philip Dormer Stanhope, 4th Earl of Chesterfield*, ed. Bonamy Dobrée, 6 vols (New York: AMS Press, 1932), 2: 314–17, quotations on pp. 314, 317.
10. *Nonsense*, pp. 2, 3. Halsband assumes her wrong-headed, asserting that black bombazine contained no wool (p. 50, n. 3) but the *Shorter Oxford English Dictionary*

defines it as 'A twilled dress-material of worsted [wool] with or without silk or cotton; *esp.* a black kind formerly much used in mourning'.

11. For her declaration of this design, see *Nonsense* VII, 14 Feb. 1738, pp. 29–33.
12. *Cobbett's Parliamentary History of England from the Norman Conquest, in 1066, to the Year 1803*, 36 vols (London, 1811), 10: 93–100, 147–48, 155. Edward Wortley Montagu had spoken against the Treaty of Commerce with France in May 1713 on the grounds that it threatened the wool industry: Isobel Grundy, *Lady Mary Wortley Montagu* (Oxford: Oxford University Press, 1999), p. 64.
13. *Nonsense*, 27 Dec. 1737, p. 5.
14. Grundy, *Lady Mary*, pp. 83–84, 89–94, 103–12.
15. For earlier criticism of levees by Richard Steele and others, see Paul Langford, 'Politics and Manners from Sir Robert Walpole to Sir Robert Peel', *Proceedings of the British Academy* 94 (1997): 114–15.
16. *Nonsense* VIII, 21 Feb. 1738, pp. 34–38.
17. Lady Mary Wortley Montagu to Lady Pomfret, [Oct. 1738], *The Complete Letters of Lady Mary Wortley Montagu*, ed. Robert Halsband, 3 vols (Oxford: Clarendon Press, 1965-67), 2: 125–26.
18. See, for example, Montagu's letters to Lady Pomfret, [March 1739], 10 April [1740], and to Lady Bute, 14 July [1758], ibid., 2: 135–37, 182–83, 3: 157. For evidence of her political activity at this time, in addition to publishing *Nonsense*, and Walpole's rejection of her offers of intelligence, see Lord Hervey to Montagu, 21/10 June 1740, ibid., 2: 195. She continued to send politically sensitive information to her husband whenever she had safe conveyance: see, for example, her letters to Wortley of 11 April 1741 and 25 March [1744], ibid., 2: 233–34, 321–23.
19. See *Nonsense* IX, 14 March 1738, pp. 39–42.
20. Montagu to Pomfret, 6 Nov. [1739], 17 May [1740], *Complete Letters*, 2: 159, 187.
21. Montagu to Lady Frances Stuart, 4 Sept. [1758], ibid., 3: 169.
22. Hertford to Pomfret, 23 Nov. 1738 O.S., and Pomfret to Hertford, 20/31 Dec. 1738, *Correspondence between Frances, Countess of Hertford (Afterward Duchess of Somerset) and Henrietta Louisa, Countess of Pomfret, between the Years 1738 and 1741*, ed. William Bingley, 3 vols (London: Richard Phillips, 1805), 1: 33, 36.
23. Pomfret to Hertford, 10 Jan. 1739 N.S.; Hertford to Pomfret, 8/19 Jan. 1739, ibid., 1: 44, 48.
24. Hertford to Pomfret, 15/26 Dec. 1738 and 6/13 March 1739, ibid., 1: 40, 90–91.
25. Hertford to Pomfret, n.d., and Pomfret to Hertford, 28 July 1739 N.S., ibid., 1: 96, 109–10.
26. Hertford to Pomfret, 10/21 June 1739, Pomfret to Hertford, 19 Aug. 1739 N.S., ibid., 1: 102–3, 115–16.
27. Hertford to Pomfret, 20 Aug. 1739 O.S., ibid., 1: 124
28. Hertford to Pomfret, 8, 13 May 1740 O.S., ibid., 1: 238–43.
29. See ibid., 2: 114, 153, 170, *passim*.
30. Montagu to Pomfret, [Feb. 1740], *Complete Letters*, 2: 174–75.
31. Montagu to Pomfret, [April 1740], ibid., 2: 182–83.
32. Pomfret to Hertford, 20 Nov., 4 Dec. 1739 N.S., *Correspondence*, 1: 155–56, 161–62.
33. See *An Account of the Conduct of the Dowager Duchess of Marlborough, from her First Coming to Court, to the Year 1710. In a Letter from herself to My Lord—*, published in 1742, reprinted as *Memoirs of Sarah, Duchess of Marlborough Together with her Character of her Contemporaries and her Opinions*, ed. William King (New York: Kraus Reprint Co., 1969; orig. Routledge, 1930), pp. 3–5, *passim*.
34. Duchess of Marlborough to Earl of Stair, 30 Jan. 1736/37, Beinecke Rare Book and Manuscript Library, Stair Papers, James Marshall and Marie-Louise Osborn Collection, no. 24, box 1, folder 6, fo. 1.
35. 6 Feb., 3 May, 6 June 1737, ibid., fos 2, 5–6A, quotation on fo. 6.
36. 21 April 1739, ibid., folder 8, fo. 45.

37. 1 Dec. 1737, ibid., folder 6, fo. 13; Memoirs *of Sarah, Duchess of Marlborough*, pp. 210–12.
38. 1, 3 Dec. 1737, Stair Papers, folder 6, fos 13–14. The sudden death of Walpole's wife had Marlborough again worrying that, if he did not recover from his grief, Hervey would fill the power vacuum: 5 June 1738, ibid., folder 8, fo. 31.
39. 4 Feb. 1737/38, ibid., folder 7, fo. 19. Later that month, Marlborough observed that the princess of Wales, though young, behaved pleasingly: 'And I think Her Conversation is much more proper and decent for a drawing Room than the wise Queen Caroline's was: Who never was half an Hour without saying something shocking to some body or other; even when She intended to oblige. And generally very improper discourse for a Publick Room': 24 Feb. 1737/38, ibid., fo. 21.
40. 10 Feb. 1737/38, ibid., fo. 20.
41. 24 Feb. 1737/38, 19 March 1738, ibid., fos 21, 22.
42. 3 April 1739, ibid., folder 8, fo. 44.
43. 20 June 1738, ibid., fo. 33.
44. See Earl of Bristol to Lord Hervey, 29 Dec. 1731, 18 Aug. 1733, 10 May 1734, 27 Nov. 1736, *Letter Books of John Hervey, First Earl of Bristol, with Sir Thomas Hervey's Letters during Courtship and Poems Written during Widowhood 1651 to 1750*, 3 vols (Wells: Ernest Jackson, 1894), 3: 80–81, 99–101, 116–18, 164–65.
45. 9 June 1733, ibid., 3: 92–93.
46. 7 Sept. 1737, ibid., 3: 170.
47. 19 Nov. 1737, ibid., 3: 177.
48. Bristol to Lord Hervey, 21 Nov., 3 Dec. 1737, and to Lady Hervey, 26 Nov. 1737, ibid., 3: 178–82.
49. For her imagined flirtations with Chesterfield and Manners, see the decoded passages in *Secret Comment: The Diaries of Gertrude Savile 1721–1757*, ed. Alan Saville (Devon: Kingsbride History Society and Thoroton Society of Nottinghamshire, 1997), pp. 1–2, 33, 109–10, 183, 202.
50. Ibid., pp. 44–45.
51. 16 Aug. 1727, ibid., p. 52. The previous day she 'like a baby' pleaded to go to Kew, only to have her mother relent after the trip she had planned fell through, which caused them to set out too late.
52. 3 Oct. 1727, ibid., p. 66.
53. 21 Aug., 6, 7, 10, 11 Oct. 1727, ibid., pp. 54, 67–69.
54. Ibid., pp. 90–91.
55. 21 Dec. 1728, ibid., p. 151. See also entries of 3, 4, 6 Dec., pp. 148–49.
56. 6 Jan. 1729, ibid., pp. 157–58.
57. 1 June 1746, 20 March, 1751, Dec. 1751, 9 Nov. 1755, ibid., pp. 272, 295, 298, 306.
58. 20 Oct. 1746, ibid., pp. 276–77.
59. See, for example, Oct. 1756, April 1757, ibid., pp. 320–21, 330.
60. Caroline Girle Powys, Annual Journal, BL Add. MS 42,160, vol. 1, 1 May 1757, fos 1–2.
61. Ibid., 25 Oct. 1760, fo. 10; 9 Dec. 1760, fo. 11; 21 March 1767, fos 19–20. For her account of the coronation, see her letter to a friend in the country, 25 Sept. 1761, in *Passages from the Diaries of Mrs. Philip Lybbe Powys of Hardwick House, Oxon. 1756 to 1808*, ed. Emily Climenson (London: Longmans, Green, and Co., 1899), pp. 87–91.
62. Powys Journal, summer 1780, fo. 76; 16 Sept. 1788, fos 116–17.
63. Ibid., 18 Jan. 1788, fo. 43; 3 June 1789, fos 130–33; 20 Aug. 1789, fos 139–40; Powys Journal, vol. 2, Add. MS 42,161, July 1799, fos 93–95.
64. Isaac Cruikshank, *The Family Party or Prince Bladduds Man Traps*, 11 May 1799, *BMC* 9382.
65. Powys Journal, vol. 2, 6 June 1788, fos 111–12; P.J. Marshall, *The Impeachment of Warren Hastings* (Oxford: Oxford University Press, 1965), pp. 52–53, 76.
66. *Diary and Letters of Madame D'Arblay, Author of 'Evelina', 'Cecelia' &c. Edited by her Niece* [Charlotte Barrett], 7 vols (London: Henry Colburn, 1854), 4: 55.

67. Ibid., 3: 59–61. For Burney's unhappy career at court, see Hester Davenport, *Faithful Handmaiden: Fanny Burney and the Court of King George III* (Stroud: Sutton Publishing, 2000). For a completely different perspective, see Mary Delany, *Autobiography and Correspondence of Mary Granville, Mrs. Delany: With Interesting Reminiscences of King George III and Queen Charlotte*, ed. Lady Llanover, 6 vols (London: Richard Bentley, 1861–62), ser. 2, vol. 3. As Clarissa Campbell Orr argues, while Delany failed to obtain an office at court, her position as 'the honoured guest of the royal family' allowed for a much closer friendship with the queen and king: 'Mrs. Delany and the Court', in Mark Laird and Alicia Weisberg-Roberts, eds, *Mrs. Delany and her Circle* (New Haven and London: Yale University Press, 2009), pp. 40, 56–62.

68. D'Arblay, *Diary and Letters*, 2: 297, 351–52; 3: 111.

69. Burney's account of the proceedings of 13 Feb. 1788 in ibid., 4: 44–76, quotations on pp. 50, 51, 52, 54.

70. Ibid., pp. 63, 64, 66, 68.

71. Ibid., pp. 79, 71, 95, 118.

72. *Early Journals and Letters of Fanny Burney, Volume V: 1782–1783*, ed. Lars E. Troide and Steward J. Cooke (Montreal and Kingston: McGill-Queen's University Press, 2012), p. 69.

73. *The Journals and Letters of Fanny Burney (Madame D'Arblay)*, ed. Joyce Hemlow et al., 12 vols (Oxford: Clarendon Press, 1972–84), 1: 196.

74. D'Arblay, *Diary and Letters*, 4: 84–85, 95–96, 116.

75. Ibid., 5: 96; Burney, *Journals and Letters*, 1: 150.

76. Burney, *Journals and Letters*, 1: 166.

77. *Early Journals and Letters of Fanny Burney, Volume III: The Streatham Years, Part I, 1778–1779*, ed. Lars E. Troide and Steward J. Cooke (Montreal and Kingston: McGill-Queen's University Press, 1994), pp. 226–30; *Early Journals and Letters of Fanny Burney, Volume IV: The Streatham Years, Part II, 1780–1781*, ed. Betty Rizzo (Montreal and Kingston: McGill-Queen's University Press, 2003), pp. 8, 77–78; D'Arblay, *Diary and Letters*, 4: 105.

78. D'Arblay, *Diary and Letters*, 4: 92, 99–100.

79. Burney, *Journal and Letters*, 3: 78; D'Arblay, *Diary and Letters*, 5: 37.

80. *Betsy Sheridan's Journal: Letters from Sheridan's Sister 1784–1786 and 1788–1790*, ed. William LeFanu (New Brunswick, NJ: Rutgers University Press, 1960), pp. 160–61.

81. Ibid., pp. 78, 35, 135; see also pp. 153, 154.

82. Ibid., p. 74.

83. Ernest Hartley Coleridge, *The Life of Thomas Coutts Banker*, 2 vols (London and New York: John Lane, 1920), 1: 297, 2: 41; for Fox's cultivation of friendship in 1787–88, see 1: 214–21, 243–45.

84. Lord Granville Leveson-Gower (1st Earl Granville), *Private Correspondence 1781 to 1821*, ed. Castalia Countess Granville, 2 vols (London: John Murray, 1916), 1: 8, 14, 18.

85. Ibid., p. 311; see p. 111 for Bessborough's recommendation of a pamphlet by Germaine de Staël hostile to Pitt for his contempt of her beauty.

86. 30 Aug. 1772, *The Letters of Richard Brinsley Sheridan*, ed. Cecil Price, 3 vols (Oxford: Clarendon Press, 1966), 1: 35, 37–38.

87. *The Journal of Thomas Moore*, ed. Wilfred S. Dowden, 6 vols (Newark: University of Delaware Press, 1984), 1: 52, 91, 171.

88. To John Grubs, [1 April 1798?], ibid., 2: 89.

89. 12 Feb. 1806, ibid., 2: 260.

90. Thomas Moore, *Memoirs of the Life of the Honourable Richard Brinsley Sheridan*, 3rd edn, 2 vols (London: Longman, Hurst, Rees, Orme, Brown, and Green, 1825), 2: 484–85. Moore dates this 1799 or 1800, but for details of this dispute, see the annotation of a letter dated 13 Nov. 1801, *Letters of Sheridan*, 2: 164.

91. Moore, *Life of Sheridan*, 2: 488–89.

92. Linda Kelly, *Richard Brinsley Sheridan: A Life* (London: Pimlico, 1998 [1997]), pp. 169–70, 206–8; see his letter to the winner of a bet that he claimed he made while drunk: *Letters of Sheridan*, 2: 64–66.

93. Kelly, *Sheridan*, pp. 206–9. Hester's dowry was £8,000 and Sheridan contributed an additional £12,000 to be held in trust for her by her cousins, Charles Grey and Samuel Whitbread.

94. To Richard Peake, [Jan. 1801]; to William Adam, 31 Jan. 1801, *Letters of Sheridan*, 2: 146–47, 149.

95. To Sir Robert Barclay, [1806–7]; to Richard Peake, [Feb. 1809?], ibid., 2: 310–11, 3: 50–51.

96. 20 April 1810, ibid., pp. 77–78.

97. Ibid., pp. 78–87, quotations on pp. 85, 86.

98. To Sir John Cox Hippisley, Sept. 1814, ibid., 3: 198. See also his letters to Thomas Grenville, 1 Dec. 1815, and to George Canning, 19 June [1816], 3: 239, 343.

99. Fintan O'Toole, *A Traitor's Kiss: The Life of Richard Brinsley Sheridan, 1751–1816* (New York: Farrar, Straus and Giroux, 1998 [1997]), pp. 423, 443, 451–52, 455–56, 461–62, 467–69.

100. Moore, *Life of Sheridan*, 2: 491.

101. Alicia Lefanu, *Memoirs of the Life and Writings of Mrs. Frances Sheridan [. . .] with Remarks upon a Late Life of the Right Hon. R.B. Sheridan [. . .]* (London: G. and W.B. Whittaker, 1824), pp. 397–403, quotation on p. 403.

102. Moore, *Life of Sheridan*, 2: 260–61. Lansdowne also objected to some of Moore's representations of Whig principles: *Journal of Moore*, 2: 858.

103. James Sayers, *Citizen Bardolph Refused Admittance at Prince Hal's*, 17 March 1794, BMC 8441.

104. Kelly, *Sheridan*, pp. 304–5; Moore, *Life of Sheridan*, 2: 456–68. See Moore's letters to Charles Brinsley Sheridan, [14] Jan., 16 April 1826, 7 Feb. 1827, and to Dr Andrew Bain, who had attended the Sheridans in their final illnesses, 17, 18 April 1826, *The Letters of Thomas Moore*, ed. Wilfred S. Dowden, 2 vols (Oxford: Clarendon Press, 1964), 2: 547–48, 554–57, 713. For his earlier efforts to verify that the prince's offer of assistance had come after Sheridan was too sick for it to do any good, see his entry of 16 Aug. 1820, *Journal of Moore*, 1: 335. For some of the debate about George IV's generosity that the work stimulated, see 21 Oct. 1825, 2: 839.

105. See 8, 10, 13, 19 Oct., 7 Nov. 1825, *Journal of Moore*, 2: 836–38, 854.

106. 7 Oct. 1825, *Letters of Moore*, 2: 539.

Chapter 7

1. Jenny Davidson, *Hypocrisy and the Politics of Politeness: Manners and Morals from Locke to Austen* (Cambridge: Cambridge University Press, 2004), pp. 7, 5; for her analysis of Chesterfield and Hume, see ch. 2.

2. See Anna Bryson, *From Courtesy to Civility: Changing Codes of Conduct in Early Modern England* (Oxford: Oxford University Press, 1998).

3. See, for example, [Catherine Macaulay Graham], *Observations on the Reflections of the Right Hon. Edmund Burke, on the Revolution in France, in a Letter to the Earl of Stanhope* (London, 1790), pp. 15–16; George Dyer, *The Complaints of the Poor People of England*, 2nd edn (London, 1793), pp. 33–34; John Oswald, *Review of the Constitution of Great-Britain*, 3rd edn (London, 1795), p. 11; William Godwin, *Enquiry Concerning Political Justice and its Influence on Modern Morals and Happiness*, ed. Isaac Kramnick (London: Pelican Books, 1976 [1798]), pp. 432–44.

4. Mary Wollstonecraft, *Vindication of the Rights of Woman*, ed. Miriam Brody (London: Penguin Books, 1985 [1792]), pp. 98–99, 121.

5. Erin Mackie, 'Boys Will Be Boys: Masculinity, Criminality, and the Restoration Rake', *The Eighteenth Century* 46/2 (2005): 129–49; Valérie Capdeville, 'Gender at

Stake: The Role of Eighteenth-Century London Clubs in Shaping a New Model of English Masculinity', *Culture, Society & Masculinities* 4/1 (2012): 13–32.

6. Margaret Talbot, 'The Public on the Private', *New Yorker*, 27 June 2011, pp. 23–24; Adam Gopnik, 'Military Secrets', *New Yorker*, 26 Nov. 2012, pp. 19–20.

7. Albert R. Jonsen and Stephen Toulmin, *The Abuse of Casuistry: A History of Moral Reasoning* (Berkeley: University of California Press, 1988), p. 233. This book gives a detailed history of the practice.

8. Keith Thomas, 'Cases of Conscience in Seventeenth-Century England', in John Morrill, Paul Slack and Daniel Woolf, eds, *Public Duty and Private Conscience in Seventeenth-Century England: Essays Presented to G.E. Aylmer* (Oxford: Clarendon Press, 1993), p. 51.

9. 'The Debts of a Great Personage', *Telegraph*, 23 March 1795.

10. *Life and Letters of Sir Gilbert Elliot, First Earl of Minto from 1751 to 1806*, ed. by his great-niece the Countess of Minto, 3 vols (London: Longmans, Green, and Co., 1874), 1: 293–95.

11. Brooke Boothby, *Observations on the Appeal from the New to the Old Whigs and on Mr. Paine's Rights of Man* (London: John Stockdale, 1792), p. 16.

12. Reports of 3, 10 Nov. 1795, National Archives, London, Home Office Papers, HO42/37/411–12, 463. See Mary Thale, 'London Debating Societies in the 1790s', *Historical Journal* 32/1 (1989): 57–86.

13. Jonsen and Toulmin, *Abuse of Casuistry*, p. 13.

Index